John Wesley

AUBURN, N.Y.
DERBY & MILLER

THE LIVES

OF

EMINENT METHODIST MINISTERS;

CONTAINING

BIOGRAPHICAL SKETCHES, INCIDENTS, ANECDOTES,
RECORDS OF TRAVEL, REFLECTIONS, &c. &c.

BY

REV. P. DOUGLASS GORRIE,

AUTHOR OF "THE CHURCHES AND SECTS OF THE UNITED STATES,"
"EPISCOPAL METHODISM, AS IT WAS, AND IS," ETC.

AUBURN:
DERBY AND MILLER.

1852.

STEREOTYPED BY
THOMAS B. SMITH,
216 William St., N. Y

PREFACE.

WERE it not that a Preface seems to be considered as almost indispensable to the existence of a book at the present time, the author would feel an inclination to let this work go to press without the usual prefatory introduction; but as custom is law, he must bow to its mandates, and detain the reader from the perusal of the body of the work long enough to inform him, that the preparation, compilation, abridgment, or whatever else the reader may please to denominate the following sketches, has required the author to examine a large number of different biographical works, such as "Lives," "Memoirs," "Journals," &c. &c. This examination, although somewhat laborious, has, nevertheless, been pleasing, as it has been the means of refreshing his memory in regard to many incidents almost forgotten, as well as putting him in possession of facts never before known to him. The labor of preparing this work, however, has been greatly enhanced, from the fact that no published "Life," or "Memoir," of several of the eminent men whose biographies are briefly sketched therein, has ever been given to the public. This is especially true of Bishops Asbury, McKendree, Whatcoat, and George, and of Dr. Olin, recently deceased. While, therefore, much ground has necessarily been gone over, the author hopes that this attempt to embody in a convenient form the leading events in the history of the *great lights* of *Methodism*, will not be unappreciated by a candid and liberal-minded public.

It is proper, also, to observe, that in some cases, there has been a great paucity of materials necessary to give even the brief and imperfect sketch connected with the names of some of the subjects in this book. On the other hand, in regard to the greater part of them, there has been no lack of materials; and the only difficulty has been to make a proper selection of the numerous facts and incidents found in the written Lives and Memoirs of those great men. One object the author has had in view,—to make the work interesting, and profitable. To accomplish these objects, *variety* was thought to be necessary; hence, the reader who deigns to peruse this work, will find many interesting and instructive anecdotes interspersed through its pages, and what is perhaps of more importance, he will learn something of the self-denial practised, and the sacrifices made, by the leading ministers of the Methodist Church in Europe and America.

In relation to the authorities consulted, it is only necessary to observe, that they are those who have received the sanction of the Church, except in a few cases, and that the facts and incidents given, may be considered authentic. Justice, however, requires that we should in this connection make particular mention of Bangs' "History of the Methodist Episcopal Church," a work which, the more we read and refer to, we learn to prize more and more, and to which, on more occasions than one, we have acknowledged our indebtedness.

The style of the work, so far as composition is concerned, will be found to be somewhat various in different chapters. This is owing partly to the fact that the authorities consulted, have written in a great variety of style, and although the author has not—except in a few instances—copied the exact words of these authorities, unless in the form of quotations, yet as he drank into the spirit of the narrative, he has no doubt in some cases been governed in the style, by that to which his attention at the moment was directed. Further: the comprehensiveness of our plan, forbade the use of an elegant or flowing style, to which the author under any circumstances could seldom lay claim; his object in the present instance has been to give *facts*, not *figures of speech;* to present a concise account of the more important events in the history of his subjects, and to induce the reader by a bare and ungarnished statement of facts, to copy, as far as possible, the example of these holy men, that a more intimate acquaintance may be cultivated with them in that "better country" where "there shall be no more death."

THE AUTHOR.

CANTON, St. Lawrence County, N. Y., 1852.

CONTENTS.

CHAPTER IX.

CHAPTER X.

CHAPTER XI.

CHAPTER XII.

CHAPTER XIII.

CHAPTER XIV.

CHAPTER XV.

CHAPTER XVI.

CHAPTER XVII.

CHAPTER XVIII.

LIVES OF EMINENT MINISTERS.

CHAPTER I.

REV. JOHN WESLEY, A.M.

ONE of the greatest lights of the eighteenth century arose to bless and enlighten the Christian world in the person of John Wesley, the father and founder of that wonderful system of religious faith and practice denominated Methodism: a system, the principles of which have obtained a lodgment in the hearts of hundreds of thousands of believers, who have left the Church militant and have fled upward to join the Church triumphant, and of millions who are still on earth fighting by faith their passage to the skies.

John Wesley was born in the parish of Epworth, Lincolnshire, Eng., in the year 1703. His father, Samuel Wesley, sen., was rector of the parish, and was a man of great moral worth, and of extensive literary attainments. His mother, Mrs. Susanna Wesley, was the daughter of Dr. Samuel Annesly, and was a woman of strong powers of mind, and suitable in every way to be the nursing mother of the future religious reformer. Mrs. Wesley was the instructress of her children in early life, she having a bad opinion of the common method of instructing and governing children, preferred to retain them under her own immediate control and government, until they were of a suitable age to send to school, where the higher branches were taught. She was led providentially to pay particular attention to the intellectual and religious instruction of John, who, when at the age of six, was the subject of a fortunate escape from death by burning, while asleep in an upper chamber of the parsonage house, which was consumed by fire. This incident led the mother to increased anxiety for the soul of her child, whom God had so mercifully and providentially delivered from the devouring flame. The effect of her increased anxiety was such, that John became very seriously disposed, and at the age of eight years was admitted by his father to the sacrament of the Lord's Supper. At the age of eleven he was consigned to the care of Dr. Walker, Head-Master of the "Charter House," where he remained until his seventeenth year, when he entered Christ's Church College, Oxford University, and pursued his studies under the direction of Dr. Wigan, a gentleman of great classical knowledge. While under this gentleman's instructions he became still more serious, and applied himself closely to the study of divinity, preparatory to taking deacon's orders in the established church. In 1725 he was ordained deacon, and in the following year was elected Fellow of Lincoln College. During the same year he was chosen Greek Lecturer and Moderator of the classes, and in 1727 took his well-earned degree of Master of Arts, and shortly afterwards obtained priest's orders at the hands of the Bishop of Oxford. Prior to his ordination as priest he became the curate of his father in Epworth, which important relation he sustained with great acceptability for nearly two years, until he was summoned by the Rector of his College to return to Oxford, which he did in 1729, and became the tutor and moderator of several classes.

During his temporary absence at Epworth, his brother Charles, who had also become a student at Oxford, had formed a small society in College of seriously disposed persons for the purpose of mutual improvement. Although strictly moral and upright, Charles possessed a lively disposition, so much so that he lost his first year in College by diversions; his second year was spent in study; and diligence in study led him to serious thinking, and to the practice of weekly communion, which he strictly attended to, in company with two or three others. This course of conduct gained for Charles and his associates the name of *Methodist*, a term which was not unknown in England before that time, as for many years previously this name had been used to distinguish the Nonconformists, and other classes of religious dissenters.

On John Wesley's return to Oxford, he at once identified himself with the little band, who had now become the objects of derision and persecution to the more volatile and less regular of the College students. In consequence of his superior age and literary attainments, he became the head of this small society, and thus unconsciously to himself, was God preparing him for the great work of *spreading Scriptural holiness over the land.* During this time, however, John Wesley and his Methodist companions were not *Christians* in the proper sense of that word. They had not attained to saving, justifying faith. Indeed it is doubtful whether they had ever supposed such a degree of faith to be possible, or the result of such faith—peace with God—to be attainable in this life. Yet they were sincere inquirers after truth, and God was leading them in a way which they as yet "knew not," to the knowledge of sin forgiven, and the blessings of a pure and perfect salvation. The sincerity of their intentions led them to improve every opportunity of doing good to their fellow-men. Hence all their spare time was employed in visiting those who were sick, or in prison, and all their spare funds were employed in relieving the wants of the poor and needy. The more faithful they became in the improvement of their time and talents, the more fiercely did the fires of persecution rage, until at length the most of those composing the little band of Methodists became discouraged and retired, leaving the two brothers to stand almost entirely alone. They were, however, greatly encouraged by their father, who exhorted them to perseverance. In 1735 he died, leaving them his blessing, and departing in the triumphs of that faith which his sons in after life were the honored instruments of diffusing more extensively throughout the world.

Shortly after the death of the elder Wesley, John and Charles received a call to go to Georgia in North America, as Missionaries. In obedience to this call, they embarked on shipboard, and in February, 1736, reached their field of labor in the western world. Here, too, persecution awaited them, and after spending a few months in Frederica, Charles returned to England as the bearer of despatches from Governor Oglethorpe to the trustees of the Colony. John, however, remained at his post until the winter of 1737, when in consequence of the illiberal and uncharitable conduct of the colonists, he hastened his departure from the scene of strife, and arrived in England in February, 1738. Although his mission to Georgia did not secure those immediate results which he had anticipated, yet it proved the means of bringing John Wesley to the knowledge of justification by faith. On the passage to Georgia, Mr. Wesley found a company of pious Moravians on board, and he particularly noticed during the prevalence of a tremendous storm, the calm serenity and composure manifested by these Moravians while expecting every moment to find a watery grave, while he himself was the subject of the most distressing fears. After the storm had subsided, he inquired the cause of so much composure, and he learned to his astonishment, that there is a degree of faith and love, which '*Casteth out fear.*" By subsequent intercourse with these unassuming Christians, he became better acquainted with the way of salvation by faith, and of the necessity of being personally *born again*, before he could enter into the kingdom of God. Hence, after his return to England, he exclaimed in the bitterness of his spirit, "I went to America to convert the Indians; but O, who shall convert me?" "I who went to America to convert others, was never converted myself."

Shortly after uttering the above language, he met with Peter Bohler, a minister of the Moravian Church, to whom he opened his heart, and from him he received such instruction in regard to the nature and exercise of justifying faith, as led him on the 24th day of May following, to *believe on the Lord Jesus Christ*, with all his heart. And in describing the change which was wrought in him, as the result of such faith, he says: "I felt my heart strangely warmed, I felt I did trust in Christ, Christ alone for salvation, and an assurance was given me, that he had taken away my sins, even mine, and saved me from the law of sin and death."

The conversion of John Wesley was indeed an important event in the history of his life, as from this time that laborious and successful ministry was commenced which immediately was rendered a blessing to thousands, and remotely to millions of the fallen race of Adam. At the time when the Apostle of Methodism began his ministry as a converted man, the English nation was enveloped by a dark, dense cloud of ignorance and superstition. The clergy of the established Church were awfully corrupt and profligate. Horse-racing, cock-fighting, card-playing, hunting and drinking were common among the clergy; and as no people can ever be expected to be farther advanced in knowledge and morals than their religious teachers, we may infer that if such was the state of the priesthood, the laity must have been in a still more deplorable condition. It is in fact asserted on good authority that the only form of prayer taught by many of the English peasantry to their children, was the one handed down from their popish ancestors, beginning with these words,

> "Matthew, Mark, Luke, and John,
> Bless the bed that I lie on," &c.,

while vice of every kind, and wickedness of every degree, prevailed to an alarming extent among all classes, high and low, rich and poor. Such was the state of morals and religion when Wesley began his evangelical labors in England.

After his conversion, Mr. Wesley took occasion to spend a few weeks at a Moravian settlement in Germany, and having learned still more perfectly the nature and effects of justifying faith, he returned to England and at once began the important work of calling upon sinners to repent and believe. London was the scene of his first labors. In this city, large multitudes went to hear him. The churches at first were generally open to receive him, but his earnestness, zeal, and boldness soon gave offence to the lukewarm indolent clergymen, and soon the Churches, one after another, were closed against him. He, however, was at no loss for places wherein to preach, as a private room or public hall would frequently afford ample accommodation. From London he went to Oxford, and in reference to both places he had the satisfaction of informing his friends in Germany and Scotland, that multitudes were crying, "What must we do to be saved?" He shortly after visited Bristol, and for the first time, preached in the open air to a congregation of more than two thousand people. Preaching in the open air was a new thing to Mr. Wesley, and seemed at first to be entirely irregular and improper, and it was only at the earnest solicitation of his friend, Rev. George Whitefield, and after having witnessed the effects produced by the preaching of the latter under similar circumstances, that he so far overcame his high church views of propriety, as to commence this method of preaching Jesus Christ to the outcasts of the nation.

In the latter end of the year 1739, Mr. Wesley formed the first Methodist Society in London. The formation of this Society was the beginning, the germ, of that large and extensive connection which has since spread itself over England, Ireland, America, and other parts of the world. At first they appear to have met in connection with the Moravians, in a place called "Fetter Lane," but during the next year—1740—they dissolved all connection with the Moravians, and met by themselves in a place called the "Foundry." The whole number of Methodists at this period, was seventy-two. Mr. Wesley, however, did not confine his labors to London, but adopting the itinerant mode of preaching, he visited Bristol, Kingwood, and other places, where his labors were greatly blessed, and where large Societies were speedily organized. As his Societies increased, it became necessary that certain rules should be adopted for the government of the members thereof. Hence in 1743, Mr. Wesley drew up a set of rules which he called the "Rules of the United Societies," which rules have always been retained in the discipline of the Methodist Church in Europe and America, with scarcely any variation. For the better government of his Societies, he divided them into smaller companies called classes, composed of about twelve members, each of which he placed under the special charge of one of their number, who was denominated the "Leader," and whose duty it was to see each member of his class once a week, in order to inquire into their spiritual prosperity, and to comfort, reprove, and exhort as occasion might require.

The increase of Societies called for an increase of laborers, but with the exception of his brother Charles, and a few of the Clergy of the established Church who assisted him from time to time, Mr. Wesley had the care of all the Societies resting upon himself. This state of things made it necessary for Mr. Wesley to employ several lay preachers to assist him in the work of the ministry, and although strongly remonstrated with upon the subject by his brother Charles, yet as Providence seemed to open the way, he in the name of the Lord authorized a number of persons—who appeared to be well qualified for the work—to preach the Gospel, and take charge of certain Societies in his absence. We have said that *Providence* seemed to open the way for the employment of lay preachers. It was on this wise. As Mr. Wesley was about leaving London, intending to be absent for some months, he left the London Society in the care of a young man by the name of Maxfield, with directions to meet them, and pray with, and advise them, as occasion might require. After being absent a short time he heard, to his utter astonishment, that Mr. Maxfield had begun to *preach*. He hastened back to London to put an immediate stop to the irregularity, but before he had silenced the young man, his mother, Mrs. Wesley, accosted him with these words, "John, take care what you do with respect to that young man, for he is as surely called of God to preach as you are; hear him yourself." He wisely took her advice, and did not venture to forbid his preaching. In this manner was the Head of the Church raising up and sending forth laborers into his vineyard.

The preaching of Wesley was attended by the divine unction. Hundreds of the *baser sort*, when they had heard, believed, were converted, and became sober, pious, praying people; but many others being stirred up by clergymen and magistrates to the commission of such unholy deeds, waged a war of persecution against Mr. Wesley and his preachers, and of extermination against all who bore the name of Methodist. The mere recital of the bloody persecutions endured by Mr. Wesley and his followers in the earlier days of Methodism is sufficient to cause the cheek of Christianity to blush, as it no doubt caused devils to rejoice, if such a thing were possible. Mr. Wesley on several occasions barely escaped with his life from the fury of the mob, who were in most instances, as before related, incited to such acts of cruelty by the clergymen and magistrates of the parish; and it was only by the direct interference of the reigning king, George III., that the storm of persecution was stayed, and religious liberty to the Methodists secured.

Mr. Wesley did not, however, satisfy himself merely with travelling and preaching. He began the work of printing, and circulating tracts and books among the people. Of the former he had "A Word to a Swearer," "A Word to a Sabbath Breaker," "A Word to a Smuggler," "A Word to a Drunkard," "A Word to a Street Walker," "A Word to a Malefactor," &c. By these little silent messengers he reached the eyes and hearts of many to whose ears he could not gain access, and in this way accomplished much good.

In the year 1744 Mr. Wesley invited his preachers, who were laboring in different parts of England, to meet him in London for the purpose of conferring with them in relation to the work of God, as progressing under their labors and superintendence. This was the first conference, and was composed of but a few persons, but was found to result so favorably, that these meetings were held annually ever after, during Mr. Wesley's lifetime, and have also been held thus after until the present time.

In 1747 Mr. Wesley visited Ireland for the first time. He went to Dublin, where Methodism had already been introduced by one of his preachers. He preached to large congregations, and after a short time returned again to England, and made arrangements with his brother Charles to proceed to Ireland, which he did shortly after, and spent several months in Dublin, Cork, and other cities of the Emerald Isle.

Up to the year 1750, Mr. Wesley remained unmarried.

In the latter year he was united to a widow lady of independent fortune, and of cultivated understanding, but the union did not prove an auspicious one, as the lady appears to have possessed a disposition of the jealous kind, which drove her to the most unwarrantable actions, and which resulted in their final separation, after an unpleasant union of twenty years. This sorrowful fact Mr. Wesley notices in his journal, and briefly adds, "I did not forsake her, I did not dismiss her, I will not recall her." Justice to his memory requires us to state that even his enemies acquitted him of all blame in the matter. It is true that at the time of the separation strong efforts were made by the lady to prejudice the public mind against him, and Mr. Wesley's friends urged him to defend his reputation against her calumnies, but his reply was, "When I devoted to God my ease, my time, my life, did I except my reputation? No!" He consequently allowed the lady to pursue her own course, and that Being to whom he had devoted his all took care of his reputation in this matter.

In 1753 Mr. Wesley visited Scotland for the second time, and in Glasgow he preached to large congregations. He was generally received by the Scotch with great respect, notwithstanding their known attachment to Calvinism and Presbyterianism. The greatest obstacle Mr. Wesley and his preachers appear to have met with in the introduction of Methodism into Scotland, was in regard to the use of hymns, instead of the old "Psalms of David in Metre," to which the Scotch were, and still are greatly attached. Many Societies, however, have been raised up in different parts of Scotland, in which the pure Wesleyan hymns are used with great delight by the worshippers.

After Mr. Wesley's return from Scotland he was taken ill with symptoms of pulmonary consumption. By the advice of his physician, he retired from active labor, and supposing that he would probably soon be called from his work on earth, he prepared his own epitaph, which, in case of death, he ordered to be placed upon his tomb. He also received a tender farewell letter from his friend Rev. George Whitefield, in which the latter expresses the sincerest attachment for his afflicted brother, and informs him, that *if prayers can detain him*, "even you, Rev. and very dear sir, shall not leave us yet." These prayers did detain him; his work was not yet completed, and in due time his health was completely restored. During his illness he spent most of his time in reading, and in writing his "Notes on the New Testament."

In the year 1766, Methodism was introduced into America by two local preachers from Ireland—Embury and Strawbridge—and through their instrumentality, Societies were organized in New York and Maryland. Mr. Wesley being anxious to provide more fully for the spiritual wants of his children in America, sent over in 1769, the missionaries—Messrs. Boardman and Pilmore—to take the charge of the Societies already formed, and to raise up and organize others. As Societies still continued to increase in the Western world, other missionaries were sent over from time to time, until at length, in 1784, after the North American Colonies had become independent of the mother country, Mr. Wesley solemly set apart the Rev. Thomas Coke, Doctor of Laws, to the important office of Superintendent of all the Societies in North America. He also empowered him to set apart Francis Asbury, one of the missionaries who had preceded Dr. Coke, as Joint Superintendent, and gave directions for the organization of these Societies into an independent Episcopal Church, all of which directions Dr. Coke faithfully attended to on his arrival in America, and the result of such provision made by Mr. Wesley for his infant Societies, in an infant nation, may be seen in the unparalleled success, and the gradual progress of the latter in population and strength.*

* It is more than probable that if the Bishops of the Church of

While Methodism was thus gaining a firm foothold in America, Mr. Wesley continued his self-denying labors in England; thousands in different parts of the kingdom were converted to God, and it is a satisfaction to know, that these

England had provided for the spiritual wants of the people in America, the Methodist Episcopal Church, as an independent branch, never would have been formed—at least, by the sanction of Mr. Wesley; but the gross and culpable negligence of the English episcopacy in this respect, rendered it absolutely necessary that Mr. Wesley should provide for these "sheep in the wilderness," in some other way. In 1780, when the Methodists in America were raising the Macedonian cry for the ordinances of the church, and were calling on Mr. Wesley, as their spiritual father, to send some one "over and help" them, the latter requested the Bishop of London to ordain a young man of unexceptionable character and ability, for that work. This, his lordship refused to do, which refusal called forth the following letter from Mr. Wesley to that bishop, under date of August 10, 1780.

"My Lord,

"Some time since I received your lordship's favor, for which I return your lordship my sincere thanks. Those persons did not apply to the Society (for Propagating Christian Knowledge), because they had nothing to ask of them. They wanted no salary for their minister: they were themselves able and willing to maintain him. They therefore applied by me to your lordship, as members of the Church of England, and desirous so to continue, begging the favor of your lordship, after your lordship had examined him, to ordain a pious man, who might officiate as their minister.

"But your lordship observes, 'There are three ministers in that country, already' True, my lord: but what are these to watch over all the souls in that extensive country? Will your lordship permit me to speak freely? I dare not do otherwise. I am on the verge of the grave, and I know not the moment when I shall drop into it. Suppose there were threescore of those missionaries in the country—could I in conscience recommend those souls to their care? Do they take any care of their own souls? If they do (I speak it with concern), I fear they are almost the only missionaries in America that do. My lord, I do not speak rashly. I have been in America; and so have several with whom I have lately conversed. And both I and conversions were not merely of a nominal character—a change from one opinion to another, or from one system of theology to another—but a radical change of heart and life, a translation from the "kingdom of darkness, into the kingdom of God's dear Son." The fruits of such conver-

they know what manner of men the far greater part of these are. They are men who have neither the power of religion, nor the form; men that lay no claim to piety, nor even to decency.

"Give me leave, my lord, to speak more freely still: perhaps it is the last time I shall trouble your lordship. I know your lordship's abilities, and extensive learning; I believe, what is more, that your lordship fears God. I have heard that your lordship is unfashionably diligent in examining the candidates for holy orders: yea, that your lordship is generally at the pains of examining them yourself. Examining them;—in what respects? Why, whether they understand a little Latin and Greek, and can answer a few trite questions in the science of Divinity. Alas, how little does this avail! Does your lordship examine whether they serve Christ or Belial? Whether they love God or the world? Whether they have any serious thoughts about heaven or hell? Whether they have any real desire to save their own souls, or the souls of others? If not, what have they to do with holy orders? and what will become of the souls committed to their care?

"My lord, I do by no means despise learning: I know the value of it too well. But what is this, particularly in a Christian minister, compared to piety? What is it to a man that has no religion? 'As a jewel in a swine's snout.'

"Some time since, I recommended to your lordship a plain man, whom I had known above twenty years, as a person of deep, genuine piety, and of unblamable conversation. But he neither understood Greek nor Latin, and he affirmed in so many words, that 'he believed it was his duty to preach, whether he was ordained or no.' I believe so too. What became of him since, I know not. But I suppose he received Presbyterian ordination, and I cannot blame him if he did. He might think any ordination better than none.

"I do not know that Mr. Haskins had any favors to ask of the Society. He asked the favor of your lordship to ordain him, that he might minister to a little flock in America. But your lordship did not see good to ordain him: but your lordship did see good to ordain and

sion were strikingly displayed in the case of the poor colliers of Cornwall, a class of people, who, prior to the labors of the Wesleys among them, were in a more debased and ignorant state than many of the heathen in Africa or America—a class of people whose days were spent in slavish toil, and whose nights were given to drunkenness and sin ; a people on whom the Sabbath could scarcely be said to dawn, only to yield them a temporary respite from their otherwise unremitting toils, and afford them an opportunity of plunging still deeper into the vortex of vice and crime—this people, having heard, believed and were converted, and their conversion resulted in "bringing forth the peaceable fruits of righteousness, to the praise and glory of God." While Mr. Wesley and his co-laborers were thus seeking earnestly to bring souls to the "knowledge of the truth," their success begat jealousy in

send into America other persons, who knew something of Greek and Latin; but knew no more of saving souls, than of catching whales.

"In this respect, also, I mourn for poor America—for the sheep scattered up and down therein. Part of them have no shepherds at all: particularly in the northern colonies; and the case of the rest is little better, for their own shepherds pity them not. They cannot, for they have no pity on themselves. They take no thought or care for their own souls.

"Wishing your lordship every blessing from the Great Shepherd and Bishop of our souls, I remain, my lord,

"Your lordship's dutiful son and servant,

"JOHN WESLEY."

The reader will readily forgive the length of this interesting letter, as it shows the great strait into which Mr. Wesley was brought on the account of his Societies in America. It shows, on the one hand, his anxiety to retain his Societies in the Episcopal Church, and the refusal of the ecclesiastical authorities of England to provide for them the ministry and the sacraments, and proves the absolute necessity of the course Mr. Wesley took in the ordination of Dr. Coke to the office of General Superintendent, and of the consequent organization of the Methodist Episcopal Church.

some of the clergymen of the establishment, and even in some of the dissenting ministers. All manner of objections were raised against him and his doctrines, and proceedings. He was assailed on one side by the Episcopal dignitaries of the church, and on the other, by the equally talented ministers of independent congregations; these objections called for replies, and rendered it necessary for Mr. Wesley and his friends to become polemics to a greater extent than was desired by themselves. Their disputations, however, and especially those of Mr. Wesley, and his friend, Mr. Fletcher, convinced their assailants that to raise objections was one thing, but to sustain them before a candid community, another, so that in spite of all opposing influences, the work of God continued to spread and grow, and the flame of revival to rise higher and higher, and spread wider and still wider.

Among the objections raised against Mr. Wesley by his illiberal opposers, was one of laying up treasure upon earth. So generally were reports of this kind circulated, and believed, that the commissioners of excise, on one occasion, wrote to him a letter in which they state that they cannot doubt but that Mr. Wesley had plate in his possession which he had heretofore neglected to report, and requiring him forthwith to make an entry of all plate, &c. in his possession. To this letter, Mr. Wesley replied:—

"I have two silver spoons at London, and two at Bristol. This is all the plate which I have at present, and I shall not buy any more while so many around me want bread.

"I am, sir, &c.,

"JOHN WESLEY."

In reference also to the same objection of hoarding up wealth, Mr. Wesley, during his sickness, before alluded to as a part of the epitaph prepared by himself for his tombstone, directed the insertion of the following words: "Not leaving, after his debts are paid, ten pounds behind him." Indeed Mr. Wesley, during his entire life, was governed by the following rule, which he frequently inculcated upon the attention of others: "Get all you can, Save all you can, Give away all you can." This rule, when properly understood, and faithfully adhered to, will prevent, as in Mr. Wesley's case, indulgence, prodigality, and penuriousness.

In the year 1784, Mr. Wesley's mind was greatly exercised in relation to the stability and government of the Methodist Society after his death, which event he foresaw could not be far distant. In order to prevent the disorganization of the Society, and to perpetuate the connection which had been established by him, he took the wise precaution of effecting a settlement of all the chapels in the connection, and giving a prospective direction to the affairs of the Conference and Society, by the enrollment in Chancery of a "Deed of Declaration," in which deed one hundred preachers, mentioned by name, are declared to be the "Conference of the people called Methodists." By means of this deed, a legal description was given to the term *Conference*, and the settlement of all chapels, &c. upon trustees was provided for. The deed also made provision for the legal occupancy of said chapels, and for the succession and perpetual identity of the yearly Conference, so that the President of the Conference should fill the place and be in fact the successor of Mr. Wesley himself. The "Deed of Declaration" thus drawn up, and enrolled, at once shows the strength of Mr. Wesley's mind, and his foreseeing sagacity. Probably no man then living but Mr. Wesley could have so well provided for the continued existence and increased stability of so large a body of preachers and people, and the history of the Connection for the past sixty years, or since the death of Mr. Wesley, proves that his efforts in the above direction were the result not of the wisdom of man merely, but of that "wisdom which cometh from above," that spirit of wisdom and sound understanding which God vouchsafes to those employed by him in carrying on his own work on earth.

Notwithstanding Mr. Wesley's advanced age, he continued to travel from place to place, visiting occasionally Scotland, Ireland, and Germany, in all places being received and honored as a distinguished messenger of God. As an illustration of the degree of esteem in which he was held even by those who differed with him theologically, we may be allowed to state, that, on one occasion, while visiting the ancient city of Perth, in Scotland, the freedom of the city was presented to him in the most becoming manner by the magistrates and corporation. Nor did his own countrymen hesitate to award to him that meed of praise which, although unsolicited and undesired by him, was nevertheless richly deserved.

In the beginning of the year 1791, Mr. Wesley took a severe cold, which finally terminated in death. His end was what might have been expected of such a holy, laborious servant of God,—eminently peaceful and triumphant. Among his last words were the oft-quoted ones, "THE BEST OF ALL IS GOD IS WITH US;" and, without a sigh or lingering groan, this eminent man—

"His body with his charge laid down,
And ceased at once to work and live."

Thus died John Wesley, in the eighty-eighth year of his age, and sixty-sixth of his ministry, on the 2d day of March, 1791. His funeral was attended on the 9th of the same month. His funeral-sermon was preached by Rev. Dr. Whitehead, to an astonishing multitude of people, including a large number of ministers of the gospel, both of the establishment and of dissenting churches. Indeed, so great were the crowds who came to see the body before the interment, that, apprehending confusion from the largeness of the multitude, his friends prudently resolved to bury the corpse at an early hour in the morning. His remains were deposited in a vault in the grave-yard of City-Road-Chapel, London.

As a scholar, Mr. Wesley had few superiors. He was a critic in the Latin and Greek classics, was well versed in Hebrew, and had a knowledge of several modern tongues. He was also well acquainted with the higher branches of mathematics, and the more abstruse sciences. He was also well read in medical science, and in natural history.

As a writer and compiler, Mr. Wesley had few equals. The very large list of works which he wrote, abridged, and edited for the press, affords sufficient evidence of his ability as a writer.

As a preacher, Mr. Wesley was more than an ordinary man. It is true he did not possess the impassioned powers of eloquence, displayed with so much success by Whitefield, but he surpassed the latter in sweetness of voice, in neatness and simplicity of style, and in easy and graceful action. His discourses were always short, seldom exceeding half an hour in length, and his subjects were always judiciously chosen, and were instructive and interesting to his usually large and attentive audiences.

In social life, Mr. Wesley was an exceedingly affable and agreeable man. In point of good-breeding, he was a perfect gentleman, and no one, not even an enemy, could be in his company long without feeling that he was in the presence of one who was able to command the respect of all with whom he had intercourse.

In labors Mr. Wesley was abundant. During the sixty-five years of his ministry he probably travelled not less than two hundred and seventy thousand miles! or more than *ten times the circumference of the globe;* or an average of four thousand five hundred miles annually. This, too, was accomplished mostly on horseback, although during the latter years of his life he was compelled, through the solicitations of friends, to use a carriage. In addition to the necessary labor of travelling, it has been estimated that he preached, on an average, two sermons daily for over fifty years of his life, or in the aggregate, of over forty thousand sermons! besides innumerable addresses, exhortations, prayers, &c., &c. If to this we add his literary labors, and his epistolary correspondence, together with the care of all the preachers and Societies subject to his direction, we need not hesitate to believe that no man since the days of the apostles, nay, not even the apostles themselves, were more abundant in labors than the apostle of Methodism, John Wesley. To accomplish so much, Mr. Wesley was necessarily very provident of his time. His hour of rising was four in the morning, summer and winter, so that while others were sleeping, Mr. Wesley had perhaps accomplished a good day's work.

Mr. Wesley's benevolence was unbounded, except by his want of means. One who well knew him, describes him as the most charitable man in England. He literally gave away all that he had, and from the income which he received, arising principally from the sale of his books, it has been estimated that he gave away for charitable purposes during his life, not less than *one hundred thousand dollars!* Notwithstanding his large income from the above and other sources, he died without leaving any property save his carriage and horses, a few clothes, and his books, which he bequeathed to the conference.

As a man of fervent piety, no person has been more preeminent in modern times, than the subject of this sketch. To doubt the piety of Wesley, would be to deny the existence of piety on earth, a species of skepticism equalled only by the profane ribaldry of a Paine, or the unblushing sophistries of a Voltaire; and yet, if John Wesley had been absolutely perfect, he had not been a mere man. "To err is human," and while we candidly believe that Mr. Wesley was as perfect as any man on earth, we would hesitate to claim for him an exemption from the frailties and infirmities incident to human nature. Of this no man was more sensible than Wesley himself; his frequent cry was,

"I the chief of sinners am,
But Jesus died for me."

Wesley, like all other pious men, was "a sinner saved by grace," and if in his deeds of piety, charity, and self-denial, he differed from others, it was the grace of God which made him to differ; and if he had qualifications fitting him for the important position of a religious reformer, and the founder of a large and respectable denomination of Evangelical Christians, to the same grace of God, he was entirely indebted for all such qualifications. Let the reader then adore the majesty of that grace, which raised up such a man as JOHN WESLEY, to adorn and bless the world, and while he adores, let the language of his heart be that of our own immortal poet:

"O, that I could all invite,
This saving truth to prove;
Show the length, and breadth, and height,
And depth of Jesus' love.
Fain I would to sinners show,
The blood by faith, alone applied,
Only Jesus' will I know,
And Jesus crucified."

CHAPTER II.

REV. CHARLES WESLEY, A.M.

THE subject of this sketch, was the third son of Rev. Samuel Wesley of Epworth, Eng., and the younger brother of Rev. John Wesley. He was born in Epworth, in the year 1708, and consequently was five years younger than his brother John. Nothing extraordinary appears to have taken place in his infancy and youth deserving of particular notice, except that he was educated at Westminster school, under the tuition of his brother Samuel, from whom, it is said, he imbibed the most ultra high church principles. After having been at school some years, a gentleman in Ireland by the name of Wesley, and possessed of a large fortune, wrote to Charles' father, offering to make the former his heir, and who subsequently sent him for several years, a sum of money annually, to assist him in his education. Finally the gentleman wished him to remove to Ireland, but Charles preferring to remain in England, the subject was dropped, and another person was selected as the heir, and who taking the property and honors left him by his benefactor, became in consequence the first Earl of Mornington, and grandfather of the present Duke of Wellington.

After pursuing his studies at Westminster School for a few years, Charles Wesley was elected to Christ's Church College, Oxford, and here, as stated in the previous chapter, he represents himself as losing his first year in diversions, the next he set himself to study ; diligence led him into serious thinking ; and he went weekly to the Sacrament, persuading two or three students to accompany him. He also strictly and methodically observed the course of study prescribed by the statutes of the University. "This," said he, "gained me the harmless name of *Methodist*." As John his brother, was at this time absent from Oxford, it would appear that Charles had the honor of being the first modern Methodist, and that he in fact laid the foundation of the religious Society which has since been distinguished by that name, although to his brother John, belongs the honor of forming the first Society of Methodists on a purely religious basis, without respect to educational interests, or merely personal improvement. In company with John, Charles Wesley spent much of his time in visiting the poor, the sick, and those in prison. These pious labors brought upon the two brothers a storm of persecution. Indeed their piety, their zeal, their devotion to the cause of God, created quite a sensation, not only within the precincts of the University, but became noised abroad, as instances of fanaticism and irregularity, so much so, that their father took a journey to Oxford that he might see and judge for himself in relation to the so called singularity of their proceedings. In writing home to his wife, he informs her, that he had been well repaid for his trouble and expense by the shining piety of their two sons.

As before stated, Charles Wesley accompanied his brother John as Missionary to Georgia, and as a prerequisite for his work, he received ordination. On their arrival in Georgia, Charles took charge of the colony at Frederica ; but here he met with much opposition from the colonists. Their licentious conduct called for frequent reproofs from their faithful pastor, and this at once made him an object of their most bitter hatred, and plots were formed either to ruin him in the opinion of Governor Oglethorpe, his friend and patron, or to take him off by violence. His enemies for a short time succeeded in prejudicing the mind of the Governor against him, who, in consequence of their falsehoods and misrepresentations, treated him with indifference, and left him to endure the greatest privations. It is said that he was obliged to lie upon the cold, damp ground, in the corner of a miserable hut, and was denied even the use of a few boards as a substitute for a bed. And as he had lost the favor of the Governor, the servants treated him coldly, and even insulted him. Thus worn out with hardship and ill-treatment, he was seized with a dangerous fever, and being possessed of an independent spirit, he, even while exposed to death through neglect, refused to let his wants be known to General Oglethorpe, who had treated him so indifferently. In this extremity he was visited by his brother John, through whose fraternal kindness, his wants were supplied, and his health partially restored. Soon after this, the Governor learned that Charles had been the victim of a base and wicked conspiracy; that the charges preferred against him were as false as they were malicious, and in consequence of this discovery, he became fully reconciled to the persecuted Missionary. Charles therefore exchanged places with John, the former taking charge of Savannah, and the latter of Frederica, but in July ensuing, the Governor sent him to England with despatches to the trustees and board of trade, and thus terminated his short mission to America, where he suffered the most bitter persecution for *righteousness' sake.*

In December of 1736, Charles Wesley again set foot on the shores of his native land, and having delivered his despatches, and discharged the duties assigned him by the governor of Georgia, he turned his attention once more to the great work of preaching the Gospel, in which work he continued, until the return of John from his foreign field of labor.*

* In August after Charles Wesley's return to England, he was made

In looking at the sacrifices and sufferings of Charles Wesley, at the sneers and scoffs of which he was the subject in Oxford, at his self-denial in leaving home and kindred for the sake of preaching Christ in a far distant land, at the contumely and reproach which he endured while there, who would hesitate to avow their firm belief that he was a *Christian* in the correct and proper acceptation of that term? And yet, Charles was but a servant of God, not a *Son*. He had not as yet received the "spirit of adoption," whereby he could cry "Abba Father." Peter Bohler had occasion to visit Charles, while the latter was lying upon a bed of sickness at Oxford. On conversing with him in relation to his hope of heaven, he learned that Charles was depending upon his own good works to secure eternal life,—that he was in fact a pharisee. And while Bohler endeavored to show the necessity of faith in Christ, and the utter worthlessness of his own righteousness, Charles was somewhat offended. After his recovery, however, by reading and meditation, he was convinced of his want of that faith which brings "peace and joy in the Holy Ghost." As he read and meditated, his convictions increased, until at length he was impelled by his sense of sin and danger, to throw himself like any other poor sinner, upon the naked merits of Christ for salvation, and he soon experienced that moral change of heart, which produced the fixed confidence of a child of God. Thus was Charles Wesley brought to *the knowledge of the truth as it is in Jesus*, a few days prior to the conversion of his brother John; and thus were these two brothers, prepared by the possession and enjoyment

the bearer of an address from the University, at Oxford, to his Majesty George III. He accordingly waited on the king at Hampton Court, and was graciously received, not only by the king, but by the archbishop. He was invited to dine with his majesty, and on the following day he dined at St. James' palace with the Prince of Wales, afterward George IV.

of personal salvation, to preach salvation to others—salvation from sin, from guilt, from fear, and from doubt in relation to the believer's acceptance with God.

During John Wesley's visit to the Moravian settlement at Hernhutt, as related in the previous chapter, Charles employed his time in preaching the doctrines of free grace and justification by faith, in the churches of London, and in holding meetings for prayer and mutual edification. He also visited Oxford, and was rendered useful to a number of his college friends. About this time also, the doctrines of predestination began to be warmly debated in their social meetings. Charles without entering fully into the merits of the case, contented himself with simply protesting against it. He also began to preach *extempore*, and although urged by his friend Mr. Whitefield to accept of a college living in Oxford, he refused to do so, for the reason, that he could make himself more useful in another sphere of action. During Mr. John Wesley's temporary absence from London, disputes arose in the Fetter Lane Society, in relation to lay preaching. Charles, whose notions in regard to the ministry were of a high-church character, protested warmly against the practice of allowing laymen to preach. But notwithstanding his high-churchism, he was strongly censured by the archbishop of Canterbury, who even hinted at the possibility of proceeding to excommunication, not on account of any erroneous doctrine promulgated by him, but simply on account of his irregularities in preaching *extempore*, &c., &c. The reproof of the archbishop threw him into great perplexity of mind in relation to what course he had better pursue, whether to recede from walking in what appeared to him the path of duty, and so obey the admonitions of his ecclesiastical superiors, or place all he had upon the altar of sacrifice, and try to do good in any place, and under any circumstances which Providence would seem to indicate. He conferred with Mr. Whitefield in relation to the matter, who advised him not to retract, but to preach in the *fields* on the next sabbath, by which step, he would render his retreat difficult if not impossible. Charles complied with this timely advice, and on the ensuing Sunday, preached to a congregation of a thousand perishing sinners in Moorfields. The Lord greatly blessed him in this effort, so that all his doubts were removed. He then proceeded to Kennington Common, where he preached to "multitudes on multitudes," and called upon them to "repent and believe the Gospel." From London, he proceeded to Oxford, and notwithstanding the opposition of the dean of the University to field preaching, he improved the opportunity of preaching to the University with great boldness, the doctrine of justification by faith. This latter doctrine, although fully taught in the XI. Article of Religion of the Church of England, had become obsolete as a matter of faith, and by most of the clergy and dignitaries of that church, was considered as a new doctrine, and not only as new, but as dangerous to the morals of the community and as jeopardizing the salvation of the soul. It was, therefore, a task imposed upon the Wesleys by the great Head of the Church, to revive this apostolic doctrine, and how successfully they accomplished this task, their subsequent history fully shows.

Among the earlier efforts of the Wesleys to benefit the poor and ignorant, was the establishment of a school in Kingswood for the instruction of the children of the poor, benighted colliers. The colliers in this locality, on account of their ignorance and wickedness, had been the terror of the entire community around them. But through the labors of Mr. Whitefield, and the Wesleys, many of them became exemplary for their piety and sobriety of conduct. The leaven thus introduced had a powerful influence, even upon the unconverted among them, as may be inferred from the following statement. On one occasion while Mr. Charles Wesley was in Bristol, he learned that the colliers of Kingswood had risen *en masse*, on account of the dearness of corn, and were marching to Bristol in a hostile manner to seek a redress of grievances. Mr. Wesley immediately rode out to meet them, to dissuade them from their purpose. Many seemed disposed to return to the school-house with him, but the more desperate rushed upon these, and violently drove them away from Mr. Wesley. He rode up to one desperado who was striking one of the pacific colliers, and asked him to strike him, rather than the collier. "No, not for all the world," replied the man, and became perfectly peaceable. Mr. Wesley seized one of the tallest of the mob, and besought him to follow him. "Yes, that I will, all the world over," replied he, and in this manner he pressed several of them into the service of peace and order, who returned with him to the school-house, singing as they went, and constantly increasing their strength and number. On arriving at the school, they spent about two hours in prayer that evil might be prevented, and the lion be chained. Soon word was brought that the mob had returned without having offered any violence to person or thing, but having simply stated their grievances to the mayor of the city. Charles Wesley found that every Methodist who had gone out with the rabble, had been literally forced to go. One of them, the rioters had dragged out of his sick bed, and thrown him into the fish-pond. Mr. Wesley adds, "It was a happy circumstance that they forced so many of the Methodists to go with them, as these by their advice and example restrained the savage fury of the others." As the Wesleys continued to gain increased influence over the hearts and minds of the colliers of Kingswood, the latter became more and more enlightened, until at length, those who had previously been but at a single remove from the brute creation in point of intelligence, and beneath the brutes in regard to their actions, became an intelligent, moral, virtuous, and pious people, "whose praise," even to this day, "is in all the churches."

Such results as the above, followed the labors of the Wesleys more or less wherever they went. The vicious, profane, and disorderly were converted into peaceable and order-loving subjects, and yet strange as it may seem, clergymen, magistrates, and officers of the army, not only opposed, and ridiculed, but even headed mobs of violent men for the purpose of preventing their preaching. Many illustrations of the truth of these remarks might be given. We will in this place give one or two instances.

In the year 1743, Charles Wesley went to visit the Society in Sheffield, who were as sheep among wolves, "the minister having so stirred up the people, that they were ready to tear the Methodists in pieces." "At six o'clock," says Mr. Chas. Wesley, "I went to the Society-house, next door to our Br. Bennett's. Hell, from beneath, was moved to oppose us. As soon as I was in the desk with David Taylor, the floods began to lift up their voice An officer in the army contradicted and blasphemed. I took no notice of him, but sang on. The stones flew thick, striking the desk, and the people. To save them and the house from being pulled down, I gave out that I should preach in the street, and look them in the face. The whole army of the aliens followed me. The Captain laid hold on me, and began rioting: I gave him for answer, 'A Word in Season, or Advice to a Soldier.' I then particularly prayed for his majesty King George, and preached the gospel with much contention. The stones often struck me in the face. I prayed for sinners, as servants of their master the devil; upon which the Captain ran at me with great fury, threatening revenge for abusing, as he called it, the King his master. He forced his way through the brethren, drew his sword, and presented it to my breast. I immediately opened my breast, and fixing my eye on his, and smiling in his face, calmly said, 'I fear God and honor the King.' His countenance fell in a moment, he fetched a deep sigh, and putting up his sword, quietly left the place. He had said to one of the company, who afterward informed me, 'You shall see if I do but hold my sword to his breast, he will faint away!' So, perhaps, I should, had I only his principles to trust to; but if at that time I was not afraid, no thanks to my personal courage. We returned to our Br. Bennett's, and gave ourselves up to prayer. The rioters followed, and exceeded in outrage all I have seen before. Those at Moorfields, Cardiff, and Walsal, were lambs to these. As there is no 'King in Israel,' I mean no magistrate in Sheffield, every man doeth as seemeth good in his own eyes." The mob now formed the design of pulling down the Society-house, and set upon their work while Charles Wesley and the people were praying and praising God within. "It was a glorious time with us; every word of exhortation sunk deep, every prayer was sealed, and many found the Spirit of Glory resting upon them." The next day the house was completely pulled down, not one stone being left upon another. He then preached again in the street, somewhat more quietly than before; but the rioters became very noisy in the evening, and threatened to pull down the house where he lodged. He went out to them, and made a suitable exhortation, "and they soon after separated, and peace was restored."

On the next day he left the place, but in passing through Thorpe, he found the people exceedingly mad against him. While turning down a lane, a large number who had been lying in ambush, arose and assaulted Mr. Wesley and his companion, Mr. Taylor, with stones, eggs, and dirt. They severely wounded the latter on the forehead, from which the blood ran freely. Mr. Wesley's horse turned from side to side, till he found his way through the mob. He then turned, and asked the reason why a clergyman could not pass without such treatment. At first the rioters scattered, but their captain soon rallied them again, and answered with horrible imprecations and stones. Mr. Wesley's horse took fright, and ran with him violently down a steep hill, the mob pursuing and shouting with all their might. Mr. Wesley barely escaped with his life, being covered from head to foot with eggs and dirt.

Shortly after the above occurrence, Mr. Charles Wesley visited Leeds, where he was treated with great respect by the resident clergymen. From Leeds he went to Newcastle, where he abounded in labors for the salvation of souls, and where his efforts were signally blessed of God. He soon after went to Nottingham, where he met his brother John, who had just returned from Wednesbury, where he had been the subject of abuse from one of the vilest mobs that ever disgraced Christendom. In referring to the meeting of the two brothers, Charles Wesley remarks: "My brother came delivered out of the mouth of the lion! His clothes were torn to tatters; he looked like a soldier of Christ. The mob of Wednesbury, Darlaston, and Walsal, were permitted to take and carry him about for several hours, with a full intent to murder him: but his work is not yet finished, or he had been now with the souls under the altar." Charles, undaunted by such usage, set out immediately for Wednesbury, that he might encourage the poor persecuted Societies.

In 1743, Charles Wesley visited Cornwall, and here he preached amidst mobs and tumults, to the most degraded and neglected portion of the inhabitants of England; and here too were his labors and those of his brother rewarded by the sound conversion of hundreds of those semi-savages; and in this unpromising soil many precious plants were subsequently reared to the praise of God, so that until the present day, Methodism has had a strong hold on the affections of the inhabitants of Cornwall, and in no part of the kingdom has it flourished more, or exerted a more benign influence upon the hearts and lives of its votaries; although at first every effort was put forth by the civil, military, and ecclesiastical authorities, to stop the flame of reformation. The members of the Society, and even the preachers were seized by the press-gang—the shame of England—and impressed into the army, but, through the abounding grace of God, the fire continued to burn, until at length poor, debased Cornwall has been redeemed through the influence of Methodism, and a large majority of the people have become identified with the "sect" which was once "everywhere spoken against."

As a further illustration of the treatment received by Mr. Charles Wesley, in his efforts to do good, we may be allowed to introduce the following statement. "The year 1745 was chiefly spent by him in London, Bristol, and Wales. In the early part of the next year, he proceeded to Cornwall. * * * On his return to London, through the introduction of Mr. E. Perronet, a pious young man, he visited the Rev. Vincent Perronet, the venerable Vicar of Shoreham in Kent. * * * Being invited to perform service in Shoreham church, 'as soon as I began to preach,' says he, 'the wild beasts began roaring, stamping, blaspheming, ringing the bells, and turning the church into a bear-garden. I spoke on for half an hour, though only the nearest could hear. The rioters followed us to Mr. Perronet's house, raging, threatening, and throwing stones. Charles Perronet hung over me, to intercept the blows. They continued their uproar after we got into the house.' From Shoreham Mr. Wesley and his young friend returned to London, and from thence proceeded to the north of England. On the way they called at Tippen Green in Staffordshire. Being in a house, without any design of preaching, and the mob being aware of Mr. Wesley's presence, beset the house, and while beating the door, demanded entrance. 'I sat still,' says Mr. Wesley, 'in the midst of them, for half an hour, and was a little concerned for E. Perronet, lest such rough treatment at his first setting out should daunt him. But he abounded in valor, and was for reasoning with the wild beasts, before they had spent any of their violence. He got a good deal of abuse thereby, and not a little dirt, both of which he took very patiently. I had no design to preach, but being called upon by so unexpected a congregation, I rose at last, and read, 'When the Son of man shall come in his glory, and all his holy angels with him, &c.' While I reasoned with them of judgment to come, they grew calmer, little by little. I then spoke to them one by one, till the Lord had disarmed them all.' "

After visiting Newcastle, he went to Hexham, where he preached in the market-place. A multitude stood staring at him, but all remained quiet. None offered to interrupt, but one unfortunate country esquire, who could prevail on no one to second his attempts at persecution. His servants and the constables hid themselves. One of the latter the squire found, and ordered him to go and take Mr. Wesley down. The constable replied : " Sir, I cannot have the face to do it, for what harm does he ?" After preaching, Mr. Wesley walked through the people, who acknowledged that what he had preached was truth. A constable followed, who told Mr. Wesley, " Sir Edward Blacket orders you to *disperse* the town ('depart, I suppose he meant,' says Mr. Wesley), and not raise a disturbance here." Mr. Wesley sent his respects to Sir Edward, and stated that if he would give him leave he would wait on him, and satisfy him. The man soon returned with the answer, that Sir Edward would have nothing to say to him, but that if he preached again and raised a disturbance he would put the law in execution against him. Mr. Wesley, however, was not so easily intimidated. He did preach again in the cock-pit, where he expected Satan would meet him on his own ground. He took for his text, "Repent, and be converted, that your sins may be blotted out." The justice's son labored hard to raise a mob, for which Mr. Wesley was to be held answerable, but the very boys ran away from him. The squire, however, persuaded a few to return, and cry "fire," but no further disturbance took place. A good influence was felt in this place, as the result of Mr. Wesley's labors.

Some time after this, Charles Wesley visited Devizes, where, while preaching in a private house, he was assailed by a furious mob, led on by the curate of the parish and two dissenters. They brought a hand-engine, and began to play into the house. A constable came and seized the spout of the engine, and carried it off. They, however, went and got the larger engine, with which they broke the windows, flooded the rooms, and spoiled the goods. The rioters continued their work of destruction until the constable read the proclamation. The greater part of them then dispersed, but the magistrate refusing to act, they took fresh courage and returned, when they made a personal attack on the house. Thinking Mr. Wesley had escaped, they rushed to the tavern where his horses were. They ordered the horses turned out, which the innkeeper did, and sent them to a neighbor's, whither the mob followed with their engine, but the man to whom the horses were sent seized his gun, and threatened to fire on them, which induced them to retreat. After enduring such treatment for a number of hours, a gentleman came and said, "Sir, if you will promise never to preach here again, I will engage to bring you safe out of town." Mr. Wesley's reply was, "I shall promise no such thing; setting aside my office, I will not give up my birth-right, as an Englishman, of visiting what place I please of his Majesty's dominions." After intimating that he had no design of preaching there again at present, the gentleman and a constable went out and influenced the mob to allow Mr. Wesley to depart in peace.

Mr. Wesley and his companion at length mounted their horses, the whole multitude pouring down upon them like a torrent, and being ready to swallow them up; such was their fierceness and malice. Through the good providence of God, these persecuted men finally succeeded in reaching a place of safety, where they raised their hymns of thanksgiving to God.

From these painful exhibitions of the depravity of the unrenewed heart, we learn the extreme danger to which the early Methodists, and especially the Wesleys, were exposed, while going about doing good; and it is certainly a matter of astonishment, that men, professed Christians, and professed Christian ministers, should not only lend their aid, but even incite, and personally participate in such disgraceful scenes of persecution; yet so it was, and these historical events leave a dark and uneffaceable spot upon the annals of that church which claimed, and still claims to be the only pure church of Jesus Christ. Volumes might be filled with accounts of such outrages upon the persons and properties of peaceable men, whose only crime was preaching the gospel of the Son of God in what some chose to call an *irregular* and uncanonical manner. But our space will not allow us to make many reflections of this character. We therefore pass to the subject more properly before us.

Shortly after the events transpired as above narrated, Charles Wesley visited Ireland, from which place his brother John had recently returned. He was accompanied by his friend Charles Perronet—son of the Vicar of Shoreham—who had become one of Mr. Wesley's preachers. A small Society had been organized in Dublin a short time previously, and the first news which Charles Wesley had when he landed, was, that a violent storm of persecution had raged against the infant society, ever since the departure of John Wesley. The popish mob had broken open their place of worship, and destroyed everything before them. Some of the rioters were sent to jail, but the grand jury refused to find a bill against them, and thus the Methodists were given up to the fury of a lawless and bigoted mob. Mr. Charles Wesley found the Society standing fast in the midst of the fiery ordeal, and he became so much attached to the members, because of their simplicity and piety, that he spent the entire winter with them, preaching and visiting daily from house to house. He also made frequent excursions into the country places around Dublin, scattering the precious seed wherever he went. He subsequently spent a part of the year 1748 in Ireland, and preached in several of the larger towns and cities, and especially in Cork, where his labors were greatly blessed to the good of the people.

In the year 1749, Charles Wesley was united in marriage to a lady every way worthy of his affection, and suitable in every way to make a useful and agreeable companion. In his marriage relations, he was more fortunate than his brother John, although it must be confessed that the charms of home in the latter part of his life, made him much more domestic in his habits, and consequently far less active, than his less entangled brother; not that he had ceased to be actively employed in his Master's vineyard, but less of his time was subsequently given to itinerant labors.

In the year 1750 there was a great earthquake in London. Charles Wesley was preaching in the *Foundry* at five in the morning, when the second shock occurred. He had just taken his text, when the building shook so violently, that all expected it would fall on their heads and crush them beneath its ruins. A great cry arose from the women and children. While the earth was moving westward and eastward, like an ocean wave, and a loud, jarring noise like thunder was produced, and while expecting every moment to be their last, Mr. Wesley rose, and cried out, "*Therefore we will not fear, though the earth be moved, and the hills be carried into the midst of the sea; for the Lord of hosts is with us; the God of Jacob is our refuge.*" The effect of this earthquake on the minds of the people of London was so great, that thousands fled from the city, and places of worship were thronged by day and night. Thousands also left their houses and sought safety in the open fields, where they remained all night. To such Mr. Whitefield preached at midnight, while Charles Wesley attempted to comfort the affrighted multitudes who remained in their houses, or resorted to the usual place of worship. This unlooked-for event was no doubt improved upon by these and other good men, so that as a result of the fears begotten in the public mind, many were led to feel their want of preparation for death and judgment, and were led to seek for pardon, and a regenerate heart at the hand of their Saviour.

Shortly after the event above alluded to, Charles Wesley appears to have accepted a commission from his brother John, to travel through the entire connection, and inquire into the character of all the preachers,—who had now become somewhat numerous—and also to inform himself in relation to their mode of administering discipline, and to become more particularly acquainted with the state of the Societies under their care. In the course of his tour of inspection, Charles saw much to admire, and also a few things which caused deep regret. Among the latter he discerned a growing disposition on the part of both preachers and people to sever themselves *in toto* from the Church of England. On his return to London, after having completed his tour, he attempted to prevail on his brother to require of every preacher employed by him a solemn pledge, that they would not make any attempt to sever the Societies from the Church, and to render this course still more successful, he persuaded John to sign an agreement by which no preacher was to be called into the work, except by the joint consent of the two brothers. This proposed plan, however, did not succeed according to the wishes and expectations of Charles. The Societies and preachers had so long been accustomed to look up to *John* as the sole fountain of authority in such matters, that any division of his power in these respects was not greatly relished, especially as John, in all his intercourse with the preachers and people, was more bland and lenient than Charles felt disposed to be. The result of such attachment to the authority of John rather than to that of Charles, very naturally led the latter to suppose that he had perhaps mistaken his true position, and led him more than ever to withdraw himself from public life, thus leaving his brother to direct solely the affairs of the large and growing connection. There was, however, no abatement of affection between the brothers, nor does there appear to have been any degree of jealousy or ill feeling engendered, although it is evident that there did exist a difference of opinion between them in relation to the attachment of the preachers and people to the Church of England. "Church or no Church," said John in a letter to Charles, "we must attend to the work of saving souls." "I neither set it up, nor pull it down; but let you and I build the city of God."

Subsequently to these events, Charles Wesley became more retired and domesticated, travelling but little, except when sickness or infirmity on the part of John made it necessary for him to supply his brother's place in preaching in London, Bristol, and other places; and it is a pleasing evidence of the continued affection of the brothers, and of Charles's unabated interest for the Societies, that he strongly urged his brother to "keep his authority while he lived, and after death to let it be given to the worthiest individuals." "You cannot," he says, "settle the succession, you cannot divine how God will settle it."

In the year 1784 John Wesley resolved on erecting his Societies in North America into an independent Episcopal Church, and for the purpose of carrying out his intentions, solemnly set apart Dr. Coke, one of his preachers, and a presbyter of the Church of England, to the important office of Superintendent. Charles Wesley's love for the "Church," awakened opposition to this course of procedure. Some letters passed between the brothers on this occasion. At first, Charles was warm, and remonstrative, but on receiving his brother's calm answer, he became mild, and assured his brother of his undying love and affection. He, however, continued to look with some degree of suspicion upon the acts of Dr. Coke, and evidently feared that after his brother's death, the Doctor would resolve the English Societies into a separate and independent Methodist Church. Such fears, however, were no doubt premature and uncalled for, as the Doctor knew full well, that what might be demanded by a Society under an independent Civil Government where there is no church establishment, might not be suitable for a Society under different circumstances; and the result of the establishment of an independent Church in America, shows that John Wesley's policy in providing for the spiritual wants of his children was by no means a mistaken one, but has been followed by the best of consequences to the Church and to the world; and had Charles Wesley lived until the present day, he would no doubt have acknowledged that his brother's course was ordered in wisdom, and that in doing as he did, he was actuated and influenced by the Spirit of God.

On the 29th of March, 1788, the Rev. Charles Wesley departed this life, in the eightieth year of his age, and fifty-third of his ministry, and was buried on the 5th of April, in Marylebone church-yard, London, the pall being supported by eight clergymen of the Church of England. He had for a long time been weak in body, and in his last moments he had the most unshaken confidence in God. Shortly before his death he dictated the following beautiful and expressive lines:—

"In age and feebleness extreme,
Who shall a sinful worm redeem?
Jesus, my only hope thou art,
Strength of my failing flesh and heart;
O, could I catch a smile from thee,
And drop into eternity!"

The character of Mr. Charles Wesley has been beautifully drawn by one of his daughters, in a letter to a friend. In speaking of some remarks made by a certain author in reference to her deceased father, she says: "Mr. Moore seems to think that my father preferred rest to going about doing good. He had a rising family, and considered it his duty to confine his labors to Bristol and London, where he labored most sedulously in ministerial affairs, and judged that it was incumbent upon him to watch over the youth of his sons, especially in a profession which nature so strongly pointed out, but which was peculiarly dangerous. He always said his brother was formed to lead, and he to follow. No one ever rejoiced more in another's superiority, or was more willing to confess it. Mr. Moore's statement of his absence of mind in his younger days is probably correct, as he was born impetuous, and ardent, and sincere. But what a change must have taken place when we were born! For his exactness in his accounts, in his manuscripts, in his bureau, &c., equalled my uncle's. Not in his dress indeed; for my mother said, if she did not watch over him, he might have put on an old for a new coat, and marched out. Such was his power of abstraction, that he could read and compose with his children in the room, and visitors talking around him. He was near forty when he married, and had eight children, of whom we were the youngest. So kind and amiable a character in domestic life can scarcely be imagined. The tenderness he showed in every weakness, and the sympathy in every pain, would fill sheets to describe. But I am not writing his eulogy; only I must add, with so warm a temper, he never was heard to speak an angry word to a servant, or known to strike a child in anger,—and he knew no guile!"

Charles Wesley was a scholar of very respectable attainments, but what will immortalize his name as long as Christianity endures, is his poetic talent. In this department of literary labor—if labor it may be called—we venture the assertion, that Charles Wesley had no superior. The justly celebrated Isaac Watts was no doubt an equal in many respects, and perhaps even a superior in others; but even he candidly admitted that Charles Wesley's "Wrestling Jacob" was superior to anything the former had ever written. To both of these clergymen the church of God is largely indebted for the soul-stirring poetry found in the devotional works of nearly all Protestant denominations. We will close this already extended article by giving, as a specimen of Charles Wesley's poetry, the following beautiful hymn, *On the Spread of the Gospel:*

"See how great a flame aspires,
Kindled by a spark of grace!
Jesus' love the nations fires,
Sets the kingdoms in a blaze.
To bring fire on earth he came,
Kindled in some hearts it is:
O, that all might catch the flame,
All partake the glorious bliss!

When he first the work begun,
Small and feeble was his day:
Now the word doth swiftly run,
Now it wins its wid'ning way:
More and more it spreads and grows,
Ever mighty to prevail;
Sin's strong holds it now o'erthrows,
Shakes the trembling gates of hell.

Sons of God, your Saviour praise!
He the door hath opened wide;
He hath given the word of grace,
Jesus' word is glorified;
Jesus mighty to redeem,
He alone the work hath wrought,
Worthy is the work of him,
Him who spake a world from naught.

Saw ye not the cloud arise,
Little as a human hand?
Now it spreads along the skies,
Hangs o'er all the thirsty land;
Lo! the promise of a shower
Drops already from above;
But the Lord will shortly pour
All the Spirit of his love!"

4

CHAPTER III.

REV. JOHN W. FLETCHER, A.M.

John William De La Flechere was born in Nyon in Switzerland (near Geneva), on the 12th of September, 1729. His father was an officer in the French army, and intended his son John for the service of the Church. He was accordingly placed while yet young at the school in Geneva, where he made great proficiency in his studies, and distanced all his competitors in their efforts to secure the customary prizes. After quitting Geneva, he was sent to a small town to perfect himself in the study of the German language, and on his return home he applied himself to the study of the Hebrew with great diligence and assiduity. In very early life he discovered the elements of Christian piety, and his thorough acquaintance with the sacred Scriptures preserved him from falling into those sins and follies so common to the young. He in fact abhorred sin from his youth up, and in a becoming manner always reproved it in others. Young Fletcher had several remarkable escapes from death ; so remarkable indeed that his biographer, Mr. Wesley, hesitates not to avow his belief, that his deliverance in one case was nothing short of miraculous. After having completed his studies at the University of Geneva, contrary to the design of his parents, and contrary to his own design hitherto, he resolved to become a soldier. His reasons for this unexpected step, as afterwards given by himself, were, 1st. His want of qualification for the high and holy calling of a minister of the gospel; 2dly. His scruples about subscribing to the doctrine of predestination, which he must do if he took orders in Switzerland; and 3dly. His disapproval of entering the sacred office for the sake of a livelihood, or to obtain preferment. Hence he went to Lisbon and accepted a Captain's commission in the service of the King of Portugal, designing to go to Brazil, but an accident prevented his sailing. About this period also his uncle had obtained a commission for him in the Dutch army, which he resolved to accept, but the declaration of peace prevented his being engaged in active service.

Being thus thrown out of active employment, he went to England, but not having made himself acquainted with the English language, he labored under serious difficulties in making his wants understood. While in an inn, Mr. Fletcher heard a well-dressed Jew speaking French, and engaged him to change his foreign money for English currency. Without due reflection he gave the man ninety pounds to exchange for him, and on making known the fact to his companions, they exclaimed with one accord, "Your money is gone; you need not expect to see a crown or doit of it any more!" As it was all the money Mr. Fletcher had, he of course felt uneasy about it, but in his extremity he commended his cause to God, and in a short time the Jew returned, and brought him the whole of the money. This little incident exhibits not only the piety of Mr. Fletcher, and his constant dependence on God under all circumstances, but it served to show him the importance of becoming acquainted with the English language. Accordingly he soon placed himself at a boarding-school for this express purpose, where he also pursued the study of polite literature. His easy and affable manners soon gained him the esteem and respect of the town's people where the school was situated, and he was a welcome guest at the houses of the first families in the place.

After remaining a year and a half at this school, and having perfected himself in the English tongue, he accepted the situation of tutor in the family of a Mr. Hill, in Ternhall, Shropshire. A little incident which transpired here, served to convince Mr. Fletcher that however pious and God-fearing he might have been, he was yet, like all others, a fallen creature, and stood in need of the pardoning mercy of God. One Sunday evening, a servant came into his room to make up his fire, while Mr. Fletcher was engaged in writing some music. The servant, seriously and respectfully, said, "Sir, I am sorry to see you so employed on the Lord's day." Although mortified at being reproved by a servant, he felt the reproof to be just, immediately put away his music, and ever after was a strict observer of the Sabbath.

When Mr. Hill went to London to attend the Parliament, he was accompanied by his family, and Mr. Fletcher. While stopping at a town on the road, Mr. Fletcher walked out, and did not return until the family had started for London. A horse, however, was left for him, and he overtook the family in the evening. On being asked why he stayed behind, he replied: "As I was walking, I met with a poor old woman, who talked so sweetly of Jesus, that I knew not how the time passed away." Mrs. Hill replied: "I shall wonder if our tutor does not turn Methodist, by and bye." "Methodist, madam! pray what is that?" "Why, the Methodists are a people that do nothing but pray; they are praying all day and all night." "Are they?" replied Mr. Fletcher, "then by the help of God I will find them out, if they be above ground." He did find them out in London, and at once became a member of the Society. Hitherto Mr. Fletcher had feared God, but he had not as yet saving faith. This he soon learned to his grief, after having heard a sermon preached on the subject of faith by a clergyman of the Church. "Is it possible," said he, "that I, who have always been accounted so religious, who have made divinity my study, and received the premium of piety from my University for my writings on Divine subjects,—is it possible that I should yet be so ignorant as not to know what faith is?" The more he reflected the more convinced he became that he was in fact a stranger to the love of God, that he was a sinner, and deserved to be damned. He finally resolved, that if sent to hell, he would serve God there, and that if he could not be an instance of his mercy in heaven, he would be a monument of his justice in hell. Soon, however, he ventured to believe in Christ as a universal Redeemer, and as his personal Saviour, and after a hard and prolonged struggle with the powers of darkness, he became a "new man" in Christ Jesus. Let not the reader think that Mr. Fletcher was beside himself, and that he was superstitious or fanatical in his efforts to obtain the favor of God. Saul of Tarsus, the two Wesleys, and hundreds of the great and good before Mr. Fletcher's time, had felt the burden of sin, and although previously moral and virtuous in their lives, and God-fearing in their disposition, were nevertheless constrained to exclaim, "O, wretched man that I am, who shall deliver me from this body of death?" and who, after having exercised faith in Christ, could also exclaim, "There is, therefore, now, no condemnation to them who are in Christ Jesus, who walk not after the flesh, but after the Spirit; for the law of the Spirit of life in Christ Jesus, hath made *me free* from the law of sin and death." And thus Mr. Fletcher attained to the adoption of a "son of God" and an heir of heaven.

After his conversion, Mr. Fletcher became an eminent instance of vital piety; his hopes, desires, and pursuits became totally changed. He now felt it his duty to call sinners to repentance, and an opening having been made whereby he could obtain a "living" in the Church of England, if he desired it, he took counsel of Mr. Wesley in relation to the propriety of taking orders in that Church, and on the 6th of March, 1757, he received deacon's orders in the Chapel-Royal at St. James, from the Bishop of Bangor, and on the following Sabbath was admitted to the order of the priesthood by the same Bishop.

The same day that he was ordained priest, being informed that Mr. Wesley had no one to assist him at West-street Chapel, as soon as the ordination service was over, he hastened to assist him in the administration of the Lord's Supper; and from this time forward fully identified himself with the Methodists by co-operating, as opportunity offered, with the Wesleys and their preachers. He soon afterward visited the country places around London, and preached in several of the churches, but his plain manner of telling the truth, and above all, the Divine unction which attended his preaching, offended several of the clergymen, who closed their churches against him.

In the year 1758 there were many French prisoners in London, who desired Mr. Fletcher to preach to them in their own language, which he did. Many of them were deeply affected, and desired him to preach to them every Sabbath. They were, however, advised to present a petition to the Bishop of London for leave, but, strange to say, the Bishop in the most peremptory manner rejected their petition. A few months after, his lordship died with a cancer in his mouth. Mr. Wesley, in reference to this event, says, "I do not think it any breach of charity to suppose, that an action so unworthy of a Christian bishop had its punishment in this world."

During the sessions of parliament, Mr. Fletcher was generally in London with his kind friends, Mr. and Mrs. Hill, the latter of whom had predicted that Mr. F. would yet be a Methodist, and whose prediction had indeed come to pass. During the recess of Parliament Mr. Fletcher might be found in his study at Ternhall, improving his mind and heart, and walking closely with his God.

In a letter written by Mr. Charles Wesley to Mr. Fletcher, the former had intimated something in relation to a salary which Mr. Fletcher should have for his labors; in reply to this the latter observes: "To what a monstrous idea had you well nigh given birth. What! the labors of *my* ministry under you deserve salary! Alas! I have done nothing but dishonor to God hitherto, and am not in a condition to do anything else for the future. If, then, I am permitted to stand in the courts of the Lord's house, is it not for me to make an acknowledgment, rather than to receive one? If I ever receive anything of the Methodist Church, it shall be only as an indigent beggar receives alms, without which he would perish."

About this time, Mr. Fletcher's friends in Switzerland were pressing him with invitations to return to his own country, but supposing their desires to be purely the result of natural affection, he preferred staying where his time could be more profitably employed in aiding the Messrs. Wesley in their work of love. About this time also he received a very polite invitation from the Countess of Huntingdon, to become her ladyship's domestic chaplain, but his engagements with the Wesleys prevented his acceptance of the kind offer; so that until the following autumn his time was mostly employed in rendering them and their Societies all necessary assistance. In the meanwhile he had frequently assisted the Rev. Mr. Chambers, Vicar of Madely—a place about ten miles from Ternhall—and had contracted a strong and growing love for the people of that parish. Mr. Chambers having accepted a living in another parish, the vicarage of Madely, through the interest of his friend, Mr. Hill, was offered to Mr. Fletcher, and after having taken the advice of the Messrs. Wesley and others, he concluded to accept the offer, and in due form was instituted Vicar of Madely, which relation he sustained as long as he lived.

At Madely, a new field of operation presented itself before him. The town was a place of considerable importance, both on account of its manufactures and population. The greater portion of the inhabitants, however, were very degraded and vicious. Ignorance, profanity, Sabbath-breaking, and drunkenness, prevailed to an alarming extent, and even the external forms of religion were ridiculed. Young persons of both sexes, at stated times, would meet and spend the entire night in dancing, revelling, drunkenness, and obscenity. These assemblages were truly a disgrace to the Christian name, and frequently did Mr. Fletcher repair to these scenes of disorder and dissipation, and administer plain, yet affectionate reproof to the thoughtless persons therein congregated, and frequently these reproofs were not in vain, for, although at first there might be a burst of indignation at the bold interference, his tears, his prayers, and exhortations, would generally be crowned with success. The great mass of the people did not attend public worship, and many gave as an excuse for non-attendance, that they could not wake early enough to get their families ready. To remedy this, Mr. Fletcher, taking a bell in his hand, sallied out every Sunday morning for some months at five o'clock, and went round to the most distant parts of the town, inviting all the inhabitants to the house of worship.

These facts are stated merely as an evidence of Mr. Fletcher's ministerial fidelity to the people of his parish. But notwithstanding his fidelity, he saw so little fruit of his labors that he was frequently on the point of leaving Madely, and giving himself wholly to the itinerant work under the direction of the Messrs. Wesley. His greatest discouragement arose from the smallness of his congregations ; but soon this cause of despondency was removed, for not only did his church become full, but many had to stand in the church-yard who could not get into the house. So great indeed was the crowd at times, that Mr. Fletcher's churchwardens spoke of hindering persons of other parishes from attending church in that place ; but their faithful pastor withstood them, and was successful in preventing such a disgraceful proceeding.

Although Mr. Fletcher was the resident Vicar of a parish, he did not confine his labors to that parish, but wherever a door opened for doing good he was ready to enter in. He frequently visited two villages not far distant from Madely, where he formed small societies of Methodists. He also regularly preached for many years at places eight, ten, and sixteen miles off. Notwithstanding his devotion to the cause of God, Mr. Fletcher, like his compeers, the Wesleys, was the subject of persecution and reproach. And it is lamentable to know, that, as in the case of the Wesleys, so in Mr. Fletcher's case, the greatest amount of persecution was caused by the unprincipled and uncalled-for opposition of church-dignitaries, and civil magistrates, who added threats to their insults, and who, if they did not stir up the unholy passions of the multitude, were perfectly willing to stand by and see a faithful minister abused and maltreated, for no other reason than that they themselves "loved darkness rather than light, because their deeds were evil."

The opposition of the innkeepers, tipplers, gamblers, &c., to Mr. Fletcher was intense, and exhibited itself in various ways. On one occasion, a stout and healthy young man, twenty-four years old, came to the church-yard in Madely with a corpse, which was to be buried, but refused to enter the church. After the burial, Mr. Fletcher expostulated with him, but his answer was, that he had bound himself not to come to church as long as Mr. Fletcher was there, and that he was prepared to take all the consequences of his refusal. As Mr. Fletcher turned away in sorrow, he could not forbear saying to the young man, "I am clear of your blood, henceforth it is upon your own head; you will not come to church upon your legs, prepare to come upon your neighbor's shoulders." The young man immediately began to waste away, and in three months was buried on the very spot where the above conversation was had. Mr. F. visited him during his sickness, when "he seemed as tame as a wolf in the trap."

Mr. Fletcher not only labored assiduously for the benefit of his parishioners, but he frequently invited Rev's. John and Charles Wesley to visit his parish, and preach in his church. He also invited Mr. Wesley's preachers to visit his parish, and take the charge of the Methodist Societies which he had raised up. He also invited the Rev. George Whitefield to visit his parish, and in his letter of invitation on one occasion he says: "Last Sunday sevennight Captain Scott preached to my congregation a sermon which was more blessed, though preached only upon my horse-block, than a hundred of those I preach in my pulpit. I invited him to come and treat her ladyship (Countess of Huntingdon) next Sunday with another, now the place is consecrated. If you should ever favor Shropshire with your presence, you shall have the Captain's or the parson's pulpit at your option." A distinction is here drawn between the "Captain's and the parson's pulpit." The "Captain" and Mr. Wesley's lay preachers not having been episcopally ordained, could not legally be admitted to the pulpit of the parish church, while Mr. Whitefield and the Wesleys, having received episcopal ordination, could lawfully be invited to preach in the same. Hence if Captain Scott and Mr. Wesley's lay preachers did not occupy Mr. Fletcher's pulpit, it was only because the law would not allow it; while the horse-block, or the desk of the Society-house, or a room in Mr. Fletcher's parsonage, were always open for the public services of those men of God who were called to the work of the ministry without episcopal authority.

In 1765, Mr. Fletcher visited different parts of England, and while spending a few Sabbaths at a place called Breedon, Leicestershire, people flocked to hear him from all the adjacent parishes. The clerk of the church being offended at the large attendance of people, because it increased his labor in cleaning the church, &c., placed himself at the door, and demanded a penny of every stranger who entered. Mr. Fletcher having been informed of the fact, at the close of the service, said to the congregation, "I have heard that the clerk of this parish has demanded, and has actually received money from divers strangers, before he would suffer them to enter the church. I desire that all who have paid money in this way for hearing the gospel, will come to me, and I will return what they have paid. And as to this iniquitous clerk, his money perish with him."

In the year 1770, Mr. Fletcher paid a visit to his native land, and in addition to visiting Switzerland, he and his friend, Mr. Ireland, travelled through the greater part of France and Italy. The five months spent in this tour were not, however, lost, as wherever Mr. Fletcher went, he tried to make himself useful to the souls of his fellow-men. He even visited the Roman Catholic monasteries and convents, and conversed freely and boldly with the most serious of their inmates. So great indeed was his boldness of speech toward many of the priests and others, that his life and that of his friend were frequently in danger. He attended the Popes chapel in Rome, accompanied by Mr. Ireland, who only consented to go after having extorted a promise from Mr. Fletcher, that the latter would not speak by way of censure or reproof at what he saw or heard. While travelling in a part of Italy they approached the "Appian Way." Mr. Fletcher directed the driver to stop, and he descended from the carriage, assuring Mr. Ireland that his heart would not suffer him to ride over that ground, upon which the apostle Paul had walked, chained to a soldier, on account of having preached the Gospel. As soon as he alighted, he reverently took off his hat, and walked with his eyes upraised to heaven, while he thanked God that England was favored with the gospel in its purity, and prayed that Rome might also share in the same glorious blessing.

Soon after his arrival in his native town, the clergy of Nyon vied with each other in doing him distinguished honor. They severally pressed him to honor their pulpits during his stay, and on the Sabbath after his arrival, he preached in one of the churches to a large and attentive congregation, and continued during his sojourn in the place to draw large and crowded audiences, who were charmed with his eloquence, and listened to him as though he was something more than man.

During his tour, he also made a visit to the Hugonots, or French Protestants, in the south of France. Such was his respect for the people, whose fathers had laid down their lives for the gospel, that he positively refused to ride to the Cevennes Mountain, where these people resided, but persisted in accomplishing the journey on foot. He accordingly clothed himself in the plainest garb, and with his staff in his hand, made his appearance among them. He was everywhere received as a messenger of God, even the profane and vicious acknowledged that he spoke with authority, and instances were given of his success in winning souls to Christ in his journeys through these mountains.

After having accomplished the object of their travels, the two friends returned to England, and such was the estimation in which Mr. Ireland held his friend, who had been his almost constant companion for five months, that had he been an angel in human form, he could have esteemed him no higher.

About this time, the Countess of Huntingdon erected a

theological seminary at Trevecka, in Wales, for the purpose of educating pious young men for the ministry, either of the establishment, the Wesleyan body, or the dissenting churches. To the superintendency or presidency of this seminary, Mr. Fletcher was called by the Countess; not that she expected him to leave his charge in Madely, but that he should occasionally visit the institution, and give advice in relation to the appointment of teachers, and the admission or rejection of students; to direct in the course of study; and judge of their qualifications for the work of the ministry. Mr. Fletcher willingly accepted the invitation, and undertook the charge without fee or reward, while Rev. Joseph Benson, one of Mr. Wesley's preachers, and Head-Master of the Wesleyan School at Kingswood, was, on Mr. Wesley's recommendation, appointed Second-Master of the Seminary under Mr. Fletcher. The visits of the latter to the Seminary were always seasons of refreshing to the pious students. Instead of haranguing them with long metaphysical disquisitions on some branch of abstruse science or philosophy, he would talk to them about the love of Jesus, and would generally close by saying, "As many of you as are athirst for the fulness of the Spirit, follow me into my room." There they would spend two or three hours in prayer, wrestling Jacob-like for the blessing of perfect love. On one of these occasions, Mr. Fletcher was so filled with the love of God, that he felt he could contain no more, and cried out, "O, my God, withhold thy hand or the vessel will burst!" In reference to this expression, Mr. Fletcher afterward told Mr. Benson, he was afraid he had grieved the Holy Spirit, and that he ought rather to have prayed that the Lord would have enlarged the vessel, or suffered it to break.

Thus did this man of God labor to improve the moral and spiritual, as well as the intellectual gifts of his students; and thus, during his superintendency of the institution, did the latter flourish and grow in utility, and more than met the anticipations of its excellent founder. At length religious dissensions began to be fostered among the patrons of the school. Her ladyship, through the influence of prejudiced counsellors, dismissed Mr. Benson from being Head-Master, because he could not endorse the doctrine of predestination. Mr. Benson, as in duty bound, informed Mr. Fletcher of the fact, and the latter in writing to the Countess says: "Mr. Benson made a very just defence, when he said he held with me the possibility of salvation for all men; that mercy is offered to all, and yet may be rejected or received. If this be what your ladyship calls Mr. Wesley's opinion, free will, and Arminianism, and if 'every Arminian must quit the college,' I am actually discharged also. For in my present view of things, I must hold that sentiment, if I believe that the Bible is true, and that God is love. For my part, I am no party man. In the Lord, I am your servant, and that of your every student, but I cannot give up the honor of being connected with my old friends. * * * Mr. Wesley shall always be welcome to my pulpit, and I shall gladly bear my testimony in his, as well as in Mr. Whitefield's. But if your ladyship forbid your students to preach for the one, and offer them to preach for the other at every turn; and if a master is discarded for believing that Christ died for all; then prejudice reigns; charity is cruelly wounded; and party-spirit shouts, prevails, and triumphs."

That the reader may understand the true position of the parties in this affair, it is perhaps necessary to remark, that the Countess of Huntingdon was a Methodist of the Whitefieldian School; that her chaplain, the Hon. and Rev. Walter Shirley, her own brother, was a violent predestinarian; and that about this time there was much controversy between the predestinarians on the one hand, and the Arminians on the other. Besides, Mr. Wesley and his preachers in Conference capacity had recently taken strong ground against the peculiar doctrines of Calvinism, and Mr. Fletcher and Mr. Benson were well known to be advisers of Mr. Wesley's course in this respect. Hence the dismission of Mr. Benson, and as might be expected the subsequent resignation of Mr. Fletcher of the presidency of the College. In the meanwhile, Mr. Shirley, above alluded to, having taken umbrage at the doctrines promulgated in the Wesleyan "Minutes of Conference," issued a "Circular Letter" to the evangelical Clergymen of England, protesting against the doctrines of Arminianism, and inviting them to meet in Bristol at the next session of the Wesleyan Conference, and go in a body to the Conference, and demand a retraction of the offensive doctrines! which they actually attempted to do, but were very properly refused an audience by Mr. Wesley and his Conference, until they were willing to meet as friends and not as belligerents.

The occasion, however, called out Mr. Fletcher in a new character, that of a polemic writer. Hitherto he appears as the pious, useful pastor; as the learned and truly dignified president of a College; but now buckling on the whole armor of truth, and seizing the sword of the Spirit, he marches out into the field of moral warfare, and bids defiance to the machinations of the prejudiced, and hurls his weapons of war into the camp of error. No sooner had he received Mr. Shirley's Circular, than he at once began the preparation of his "Checks to Antinomianism;" a work which does immortal honor to the head and heart of the author, and which no doubt will be read and admired as long as error shall demand an antidote. In speaking of these "Checks" Mr. Wesley observes: "How much good has been occasioned by the publication of that Circular Letter! This was the happy occasion of Mr. Fletcher's writing those 'Checks to Antinomianism,' in which one knows not which to admire most, the *purity* of the language (such as scarce any foreigner ever wrote before);

the *strength* and *clearness* of the argument; or the *mildness* and *sweetness* of the spirit that breathes throughout the whole. Insomuch that I wonder not at a serious Clergyman, who being resolved to live and die in his own opinion, when he was pressed to read them replied, 'No, I will never read Mr. Fletcher's Checks: for if I did I should be of his mind.'"

Thus was Mr. Fletcher, before he was aware of it, a controversial author, and it was because of his peculiar fitness for this particular part of ministerial duty, that ever after his well-pointed pen was employed almost constantly in defence of what he sincerely believed to be truth. His numerous polemic works were printed at Mr. Wesley's press in London, and in this way he rendered the latter much more efficient service, than though he had been actively employed in the itinerant field. And in engaging in controversy as much as Mr. Fletcher did, he felt in his own soul, as though he was serving the interests of the bleeding cause of Christ as much, or more than he could do in any other way. To give his views on the subject of controversy and also to show his command of the English language—Swiss though he was—we will favor the reader with an extract from one of his controversial works: "Some of our friends will undoubtedly blame us for not dropping the contested point; but others will candidly consider that controversy though not desirable in itself, yet properly managed, has a hundred times rescued truth groaning under the lash of triumphant error. We are indebted to our Lord's controversies with the Pharisees and scribes, for a considerable part of the four gospels. And to the end of the world the Church will bless God for the spirited manner in which St. Paul in his Epistles to the Romans, and Galatians defended the controverted point of a believer's present justification by faith, as well as for the steadiness with which St. James, St. John, St. Peter, and St. Jude carried on their important controversy with the Nicolaitans, who abused St.

Paul's doctrine to antinomian purposes. Had it not been for controversy, Romish priests would to-day, feed us with *Latin masses*, and a *wafer-god*. Some bold propositions advanced by Luther, brought on the Reformation. They were so irrationally attacked by the infatuated Papists, and so scripturally defended by the resolute Protestants, that these kingdoms opened their eyes, and saw thousands of images and errors fall before the ark of evangelical truth."

Previous to the year 1773, Mr. Fletcher's health had been somewhat on the decline, in consequence of his exposure to all kinds of weather, at all seasons of the year, which greatly impaired his strength and constitution. He was able however to perform all his clerical duties without much intermission. In the former part of this year, he wrote a long letter to Mr. Wesley, in which he intimated that he had doubts about the propriety of his remaining longer at Madely, and expresses his willingness, if Providence opened the way, to resume his office as Mr. Wesley's "deacon." "And as the little estate I have in my own country," he observes, "is sufficient for my maintenance, I have thought I would one day or other offer you and the Methodists my *free* services." "I can never believe," says Mr. Wesley in referring to this letter, "that it was the will of God that such a burning and shining light should be hid under a bushel. No, instead of being confined to a country village it ought to have shone in every corner of the land." But the way for his leaving Madely did not seem to open, so that he continued his pastoral relation to that parish, as before stated, while he lived. His health, however, being poor, he supplied his parish with a curate, and accepted an invitation from Mr. Wesley to accompany him in a tour through different parts of England. Accordingly, he spent the greater part of the year, in travelling with the latter some twelve hundred miles, mostly on horseback, and only stopped in his tour for the purpose of writing an answer to a work which had been lately published by a Mr. Evans and Dr. Price, and also to supply the pulpit in Madely, as his curate had left the parish. His return to active labor, however, increased the violence of his disease, so that his physician forbade his preaching. He consequently secured the services of another curate, and spent the greater part of the ensuing summer at the Hot Springs, but without any material improvement of his health.

In the fall of 1776, he again joined Mr. Wesley in a tour through various parts of England, and at the close of the same accompanied him to London, but in the winter he retired to a friend's house in Newington, where he spent the most of the time in writing Christian letters to his parishioners and other friends, although his disease (spitting of blood) would not allow him to converse much. In the spring of 1777, he went to Bristol, and Bath, and in the latter part of the summer, as his health still continued poor, resolved on making another journey to Switzerland. But he did not leave England until the beginning of December, when in company with Mr. Ireland, and two of his daughters, he sailed for the south of France. His journey appearing to benefit him, he proceeded to Rome and various parts of Italy. While in Rome, as he and Mr. Ireland were one day going through the streets in a coach, they met the Pope in an open carriage; and as the custom was for all to leave their carriages and kneel when they met the pope, and as a refusal to do so would draw on them the vengeance of the multitude, our friends were placed in somewhat of a strait in reference to how they ought to act. To kneel to a pope they could not; the coachman was terrified, and knew not what to do; he finally succeeded in reining his horses into a narrow passage, until his Holiness had passed by.

After having visited various parts of France and Italy, he proceeded to Nyon, his native place, from which he wrote to

John and Charles Wesley. In Nyon, he was able to preach but three or four times, but he spent much time in instructing and catechizing the children, and in writing epistles as usual to friends in England. His health during his prolonged stay in his native country was so vacillating, that it was not till the summer of 1781 that he ventured to return to England. After having visited London and preached in the Wesleyan New Chapel, he proceeded to Bristol, near which he had an opportunity of seeing Mr. Rankin, who during his absence had returned from America, and while Mr. Rankin was relating the progress of the work of God in that distant portion of the field, Mr. Fletcher would frequently stop him, and pour out his soul to God for the prosperity of the American brethren. After a few days he set out for his beloved parish, and was affectionately received by his people, who were warmly endeared to him by a thousand sacred ties.

Hitherto Mr. Fletcher had led a single life, having never been married. In early life he had formed an acquaintance with a devotedly pious and estimable young lady, but without having seriously entertained thoughts of marriage. After his return from Switzerland the second time, he providentially renewed his acquaintance with the same person, who had suffered much during her life, for her devotion to the cause of Christ. As there appeared to be no impediment to the union, Mr. Fletcher and Miss Bosanquet were united in holy matrimony. This lady was of respectable family, and was possessed of a competent fortune. In early life, she became a subject of saving grace, and soon united with one of Mr. Wesley's Societies. It appeared from subsequent developments that both of these persons while young had formed an attachment for each other, and had concluded in their own minds, that if they ever married it would be to each other. But Mr. Fletcher, who had imbibed a disrelish for the marriage state, solely on the ground that he believed a person could not be as holy and useful in this, as in a single state, prudently and with great sacrifice of feeling no doubt, abstained from making his attachment known to the lady, and she perhaps for similar reasons, had hid her own feelings within her own heart. At the time of their marriage, however, providence seemed to open the way for their union, and the pious and useful Miss Bosanquet became the holy devoted wife of Mr. Fletcher. This union was followed by the best of consequences, for instead of drawing their affections in any measure from God, it only served to increase the flame of divine love, and make their united labors more acceptable and efficient to the church of Christ. Like Zacharias and Elizabeth of old, these holy persons "walked in all the ordinances and commandments of the Lord blameless."

In the summer of 1784, Mr. and Mrs. Fletcher having been repeatedly urged and invited by several pious people in Dublin to visit the Methodist Society in that city, they accepted the invitation, and although they remained there but a short time, they were instrumental in accomplishing much good, and when they returned to England they left behind them a large circle of warm-hearted pious friends, whose attachment to them had become ripened by the influence of Christian love and affection.

About four years after his marriage Mr. Fletcher was seized with his last illness, which was only of a week's continuance, and on the 14th of August, 1785, he departed this life in hope of a blissful and glorious resurrection. Thus died one of the holiest men that probably had lived from the days of the Apostle John—"a pattern of holiness"—as described by Mr. Wesley in the notice of his death in the Minutes of the Wesleyan Conference,—a man who of all others had an eye single to the glory of God, and one who, next to Wesley, did more than any other man of his times to advance the cause of Wesleyan theology and sound Arminian doctrine. He was buried in Madely church-yard, honored and lamented by all who knew him, and by none more so, than his friend and brother the Rev. John Wesley.—"PEACE TO HIS ASHES."

CHAPTER IV.

REV. JOSEPH BENSON, A.M.

This distinguished Methodist minister was born in Melmerdy, County of Cumberland, England, on the 25th day of January, 1748. His father was a farmer of good character, and in comfortable circumstances; and who designed his son for the ministry of the English established Church. At a very early age Joseph became the subject of serious religious impressions, which never wore off, until he became the happy partaker of the saving grace of God through faith in Jesus Christ.

While yet young, Joseph was placed at the village school, and afterwards under the care of a Presbyterian minister named Dean, who was pastor of the Presbyterian Church, in the village where his father resided. He continued under this gentleman's instruction pursuing a course of classical study, until he was sixteen years of age, when he became a teacher in a school in a neighboring town, where he remained for one year. It was while engaged in this school, that Joseph became convinced that notwithstanding his morality he must be born again before he could see the kingdom of God. Through the influence of a pious cousin, and the knowledge gained by reading Mr. Wesley's sermons, and hearing Methodist preaching he was at length constrained to trust in Jesus Christ as his personal Saviour, and he obtained the witness of his adoption into the family of God.

After his conversion, he united with a Methodist Society.

This step gave great offence to his father, who was a zealous son of "the church," and believing that he would take but little comfort at home, on account of his father's opposition, and there being but little opportunity for improving his mind there, Joseph with his father's consent, left the parental mansion, and parted from his father, both being overcome by a flood of tears. The farewell words they spoke were the last they ever spoke to each other, as father and son never met again on earth.

At this eventful period in the history of his life, Mr. Benson was only seventeen years of age—an age of all others when a young man needs the aid of parental restraint and advice. Besides, he had but a small portion of this world's gear to take with him—so little indeed, that his legs and feet had to answer in the place of horses and carriage while pursuing his outward journey. Before leaving home, Joseph had heard that there was a vacancy in the office of Classical master in Mr. Wesley's school in Kingswood. He accordingly bent his steps towards Newcastle-upon-Tyne, where he hoped to meet Mr. Wesley; the latter, however, had left for London before he arrived. Being disappointed in securing a passage on board of a vessel to London, Mr. Benson commenced the journey on foot, although in the depth of winter. He had not proceeded far, however, before he fell in company with a gentleman who was acquainted with Mr. Wesley, and who after learning the particulars of young Benson's case, kindly paid his stage fare to London. On his arrival at the latter city he was again disappointed about meeting Mr. Wesley; he, however, remained in the city about four weeks, and shortly after received the appointment of Classical master in Kingswood School. The appointment thus conferred upon him, shows the confidence which Mr. Wesley had in the piety and classical attainments of one so young; and this confidence was not misplaced, as Mr. Benson's subsequent history proves.

After his arrival at Kingswood, he entered upon the duties of his office with a degree of zeal and ardor peculiar to himself, and by his knowledge of the classics, and his manner of imparting instruction, soon gained not only the confidence of his pupils, but the further confidence and respect of Mr. Wesley.

While engaged in Kingswood he made his first attempts at preaching. Being destitute of natural talents for extemporaneous efforts, it was with some difficulty that he could be prevailed upon to pray publicly, and preach to the colliers in the neighborhood. But although slow of speech, his labors were greatly blessed to the good of the scholars committed to his care, so much so, that several of them were awakened to a sense of sin, and were led to Christ. He remained at the school in Kingswood for nearly four years, and when he left it, he was followed by the best wishes and respects of all who knew him, or had been benefited by his instructions.

In 1769 the Countess of Huntingdon founded a college in Wales for the benefit of young men who were candidates for the ministry in the established Church, or in either of the evangelical dissenting churches. To the presidency of this institution, Mr. Fletcher, as stated in the preceding chapter, was duly appointed by her ladyship. On the recommendation of Mr. Wesley, and the advice of Mr. Fletcher, Mr. Benson was appointed Head Master of the College, a situation at once awfully responsible, and the duties of which were complicated and arduous, especially for a young man of twenty-one years of age.

In the spring of 1770, he took up his residence at Trevecca, the place where the College was located, and became well satisfied with his situation and the flattering prospects of the College. He was also much beloved and respected by the gentlemen students and the patrons of the College.

Mr. Benson during the succeeding winter vacation was absent at Oxford "keeping terms," and during his absence, a zealous advocate of the Calvinistic Creed visited the seat of the College, and propagated the seeds of dissension and disunion among the students, and others connected with the College. It should be known to the reader, that at this period, much excitement prevailed in England and Wales, in relation to the doctrines of Calvinism on the one hand, and of Arminianism on the other. This excitement was mostly felt in the two Methodistic bodies, known as the Whitefieldian, and the Wesleyan, and at this particular period, was at its height. Mr. Whitefield, Lady Huntingdon, and others were disposed to defend the Calvinistic views: while Mr. Wesley, Mr. Fletcher, and Mr. Benson, arrayed themselves on the opposite side of free grace, and God's impartial love to all mankind. It was at length determined by the countess, to dismiss all Arminians from her College, whether teachers or students, and consequently Mr. Benson had to take his leave after a short but useful term of nine months' duration, as Head Master. On leaving the College, Lady Huntingdon cheerfully gave him a testimonial of her high regard for his character, as a gentleman and as a teacher. As before stated, Mr. Fletcher on hearing the fact of Mr. Benson's abrupt dismissal on account of his religious views, immediately resigned the Presidency of the College.

We have stated above that Mr. Benson was at Oxford keeping terms. He had in March 1769, entered his name on the books of the University, and from that period he regularly and systematically cultivated every part of a University education. After having been at the University two years, and having pursued all the branches pre-requisite to ordination in the Church of England, he concluded in the fear of God to take upon himself holy orders. It was necessary, however, previously to ordination, that his tutor in the University should sign his testimonials, but on hearing that Mr. Benson had been a local preacher under Mr. Wesley, and that he had actually dared as such to preach to the poor colliers of Kingswood, he peremptorily, and in the true spirit of bigotry refused to sign such testimonials, or even to act longer toward him in the capacity of tutor. Mr. Benson remonstrated in the spirit of kindness against such ill-usage, and although seconded in his effort to obtain his testimonials by the principal of St. Edmund's Hall, yet the tutor remained inflexible in his refusal, and Mr. Benson left Oxford.

After leaving Oxford, Mr. Benson obtained testimonials from a respectable clergyman in Wales, and a large and respectable parish was obtained for him. His testimonials were countersigned by the bishop of St. David's, but as the parish which had been presented to him, was within the diocess of Worcester, he applied to the Bishop of Worcester for ordination, but the latter refused to ordain him, ostensibly for the reason, that he had not received his Academical degree, but truly, as it is to be feared, for the same reason that his bigoted tutor would not sign his testimonials.

We have before stated that Mr. Benson did not naturally possess a capacity for extemporizing. For this reason probably he was the more anxious to obtain orders in the Established Church, as in that case the prayers and sermons required of him would all be written, and extemporizing be unnecessary. But the great Head of the Church had other fields of labor for him to occupy, and more extensive work for him to do than to shut himself up in an obscure country parish; hence, he ever after considered these obstacles in the way of procuring episcopal ordination, as so many providential hindrances, closing up what to him then appeared to be the path of duty, but in reference to which he was afterwards convinced was a mistake.

After leaving Oxford, he visited Bristol and preached almost every day, and at the session of the Methodist Conference in

August 1771, he was received on trial as an itinerant preacher, and was appointed by Mr. Wesley to labor on the London circuit, where he continued one year with more or less success. At the ensuing Conference, he was received into full connection, and was appointed to Newcastle circuit. In 1773 he was appointed to Edinburgh circuit in Scotland ; and although at first he felt rather opposed to the idea of going into a strange country, and among a people so different in their habits and religious views and practices from the people of England, yet he made up his mind fully to acquiesce cheerfully in the allotment of Providence, as indicated by the appointment.

Mr. Benson labored in Edinburgh for three years, and near the close of the third year he remarks in his diary: "My heart is so united to this people, that I find it very hard to leave this place. I never was among a more kind and loving people than those in our Society at Edinburgh. Many a happy and edifying hour, have I spent among them. Many a time has my soul been blessed in answer to their prayers, both in public and in private. May the Lord continue to favor them with his presence, and reward them for all their kindness to me." After leaving Edinburgh he was again appointed to Newcastle circuit, where he remained for two years with great honor to himself and profit to the cause of God in that place. In 1778, Mr. Benson was stationed in Manchester, and while laboring in this place he was united in marriage to Miss Thompson, a pious and intelligent lady, who resided in Leeds. In company with Mrs. Benson he immediately returned to his circuit, and proved himself to be no less arduous and engaged after, than before his marriage.

At the Conference of 1780, Mr. Benson was appointed to the Leeds circuit, which at this period was large and extensive. During the period of his ministry in other places he had in a great measure overcome his want of capacity for extemporizing; he had in fact become not only a forcible but an eloquent extemporaneous speaker. This combined with his zeal and literary acquirements rendered his labors acceptable wherever he was stationed, and being attended with the divine blessing were not only acceptable, but highly useful. After spending two years in Leeds he was appointed to Bradford circuit, and in 1784, was stationed in the Sheffield circuit, where during his pastoral labors among them, the members of the Society increased three hundred and fifty in number. From Sheffield he removed to Hull, where he spent one year, and from thence he was stationed in Birmingham. It was during his residence in this city that the venerable and apostolic John Wesley departed this life. The intelligence of his death, which he obtained on the day following his decease (March 2d, 1791), greatly affected Mr. Benson. On the 13th of March he delivered a discourse on the occasion, his text being 2 Kings ii. 12, "My father! my father! the chariot of Israel, and the horsemen thereof!" Many hundreds came to hear the sermon who could not gain admission to the chapel. The discourse being lengthy he did not finish it at that time, but deferred the remainder until the 15th, when the chapel was again crowded to its utmost capacity.

Birmingham was the scene of many disgraceful riots of a political character during Mr. Benson's residence in that place. Referring to the same, he says in his journal under date of July 15th, 1791: "Yesterday, according to appointment, several gentlemen met at the hotel in this town with a view to commemorate the French revolution. The mob collected and hissed them as they went in; and in the dusk of the evening gathering in greater numbers they broke all the windows of the hotel. Then hastening to Dr. Priestley's meeting-house, in a little time they burned it to the ground. They then proceeded to what is called the Old Meeting House, and burned it likewise. This morning they set fire to Dr. Priestley's dwelling-house, which is about two miles from town, and burned it also with all its furniture. The same destructive work they have pursued all day."

Under date of July 16th, Mr. Benson continues: "This day we have been in continual alarm. The mob reigns without control. The attack made upon them by the constables yesterday only inflamed them the more; and to-day, they are continuing their depredations. Hundreds of families are removing their property, and the whole town is in utter consternation. May the Lord be our defence and habitation. On the succeeding day—Sunday—a body of light-horse arrived in town, which effectually put a stop to further rioting."

Shortly after this, Mr. Benson was in imminent danger of losing his life by being thrown from his horse, which had taken fright and become unmanageable. He was trodden under the horse's feet, and by some means was dragged a considerable distance before he became disengaged from the animal. His under, and over-coats were torn to pieces, but excepting a few slight bruises, himself escaped without further injury. "Surely," said Mr. Benson, "I am laid under fresh obligations to live to the glory of my great deliverer!"

In May, Mr. Benson removed to Manchester, and while there he volunteered his services in connection with other ministerial brethren to proceed to Liverpool, for the purpose of healing certain dissensions which had arisen in the Methodist Society in that place, growing out of holding service in Church hours, and of the administration of the Lord's Supper in the Chapel of that place. To understand the cause of division it may be necessary to state, that previous to this time, the Methodists in England, were considered as an integral portion of the Church of England, and were required by the rules of the Society, to attend the services of the Established Church, as also, to receive the Lord's Supper there, if permitted by the officiating clergyman to do so. The Methodist services were held at such hours as did not interfere with the services of the

Church. About this time, however, it was thought proper by the Conference to allow in cities, and large towns, the holding of Methodist services in church hours, and if the preacher stationed among the people in those places was ordained, they were permitted to receive the sacrament in their own house of worship. This practice at first was considered by many of the Methodists, as a bold and dangerous innovation. And as the Society in Liverpool had just had the innovation introduced among them, an unhappy division arose among the members in relation thereto. Mr. Benson and his brethren, however, were by the divine blessing, rendered instrumental in healing the dissensions, and restoring peace between the parties.

In 1794, by the earnest request of the trustees of the chapels in Bristol, Mr. Benson was stationed in that city. In this place also, divisions and distractions had existed for several months, which induced Mr. Benson to doubt the propriety of his being stationed there, and which rendered his situation for a portion of the time he there remained, unpleasant in the extreme. But he went to his appointment in the name of the Prince of Peace, and was instrumental in adopting measures which secured not only a lasting peace to the Societies in Bristol, but by his "plan of pacification," laid the foundation of that general union, which has since continued with scarcely any abatement throughout the connection.

While in Bristol, he made a tour of several weeks' continuance to the west of England. It was not, however, a tour of leisure to him, as his journal abundantly proves. Day after day, and week after week, he preached to large congregations wherever he went, and such was the power of the word of God, as administered by him, that hundreds trembled, and scores were brought to the "knowledge of the truth." After his return to Bristol, he spent the remainder of the conference year in strengthening and confirming the hearts of the people of his important charge, with the assurance that his labors among them had not been "in vain in the Lord."

In 1795, Mr. Benson was again appointed to Leeds, where he remained for two years, and during this period he labored with his usual diligence to secure the salvation of souls. His talents and zeal were in some measure appreciated by the vast crowds of people that from time to time went to hear him, and his labors were attended with great success, as God gave him in this place, many seals to his ministry. After leaving Leeds, he went to Hull. At the latter place he again narrowly escaped death by a fall from his horse, which having fell down upon his knees and face, suddenly pitched Mr. Benson over his head. Mr. Benson, however, escaped with very little injury.

In 1798, by the partiality of his brethren, Mr. Benson was elected to the responsible station of President of the Conference. This station he filled with acceptability to the Conference, with honor to himself, and with profit to the connection.

In 1800, Mr. Benson was appointed Superintendent of the London circuit, which was a great and important charge. During his stay here, he records one or two instances of sudden death, the recital of which may be interesting to the reader. On the 12th of April, while Mr. Benson was praying before sermon in the Queen-street Chapel, a Mr. Falzham was taken suddenly ill, and after groaning for a few moments, expired on the spot. "Some of the friends," says Mr. Benson, "bore him down into the vestry, where I found him on the table, on his back, much altered, when the service was over. It was an awful and affecting scene to those who were present." Another instance which greatly affected Mr. Benson, was the sudden death of Mr. Pine of Bristol. He was attending a prayer-meeting. After two or three had prayed, Mr. Pine observed that they would no longer meet together as they had done; and the very next morning he died in his bed, with scarcely a moment's warning.

After having spent three very pleasant and profitable years as Superintendent of London circuit, Mr. Benson was elected sole editor of the Methodist Magazine, a periodical which had been commenced by Mr. Wesley, and which had been continued since his death with great and increasing patronage. Mr. Benson was elected to this office by the unanimous vote of the Conference, which at once shows the confidence which that body placed in his talents and piety. The office to which he was thus elected, he continued to fill with great acceptability, until the time of his death; his residence, as a matter of course, being thenceforward fixed in London. But although called to labor in another sphere, he continued to exert himself as a minister of Jesus Christ, by preaching frequently as occasion might require, or doors of usefulness open. On one of these occasions, while preaching at Lambeth, he gave an account of the conversion and happy death of a once noted actress of great popularity, by the name of Mrs. Boothe. "After returning home from the theatre on a certain evening, the house in which she lodged was so suddenly consumed by fire, that it was with much difficulty she made her escape from the flames. Her exertions on the occasion, together with her mental agitation, brought on a fever, during the continuance of which, she was convinced that her mode of life was opposed to the spirit and practice of religion. She left the stage, and sought for rest and peace; but in vain at first. She felt an aching void; and nothing she could do, or enjoy, afforded her the least degree of happiness.

"She retired to reside in a village in which a Sunday-school was established, and occasionally heard an exhortation from some of the teachers employed in it. By means of these pious men, she soon learned that what she needed in order to her happiness, was a living faith in the Lord Jesus Christ, together with its concomitants—pardon, peace, and joy. She became a teacher in the school just noticed, and was grateful to God for so far subduing her proud heart, as to make her willing in a sphere so humble, to make some good use of the talents which she had so much abused.

"After changing her residence to Lambeth, she frequently heard preaching at the Methodist chapel. She soon was enabled to exercise faith in Christ as her Redeemer, and was filled with peace and joy in the Holy Ghost. She joined the Methodist Society, of which she continued a worthy and exemplary member until her decease. For some days before her death, it was evident to herself that her race was nearly run. She spoke frequently, and with great animation, of heaven and its glories. Her death, although sudden, was not so much unexpected as to induce alarm. Though she was rather unwell, she attended preaching as usual, on Thursday evening. On the night of the following Sabbath, she entered the eternal world. Was not this a brand plucked from the fire?"

In 1808, the Conference, by vote, requested Mr. Benson to write a commentary on the Bible, and in compliance with such request, he in the following year began the onerous task—a task for which he was well qualified, and in the accomplishment of which he at length succeeded, to the satisfaction of the Church. His "Commentary on the Old and New Testament," is an enduring monument of his piety, and extensive biblical knowledge, as well as of his general erudition.

In the year 1810, Mr. Benson had the misfortune to lose his beloved wife with whom he had lived and travelled for thirty years. This affliction bore heavily on his stricken mind, but although "cast down" by the dispensation of divine Providence, he was "not destroyed." Yet it was only by looking to the Lord, that he obtained support and consolation. During the same year in which his wife died, he was the second time elected President of the Conference, an evidence that his brethren appreciated his services in that capacity during his former term of office. The duties of this office, together with those of editor of the Magazine, and the task of writing his commentary, were duties sufficiently oppressive to break down the constitution of a more healthy man than Mr. Benson. One evening as he kneeled down to offer family prayers, he fell on his face like one dead. His daughters lifted him up, when he gradually recovered his strength and consciousness. Thus did this good man spend his strength, for the good of the Church and the world.

While Mr. Benson was thus laboring for the good of mankind, he was frequently made the distributer of the alms of the benevolent. In 1812, an unknown friend sent twenty pounds ($90) to be distributed among the poor, by Mr. Benson. One year after, the same friend gave him forty-five pounds for a similar purpose, and in another year he called on Mr. Benson, and left with him seventy pounds (over $300) for the same object, adding as he gave it, "The more I give the Lord, he blesses me the more." Mr. Benson desired to have his name, but he declined making it known, thus practically carrying out the precept of Christ, "When thou doest alms, let not thy left hand know what thy right hand doeth."

Another instance of benevolence is recorded by Mr. Benson. In 1816 he preached in a neat Methodist chapel which had been lately erected in Cambridge, through the exertions of a Mr. Babcock. This person was a plasterer by trade, and on going to Cambridge to work at his trade, he found a small Methodist Society, having no place of worship. Resolving if possible to build one, he mentioned the subject to several pious friends, some of whom could not encourage the undertaking, and others who were willing to encourage and aid to a limited extent. Mr. Babcock however purchased a lot of ground, procured the materials, and proceeded with his own hands —frequently without the help of any other laborer—to lay the brick, plaster the inside, and slate the roof. His labor was given gratuitously, besides a handsome donation towards defraying the expenses of materials, &c. Such an instance of liberality on the part of a comparatively poor man, deserves to be recorded to his honor.

In 1818, Mr. Benson completed his Commentary on the Bible, which he had commenced eight years previously, and to finish which, and attend to his editorial, and other duties made it necessary for him to write day after day, from five o'clock in the morning until eleven at night, and this too, at the age of more than seventy years. Besides which, he generally preached twice or thrice on the Sabbath, and walked from eight to twelve miles with a body somewhat enfeebled by disease.

On the 26th day of November, 1820, Mr. Benson preached his last sermon. He had been growing more and more infirm for some time, although able to attend to his editorial duties. But his work was now nearly done, and the father in Israel was about to take his departure to the land of spirits. During his last sickness of ten weeks, he preserved the utmost composure of mind and conversed frequently and freely on the subject of death, asserting the utmost confidence in Christ, as an all-sufficient Saviour. A day or two before he died, he was visited by Dr. Clarke, and Rev. Jabez Bunting. The Doctor was very much affected at seeing him so much reduced, and said, "You know me, sir?" "O yes; it is Dr. Clarke." "Well, sir, you are not far from the kingdom of God." "I am not only not far from the kingdom of God, but I am sure of finding God in that kingdom," was the reply. He afterwards said to the Doctor, "I have no hope of being saved but by grace through faith," and to Mr. Bunting he remarked, "I have no sufficiency for anything good in myself," and on being asked if he now realized those truths he preached so often to others, he answered, "Yes! O yes!"

On the 16th of February, 1821, Mr. Benson bade farewell to earth. He died without a struggle, or a groan, in the seventy-fourth year of his age, and the fiftieth of his ministry in the Methodist connection.

His remains were deposited in the burying-ground of City Road Chapel, London, on the 22d day of February, there to remain until the resurrection of the just. The corpse was preceded by four of the senior members of the Conference, and was followed by the relations, and by twenty-four travelling preachers, twenty lay gentlemen—personal friends of the deceased—thirty local preachers, twenty stewards, and forty other members of the Society, all of whom appeared in mourning cloaks, as the representatives of the bodies to which they respectively belonged, and who were deputed to honor the remains of the faithful but departed Benson. Mr. Bunting, as President of the Conference, conducted the funeral services, while Dr. Clarke delivered a funeral discourse to the thousands who were assembled together on the solemn occasion.

Thus died, and thus was buried, the Rev. Joseph Benson; a man who, although inferior to a few more talented ministers, was superior to many, yea, to the great mass of ministers, in point of talent, education, piety, usefulness, and diligence. His works still praise him. Not only was he the author of the Commentary on the Bible, but he wrote various works of other kinds, and among these, his excellent life of Mr. Fletcher will not only often be read, but be greatly admired, while his Commentary, as before stated, will be a lasting, living, speaking monument of his piety and erudition. "HE RESTS FROM HIS LABORS, AND HIS WORKS DO FOLLOW HIM."

CHAPTER V.

REV. THOMAS COKE, LL.D.

THOMAS COKE was born at Brecon, in Wales, on the 9th of September, 1747. His father was an eminent surgeon, and magistrate in Brecon, and gave his only child, Thomas, such an education as would qualify him for usefulness in after life. His mother was a Methodist, and died a member of the Wesleyan Society in Bristol. At a proper age, Thomas was placed under the charge of the Rev. Mr. Griffiths, master of the college school in Brecon, and at the age of sixteen, was entered at the University of Oxford as a gentleman commoner of Jesus College.

While at the University, his mind was poisoned with the principles of infidelity. These principles were easily instilled into his youthful mind by the artifice and sophistry of his fellow-students, many of whom were openly avowed infidels. The religious principles of Thomas, being thus tainted, very soon produced a pernicious influence upon his daily practice. The company into which he was thrown, led him into scenes of dissipation and vice, at which his yet moral feelings often revolted, and had it not been for the loud upbraidings of his conscience, he would have fallen an easy prey to the natural passions of a depraved heart. But although by the influence of an enlightened mind, he was kept from the commission of the grosser crimes in which his associates greedily indulged, he yielded himself at once to the fashionable vices and follies which even the reputed virtue of the age did not hesitate to allow.

Young Coke, however, was far from being happy. Having sacrificed his religious principles upon the altar of infidelity, and having found the follies and sins of fashionable life insufficient to satisfy the longing desires of an immortal mind, he was illy at ease, and sighed in solitude for that peace of mind, which he had in some measure frequently enjoyed, but to which he was now an entire stranger. In this sorrowful state of mind, he paid a visit to a popular clergyman of the establishment in Wales. On Sunday the minister preached an able sermon on the more important doctrines of the Gospel, which served to convince his guest of the falsity of his skeptical principles, and the truthfulness of that system of faith which he had discarded. He began toward the close of the sermon, to resolve on an abandonment of his infidel sentiments, and on a return to the path of truth and virtue. On returning from church, while the heart of young Coke glowed with gratitude to the clergyman for his able defence of Christianity, and while he was proceeding to state the exercises of his own mind, and his desire to return to the path of duty, what was his astonishment when his reverend friend darkly smiled at his simplicity, and bluntly and frankly informed him that he himself was not a believer in Christianity, and that he did not believe a word of what he had been preaching!

As might have been expected, young Coke was exceedingly disgusted at such perfidy of conduct on the part of a professed minister of Jesus Christ, and yet, who was a frankly avowed infidel. Thomas, however, at this early age, was too much of a logician to lay the blame of his misconduct at the door of Christianity. He saw at once, that it was infidelity in disguise—a wolf in sheep's clothing—Satan clothed in garments of light. He returned to Oxford with the fixed determination of either openly avowing the principles of infidelity, or taking such steps as should convince him of the truth of Christianity. To live "halting between two opinions," was to him, as it is to all others who attempt it, a life of misery. Providentially falling in with Bishop Sherlock's discourses and dissertations in favor of the Christian religion, he read them carefully, and meditated upon them prayerfully, and by the blessing of God was again confirmed in the truths of Christianity. Again was Coke a Christian in theory, and his conversion thus far, resulted in his total abandonment of his infidel associates, and of their wicked practices.

At the age of twenty-one, Mr. Coke was chosen common councilman of the borough of Brecon, and at the age of twenty-five, was elected chief magistrate or mayor of the corporation, which important office he filled with great acceptability. The important station thus filled by him, brought him in contact with those who were possessed of much authority, both in civil and ecclesiastical affairs, and as Mr. Coke had now fully made up his mind to enter into orders, he was flattered by his influential friends to expect preferment in the Church. A prebend in the Cathedral of Worcester was held out to him, and other promises given of an exalted station in the Church, when he should enter into orders.

In June, 1775, he took his degree of Doctor of Civil Laws at the University, and having received ordination, he obtained a curacy in South Petherton, in Somersetshire. Although still a stranger to vital godliness, he entered on his new field of labor with an intense desire to be useful to his parishioners. This desire manifested itself in his animated manner, his burning zeal, and tender expostulations which were connected with all his pulpit performances. The result of such a kind of preaching, as they had before been unaccustomed to, served soon to enlarge his congregation to such an extent, that the church became too small for their accommodation.

He therefore applied to the parish vestry to have a gallery built at the expense of the parish. His application, however, was unsuccessful, and he accordingly employed workmen, and built a large and handsome gallery at his own expense. This liberality on his part, was a matter of surprise to the honest farmers of his parish, who had never before seen things done in "that fashion," while a few of the more knowing ones, suspected him to be tainted with Methodism.

Up to this time, however, he had had no intercourse whatever with the Methodists either as individuals or as a society, but shortly after this, Dr. Coke was visited by Mr. Maxfield, one of Mr. Wesley's preachers. The subject of their conversation during this first interview was the nature and necessity of the New Birth, the Witness of the Spirit, &c., which doctrines, although somewhat novel to Dr. Coke, commended themselves to his attention and candid inquiry. By subsequent interviews his mind became more and more enlightened, his doubts began to leave him, and in due season he became a sincere seeker of personal salvation. He accordingly availed himself of the knowledge to be derived from reading books which treated on the subjects of his inquiry. Among other works which fell into his hands, were "Fletcher's Appeal" and his "Checks to Antinomianism," and were the means of bringing him among the despised people called Methodists.

An incident is related as taking place about this time which is worthy of being noticed. A certain Mr. Hull, a pious Calvinistic dissenting minister, hearing something of Dr. Coke's state of mind and wishing to assist him in his inquiries after truth, proposed having an interview with the Doctor; but such were the prejudices of the latter in reference to all who dissented from the Established Church, that he declined *receiving* a visit from Mr. Hull, neither would *he go* and visit the latter. A meeting, however, subsequently took place on neutral ground, when the doctor became convinced that piety and intelligence could exist out of the establishment. Mr. Hull appears to have been as sincerely desirous of knowing the truth, as was the Doctor himself. On one occasion while preaching to his congregation from the text, "Of a truth, I perceive God is no respecter of persons," &c., he pledged himself to show the harmony existing between the Scriptures and the system of doctrine called Calvinism. But before he had advanced far in his discourse, he perceived that instead of there being a harmony existing between the two, there was in fact a perfect discordancy. He became embarrassed and bewildered, and was at length obliged to dismiss his congregation without having fulfilled his pledge. After due reflection and prayer he saw his error, and on the following Sabbath renounced his Calvinism, and preached the doctrine of God's impartial love to all mankind; and God set his seal to his ministry, by giving him great success among the people.

While on a visit to a family in Devonshire, the Doctor learned that there was a poor laborer employed by the family who was a Methodist, and the leader of a small class. Soon the Doctor found him out, and after conversing freely on the subject of experimental religion, they had a season of prayer together. There was such a union of feeling between the learned Doctor of Laws and the poor laboring peasant, that the former ever after wanted to know more of the Methodists. Soon after his return to his parish, while preaching on the greatness of redeeming love, it pleased the God of grace to speak unutterable peace to his soul, so that his heart was "full of glory and of God."

He soon announced the fact of his conversion from the pulpit, and laying aside his carefully prepared manuscripts, he began to preach *extempore*. His exhortations were powerful; his reproofs were cutting to the conscience of the sinner; and his general earnestness of manner began to give great offence, so much so indeed, that the parish was in a complete uproar—

an uproar as great as if their minister had committed the crime of murder, and much more so than if he had been found overtaken in drunkenness, or had committed some other venial crime. Not only did the people of his own parish conspire against him, but the neighboring clergy who were rebuked by his zeal and labors, joined with his parishioners in raising the storm of opposition. At length, charges of irregularity, &c., were formally preferred against him to his bishop, but the bishop took no notice of the affair. Another application was made to the Bishop of Bath and Wells, with no better success. His enemies at length applied to the rector to remove him from the parish ; and on a certain Sabbath, without having given the Doctor any previous notice whatever of the intended dismissal, he was to the great satisfaction of his enemies, publicly discharged from the office of curate ; and to add to his disgrace if possible, his foes caused the parish-bells to chime him out of doors.

The *fact* of his dismissal gave the Doctor very little uneasiness, but the *manner* of the same caused him some sorrow, especially as the precipitancy of the measure prevented his preaching a farewell discourse to the people. His friends advised him on the two following Sabbaths, to place himself at the church doors as the congregation was coming out, and preach to those who were willing to hear him. He did so, and was permitted to preach without molestation to both friends and foes. On giving out an appointment for the next Sabbath at the same place, his enemies became perfectly exasperated, and threatened to stone him if he made the attempt. The attempt, however, was made with full success, notwithstanding the precaution of his enemies in having collected together a large pile of stones to throw at the Doctor. Among his friends present were a young gentleman and his sister, who, when the Doctor began to preach, placed themselves on either side of him, while others of his friends and the lovers of religious liberty rallied round him so closely, that it became a matter of prudent calculation among his foes, who should "cast the first stone." The result was, that he finished his discourse without any interruption whatever.

As Dr. Coke was now released from his parish on account of his Methodism, he was at liberty to form a connection with Mr. Wesley, which he did in 1776. At the Conference of 1778, he was stationed in London, where his popularity was very great, and his congregation was exceedingly large. In 1780, the Doctor received no particular circuit, but travelled from this time forward while in England all over the connection according to the directions of Mr. Wesley. In the course of his travels he visited his former parish, but such in the meantime had been the change of public sentiment in relation to him, that those who a few years before had chimed him *out* of his church, now rung him *in*, and thus in part atoned for their former error and prejudice.

Mr. Wesley's celebrated deed of Declaration was mostly drawn up by Dr. Coke, in 1783, and during the previous year the Doctor had been commissioned by Mr. Wesley to hold the first Irish Conference, which he did greatly to the satisfaction of the preachers over whom he presided. This post of honor, he also filled for nearly thirty years, an evidence of the high estimation in which he was held by Mr. Wesley, the English Conference, and the Irish brethren.

In the year 1784, Mr. Wesley with the most parental regard for his Societies in America, saw fit to empower Dr. Coke to proceed to that distant field of labor, and organize such Societies into an independent Methodist Church. Methodism had been introduced into America, in the year 1766, by the preaching of Philip Embury, an Irish emigrant. After that period, it had increased to such an extent, as to require many preachers, some of whom were sent from England from time to time as missionaries, by Mr. Wesley. In the year

1776, American Independence was declared by the Continental Congress, and all connection between Church and State in America ceased, properly speaking, from this period. Hitherto the Societies in the colonies had been considered by the Father of Methodism, and by the preachers generally, as *societies* simply, and as being merely an appendage, or addition to the Church of England. During the war, however, the most of the Episcopal Clergy, had forsaken their flocks, and on political grounds had returned to England. As the Methodist preachers were unordained, themselves and flocks looked exclusively to the Episcopal Clergy, for the sacramental ordinances; and as the most of the Clergy had left as above described, the consequence was, that the Methodists for seven or eight years, were deprived of these ordinances almost entirely. Petitions were frequently sent to Mr. Wesley for relief, and at the close of the war, as the ecclesiastical, as well as the civil relation of the colonies was now completely severed between them and Great Britain, it became necessary for Mr. Wesley to provide for his "sheep in the wilderness."

Accordingly, after due consultation with several eminent divines in England, and being convinced that the high Church claim of uninterrupted succession was a mere chimera of the brain, and that he himself was as much a bishop in the *proper sense of that term*, as any man in England, Mr. Wesley on the 2d day of September, 1784, set apart by the imposition of hands, and prayer, Dr. Coke as a superintendent or bishop of the Societies in America. He also commissioned him to organize in due form an *Episcopal Church*, preferring as he did, this form of Church government, to every other. He also instructed him to set apart Francis Asbury as joint Superintendent of the Church. After receiving ordination, Dr. Coke sailed for America, and arrived in New York, on the 3d of November following. He proceeded with the approbation of the preachers, to call an extraordinary session of the Conference to meet in Baltimore on the 25th day of December of the same year. In obedience to this call, a large majority of the preachers met on the day appointed, at which time, the Doctor explained the steps taken by Mr. Wesley for their relief. The Conference then resolved itself into the *Methodist Episcopal Church of the United States of America*, and as the Doctor was unwilling to serve as their bishop—although set apart to the office by Mr. Wesley himself—unless the Conference would elect him by their own suffrages to that office, they proceeded to elect him to the said office, and in further accordance with the expressed wishes of Mr. Wesley, to elect Francis Asbury to the same office as joint Superintendent, the latter being publicly and solemnly ordained by Bishop Coke. The preachers who were present, and who were eligible, were ordained deacons of the Church, and authorized to baptize and celebrate marriage, and a few of the senior ones, were ordained elders. After these transactions the Conference adjourned, the preachers returning to their respective fields of labor, and meeting everywhere with the congratulations of the people in view of their new position as a distinct ecclesiastical body.

The lapse of nearly seventy years since the organization of the church, has proved the far-seeing wisdom of Mr. Wesley, and the deep penetration of Dr. Coke, in providing for the future well-being of the infant American Societies, which have since become the most numerous protestant people, both as it respects members and adherents, that exists on the American continent.

Immediately after the adjournment of the General Conference of 1784, Bishop Coke took his leave of Baltimore and began a course of extensive travel through the United States, visiting the Societies and being everywhere received as the messenger of God. He also in connection with Bishop Asbury, collected funds for the establishment of a Methodist

College near Baltimore. This edifice, however, a few years subsequently fell a prey to the ravages of fire, and although another suitable building was afterwards procured in the city of Baltimore, that, like the former, was consumed by fire.

Having discharged the duty assigned him by Mr. Wesley, in the organization of the church, and having made proper provision for its government, and believing that his services were not immediately called for in America, on the 3d of June, 1785, he bade a partial farewell to the American church, and returned to England. After having reached the shores of his native land, he commenced travelling through different parts of the kingdom, visiting Scotland, Ireland, and the Isle of Man, and everywhere endeavoring to awaken an interest in behalf of the American church, as also, in behalf of the Methodists of Nova Scotia.

On the 24th of September, 1786, he again set sail for America, intending to stop at Halifax by the way, and establish a mission in that place. But his voyage on this occasion was attended by many dangers and disasters, so much so, that he did not reach Halifax at all. For the first five days after his embarkation, the ship made no progress in consequence of head winds. On the 28th of September, they were nearly run down by another vessel. On the 30th, they were forced to take shelter in the harbor of St. Helena, where they remained for some days, and it was not until the 14th of October that they were able to put out to sea with the prospect of a safe and speedy voyage. After being out three days, they discovered that the vessel had sprung a leak, and to add to the danger, the leak was in a part of the ship where it could not be reached, and to heighten their alarm for the safety of the ship, a violent gale arose, which increased the leak. They, however, continued on the wide ocean, the sport of the winds and waves, until the 25th of November, when one of the masts gave way, and on the 30th, a storm still more fierce and terrible threatened them with seemingly inevitable destruction. The captain's wife cried out in the most frantic manner, and one of the passengers ran to the Doctor, saying, "Pray for us, Doctor, pray for us; we are just gone!" The ship was indeed on her beam-ends, and the crew were cutting away the main-mast, as the only remedy. Dr. Coke and his companions went to prayer, and soon the ship righted, without having to cut away the mast.

On the night of the 4th December, they experienced another dreadful gale. The leak in the ship increased, the sails were torn to fragments, and some of the rigging was carried away. On the next day, it was determined by the captain and crew to make one of the West India Islands, if possible. Still the storm raged, and Dr. Coke and his associates betook themselves to prayer, but the captain, instead of joining in their devotions, became superstitiously agitated, and imagining he must have a Jonah on board, paced the deck in a state bordering on that of phrenzy. At length he entered the Doctor's cabin in a paroxysm of rage, seized his papers and books, and threw them overboard, and then proceeded to the Doctor to bestow upon him like treatment, but after grasping the Doctor's person, and shaking him violently, with oaths and curses and the most bitter language, he concluded to let poor "*Jonah*" escape for this time, but declaring, with an oath, that if he made another prayer on board, he would throw the Doctor after his papers. After the gale had subsided, however, the captain's good nature returned, and continued during the remainder of the voyage.

On the 25th of December, the weather-beaten bark reached the island of Antigua, and the Doctor on going on shore, much to his gratification, found a Mr. Baxter, a member of the Society, who was employed as a ship-builder in the Government dock-yard at Antigua. A Methodist Society had been in existence in this island for a number of years, a Mr. Gilbert, speaker of the House of Assembly, having introduced Methodism about thirty years previously. After his death, Mr. Baxter, above alluded to, on his arrival, found the remnant of a Society which had been raised by Mr. Gilbert. Being himself a local preacher, he felt it his duty to preach occasionally, and through his instrumentality the Society became enlarged to the number of two thousand persons, mostly blacks, and a neat chapel had been erected in 1783.

As the Doctor was obliged to wait for the sailing of a ship for the American Continent, he spent his time on this and other islands, in preaching and visiting both whites and blacks; and so great was the estimation in which he was held by the former class, that he was offered £500 (two thousand dollars) a year, if he would remain among them. He was also cordially received by the higher circles in society, and had the honor of dining on one occasion with the Duke of Clarence, afterward William the Fourth, King of Great Britain, who happened at that period to be on the island.

While visiting the island of St. Eustatius, Dr. Coke became acquainted with the history of a poor negro, named Harry, whose pious labors for the salvation of souls, and his heroic fortitude under persecution, deserve to be long remembered. Harry had been a slave on the American Continent, and had been imported from thence to Antigua. He had been a member of the Methodist Society in America, and on his arrival on the island he found himself destitute of pious associates, and of the means of grace. He had, however, a burning zeal for the salvation of souls, which led him, in his way, to bear public testimony for Christ among his fellow-slaves. The novelty of a negro slave's preaching, drew many, both white and black, to hear him, and among the rest, the Governor of the island, who approved of his course. Under the labors of Black Harry, a reformation among the negroes took place. As is characteristic of that people, there was much enthusiasm, and perhaps some wild fire among the converts, which so discomposed the minds of the planters, and especially of the Governor, that Harry was peremptorily ordered by the latter to stop his preaching.

Harry was obedient to the mandate for some time, till at length supposing that the storm had blown over, he ventured to pray with his associates. A complaint, however, was lodged against him, and he was sentenced by the governor to be pubicly whipped, imprisoned, and banished from the island. The sentence was executed to the letter, and after his imprisonment he was secretly removed by the authorities, so that nearly all were ignorant of his fate. Prayer, however, was offered for him, not only in the islands, but in England where his history had become known. About ten years afterwards, Dr. Coke had the pleasure of meeting this sable son of affliction in the United States, and learned to his satisfaction that Harry, whom he feared was dead, was still alive, in possession of his freedom; and better than all, still on his way to the Kingdom.

In February, 1787, Dr. Coke left the West India Islands, after having made arrangements to afford them a partial supply of preachers and missionaries, and in eighteen days arrived in Charleston, S. C. During this second visit to America the Doctor was greeted with great affection and esteem, except by a few who were not on very friendly terms with him, on account of his known hostility to the institution of American slavery. At that early day, as now, the interests of this institution were watched with a jealous eye; and the man who dared openly to lift his voice against it, might expect opposition. As Dr. Coke, during his former as well as his present visit, considered it his duty thus to oppose slavery in all its forms, a degree of unreasonable hostility was evinced by some against him. A bill of indictment was found against the doctor by a southern grand jury, and ninety men went in pursuit of him to force him back to the county where the bill had been found. They, however, did not proceed far before they grew weary of their journey, and returned without him. From the south the Doctor proceeded northward, and after having spent about three months in travelling from place to place, in the latter part of May he sailed from the port of Philadelphia for Dublin, where he found the Irish Conference in session with Mr. Wesley presiding. From Ireland he proceeded with Mr. Wesley to England and the Norman Isles, and spent all his time during this year in aiding Mr. Wesley in his arduous work.

After the English Conference of 1788, Dr. Coke and three missionaries sailed for the West Indies, where he remained visiting from island to island, and establishing missions, until the next February, when he again set sail for the United States. On his arrival at Charleston, S. C., he immediately directed his course northward for the purpose of meeting Bishop Asbury, and attending the Conferences in connection with him. During this, his third visit, he remained from February to June, travelling through nearly all the States, and performing a vast amount of labor.

On the 5th of June, 1789, he sailed for Liverpool, which he reached on the 17th of July following, and immediately proceeded to the Conference to plead the cause of the poor West India negroes, and beg for missionaries. The Conference appointed him an agent to collect funds to sustain the missionaries; and for the ensuing sixteen months, in this department of the work he was greatly successful, not only in securing pecuniary aid, but in awakening missionary zeal among the Methodists of England, which has not abated to the present day.

In October, 1790, he again sailed for the West Indies in company with a reinforcement of missionaries. After his arrival, he found that the work of God had been spreading in the islands during his absence. While preaching in one of the islands on a certain occasion,—the room having been formerly a theatre,—such was the power of the Doctor's eloquence that the audience became perfectly enraptured, and strangely forgetting the occasion, if they remembered the place, gave vent to their approbation by crying out, "Encore! encore!"—a French theatrical phrase, which means a repetition of the performance. He was not, however, so popular in some other places, nor were his sermons always so well appreciated as by the Shaksperian congregation alluded to above. Some of the newspapers teemed with malicious libels against him. It was even asserted that he had been tried in England for horse-stealing, and had come to America to escape the gallows. Riots were frequent, and when in one case, the rioters were complained of to the grand jury, the latter dignified body gave it as their opinion, that both the preacher and the chapel ought to be indicted as nuisances.

In February, 1791, he again landed in Charleston, S. C., for the purpose of making a fourth visit to the United States brethren. He met the Conference which was in session in Charleston, and after its adjournment proceeded on a tour of visitation, which he continued until the fourteenth of May; when, having heard of the death of Mr. Wesley, he returned to England to join his tears and sorrows with those of his ministerial and lay brethren at home.

At the ensuing English Conference, Dr. Coke was elected Secretary of the same, an evidence of the high estimation in which he was held by his English brethren. Some time after this he visited France for the purpose of introducing Wesleyan missionaries into that nation, and then returned to London for the purpose of preparing a life of Mr. Wesley for the press, where he remained until after the next Conference, when he again sailed for the United States. After his arrival he attended the Conferences, and travelled over different States of the

Union until December, when he made another visit to the West Indies, where the fires of persecution had been raging violently against the Methodists since the time of his former visit. But notwithstanding these persecutions, Methodism by the blessing of God continued to spread, so that at this period the number of members in Society was not far from seven thousand, with twelve regular missionaries, and ten mission stations. Having met these missionaries in Conference, he sailed for England, where he arrived in June, 1793.

On his visit to one of the West India islands,—St. Vincent—he found Rev. Mr. Lamb, the missionary in that island, confined in the common jail, for having dared to preach the Gospel without a license from the legislature of the island, which no one could obtain until they had resided twelve months on the island. Rectors of parishes, were exempt from the requirements of this law. The penalty for violating this law was, for the first offence, fine, or imprisonment for from thirty to ninety days; second offence, whipping, and banishment; and a return from banishment, death! As Mr. Lamb had preached in the chapel, he as above stated, was undergoing the sentence of the law, being confined in the same room with a capitally convicted criminal. An effort was made by the Doctor to procure the liberation of Mr. Lamb, but this he could not succeed in doing, unless he would pay an exorbitant fine, which had been imposed in addition to the imprisonment, which fine, neither Dr. Coke, nor Mr. Lamb would consent to pay, as they would thereby seem to acknowledge the justice of the law. As soon, therefore, as the Doctor arrived in England, he posted with all speed to the colonial office, and made a proper statement of facts to the Home government; and in a short time he had the satisfaction of being officially informed by one of his majesty's secretaries of state, that the law under which Mr. Lamb was imprisoned had been repealed by the supreme power. The Doctor also visited Holland for the purpose, if possible, of obtaining permission of the Dutch Government for Missionaries to be allowed to preach in the Dutch West India islands, but all his efforts, although backed up by the recommendation of the Right Hon. Henry Dundas, one of his British Majesty's secretaries of state, were ineffectual in gaining the desired permission.

The Doctor next projected the establishment of a Wesleyan mission in the neighborhood of Sierra Leone, Africa; and for this purpose he travelled extensively for the collection of funds, as also to provide suitable persons to undertake the mission. After a length of time, some five or six respectable and professedly-pious mechanics, and their wives, were engaged to emigrate for the purpose of teaching the arts of civilization to the African race. But although thus successful in obtaining money and persons for the mission, and these persons actually went to Africa, yet partly through the secular nature of the intended enterprise, and mostly through the unworthiness of some of the persons selected, the mission for that time proved a failure; but still the Doctor continued his efforts in behalf of various missions, approaching high and low, rich and poor, and not without success. On one occasion he called on the captain of a British frigate, and pleaded the cause of the poor negro, and received from the captain a handsome donation. As the latter was totally unacquainted with Dr. Coke, he afterwards made inquiry of a gentleman in reference to him, "Pray, Sir," said the captain, "do you know anything of a little fellow, who calls himself Dr. Coke, who is going about begging money for missionaries to be sent among the slaves?" "I know him well," was the reply. "He seems," said the Captain, "to be a *heavenly minded little devil*, he coaxed me out of two guineas this morning."

On the 6th of August 1796, Dr. Coke again set sail for America. He had paid eighty guineas for his passage, but soon found that the provisions, &c., laid in for the voyage, were of the meanest and coarsest quality. To add to the wrong thus practised upon the passengers, the captain was one of the most abandoned wretches, that ever walked the deck of a ship, and who conspired with another captain who was on board, to make the voyage as disagreeable to the Doctor as possible. The treatment received by the latter, brought on a fit of sickness, which lasted three weeks. After having been to sea some weeks, they came across the wreck of a ship, with the remainder of the crew in a most wretched situation. These poor fellows were rescued from a watery grave, and from death by starvation, and on the 3d of October came in sight of the American shore.

Dr. Coke immediately on his arrival, proceeded to Baltimore, and subsequently attended the sessions of the Conference, and travelled and preached extensively for four months, when he again returned to Europe. On the passage homeward, an amusing instance of a sailor's simplicity occurred, which is worth recording. When the ship left Charleston, they were wafted by a severe gale across the Atlantic, so that in four weeks they made the Irish Channel. The gale now gave place to a great calm, which lasted for sixteen days. The Captain attributed this calm to Dr. Coke's reading a large folio volume. During the first few days, he hinted his wishes that the perusal of the book was finished. Growing out of patience, he at last told the Doctor, that they never would have a wind, till the reading of that book was finished. The Doctor at once offered to lay the book aside; "No, no," rejoined the Captain, "that will not do; it must be finished, or we shall have no wind." The Doctor to please him finished the book as rapidly as possible, and just as he had finished the wind sprung up, and in thirty-six hours, they were wafted into harbor.

Before leaving America the last time, the Doctor had made up his mind to comply with the wishes of the American preachers to settle permanently among them, and engaged himself to do so after having made another visit to England. The English Conference, however, could not consent to his leaving them, and requested the American brethren to cancel the Doctor's engagements in this respect, and allow him to settle in England. Having remained in the latter country about four months, he again embarked for America, where he remained until the spring of 1798, attending to all his duties as a superintendent, or bishop of the Church. The General Conference having taken into consideration the urgent request of the British Conference, consented to "*lend*" the Doctor to the latter for a season only.

On his return to England, he resumed his labors of preaching, and writing, besides soliciting aid for missions. He also projected a plan for the introduction of a protestant ministry among the degraded Romish peasantry of Ireland. He also obtained the rescinding of a municipal law by which the inhabitants of the isles of Jersey, and Guernsey, were required to attend military trainings on the Sabbath, on pain of banishment from the islands. Some correspondence also passed between him and the Bishop of London, and the Archbishop of Canterbury in relation to the propriety of their lordships' making some provision whereby a total separation of the Methodists in England, from the establishment, might be prevented. The bishops returned courteous answers, but declined making the desired provision by ordaining any of the preachers.

In 1800, Dr. Coke made his eighth visit to America, where he spent several months in the discharge of the usual duties of his high and holy office. He also visited the West Indies, and near the close of the year returned to England. After his arrival, he formed a plan for the introduction of Wesleyan Methodism into Wales, by which the natives of that principality might hear the doctrines of a free and full salvation proclaimed in the Welch tongue. This enterprise, when first mentioned, was thought to be altogether too romantic a one to be seriously engaged in; but otherwise thought Dr. Coke, and the lapse of ten years proved that the object was not a mere visionary one, as the sixty Wesleyan chapels, the thirty-six travelling preachers, and the five thousand members of that period, abundantly proved.

In the year 1801, Dr. Coke published his Commentary on the Old Testament, a work which nine years previously, at the request of the English Conference, he had began to prepare. It was issued in numbers, and met with a ready sale, the delivery of those on the New Testament being completed in 1807.

In 1803, he made his ninth and last visit to the United States. Here he spent several months, presiding in the Conference, and travelling extensively, until his return to England in 1804. In 1805, he was united in marriage to a Miss Smith, of Bradford, Wiltshire. This lady, possessed of an independent fortune, was every way worthy of so distinguished a companion as Dr. Coke. His first acquaintance with her, was formed by soliciting aid for missions. On being recommended by a friend to apply to the lady for aid, she generously subscribed one hundred guineas, nearly $500. On calling on her at her residence, to receive the above, the lady doubled the amount, and gave him two hundred guineas. The Doctor, admiring such acts of benevolence, contracted marriage with the lady. She only lived in his society till 1811, when she died in London, having in the meantime, devoted a large share of her wealth to the cause of spreading scriptural holiness through the world.

After his marriage, the Doctor still continued to devote himself to the good of mankind, by writing, preaching, praying, begging for missions, and keeping a constant lookout for any encroachment upon the rights and privileges of the Societies at home by the Government, or its officers; and of those of the preachers and negroes in the West Indies, by the colonial authorities; and such was his influence with the King and his privy council, that scarcely any remonstrance that he presented to them, was unheeded, or any grievance complained of, unredressed. The Doctor also gave from his own private purse, nearly three thousand dollars, for the establishment of a mission in Sierra Leone.

After the death of his beloved wife, he married again. The maiden name of the latter lady was Miss Ann Loxdale, of Liverpool, who had for a number of years been an esteemed member of the Methodist Society in that city. But, alas! for human hopes, she too, died in about a year after her marriage, and her remains were deposited beside those of his former companion, in the family vault in Wales.

In 1813, Dr. Coke conceived the Utopian plan of visiting India, and of personally superintending the establishment of a mission in that distant land. He found seven preachers who were willing to volunteer for that field of labor, whose names he presented to the Conference. The only objection to the establishment of the mission, was the cost of the outfit, nearly $27,000. To remove this objection, the Doctor offered to bear the whole expense himself, and accordingly, with the approbation and prayers of the Conference, the party sailed from England on the 31st of October. The missionaries continued their voyage until the 3d of May following, at which time they were in the Indian Ocean. Nothing special had transpired, except the death of one of the female missionaries. On the 1st of May, Dr. Coke felt somewhat unwell, and took a little medicine. On the 2d, he was still a little indisposed, but was up on deck. On the morning of the 3d, his servant knocked at his cabin-door, when receiving no response, he ventured to open the door, and to his utter astonishment found the Doctor lying on the floor, lifeless and cold. His death was no doubt caused by a fit of apoplexy, and it being impossible to preserve the body so as to send it to England, it was enclosed in a heavy coffin, and amidst the tears and prayers of his pious, but now forsaken associates, was committed to the bosom of the great deep.

Thus died the Reverend Bishop Coke, on the 3d of May, 1814, in the 66th year of his age—a man whose time, talents, wealth, ease, honor, and fame, were placed upon the altar of Methodism, for the good of mankind ; a man who had eighteen times crossed the Atlantic Ocean to promote its interests ; a man who had travelled hundreds of thousands of miles, and had endured all manner of contumely and reproach for its sake. Such an event could not transpire, without causing a sensation of deep sorrow through all the ranks of Methodism. Indeed, what portion of the world is there, where Methodism now exists, that has not been benefited directly or indirectly by the good Doctor's labors ? Truly it may be said of him, that "He being dead, yet speaketh," and that when he died, "A great man in Israel had fallen."

CHAPTER VI.

ADAM CLARKE, LL.D., F.A.S.

This extraordinary man was born in the village of Moybeg, county of Londonderry, Ireland. The precise date of his birth is not known, as no registry of this event or of his baptism could ever be found in the records of the parish church, to which his father belonged. It was probable, however, that he was born in the spring of 1760, as the minister who baptized him died shortly after this date. Adam was the second son of John Clarke, M.A. of Trinity College, Dublin, whose hopes of preferment in the Established Church being blasted on account of his marriage, induced him to resolve on emigrating to America, which resolution he was only prevented from executing by the remonstrances of friends. After having changed his purpose he retired to the obscure village where Adam was born, and where the father gained a livelihood by teaching school—an employment for which he was no doubt well qualified by inclination, as well as by learning.

At the age of five years, Adam was attacked severely with the small-pox. His medicine consisted mostly of spirituous liquors given for the purpose of driving out the "pock," while the patient was covered over with a large quantity of clothes in a warm bed, and the curtains drawn so as to exclude every particle of external air! Against such fond yet foolish treatment young Adam rebelled, and as often as opportunity offered ran out of doors entirely naked; and although forewarned of consequences as dreadful as death itself for so doing, he persisted in exposing himself to the open air; and although covered with pustules from the crown of his head to the soles of his feet, he mercifully recovered without having a single mark left upon his person.

At an early age, Adam was sent to the village school to learn the alphabet, &c., but so slow was he in acquiring a knowledge of the first rudiments of learning, that his teacher pronounced him to be a *grievous dunce.* Another teacher, however, who happened to be present when the last remark was made, placing his hand on Adam's head, encouragingly said, "This lad will make a good scholar yet." After having acquired a knowledge of reading, his father put him to the study of the Latin grammar. Some portions of his text-book he committed to memory with great difficulty, but other portions were perfectly incomprehensible to his juvenile mind. In perfect despair he threw by his grammar, and taking up an English testament he went into an English class, determined to study English only. His teacher perceiving his intentions, exclaimed in terrific tones, "Sir, what brought you here? Where is your Latin grammar?" Adam began to weep, and said, "Sir, I cannot learn it." "Go sirrah," said the teacher, "and take up your grammar: if you do not speedily get that lesson, I shall pull your ears as long as *Jowler's* (a dog), and you shall be a beggar to the day of your death." Poor Adam went to his seat, and was accosted by one of his classmates with the words, "What, have you not learned that lesson yet? O, what a stupid ass!" This was too much for Adam to endure without making an effort to redeem his character. His mind was made up to show to the teachers and scholars that he was not a *jackass.* He seized his grammar, and in a few moments committed his lesson to memory and recited it without missing a word; and finally wearied his teacher with the frequency of his recitations. Thus, through the taunts and jeers of a school-fellow, was the hidden spark of genius in Adam Clarke suddenly brought to light, and gave tokens of the future greatness of the man.

Adam now became very fond of reading, and all the money he obtained as presents, he carefully expended for books. At first his means were small, and he was obliged to content himself with penny or two-penny books, such as *Tom Thumb*, *Jack the Giant Killer*, *Babes in the Wood*, &c. &c. By reading such works his mind became somewhat attached to romance; and he even ventured on the study of magic, but his mind becoming somewhat enlightened on the subject of that art, he, from conscientious scruples, brought his studies in that *bewitching* department abruptly to an end.

Adam's father, as before intimated, was a member of the Church of England. His mother, however, was a Presbyterian of the Puritan stamp, and early inculcated upon the minds of her children the importance of religion; but Adam was too much engaged in the pursuit of knowledge as well as in the amusements peculiar to youth, to pay much regard to religious counsels any farther than to obey his parents and lead a moral life, until he was about seventeen years of age. At this time, the neighborhood where he lived was visited by certain Methodist preachers. On one occasion, Adam was invited by a young man to attend the Methodist meeting for the purpose, as he expressed it, of having some *fun*. Such an object was a strange one in the opinion of Clarke. He had attended balls and parties for the sake of the "*fun;*" but although he had very little if any acquaintance with the Methodists, he knew that a religious meeting of any kind was no place to seek for amusement. He, however, concluded to attend for the sake of information, and was so much edified with the discourse of Mr. Brettel (the gentleman who preached), that the next week he went to another neighborhood to hear him.

Mr. Brettel was succeeded on the circuit by Mr. Barber,

and under the labors of the latter gentleman, young Clarke and his mother became deeply interested in the subject of personal salvation; and having attended class-meeting became still more serious, until at length Mr. Barber enrolled Adam's name as a member of a small class which had been formed. He shortly after, for the first time, received the sacrament at the hands of the parish minister, but still he was a stranger to pardoning mercy. He became about this time the subject of strong temptation in relation to the propriety of praying to Jesus Christ, which some of his Socinian friends alleged was an unscriptural and idolatrous practice. Giving way to the temptation, he ceased praying to the Son, and made his petitions to the Father without ever mentioning the name of Christ. Being under strong convictions for sin, he was led frequently to call upon God to have mercy upon him, but all his prayers seemed to be in vain. While one day in a field alone praying for pardon, he wrestled with God until his strength was exhausted, and he could no longer speak or pray. In this his hour of extreme agony, the Spirit whispered, "*Pray to Christ.*" He at once complied with the suggestion, and soon his whole soul was overwhelmed with a sense of the divine presence and approbation. But still he was ignorant of the fact that he was *converted;* and it was not until some time after, when being at the same spot in company with Mr. Barber, that he obtained the Witness of the Spirit, and became satisfied in regard to the nature of the work wrought in his heart.

As soon as Adam became convinced that he was a child of God, he returned home to tell what great things the Lord had done for his soul. He also, notwithstanding his youth, erected a family altar in his father's house, and through his pious counsels and fervent prayers in their behalf, the most of the family finally became the subjects of converting grace, as did also some of his school-fellows.

In the above, and other ways, young Clarke began to render himself useful in the vineyard of Christ. He frequently went several miles from home, for the purpose of attending class-meeting, and giving the "word of exhortation." He would even go from village to village, and entering into a house, would say, "Peace be to this house," and request them to call in their neighbors, which if they consented to do, he would pray for, and exhort them, and then repair to the next village for a like purpose. In this way, Adam Clarke, almost unconsciously to himself, became an itinerant preacher, while his extreme youth and interesting deportment, made him a favorite wherever he went.

As it was now time that Adam should engage in some employment by which he could in subsequent life gain a subsistence, and as neither he nor his parents, ever supposed that he would become a Methodist preacher, he was put as an apprentice to a linen-draper, in Coleraine, by the name of Bennet, where he remained nearly a year, but without being indentured. While remaining at Mr. Bennet's, young Clarke's religious friends suggested to him their belief, that God intended him for the ministry, and becoming persuaded in his own mind that such indeed was the fact, he parted from his friend Mr. Bennet, with the kindest feelings, having been instrumental while there, in the conversion of one of his domestics.

After leaving Mr. Bennet, young Clarke not having received what he considered to be a satisfactory call as yet, to the regular work of the ministry, waited patiently for any indications that Providence might give him in relation to duty. Shortly after this, he was invited by Mr. Bredin, the circuit preacher, to visit him for a week or two. Adam accepted the invitation, and being requested by Mr. Bredin to go and fill his place the next evening, and to be sure and take a text, he reluctantly consented to go, and on the 19th of June,

1782, he preached his first sermon from 1 John v. 19. In the meantime, Mr. Bredin had written to Mr. Wesley in England, about Mr. Clarke, and the former having received an appointment in England, was requested to bring Adam with him, that he might be placed in Kingswood School for the purpose of improving his classical knowledge. Adam having laid the matter before his parents, found them to be highly displeased with the proposal. His father was enraged, and his mother threatened him with God's displeasure, and informed him that if he went, he should have a parent's curse, and not her blessing to go with him. Under these circumstances, not daring to leave home with a mother's curse, he had recourse to prayer, and was surprised a few days afterward to find that his mother had changed her mind in relation to the matter, and that both parents were willing to submit to the indications of Providence.

In the course of a few days, he left the parental mansion, and being disappointed in not having the company of Mr. Bredin, he set sail from the port of Derry for Liverpool, having purchased, previously to embarking, a loaf of bread and a pound of cheese, as provision for the voyage. In two days, they arrived in Liverpool, but while ascending the river Mersey, they were boarded by a press-gang, who were raising supplies for the navy. Two young men who were on board, hid themselves, but Adam stood his ground, all the while lifting his heart to God in prayer. The press-gang searched the vessel, and finding one of the young men who had hidden himself, took him with them, but for some reason left Adam unmolested, saving the utterance of a horrid oath by the lieutenant of the gang, followed by the words "you'll not do." Mr. Clarke ever after this, had an enduring hatred for the system of impressment as pursued in England; and well he might, for as he himself remarks in relation to it, "What Briton's bosom does not burn against this infringement of

British liberty? This unconstitutional attack on the liberty of a free-born subject of the Sovereign of the British Isles? While the impress service is tolerated, in vain do we boast of our constitution. It is an attack upon its vitality ten thousand times worse than any suspension of the *Habeas Corpus* act. Let Britons know, that it is neither any part of the constitution, nor any law of the land, whatever some venal lawyers have said, in order to make it constructively such. Nothing can be a reason for it, but that which justifies a *levee en masse*, of the inhabitants of the nation. It is intolerable to hear those plead for it, who are not exposed to so great a calamity."

On Adam's arrival in Liverpool, he was kindly entertained in the family of the captain of the vessel which had brought him over. The captain's name was Cunningham, a Scotchman, and he and his excellent lady conspired to make his stay with them as pleasant as possible; and while enjoying their hospitality, Mr. Clarke endeavored to make himself as useful in a spiritual sense, as he could. When he left them, he expected, as a matter of course, to pay his bill like all other private boarders, but Mrs. C. informed him that he had nothing to pay, "You owe nothing here; Captain C., myself, and all the family, are deeply in your debt. You have been a blessing to our house, and were you to stay longer, you would have no charges."

The distance from Liverpool to Bristol, near which Kingswood is situated, is about two hundred miles. This distance, Adam resolved to pursue on foot, as his finances were by no means very abundant. He was, however, persuaded by a friend to relinquish this mode of travelling, and to procure an outside seat on a stage-coach to Birmingham. At the latter place, he met with a brother of his friend, Rev. Mr. Brettel, who showed him great kindness, but cautioned him against forming too high an opinion of Kingswood School, as he might there be doomed to suffer pain and discouragement. After remaining here a few days, he took his departure for Bristol, having no other refreshment on the road than a penny loaf, and a half-penny worth of apples, during a journey of seventeen hours. Arriving at a late hour in the evening, he put up at the inn, and in the morning when his bill was paid, he had but three half-pence left to pay his expenses at Kingswood.

In the morning, he went to Kingswood, and having found Mr. Simpson, the head-master of the school, he presented to him a letter from Mr. Wesley, authorizing his admission as a student. Mr. S. informed him, that there was no room for him in the school, and that he must go back to Bristol, and wait for a fortnight, until Mr. Wesley himself should come. Adam told Mr. S. that he could not go back, as his money was all gone.

After some farther conversation, Mr. S. gave Adam permission to remain, provided that he would occupy a small room at the end of the chapel, and that he would stay in that room, and not come into the house. He was also informed, that his food would be brought to him daily by one of the servants. Adam felt, indeed, as though this was rather ungenerous treatment of a stranger in a strange land. He, however, found out during the day, that as he was an *Irishman*, he was suspected of having the *itch*, and that on this account, Mrs. S. could not allow him to mingle with the family. Adam resented the imputation by opening his vest and shirt bosom, and showing Mr. S. as white a skin as ever crossed the Tweed—Mr. S. was a *Scotchman*—but all to no purpose, the itch might be cleaving somewhere to his person, and nothing would satisfy them until he had rubbed himself from head to foot, with a box of "*Jackson's Itch Ointment.*"

It is proper here to remark, that Kingswood School at this time, was under the supervision of very improper persons.

Mr. Simpson and his wife were illiberal, tyrannical, and parsimonious; and although frequent complaints had been made to Mr. Wesley, of their treatment of the students, yet as he was in his 80th year, and was disposed to believe evil of no one, he had suffered them to remain at the head of the institution. That the reader may know how to sympathize with the young Irish stranger, we will give a few paragraphs from his life in his own words. "It was only my strong hold of God, that kept me from distraction. But to whom could I make my complaint? Earthly refuge I had none. It is utterly impossible for me to describe the feelings, I may justly say, the agony of my mind. I surveyed my apartment; there was a wretched old bureau, wainscot-bedstead, not worth ten shillings, and a bed and bed-clothes, not worth much more; but the worst was, they were very scanty, and the weather was cold and wet. There was one rush-bottomed chair in the place, and besides these, neither carpet on the floor, nor at the bedstead, nor any other kind of furniture. There was no book, not even a Bible in the place; and my own box, with my clothes, and a few books was behind at the Lamb Inn, in Bristol; and I had not even a change of linen. Of this I informed them, and begged them to let the man (as I found he went in with a horse and small cart three times a week) bring out my box to me. To this request often and earnestly repeated, I got no definite answer, but no box was brought.

"*Jackson's Ointment* was brought, it is true; and with this unguent, I was obliged to anoint myself, before a large fire (the first and last I saw while I remained there) which they had ordered to be lighted for the purpose. In this state smelling worse than a pole-cat, I tumbled with a heavy heart, and streaming eyes into my worthless bed. The next morning, the sheets had taken from my body as far as they came in contact with it, the unabsorbed parts of this tartareous compound: and the smell of them and myself, was almost insupportable. I begged the woman that brought my *bread and milk* for breakfast, for dinner, and for supper—for generally I had nothing else, and not enough of that—to let me have a pair of clean sheets. It was in vain: no clean clothes of any kind were afforded me; I was left to make my own bed, sweep my own room, &c. &c. as I pleased! For more than three weeks no soul performed any kind act for me. And as they did not give orders to the man to bring out my box, I was left without a change of any kind, till the Thursday of the second week; when I asked permission to go out of my prison house, to Bristol for my box, which being granted, I walked to Bristol and carried my box *on my head* more than four miles, without any kind of assistance! It was then no loss that my wardrobe was not extensive. As for books, I brought none with me but a small 18mo. Bible, a 12mo. edition of Young's Night Thoughts, Prideaux' Connections, and Buck's 8vo. Greek Testament.

As both the days and nights were very cold, the season then being unnaturally so, I begged to have a little *fire*. This was denied me, though coals were very cheap; and had it been otherwise, they were not at *their* expense; they were paid for out of the *public collections* made for that school, to which many of my friends made an annual offering.

One day having seen Mr. Simpson walking in the garden, I went to him and showed him my fingers, then bloodless through cold! He took me to the hall, showed me a cord which hung from the roof, to the end of which was fixed a cross stick; and told me to jump up and catch hold of the stick, and swing by my hands, and that would help to restore the circulation. I did so: and had been at the exercise only a few minutes, when Mrs. S. came and drove both him and myself away, under the pretence that we should dirty the floor! From this woman I received no kindness. When nearly crippled with cold, and I had stolen in the kitchen to warm myself for a few moments, if I heard her voice in the hall, I have run as a man would who is pursued in the jungles of Bengal, by a royal tiger.

"This woman was equally saving of the *candles*, as of the coals; if my candle was not extinguished by nine o'clock, I was called to account for it. My bed not being comfortable, I did not like to lie much in it, and therefore kept out of it as late, and rose from it as early as possible. To prevent Mrs. S. from seeing the reflection of the light through my window (for my prison house was opposite the school over the way), I was accustomed to set my candle on the floor behind my bureau-bed, take off my coat, and hang it on my chair-back, bring that close on the other angle, and then sit down on the floor and read!"

We might enlarge these extracts for the purpose of showing the wretched situation in which Adam found himself when he first became an inmate of Kingswood, but these must suffice. Should the reader wonder at the tameness of his spirit, and be led to inquire why he submitted to such treatment, the answer is very easy. He was a youth, a stranger, without money, and without friends; he lived in expectation of soon seeing Mr. Wesley, when he expected an improvement in his situation; and for these and other reasons, he preferred suffering for awhile, rather than leave the institution and be foiled in his attempts to secure an education. Besides, he soon became acquainted with Mr. Rankin, the Superintendent of the circuit, who became his friend, and invited him to preach in a distant neighborhood, and from this period his condition was somewhat improved.

For the sake of exercise, Adam sought and obtained permission to work in the garden connected with the School. While thus employed, one day he found a half-guinea, embedded in a clod, which he was breaking with a spade. He took the piece of money to Mr. Simpson, who stated it might be his, but did not recollect having lost any, and advised Adam to keep it until an owner was found. Adam did so with reluctance. The next day learning that a Mr. Bayley had lost a half-guinea, he gave it to him, but in three days after, Mr. Bayley restored to Adam the possession of the piece, saying, "Mr. Clarke, it is true that I lost half a guinea, but I am not sure that *this* is the half-guinea I lost; unless I was so, I could not conscientiously keep it; therefore, you must take it again." Adam replied, "It is not *mine;* probably it is *yours*, therefore I cannot take it." Mr. B. replied, "I cannot keep it. I have been uneasy in my mind ever since it came into my possession," and while saying this, he forced the gold into Adam's hand. So the latter was obliged to keep it, and as no owner could be found for it, it formed quite an addition to the purse, that contained but three halfpence.

After having been at Kingswood about five weeks, Mr. Wesley arrived in Bristol, and Adam hastened to pay his respects to him. The old gentleman received him kindly, and asked him if he wished to devote himself to the work of the Lord. His reply was, "Sir, I wish to *be*, and *do*, what God pleases." Mr. Wesley accordingly requested him to hold himself in readiness to go to Bradford circuit, where there was a vacancy, after which he laid his hands upon his head, and blessed him in the name of the Lord.

On the 27th day of September, 1782, Adam Clarke began his labors as an itinerant Methodist preacher. At one place where an appointment had been given out for him, there was a large assemblage of young persons brought together from motives of curiosity, to hear the youthful preacher. After having preached, he gave out the well-known hymn, beginning with the words, "Vain delusive world adieu," &c. After singing, in which the audience all joined, Mr. Clarke addressed himself to their consciences, by reminding them of what they had sung, and inquiring whether they intended to keep the vows they had verbally made while singing the hymn. Such was the effect of this appeal to them, that during that evening and next morning, thirteen young persons came to him, desiring to know what they must do to be saved? A revival of religion immediately took place, and Methodism was thenceforth established in that village.

A circumstance shortly after this, occurred, which came very near putting an end to Mr. Clarke's classical pursuits. At one appointment where he was in the habit of preaching, he observed a Latin sentence pencilled on the wall of the room where his lodgings were. Admiring the sentence, he subjoined an appropriate Latin quotation from the Æneid of Virgil. Shortly after this, one of his colleagues on the circuit being in the same place, and also in the same room, observed the quotation, and without being able to read it, he judged it was Latin, and that Mr. Clarke had written it. Not being able to bear an equal, much less a superior in knowledge, he wrote under Mr. Clarke's quotation, the following words:

> "Did you write the above
> to show us you could write Latin?
> For shame! do send pride
> to hell, from whence it came.
> O, young man, improve your
> time, eternity's at hand."

On Mr. Clarke's return to that place, he noticed the reproachful effusion, and in a moment of temptation, he knelt down and solemnly promised his Maker never more to meddle with Latin or Greek! The next time he saw the ignorant and conceited author of the reproof, he ventured to inquire why the latter had not reproved him privately, instead of publishing it in a manner whereby many persons might see and read it! The preacher replied, that he thought he pursued the best mode to produce a cure. Mr. Clarke then told him of the vow he had made, and was warmly applauded for so doing, by this mistaken man. For nearly four years he abandoned the study of Latin and Greek, and confined his attention principally to French and Hebrew. At length he received a letter from Mr. Wesley, in which he was charged to cultivate his mind as far as possible, and not to forget anything he had ever learned. This timely advice, broke the spell by which Mr. Clarke had been bound, and he concluded that his vow was not only rash, but wicked, and that it would be more acceptable to God to break the same, however solemnly made, than to persist in keeping it. He accordingly resumed his Greek and Latin, and neither himself nor the Church have had reason to repent his change of purpose in this respect.

After having travelled as a preacher for nearly a year, he was received into full connection by Mr. Wesley, at the Conference in Bristol, in 1783. A circumstance occurred at his examination, which shows his strict regard for truth. One of the questions asked by Mr. Wesley—and indeed by all his successors, whether presidents or bishops—of every preacher eligible to full connection in the Conference, was, "Are you in debt?" The day before Mr. Clarke's examination, he had borrowed a half-penny of a brother preacher, for the purpose of bestowing it upon a poor man. During the day, the preacher had left town before Mr. Clarke had an opportunity of paying him back the half-penny. Knowing the question would be asked him as usual, "Are you in debt?" he was at a loss to know what answer to give. If he should reply negatively, it would not be strictly true; if he replied that he was, and should be asked the amount, he feared his brethren might think him a fool. He, however, relieved himself from the dilemma by replying, "*Not one* PENNY."

During the eleven months he was on Bradford circuit, he preached five hundred and six times, besides delivering a large number of exhortations, &c., which shows to some extent the arduous labors of the early Methodist preachers. At the Bristol Conference, Mr. Clarke was appointed to Norwich circuit, having the venerable Richard Whatcoat, afterwards Bishop Whatcoat, for his colleague. The circuit was poor, and could not afford Mr. Clarke a horse, he consequently was often obliged to walk to his appointments, and carry his own saddle-bags. The next year he was appointed to St. Austell circuit, in Cornwall, a distance of about four hundred miles from Norwich. He had but a guinea and a half-crown, to bear his expenses to that distant field of labor, but he set out trusting in the Lord. Soon after his arrival on his circuit, he went to one of his appointments, and as directed, called at the house of a farmer P. for entertainment. When he entered, he found only the good woman within, who gave him for his dinner cold apple-pie and cream, this being the best the house afforded. After satisfying himself, he went to the stable to clean his horse, and waited till the farmer came in from the field. The following dialogue then took place: "*Who art thou?*" "I am a Methodist preacher; my name is Adam Clarke." "*And what is thee coming here for?*" "To preach to yourself, your family, and your neighbors." "*Who sent thee here?*" "I received the plan from Mr. W." (the superintendent of the circuit,) "and your place stands for to-night and to-morrow morning." "*I expect other friends to-morrow, and thou shalt not stay here.*" "Why, will you not have the preaching?" "*No, I will have none of thy preaching, nor any of thy brethren.*" "But will it not be wrong to deprive your family and neighbors of what may be profitable to them, though you may not desire it?" "*Thee shalt not stay here, I will have no more Methodist preaching.*" "Well, I will inform Mr. W. of it, and I dare say he will not send any more, if you desire it not; but as I am a stranger in the country, and know not my way, and it is now toward evening, I hope you will give me a night's lodging, and I will, please God, set off to-morrow morning." "*I tell thee thou shalt not stay here.*" "What, would you turn a stranger out into a strange country, of which he knows nothing, and so late in the evening, too?" "*Where was thee last night?*" "I was at Palperr." "*Then go there.*" "It is out of my reach, besides I have to preach at Bodmin to-morrow evening." "*Then go to Bodmin.*" "I have never yet been there; am not expected there to-night; and know no person in the place: pray give me the shelter of your roof for the night." "*I tell thee thou shalt not stay here.*" "Are you really in earnest?" "*I am.*" "Well, then, if I must go, you can direct me the way to Buthernbridge; I was there on Thursday, and am sure I shall be welcome again." "*Thee must inquire the road to Bodmin.*" "How far is Ruthernbridge hence?" "*Almost fifteen or sixteen miles, so thou hadst best be getting off.*" "I will set off immediately."

On being thus denied a night's lodging, Mr. Clarke repacked his loose articles and saddled his horse, the farmer all the while looking on, but offering to lend no assistance. Having mounted his horse Mr. Clarke said, "Now sir, I am a stranger, and you have refused me the common rites of hospitality; I am a messenger of the *Lord Jesus*, coming to you, your family and your neighbors with the glad tidings of salvation by Jesus Christ, and you have refused to receive me: for this, you must account at the bar of God. In the meantime, I must act as my Lord has commanded me. Remember! a messenger of peace came to your house with the Gospel, and you have rejected both him and his message!" So saying, he shook off the dust from the soles of both feet as a testimony against the inhospitable farmer. The result off his conduct was the withdrawal of Methodist preaching from the neighborhood, ruin came upon the man, his family became corrupt, and he himself soon died.

Mr. Clarke, while on this circuit, met with a severe accident by the stumbling of his horse which nearly deprived him of life, and the effects of which he felt for several years after; although, by the goodness of God, he was not prevented thereby from attending to his work. At the Conference of 1785, held in London, Mr. Clarke was appointed to Plymouth Dock circuit, where a secession of some fifty members had taken place from the Society. Such was Mr. Clarke's influence, that most of the seceders returned in the course of the year; and at the close thereof, the Society was found to have doubled its number. In the meanwhile, Mr. Clarke was improving every leisure moment in pursuing his classical studies. He also through the kindness of friends who appreciated his thirst for knowledge, became the owner of a few valuable classical works, which greatly assisted him in his researches. At this time, his salary as a preacher was only twelve pounds (about $50) per annum, so that he could not from his own resources purchase such books as were necessary; but Providence furnished the means through the liberality of friends, and frequently in the most unexpected manner. In consequence of Mr. Clarke's knowledge of the French language, he was, at the Conference of 1786, appointed by Mr. Wesley to the Island of Jersey, one of the Norman Isles, where he was most hospitably received and entertained in the family of Henry De Jersey, Esq. The next year, Mr. Wesley and Dr. Coke visited these islands, and on their return were accompanied by Mr. Clarke. He was, however, reappointed to the same field of labor, and remained there until 1789, when he was appointed to Bristol. In 1788, Mr. Clarke was united in marriage to Miss Mary Cooke, of Trowbridge, Wiltshire, a young lady of fervent piety, a highly intellectual mind, and withal, a strict Methodist. This union was followed by the best possible consequences to both parties; and was attended with no loss of honor to the lady or her friends, although some of the latter opposed the marriage, and in fact delayed it for a year, because they imagined that she would be degraded by an alliance with a poor Methodist preacher.

In 1790, Mr. Clarke was appointed to Dublin. This was an important appointment, inasmuch as the preacher in Dublin was considered Mr. Wesley's representative in Ireland, and had charge of all the circuits and stations in the kingdom. While in Dublin, he heard of the death of his father and friend, Mr. Wesley. The news, though not entirely unexpected, was so affecting to the sensitive mind of Mr. Clarke, that he could scarcely read the account of his death. After remaining in Dublin one year he was appointed to Manchester circuit, and while in the latter place he formed the well-known Stranger's Friend Society, which as it became known was introduced into many of the cities and large towns of England.

Mr. Clarke remained in Manchester two years, and in 1793, was appointed to Liverpool. While in this place and while returning from an evening appointment in the country, he was attacked by several Roman Catholic ruffians who had waylaid him. He was in company with his brother and another friend at the time. As they passed the place where the ruffians lay concealed, Mr. Clarke was struck by a large stone on the head which caused a deep wound. He was immediately carried to a neighboring house and was left in charge of the friend, while his brother ran back to pursue the assailants. He found them and charged them with the act. He had them arrested, and then returned to attend to his wounded brother. The inhabitants of the house on hearing that Mr. Clarke was a Methodist preacher, and that the men who had assailed him were Roman Catholics, and being Roman Catholics themselves, declared that he was well served, and that it was a pity they had not killed him. His friends seeing how matters stood, had him carried to his own house in Liverpool, where he was laid up for a month in consequence of his wound. The ruffians were at last released from confinement through the merciful disposition of Mr. Clarke, who refused to prosecute them for the assault. They both, however, soon came to an untimely and tragical end.

In 1795, Mr. Clarke was appointed to the London circuit, where he continued three years; and while here he commenced taking notes for his Commentary, which may, in fact, be considered as the beginning of that literary career, which afterwards made him so famous as a scholar and as an author. We are not, however, to suppose that Mr. Clarke's literary pursuits rendered him less diligent as a pastor. It has been computed that during his three years' stay in London, he *walked at least seven thousand miles* in attending upon his pastoral duties. After his three years in London had expired he was appointed to Bristol, and while here he had the misfortune to lose his beloved father by death. Mr. Clarke senior, had remained a few years previously with the younger members of his family from Ireland to Manchester, at which place he died, and where his remains lie interred. As an instance of filial affection, it is recorded that ever after when Mr. Adam Clarke was passing the burying ground where his father lay interred, whether riding or walking, he would reverently uncover his head, and keep it uncovered while passing by.

The greatest difficulty Mr. Clarke had to contend with while writing his Commentary and other valuable works, was the want of books. At this period he was greatly in want of an Arabic Dictionary. There was but one work which he could obtain to supply this deficiency in this respect, but to obtain it he must pay forty pounds sterling (nearly $200). Not having the money he tried to borrow it of a friend, but the latter considering him almost insane to pay so much money for a single book, refused to lend him the desired sum. He was, however, more successful in another direction, and the book was obtained.

Mr. Clarke now became an author on an extensive scale. In 1800, he translated and published Sturm's Reflections, a very valuable work. In 1802, he published a "Bibliographical Dictionary" in six volumes. About the same time he published "A Succinct Account of Polyglott Bibles," and also "A Succinct Account of the Principal Editions of the Greek Testament." All these works demanded great labor and research, and for this no man was better fitted by nature and education than Mr. Clarke. After remaining in Bristol three years, Mr. Clarke was appointed again to Liverpool, and while here he projected the formation of the "Philological Society;" but his arduous labors were undermining his constitution, hence in 1802, he was obliged to repair to London to seek medical advice. His physician plainly told him that unless he would abstain totally from reading, writing, preaching, &c., in less than a year he would be a dead man. God, however, saw fit to spare him to a good old age. To add to his afflictions while in Liverpool, he lost his brother by death; but God was his supporter and his strength amidst all his troubles and afflictions.

After leaving Liverpool, Mr. Clarke went to Manchester, where he met his daughter Agnes, and while here in 1804, he published "Memoirs of the Ancient Israelites," and in the following year, he issued a new edition of the same work. On leaving Manchester he was again stationed in London, and in 1806, was elected President of the Conference, contrary to his expressed wishes. The British and Foreign Bible Society also, elected him a member of its executive committee, a station for which he was well qualified by his extensive knowledge of the ancient languages. His duties in this department were principally confined to the printing of the Bible in the

Arabic tongue; and so well were his labors appreciated in this direction, that the committee requested his acceptance of fifty pounds, which they sent to him in the most handsome manner, but which he peremptorily declined to accept, and which he immediately returned with great respect. During the year of his Presidency of the connection, he visited his first circuit, and preached in the same chapel where he preached his first sermon, as an itinerant, about twenty-four years previously. Old scenes were of course presented afresh to his memory, and he distinctly remembered hearing a man say when he first presented himself, as the youthful and diffident itinerant, "*Tut, tut, what will Mr. Wesley send us next?*"

On the 31st of January, 1807, Mr. Clarke received in the most flattering manner, the degree of Master of Arts, from the University of Aberdeen in Scotland, and in a year from that time, the same College as a further testimonial of esteem, and appreciation of his merits, bestowed on him the degree of Doctor of Civil Law. The diplomas were sent to him, the College refusing to accept the customary fee given on such occasions.

In 1808, Dr. Clarke received an invitation from the British government, to undertake the completion of a collection of State Papers, embracing all the leagues, treaties, alliances, capitulations, and confederacies, which had been entered into by the British Crown and other States, or princes. This voluminous work had been commenced in 1693, and had been published from time to time, down to the year 1717, since which time, little appears to have been done toward its completion. As this was a work of great importance, it became necessary for the government, to select one of the ablest men in the nation to make the completion. The selection fell on Dr. Clarke, who was requested by the secretary of the Commission, to accept the appointment. The Doctor refused on the ground that his researches had always been directed to other and totally different subjects. The Secretary smiled, and requested him to have the goodness to *try*. Before coming to a conclusion in reference to the matter, he resolved to ask the advice of the London Wesleyan preachers at their meeting at City Road Chapel. Some objected that it would interfere with his ministerial duties; others, that it was a trick of the devil to prevent his usefulness; others, that it was a call of Providence to greater usefulness, and advising him to accept the appointment by all means. As the most of his brethren were of the latter opinion, he reluctantly concluded to accept the appointment. He was immediately appointed Sub-commissioner, with authority to employ all the assistants necessary to the completion of the work, and with liberty to examine all the public records necessary to the undertaking. This work in which Doctor Clarke engaged was completed by him in ten years, to the entire satisfaction of the government.

While thus rendering his valuable services to the government, he by no means neglected his duties as a Methodist preacher. He attended all his appointments, visited all the classes and proceeded with the preparation of his Commentary, as time and circumstances would allow. In 1810, the first part of the work was published, and the receipt of a copy thereof acknowledged in the most flattering terms by the Right Honorable the Speaker of the House of Commons.

In 1811, Dr. Clarke and son visited Ireland. He went to the house where his father lived, when the Methodists first came into the place, and where Adam lived when he was converted. The house had now become old and dilapidated. Dr. Clarke asked permission of the woman to enter. She replied, "It is too mean a place for such a gentleman as you to enter." "Good woman," replied the doctor, "do not say so; I have spent several years in this very house." The woman was astonished! He entered, and before taking his leave gave each of the children a piece of silver.

The first part of his Commentary, was generally received by a discerning public according to its real merits. There were, however, a few who took exception to the Doctor's interpretations, especially to his rendering of the term *serpent* in Gen. iii. 1, by another word, which he thought more significant—a monkey. The objections of these critics, called forth from the Rev. Richard Reece,—who was a great admirer of Dr. Clarke,—the following ingenious lines:

"The Rev. Doctor Adam Clarke asserts,
 It could not be a serpent tempted Eve,
But a gay monkey, whose fine mimic arts
 And fopperies, were most likely to deceive.

Dogmatic commentators still hold out,
 A *serpent*, not a *monkey*, tempted madam;
And which shall we believe? Without a doubt
 None knows so well who tempted *Eve* as *Adam*."

In 1813, Dr. Clarke was elected Fellow of the Society of Antiquarians, an honor which was richly deserved, and greatly appreciated by the Doctor himself. In 1815, the state of his health rendered it necessary for him to leave London, and retire into the country in the neighborhood of Liverpool, where he had purchased an estate, and which he called Millbrook. At this place he built a Methodist chapel at his own expense, and as the winter of 1816 was very severe, hundreds of sailors in Liverpool were without means of support. Dr. Clarke immediately on hearing of the distress of this neglected class of men, prepared some untenanted cottages on his estate, for the reception of twenty of them, and provided them with regular meals in his kitchen every day during the winter. He gave them also some slight employment to keep them from idleness.

In the summer of 1816, the Doctor made another visit to Ireland, as also to Scotland, and on his return was warmly greeted by his family and dependants. In 1817, he was elected member of the American Antiquarian Society. In 1818, he took under his charge and tuition two young heathen priests, who had just been brought over from the island of Ceylon, for the purpose of being instructed in the theology and science of Christendom. Many anecdotes are related of these youths, while under Dr. Clarke's care. One or two we will give: They had been instructed in the Doctor's family, that in winter the ground would be covered with snow, and that water would be frozen, so that it would bear a person to walk on its surface. They were, however, incredulous about these matters, until one morning in the beginning of winter, they arose from their beds, and to their utter astonishment, the world was white before and around them! Surprised and fearful, they ran for the Doctor, who soon allayed their fears by going out with them into the garden, and taking some of the snow in his hands, taught them its nature and properties. Soon after, the fish-pond was frozen over, and this also was a matter of astonishment. They could not be prevailed to venture upon it, until the Doctor and the ladies of the family had set the example. These priests remained for two years in the family of Dr. Clarke, and during that period had been soundly converted to the Christian faith, and received at the hands of the Doctor, in Richmond Chapel, Liverpool, the rite of Christian baptism, in the presence of a large congregation. As these youths had been committed to his care by Sir A. Johnstone, Chief Justice of the island of Ceylon, it became necessary on the appointment of his successor, Sir Richard Ottley, to the same distinguished office, to allow these Cingalese converts to return to their own land, which they did after shedding many tears of sorrow, at being obliged to leave the kind-hearted Doctor and his family.

In July, 1821, Dr. Clarke was elected member of the Royal Irish Academy, an institution on whose list of members were enrolled some of the most honorable and distinguished names in the land. In July of 1822, he was for the third time elected President of the Wesleyan Conference, a mark of honor which he esteemed more highly than all the literary degrees which had been conferred upon him. In 1823, he was elected Member of the Geological Society of London, and during the same year, became an original member of the Royal Asiatic Society. To pass over a portion of Dr. Clarke's history, we find him in 1825, the honored guest of his Royal Highness the Duke of Sussex. This nobleman was ever the patron of sound learning, and a great admirer of Dr. Clarke. On the occasion just referred to, he had been invited by the Duke to meet another distinguished nobleman, the Duke of Hamilton, at the palace of the former, for the purpose of a mutual introduction; and without entering into details in reference to the honor shown him at this visit, we cannot avoid contrasting his present position in society, flattered and honored by royalty itself, with the condition in which he found himself when he first arrived in England, and especially on his arrival at Kingswood School, where he had literally to beg for a place to stay, and for a bed whereon to rest his wearied limbs.

Previous to this, he had sold his estate at Millbrook, and had purchased another in the vicinity of London, which he called Haydon Hall; and at this latter place in 1826, he finished his Commentary on the Old and New Testaments, a work on which he had been engaged for *forty years* of his precious life. The last sentence of that work was written upon his knees, and when completed he returned fervent thanks to God, that his life had been spared to see the completion of a work which had cost him so many wearisome hours of labor and research, without aid from any person, not even an amanuensis. On the completion of his Commentary, he was invited by his children to a family dinner, at the nouse of one of his sons. After dinner, a splendid silver vase was brought in, and placed at the head of the table. This vase had been prepared by his children, as a solemn offering upon the occasion, without the Doctor's knowledge. The Doctor's eldest son arose, and uncovering the vase, and with an appropriate and affectionate address, he in the name of each child in the family, offered it to their revered parent. The good Doctor was taken by surprise ; for a few moments he sat incapable of utterance; then regarding them all, he rose, and spreading out his hands, pronounced a father's blessing upon them, individually and collectively. Such a scene would be worthy the attention of the artist.

In June, 1826, the Doctor, accompanied by one of his sons, started on a visit to the Shetland Isles, for the purpose of promoting the good of the Wesleyan Missions in that much neglected portion of the British Isles. On the voyage, they experienced a tremendous storm ; to add to their danger, they were pursued by a royal revenue cutter, who supposed them to be engaged in the smuggling trade. The cutter made a signal, which the other vessel, on account of the derangement of its rigging, was unable to answer. Finding the signal unanswered, the cutter fired a blank cartridge ; still the flag was entangled in the shrouds. The cutter was on the point of firing into her, when discovering the cause of her failure to reply to the signal, and also that she was engaged in the Shetland Island service, suffered her to proceed. After reaching the port of his destination, and spending a short time with the simple, yet hospitable inhabitants of those Islands, he returned again to England, by way of Scotland. Having acquired by his visit to Shetland a much better knowledge of the wants of the people, he exerted himself to awaken an interest in the bosoms of Christians at home, for the spiritual welfare of those distant sheep ; and during the next summer, accompanied by several ministers, and other gentlemen, he made a second visit to the islands. During this second visit, he laid the corner-stone of a new Wesleyan chapel, and after remaining nearly a month, returned with his company to England.

In 1830, Dr. Clarke was elected a Fellow of the Eclectic Society of London, an honor conferred only on the most eminent of scientific men. In April of this year, he visited Ireland again, and towards the close of this year we find him exerting himself to establish schools among the peasantry of his native island, which he subsequently succeeded in doing, and which he fostered with a parent's care.

During the year 1831, and until the close of his life, Dr. Clarke sustained a supernumerary relation to the Conference. This relation was not sought by him; indeed, it was given him in opposition to his own feelings and judgment in the matter, a circumstance which somewhat afflicted him. It however gave him a little more liberty to travel where he chose. In the latter part of the year, he received an affectionate letter from the Board of Managers of the Missionary Society of the Methodist Episcopal Church in the United States, inviting him to visit America. To this invitation he was obliged, through the multiplicity of engagements, to return a negative answer, but assuring the worthy brethren who extended the invitation, that he loved the Church they represented, and respected and wished well to the State of which they were citizens, and asserting his belief that their "nation is destined to be the mightiest and happiest nation of the globe," and their "Church the most extensive and pure in the universe."

In the spring of 1832, Dr. Clarke again visited Ireland, for the purpose of seeing to his Irish schools, but while here he became seriously indisposed, so much so, as to unfit him for active employment. After a partial recovery from his attack of rheumatism, he proceeded to visit several places, but learning that his son, who had started from home to attend to the Doctor during his illness and accompany him home, had met with a serious accident on the way, by the upsetting of the stage-coach, he hastened to Belfast, where he took passage in a steamer for Liverpool; but such was his weakness that he did not reach his home, until the 2d of July. At this time, the cholera was raging in Liverpool, and the session of the Conference was to be held in that town during this year. Dr. Clarke, notwithstanding his bodily infirmities, had a great desire to attend the Conference. Strong objections were interposed by his family to his going to Liverpool. Believing, however, that duty required his presence, he went there, and found that many of his dear friends were falling victims to the pestilence. He preached the annual sermon at the request of the Conference, and received as a supernumerary, an appointment to Windsor with a note appended to his name, that he was not bound to that circuit, but was respectfully requested to visit all parts of the Connection, and labor as strength and convenience would permit.

On the 25th of August, having promised to preach at a place called Bayswater, a few miles from Haydon Hall, on the next day, Sabbath, he rode out in a chaise with his friend Mr. Hobbs, who called for him. On his way to Bayswater, he was quite cheerful, but on his arrival, he appeared quite languid and wearied. During the night, his indisposition increased so that he passed a painful night. On Sunday morning he arose early, and at six o'clock sent for Mr. Hobbs, who found him with his great-coat on, and his travelling bag in his hand. Dr. Clarke informed Mr. Hobbs, that he wanted to go home immediately, as he could not possibly preach that day. Mr. Hobbs went to procure an easy carriage, but while absent the Doctor became quite cold and distressed, so that his removal was out of the question. Physicians were called in, who pronounced it a case of cholera. Mrs. Clarke was sent for, and all that love and affection could do to "retain the spirit," was done, but all in vain; a little before midnight he closed his eyes in death. And thus ended the mortal career of Adam Clarke, on the 26th of August, 1832, in the seventieth year of his age, and fiftieth of his ministry as a Wesleyan preacher. His remains were interred in the burying-ground of City Road Chapel, near those of the Rev. John Wesley.

Thus fell a man, who from the most obscure and humble station in life, pressed his way onward and upward to a position in society, where he could literally claim to be the companion of princes and nobles; of the wise, the great and the good among men. His best eulogy may be found in the words of his eldest son, the Rev. J. B. B. Clarke: "*My God, I bless thee, that I had such a father.*"

CHAPTER VII.

REV. RICHARD WATSON.

THE eminent man whose name stands at the head of this chapter, was born in Barton, Lincolnshire, England, on the 22d of February, 1781. He was the seventh son of a family of eighteen children, all of whom died in early life excepting Richard, and three sisters. While an infant his health was very feeble, but at a proper age he was sent to school, and his aptness to learn caused his instructress to exclaim frequently, "Bless thee! thou wilt be a great man!"

At the age of six years, he was sent to a school, kept by an Episcopal clergyman, where through the advice of his teacher, he commenced the study of Latin. This study he pursued with great success for one so young, as he did other branches of science and literature. As an evidence of his proficiency, it is said that before he was six years of age, he had read with intense interest, sixteen, or eighteen volumes of the "Universal History," which his father had purchased for him.

Richard was blessed with an extraordinary memory, so much so, that he could get any lesson in his Latin Grammar without any difficulty. Being confined at home with sickness, he would recite his Latin lessons to his eldest sister, so that she became nearly as well acquainted with the language as himself. And on one occasion while both were confined by sickness, they committed nearly the whole of "Fenelon's Telemachus" to memory.

RICHARD WATSON.

Richard's father was a saddler by profession, and at this period, was a Calvinistic dissenter. He was a pious, upright man, one who feared God, and whose practical motto was: "As for me, and my house, we will serve the Lord;" hence his family were brought up "in the nurture and admonition of the Lord," and as the result of such parental training, his children "remembered their Creator in the days of their youth." Little Richard, at a very early age, manifested signs of love to God, and was often found in prayer, and often delighted to sing hymns of praise to God.

When Richard was eight years of age, Mr. Watson, sen., and his family removed from Barton, to Lincoln. At this place, Richard attended a private seminary for about two years, when he was removed to the grammar-school at the same place. Here he read Cæsar, Virgil, Horace, and other classical works. He also eagerly perused large volumes of classical history, as also those containing the history of England. So passionately fond was he of the latter kind of reading, that he desired permission to sit up all night to peruse his favorite works, and when his request was denied, he sometimes resorted to stratagem to effect his purpose, which practice in more mature years, he did not feel disposed to justify.

Mr. Watson, sen., had not the means to give his son a University education, so as to fit him for one of the learned professions, consequently Richard, at the age of fourteen, was apprenticed to a respectable carpenter and joiner, for the purpose of learning that branch of business. It was agreed, however, that he should, in consequence of feeble health, continue to board and lodge in his father's house. His appearance at this time was quite singular: his height was six feet two inches; his hair was jet black, and long and lank, while his countenance was that of a mere boy. His morals at this time also, appear to have become more lax, so that he engaged in all kinds of mischief with the greatest delight. One of the worst species of mischief in which he seemed to take delight was misbehavior in the house of God, and in ridiculing, and insulting the people of God, especially those who were stigmatized with the name *Methodist.* So far did this love of frolic lead him, that in defiance of his parents' example and authority, he has frequently been known to pelt with stones, and other missiles, the people with whom his father worshipped, while on their way to the house of God. Connected with this course of conduct, there was of course a habitual disregard of the ordinances of religion, and the observance of the Sabbath ; with a love of evil company, and wicked associates. Such a course of conduct was painful in the extreme, to his pious father, who had by this time become a Methodist himself, and almost led him to doubt the truth of the declaration in reference to those who are trained up in the way they should go, that "when they are old they will not depart from it." But God, who "moves in a mysterious way, his wonders to perform," had thoughts of mercy toward Richard, wicked as he had become, and in a very unexpected manner, brought his "conscience to a stand."

There lived in Lincoln a gentleman whose wife was a zealous Calvinist, and whose house Richard frequently visited. As Mr. Watson's family had forsaken the Calvinists, the good woman of the house was extremely anxious to convince Richard of the wrong his parents had committed in joining the Methodists. This led to disputation, and as she advanced arguments which Richard could not on account of his ignorance in these matters readily answer, he resolved to attend the Methodist chapel a few times for the purpose of learning some arguments wherewith to confute and silence his opponent. He accordingly attended, and during the first sermon he was deeply convicted of sin, and learned that there were matters of even greater importance to be attended to, than those which had brought him to the house of God. His great concern now was, how he should escape "the wrath to come;" and in this state of mind he went to another place of worship, where his convictions of sin were deepened. So heavy was the load which now weighed him down to the earth, that he could not conceal his state of mind from his pious friends; indeed, he had no desire to conceal his feelings. Such was the intolerable anguish of his broken spirit, that he gladly availed himself of the prayers of those whom he had before persecuted and insulted. And such prayers were as gladly offered up in his behalf. Indeed, there is, perhaps, no description of persons for whom pious Christians can more devoutly and sincerely pray, than for those who "despitefully use and entreat" them. And such was now the case. Fervent prayer was offered with, and for him; and in answer thereto, peace and pardon, through Jesus' blood, was imparted to the broken-hearted penitent. To the end of his life, Mr. Watson ever retained a vivid recollection of his feelings and the occurrences of that momentous occasion. His transition from "darkness to light" was so clear and convincing to his own mind, that he never after could doubt the fact of his conversion to God.

The fruits of his conversion immediately followed. He forsook his ungodly associates; his passion for folly and mischief was entirely subdued; his love for the people of God was established; he became at once a faithful member of the Methodist society; he submitted to all the contumely and insult bestowed upon the people of his choice; and his attention to business became serious and constant. In every respect Richard had become a "new creature" in Christ Jesus, "old things having passed away" with him. His conversion, as might have been expected, excited the ire of his former associates, who became still more outrageous in their conduct towards the Methodists, and who made Richard the butt of their ridicule; but all these things he endured with patience and resignation. He now became a constant attendant of the class and prayer-meetings. So eager was he sometimes to reach the place of worship in proper season after his work was done, that on two several occasions he stumbled and fell, and broke his arm.

On the 10th of February, 1796, Richard for the first time publicly began to call sinners to repentance on the occasion of the death of his grandmother, whose sudden departure from time constrained Richard on the evening of the same day to arise in the congregation, and exhort his fellow-creatures to be "prepared to meet their God." At this time Richard was only fifteen years of age, and on the 23d of the same month, when he was fifteen years and two days old, he preached his first sermon in a private dwelling near Lincoln. Such was the precocity of his mind, that at this early age he was in more senses than one prepared to become a "teacher in Israel." From this period till called into the travelling ministry, he labored zealously and successfully as a local preacher. At that time on Lincoln circuit, there was but one chapel belonging to the Methodists, while there were quite a number of villages within its bounds. The travelling preachers with six other local preachers, contrived to supply the most of these villages with preaching; although for want of a house to preach in, the services were often held in the open air. These out-door services frequently exposed the preachers to the ill-treatment of the rude and profane; and Richard, notwithstanding his youth, came in for a full share of the abuse usually given on such occasions. On his return home, his clothes often gave evidence of the rough treatment he received at the hands of his persecutors. On one occasion, he was preaching in a village where his uncle, a respectable farmer, resided; and while there, was attacked with rotten eggs and other missiles. His uncle instead of protecting him, exclaimed, "Pelt him well, lads; my nephew can *stand fire.*"

The labors of young Watson could but excite great attention wherever his name was known, so that numerous invitations were sent to him from a distance to come and preach. On one occasion, he complied with a request to preach in the Methodist chapel in Newark, where he was personally unacquainted. As the youthful preacher ascended the pulpit, his appearance excited irrepressible apprehensions of a failure on the part of the congregation. These apprehensions were insreased when he announced as his text, "God is a Spirit," &c., but when he proceeded in his discourse, and unfolded to their minds with a correctness of language, and a fervor scarcely imaginable some of the more important doctrines of Christian theology, their fears subsided, and their apprehensions gave place to wonder and admiration.

As his time and attention were now greatly occupied with his favorite work of preaching, his master, who was desirous of promoting his usefulness, generously offered to release him from his indentures. Being but sixteen years of age he had still five years of apprenticeship to serve, and believing that God had called him to the work of the ministry, he thankfully received his release. At this juncture the health of one of the preachers on Newark circuit failed, and those who had been so agreeably disappointed at Richard's preaching as above stated, sent for him to supply the vacancy for the time being. He accepted the invitation and went to Newark, but here his feelings overcame him in view of the responsibilities of his calling and his own youth and want of experience, and he wept like a child. He was, however, greatly encouraged by Mr. Cooper, the preacher whose place he was expected to fill, and he commenced his labors as an itinerant with redoubled zeal and success.

On a distant part of Newark circuit where his fame had not preceded him, the family with whom he put up for entertainment could not repress their feelings of disappointment at the non-appearance of Mr. Cooper, who was indeed highly and deservedly popular, and at the youthfulness and inexperience of his substitute. Their unkind and imprudent expressions of regret were listened to in sorrowful silence by the young itinerant. He, however, raised his heart to God, and when service commenced he arose and gave out the beautiful hymn of Charles Wesley, beginning,

"How happy is the pilgrim's lot," &c.

He read it with such seriousness and emphasis, that he immediately won the hearts of his hearers; and as he proceeded with the rest of the service, they became so delighted with him that his host begged pardon for his unkind remarks, and earnestly desired him to visit them again, even if it must be in Mr. Cooper's place.

About this time, it became necessary for Richard to obtain a certificate of his profession as a preacher, under the "Toleration Act" of Parliament. The magistrates, however, objected to giving him a certificate, on account of his boyish appearance, but being reminded by one of their brethren on the bench, that the act specified no particular age, they were forced rather reluctantly to administer the oath, and give him a license.

Mr. Watson, as we shall now call him, though not yet sixteen years of age, remained on Newark circuit until the next session of the Wesleyan Conference, in 1796. At this Conference, Mr. Cooper strongly urged the reception of Mr. Watson as a preacher on trial, but his entreaties were urged in vain; the Conference thought Mr. Watson altogether too young for such an important work. Mr. Cooper, however, on going to his new circuit, called Ashby-de-la-Zouch, found that he could profitably employ Mr. Watson. He therefore ventured to send for him, notwithstanding the decision of the Conference. Mr. Watson at once complied with his request, and labored efficiently and profitably during the year, so that at the next Conference, not only was Mr. Cooper not censured for employing him, but the year thus spent was reckoned as one year of probation. Although his colleagues, Messrs. Cooper and Birdsall, were men of superior talents, yet Mr. Watson commanded as large congregations as they did, and labored with equal acceptability.

At the Conference of 1797, he was appointed to Castle Donington circuit. Here he came in contact with the doctrine of the restoration of all men to final holiness and happiness, as taught by Mr. Winchester. Against this doctrine, young as he was, he felt it his duty to raise a warning voice. During his stay on this circuit, he had occasion to preach in Leicester, having exchanged pulpits with a preacher for one Sabbath, and such was the gratification of the people of that place at his two sermons, preached from one text, that at the next Conference they sent a request to have him appointed to Leicester circuit the ensuing year. He was accordingly appointed to that place, under the superintendency of Rev. J. Edmondson, who being a man of extensive literary attainments, proved himself a valuable friend and instructor to his youthful colleague. In 1799, Mr. Watson was appointed to Derby, a station of some importance. On the first Sunday after his arrival, two persons were converted under his preaching. During his stay in Derby, Mr. Watson began his career as an author. An Episcopal clergyman of that city, had volunteered an unprovoked attack upon the Methodists, in the form of a pamphlet, which among other hard sayings contained in it, accused the Methodist preachers of preaching enthusiastic doctrines; of depriving men of innocent gratifications; and subjecting them to needless alarm, &c. &c. At the request of the friends in Derby, Mr. Watson published a reply, under the title of "An Apology for the People called Methodists," &c. In this reply, Mr. Watson states, "We *distress* the minds of those *well-meaning* people, who perhaps may be at the same time drunkards, swearers, liars, Sabbath breakers, &c. We distress those well-meaning people, by telling them that they are sinners, and must come to Jesus Christ for salvation, and that if they obstinately refuse, they must all perish. Is not all this Scriptural? And will they not have reason to bless God for this *distress*, if it leads them to believe on 'him who justifieth the ungodly?' And ought not you, sir, instead of reviling, to say with the apostle when some of his poor, ignorant, well-meaning followers were distressed, 'Now I rejoice, not that ye were made sorry, but that ye sorrowed to repentance?' "

In August, 1800, Mr. Watson having travelled four years on trial, and being in his twentieth year, was received into full connection, and appointed to Hinckley circuit. While on this circuit, he commenced the study of the Hebrew language, in accordance with the advice of Mr. Edmondson, and in a month from the time that he commenced, he was able to read and translate the first Psalm in Hebrew, and account grammatically for every word. He had previously to this time, mastered the Greek language.

Thus far we have followed Mr. Watson from his entering into the ministry, until the present period, and have discovered nothing but the most flattering prospects before him, as a minister and student; we have seen his success and acceptability as a Methodist preacher, but trials awaited him of a serious nature, which it is now our duty to record.

After being on Hinckley circuit for some time, and having in the meanwhile been engaged in reading certain authors on the Trinity of the Godhead, he was led casually to make an unguarded remark in relation to the subject of the Trinity, which being misunderstood, brought him under suspicion of being unsound on that point. Reports now began to circulate in reference to his heretical opinions, as they were called; and such was the influence of such false statements, made in his absence, that on going to an evening appointment, he found the place of worship closed against him, and he was even denied a night's lodging where he had often been received as the messenger of God. Until this time, he had not been aware of the reports in circulation, and on being informed of the state of the public feeling on this matter, he resented the treatment so highly, that he immediately withdrew from the work as an itinerant minister. This was a hasty and injudicious step no doubt, and a step which he afterward sincerely regretted having taken; but we cannot too highly condemn the proceedings of those, who without giving him an opportunity to explain his meaning, defamed his character, and stabbed him in the dark. At the succeeding Conference, the matter came up, and the return ordered to be made on the minutes was, "Richard Watson has desisted from travelling by his own choice."

After leaving the travelling connection, Mr. Watson did not for some time, unite with any other church. He entered into business with a respectable local preacher in Hinckley, but he soon changed his mind, and went to live at Castle Donington, where he soon after married Miss Henshaw, a young lady of deep piety, and suitable accomplishments. His father-in-law was a local preacher in the Methodist New Connection, through whose influence, undoubtedly, Mr. Watson was induced to unite with that branch of the Methodist Connection. He joined as a simple private member, and his class-leader was a farmer's laborer, of plain manners, and not very lofty capacity, and the other members were mostly of the same humble rank in life; yet Mr. Watson regularly met in class every week, and being an early attendant, he often had to act the part of sexton, in opening the house, &c. After a painful interval of two years as a private member, he was urged to become a local preacher among his new friends, and shortly after, he became a regular itinerant among them, and was stationed in Manchester. Here he lived on terms of intimacy with many of his old Wesleyan friends, and was deservedly popular among his own people. After a stay of two years and a half in Manchester, he was sent to Liverpool in 1806, and while in this place, many of the Wesleyan preachers and members sat with delight under his ministry. In 1807, he was re-appointed to Liverpool, having in the meantime been received into full connection in the Methodist New Connection Conference. He was also elected secretary of the Conference.

While in Liverpool during his second year, he published a history and description of Liverpool, which was well received. He also wrote a Life of George III., as a continuation of Goldsmith's History of England. He also assisted editorially, in the management of a weekly paper published in Liverpool, all of which duties he attended to with great credit to himself. In 1808, he was appointed for the third year to Liverpool, having served his Conference the second time as Secretary. In 1809, on account of partial ill health, he was made supernumerary, and re-appointed to Liverpool. His being allowed to desist for a time from preaching, enabled his lungs which had become much diseased, to regain their strength in part, and although at first the blood "oozed from his lungs," he in the course of a few months was able to resume his ministerial duties.

At the next Conference of 1810, Mr. Watson was appointed to Manchester, after an absence of four years. While here he first became acquainted with Rev. Jabez Bunting of the Wesleyan Connection. In the early part of 1811, a bill was introduced into the House of Lords, by Lord Sidmouth, so as to prevent improper persons from taking the necessary oaths to obtain the civil license, to preach according to the "Act of Toleration." The wording or verbiage of the bill was such, as in the opinion of many, would make the proposed amendment exceedingly oppressive to all classes of dissenters, especially to the Methodists. Mr. Bunting accordingly, requested Mr. Watson to publish in the Manchester papers, an appeal to the dissenters to oppose the passage of the bill. Mr. Watson did so; the appeal was copied into other papers, and on the day set apart for the second reading of the bill, parliament received six hundred petitions against its passage, so that the bill was rejected. Two hundred and fifty of those petitions, were from Methodist Societies, bearing the names of thirty thousand persons, which names were all obtained in the space of five days. They were presented to the house by Lord Erskine, who took occasion to eulogize the Methodists for their loyalty, and especially the founder of Methodism, whose labors he declared had not been equalled since the days of the apostles, for usefulness to his fellow-men.

At the Conference of the New Connection in 1811, Mr. Watson was re-appointed to Manchester, but before the close of the year his health failed, and he removed to Liverpool. Mr. Watson ever since his connection with the body to which he had belonged for several years, had felt unhappy in his new relations. In fact he did not feel at home among that people. His views and theirs, differed much in relation to Church government, and he felt that he did not have that degree of confidence in the system of Church polity adopted by the New Connection Methodists, necessary to render his labors abundantly useful among them. After advising with some of the most intelligent and confidential of his friends among them, he resolved quietly to withdraw his connection from them, which he did, a few months after his removal to Liverpool as above described. No feelings of bitterness or hostility were manifested on either side, by his withdrawal, and Mr. Watson ever after retained a strong affection for the people from whom he had received nothing but kindness.

Being laid aside for want of health, he could have entertained small hopes of ever joining the travelling connection again; he, however, felt that it would be a privilege to belong to the Wesleyans as a private member, in order that he might continue to enjoy the providential means of grace to which he had so long been accustomed. He accordingly offered himself, and was received as a private member of the Wesleyan Society in Liverpool, and after having done so, he feelingly remarked, that his mind was now fully at rest for the first time in eleven years.

Having thus retired into the more private walks of life, he began the other duties of an editor in Liverpool, and with so much success that persons in authority in London, offered him every inducement to remove to London, and employ his pen in the service of the government. His health in the meantime began to improve; his bleeding of the lungs subsided, and he found himself able to preach occasionally as a local preacher in the Wesleyan pulpits of Liverpool, and other places. The Wesleyan preachers, and especially Mr. Bunting, unwilling that Mr. Watson should confine himself to a local sphere, besought him to allow them to offer his name at the next Conference as a candidate for membership. After due deliberation and prayer, he yielded to their entreaties, and at the next Conference was received with great cordiality by his former friends, and reinstated without any probation in the Wesleyan Ministry. Mr. Watson from this time forward, enjoyed uninterrupted friendship and union with his Wesleyan brethren.

By the Conference, Mr. Watson was stationed in Wakefield, to which he immediately repaired, and shortly after his arrival was invited to preach the opening or dedication sermon of a new chapel in Halifax. His sermon on this occasion, was considered by good judges to be one of the best specimens of pulpit eloquence that they had ever heard. After the lapse of a year from the time of his readmission, Mr. Watson was re-appointed to Wakeley circuit, and it was during his second year at this place that the Wesleyan Missionary Society was formed, toward the formation of which Mr. Watson exerted himself with all the ability which he possessed. Indeed Mr. Watson had the honor of having delivered the first sermon in behalf of Methodist missions, with the distinct object of producing a systematic course of action in relation to their support. On the afternoon of the day on which this sermon was preached, the first Missionary meeting was held in the Chapel in Leeds. On this occasion the meeting was addressed by Mr. Warrener, who was one of the first missionaries to the West India Islands, under the superintendence of Dr. Coke. Mr. W. related several interesting anecdotes in relation to the power of the Gospel in converting the negro. One of these anecdotes, we will give to the reader. "On the estate of a Mr. G. some pious negroes resided, who repaired to the means of grace, whenever they could go without detection. Mr. G. being about to sail for England, his manager was heard to say before his departure, 'Mr. G. is going to England; I will then soon put an end to all this praying among the negroes.' One day soon afterward, Mr. G. was walking between two cane pieces, when he saw some ripe peas wasting; on which he said to his watchman who was near, 'Why do you not gather those peas?' 'O, massa,' said he, 'they no my peas.' 'Not your peas, you rogue,' said Mr. G., 'do not you all take peas or anything else which you can get?' 'O, massa,' rejoined the watchman, 'we *negers* who go to prayer never *teeve.*' Mr. G. said, 'What do you say? that you negroes who go to prayer never thieve?' His reply was, 'O no, massa.' Mr. G. as he walked to his house said to himself, 'What have we been doing not to encourage the negroes to attend preaching.' He then called his boy and said, 'Go tell Mr. —— the manager,—to address a note in my name to the missionary, and to inform him that he is welcome to preach on my estate at any time.' Thus was a wicked design frustrated, and the good hand of God being with us, we erected a chapel on that very estate, worth £400 currency."

After two pleasant and profitable years spent in Wakefield, he was stationed in Hull, where as he informs us he spent "two of the happiest years of his life." There were three chapels in this place, and one in process of erection. The dedication services of the latter, took place in Oct. 1814, at which time sermons were preached by Rev. Messrs. Bunting, Watson, Newton, and Birdsall. Owing principally to the stated ministrations of Mr. Watson, a large and respectable congregation was at once secured; and as it is the universal practice among the Wesleyan Methodists to rent the pews or slips in their chapels, reserving simply a sufficient number of free seats for strangers and poor persons, every sitting was let, while eight hundred were reserved for the latter purpose. But better than all, his labors were attended by a gracious outpouring of the Spirit of God upon the people.

At the Conference of 1816, Mr. Watson was appointed to the East London circuit. He was also appointed one of the missionary secretaries, an office for which he was eminently qualified, and which he retained during life. In 1817, he was re-appointed to the same circuit, and shortly after Conference, he assisted in the opening of Queen-street Wesleyan Chapel, being the largest chapel in London, save the City Road, and also the most elegant and costly. During the next year, 1818, Mr. Watson published a defence of the doctrine of the eternal sonship of Christ, in opposition to the objections of Dr. Adam Clarke in relation to the commonly received opinion on that subject. This was a masterly production, which called forth the highest commendations, and proved that Dr. Clarke had in Mr. Watson an opponent of no ordinary strength of mind. During this year also, he prepared the plan of a General Wesleyan Missionary Society, in accordance with the vote of the previous Conference. This plan proposed the enlistment of lay-members of the Church, as the managing committee of missions, reserving to the ministry only the examination and appointment of missionaries, and all cases of discipline, according to the usages of the body. This plan was approved and adopted by the ensuing Conference of 1818.

At the Conference held the latter year, Mr. Watson was appointed to the West London circuit, and while here, he in company with Mr. Bunting, visited the counties of Cornwall and Norfolk, for the purpose of advocating the missionary cause from the pulpit and platform. In 1819, Mr. Watson was re-appointed to West London circuit, and at the Conference of 1820, he drew up that admirable document in reply to the Address of the General Conference of the Methodist Episcopal Church in America, which has been esteemed among the latter as a paper of great interest. In 1820, he was returned for the third year, to the West London circuit, and was also continued with his two associates in the office of missionary secretary, and on him devolved the task of corresponding with all the missionaries, then numbering about one hundred and fifty.

As the session of the Conference of 1821 was approaching, Mr. Watson was uncertain where his lot in future would be cast. He had spent six years in London, as an itinerant preacher, three years on each of the circuits, and the rules of the Society did not allow of a re-appointment to either of them, until after an absence of seven years. So anxious was the Conference, however, to retain his services as missionary secretary, that they appointed him one of the resident secretaries, so that his services might be wholly given to the cause of missions, which office he continued to fill with great acceptability for the ensuing six years. Being now freed from the cares and labors of a pastorate, he was able more fully to give his mind not only to the cause of missions, but to literary pursuits, his evenings being mostly spent in his study; but he felt the loss of those frequent social meetings which he had so long enjoyed with his brethren. To make up in part for the loss thus sustained, he entered his name as a private member of a class, under the care of a pious and much-esteemed leader. The class consisted mostly of poor laboring people, and with them Mr. Watson would meet once a week, and enjoy with them the communion of saints. Mr. Watson did not confine his labors in behalf of missions to the discharge of the duties of the office in London, but frequently made journeys of greater or less extent for the purpose of pleading in their behalf, and during such seasons he usually pleaded with so much earnestness of feeling, as to draw not only tears from the eye, but generous contributions from the pocket.

In the winter of 1823, Mr. Watson was under the necessity of repairing to Brighton, for the benefit of his enfeebled health; from this place he frequently addressed letters to his friends, and members of his family. As an example of his lively style of corresponding with the latter, we will give an extract from one of his letters to his son Thomas.

"BRIGHTON, Feb. 18th, 1823.

"Dear Tom,—After having been cheated in the Angel Coach, in the fare, and squeezed up in a six-inside old Islington stage, we arrived safely here. Through the mercy of God, I feel my health improved; though the weather is cold, I got out to chapel twice yesterday, and was thankful that again I was brought by Providence into the house of God, to worship at his footstool.

"Thursday was a calm day; but Friday and Saturday brought us gales and wind, and your mother was all wonder at the waves. The roar of the sea was in our ears night and day, and filled the mind with sublime thoughts of the power of the elements, and the might of their great Ruler.

"We live in a curious sort of style, having every little thing to provide. Sometimes we are without butter when the meal comes, and we have to send out; and then we wonder whether our remaining piece of bread will serve us for breakfast, or tea; so that we need a good deal of contrivance, and our forgetfulness is often amusing.

"I hope you are diligent while at study, and that you will leave yourself by application, the leisure for exercise. You are now approaching man's estate, and must 'put away childish things.' Be thoughtful for your future prospects in life; and above all, give your heart to God. Seek him *first*, and you will not be without his providence to direct you in life; and without that, you will be wretched. Make a point of reading a portion of Scripture every day, with prayer that you may obtain pardon and experience that *conversion*, without which, you can never enter the Kingdom of God. Write this upon your heart."

After Mr. Watson's return to London, he found his health materially improved, so as to continue writing a work on systematic divinity, for the special benefit of theological students and junior preachers, commenced some time previous. The first part of the work, called "Theological Institutes," accordingly appeared in the spring of 1823, and was so well received, that a second edition was soon called for. In about a year after, the second part was published, and was received with like favor. In the autumn of 1825, he published the third part, and in a year or more, the fourth part was published. It is perhaps not too much to say, in the praise of this work, now that the lamented author "sleepeth," that there is no work in the English language, the Bible alone excepted, that contains as much sound reasoning and legitimate argument, as this one work of Richard Watson. It is, indeed, a complete body of divinity in itself, and the student who will peruse it carefully, so as to make himself acquainted with its contents, will arise from its perusal a much wiser, if not a better man, and will, we venture to say, know more of theology than was ever taught in Oxford or Cambridge. This one work has made the author's name immortal. As an instance of the author's liberality, it is proper to state, that after undergoing the risk and expense of publication, and when it was found that the merits of the work were duly appreciated, that then, and not till then, did he in the most delicate manner, present the copyright to the Conference.

In the early part of Mr. Watson's ministry, he had been very much opposed to instrumental music in churches, so that on one occasion he wrote a humorous pamphlet against the practice. In the latter part of his ministry, however, his views underwent a change in reference to this matter. Toward the close of the year 1823, a portion of the Society in Wakefield designed erecting an organ in their chapel. Another portion of the Society were opposed to this innovation, and wrote to Mr. Watson, desiring his views in relation to the matter. These he gave in the following language:

"Dear Sir,—I am unable to say anything but what is exceedingly obvious in the case of the introduction of organs into our chapels: and I think the only question to be considered is, whether they serve, or obstruct congregational singing. On this, opinions differ; some affirming, and others denying as positively, that the congregation trusts to the organ and listens, rather than joins in the service. As far as my observation goes, this does not necessarily follow. In churches where the congregation are irreligious it is so; but it would be the same if there were only a clerk, or an orchestra of singers and fiddlers. In many churches I know, where the minister is evangelical, and the congregation is devotional, the organ is scarcely heard but at the commencement of the tune, its sounds being mingled with the full swell of the voices of the worshippers.

"Among ourselves at Brunswick Chapel, Liverpool, the congregation joins with as much order, as if there were no organ. This also is the case at Bath, in both the chapels; at Margate, and at Newark. These facts have fixed my opinion in favor of organs in large chapels, and where they are prudently and constitutionally introduced. The only exception I know is one in which the tone of the organ is so intolerably harsh, that no sound in heaven or in earth, can commingle with it. I believe, however, that even there, the people sing; but after all, the tones of the organ like the voice of a fish-woman in a market, keep a lofty distinction above all the others. This exception only proves that it is of importance to have an instrument of full and mellifluous tone.

"On the other hand, we shall regret the day, when the liberty to introduce organs into our chapels under certain circumstances was granted, if we are to have organists also, who seek to display their talents, and to tell a gaping crowd below, with what elasticity their fingers can vibrate, and how many graces and trills they can add to the composition before them;—men, who could not think the sun shone bright, unless they looked at his beams through a painted transparency of their own, and who would fancy they heightened the sublimity of a peal of thunder, by the ringing of hand-bells during the storm. The attempts of such organists, to embellish and garnish the noble compositions of our great masters in psalmody, is disgusting beyond endurance. Voluntaries are equally objectionable for a different reason. If good, they are out of place; if bad they do not deserve a place anywhere."

We have not room for the whole of his letter, but sufficient has been given to show what Mr. Watson's views in after life were, in regard to organs and congregational singing; but to pursue our narrative.

Mr. Watson during the year 1824, continued to labor in behalf of missions, and his heart was cheered by the princely donation made to the cause of Wesleyan Missions during this year, by his friend, and the friend of Wesley, and Coke, the Rev. W. Dodwell, Vicar of Welby, an exemplary and pious clergyman of the Church of England. This excellent man instead of prating about "apostolic succession," and "infatuated Methodists," bestowed the sum of *forty-seven thousand, five hundred dollars* upon the Wesleyan missionary treasury!

In 1826, Mr. Watson was elected President of the Conference, and discharged the duties of that high office, in such a manner, as to secure more and more the esteem and affection of the members. During the year also, notwithstanding his bodily infirmities, he attended faithfully to the general interests of the connection. In the spring of 1827, accompanied by Mr. Bunting he visited Scotland for the purpose of meeting the preachers stationed in that country. Having finished the business, which called him to Edinburgh, he returned to England, and thence proceeded to Ireland, to preside over the Irish Conference, which during that year was held in Belfast. At the Conference of 1828, having in due form resigned the presidency of the Connection, he was appointed to Manchester circuit. He had been a resident of London during eleven years, and as the change of residence would necessarily interfere with the duties of resident missionary secretary, he was under the necessity of resigning that post. Such was the wish, however, to retain him as much as possible in connection with the missionary enterprise, that he was elected honorary secretary, and at the ensuing Conference of 1829, after a long debate about where his services were most needed, it was resolved that he be returned to London, as the superintendent of London North (or city Road) circuit. In 1830, he published his book called "Conversations for the Young," a small, but extremely valuable work, and at the Conference of 1830, he was requested to write a life of Mr. John Wesley, with which request he complied as soon as his numerous engagements would allow; and while engaged in this work, he was invited to fill the chair of professor of Belles-Lettres and Moral Philosophy, in the Wesleyan University in Middletown, Connecticut, which invitation he respectfully declined accepting. When his Life of Wesley was completed, he generously presented the copy-right to the Conference. The Conference of 1831, also requested him to compile a Biblical and Theological Dictionary, the Book Committee urging him to receive a pecuniary consideration for his labor, but although he had been for some length of time collecting materials for such a work, with the intention of appropriating the profits of its sale to the benefit of his family in case of his decease; yet on the request being made without knowing his previous intention, he refused to appropriate any portion of the profits to himself or family, and again presented, when the work was completed, the copy-right to the Conference. The work was completed in 1832.

The Conference of 1832 was held in Liverpool, and during the time of its sittings, the cholera prevailed to an alarming extent, yet the preachers and the families by whom they were entertained were all mercifully preserved in answer to prayer. Before the meeting of this Conference, Mr. Watson executed a deed, whereby he conveyed to trustees for the benefit of the Conference, the copy-right of all his works, except the "Conversations for the Young." This he did in view of the uncertainty of life, and his wish that the copy-rights might be fully, and forever secured to the Connection. At this Conference, on account of increasing ill-health, he was elected resident Missionary secretary again; and during a portion of this year his leisure time was mostly occupied in writing "An Exposition of the Gospels."

The Conference year of 1832–3, will long be remembered in the annals of Methodism, as one of great mortality among the talented and aged members of the Church. Dr. Clarke had been suddenly called to his rest. Rev. Thomas Stanley had followed even more suddenly; and before the year terminated, Rev. John James, one of Mr. Watson's colleagues in the Missionary department, was summoned suddenly into eternity. And now Mr. Watson himself began to wear away by slow degrees, until at length on the 8th day of January, 1833, his happy spirit took its flight to the paradise of God, to mingle with the spirits of Wesley, Fletcher, Coke, Clarke, and others who had preceded him. He died in the fifty-second year of his age, in the most peaceful, and even triumphant manner. His remains were interred in City Road Cemetery, near the tombs of Wesley, Clarke, Benson, &c.

Thus died one of the brightest ornaments of the Methodist Connection in England: but for him "to live" was "Christ; to die," was "gain."

CHAPTER VIII.

REV. GIDEON OUSELEY.

THIS extraordinary Irish minister and missionary, was born in the town of Dunmore, County of Galway, Ireland, in the year 1762, and was descended from an ancient Irish family of great respectability.

While a boy, being the eldest son, he was not designed by his father for any profession, but being the heir-apparent to his father's estate, he received such an education as was common for gentlemen of respectability to give their eldest sons; that is, he received a thorough mathematical and classical education. His younger brother was educated for the army, and was afterward distinguished as Major General, Sir Ralph Ouseley.

At an early age, Gideon was the subject of deep religious feelings, and when he attained to man's estate, his serious impressions, instead of wearing off, gradually increased, until at length his seriousness deepened into pungent conviction for sin, and he would often cry out, "Lord, help me! What shall I do? Who will teach me? Priest and minister no better than myself—as great fools as I am. We are all a pack of fools together!" While in this state of mind, bordering on skepticism on the one hand, and despair on the other, his native village was visited in 1789, by certain Methodist preachers. From these men of God he received much light in regard to spiritual things, but it was not until 1791, that his convictions assumed a decidedly evangelical character. During the latter year, he attended Methodist preaching one evening, and after sermon, the preacher invited the Society to remain, and also other seriously disposed persons. Mr. Ouseley having been a sincere inquirer after the right way, felt inclined to stay, but feared there might be some secret proceedings, with which he could not concur, if he did remain. "I'll wait," said he to himself, "until I see what they are about; but if I find any juggling—any free-mason's tricks, among them, I'll have nothing to do with them." He did stay, and the fact of his having attended again, and again after that, proves that his fears in the first instance were uncalled for. This means of grace—class-meeting—for such it was, was rendered a peculiar blessing to Mr. Ouseley, as it led him to examine more closely his own heart, and to learn where absolution of sin must be obtained, if obtained at all; and so great was his anxiety of mind increased, that he has frequently been afterward heard to say in reference to that period, "I got such a sight of hell, and of going into it, never, never to be released through all eternity, that I cried from my heart, 'O, Lord, I will submit!'" And when he did thus fully submit, "pardon, and peace, and heaven," were infused into his mind. The fruits of justification were immediately manifested by him, by going from house to house, and from neighbor to neighbor, inviting them to come to Christ.

Rev. Mr. Woodrow was at that time on the circuit where Mr. Ouseley lived, and to that holy and gifted man was he greatly indebted, as an instrument of his conversion to God. At one of the places on the circuit, the Episcopal church was undergoing repairs, and the Church service was held in the Methodist chapel. The late Archdeacon of Tuam, the Hon. and Rev. Dr. Trench, was at that time rector of the parish. Mr. Woodrow would frequently hear the rector at noon, and the rector in turn would hear Mr. Woodrow in the evening.

After hearing the latter preach one evening, on the doctrine of the new birth, he remarked, "If all the Methodist preachers can preach like that good man, it is not surprising that the whole world follow them." This same Dr. Trench, when Archbishop of Tuam, invited the Wesleyan missionaries into his province, and recommended them to some of the leading families in the country, so that Methodism in this part of the country was patronized, and its ministers honored by many of the influential in Church and State.

But to return to our subject. Mr. Ouseley could not long satisfy his conscience with merely warning his neighbors to flee from the wrath to come. He believed that a dispensation of the Gospel was committed to him; yet he felt his own weakness and unworthiness so much, that he scarcely dared to venture on errands of mercy to others. He would exclaim, "Lord, I am a poor ignorant creature; how can I go?" Then it would rush into his mind, "Do you know the disease?" "*O yes, Lord, I do!*" "And do you not know the cure?" "*O yes, glory be to thy name, I do.*" "Then go and tell them of the disease and the cure." So that with only these two things, as he sometimes said, the knowledge of the disease and the knowledge of the cure, he went forth to preach the Gospel. Mr. Ouseley's first sermon was preached in a church-yard, at a funeral, which was attended of course by another officiating clergyman, and from this time forth, he preached in the streets and church-yard, at fairs and markets, at wakes and funerals, wherever in fact he could find a congregation assembled, whether Protestant or Catholic.

One day, Mr. Ouseley, while on a missionary tour, rode up to a Catholic chapel, where a priest was celebrating mass; the large congregation were on their knees; Mr. Ouseley knelt with them, and rendered every Latin word which the priest spoke, into Irish; and when he wished any particular part of the service which was Scriptural impressed on the minds of the people, he would emphatically exclaim, "Listen to that." The people became deeply affected, and the priest not knowing who he was, was thunderstruck. When the service was ended, Mr. Ouseley and the congregation rose on their feet, and before they retired from the house, he delivered a warm-hearted exhortation to them, to repent and forsake their sins, and believe in Christ. When he had finished his exhortation, the people cried out to the priest, "Father, who is that?" "I don't know," he replied; "he is not a man at all, he is an *angel;* no *man* could do what he has done." Mr. Ouseley mounted his horse, amid the prayers and blessings of the people, and rode off to seek another opportunity of doing good.

In this way he would go from town to town, and from county to county, preaching and exhorting wherever an opportunity offered; and this practice he followed for seven years, prior to his connection with the Irish Methodist Conference. But it was not only by public preaching and exhortation, that he sought to do good. On one occasion, he met a man who had, by orders of the priest, taken a pilgrimage of forty Irish miles, as a penance; "Where have you been?" said Mr. Ouseley: "*At the reek,*" was the reply. "What were you doing there, poor man?" "*Looking for God.*" "Where is God?" "*Everywhere.*" "Where would you go to look for the day-light when the sun rose this morning? Would you go forty miles to look for the day-light, when it was shining into your own cabin door?" "*O the Lord help us, I would not, sir.*" "Then would you go on your feet forty miles to look for God, when you could get him at your own door?" "*O, then may the Lord pity us, gentleman! It's true for you! It's true for you!*"

Some time after this, while riding along the road, he overtook a countryman, whom he addressed as follows: "My dear man, would you not like to be reconciled to God, have his peace in your heart, and stand clear before the great Judge, when he will come in the clouds of heaven to judge the world?" The man replied: "*O glory be to his holy and blessed name! Sir, I have his peace in my heart, and the Lord be praised that I ever saw your face!*" "You have! What do you know about this peace? When did you see me?" "*Don't you remember the day when you were at the burying, when the priest was saying mass?*" "I do very well, what about that day?" "*O, gentleman, you told us then how to get that peace; and I went, blessed be his holy name, to Jesus Christ my Saviour, and got it in my heart; and have it ever since.*" Thus Mr. Ouseley began to see the fruit of his labor among the ignorant and debased Catholic population of his own country, for whom his soul, like that of Jeremiah, was "in affliction," and who like the same prophet, would frequently exclaim, "O, that my head were waters, and mine eyes a fountain of tears, that I might weep day and night for the slain of the daughter of my people."

Previously to Mr. Ouseley's conversion, the Lord had raised up in different parts of Ireland, a number of eminent Methodist missionaries. Among these, may be named Rev. Thomas Walsh, a young man who was so thoroughly acquainted with the original Scriptures, that if he was questioned concerning any Hebrew word in the Old, or Greek word in the New Testament, he would tell how often the word occurred in the Bible, where it might be found, and what it meant. Mr. Wesley pronounced him the greatest master of biblical knowledge that he ever saw, or ever expected to see again. Mr. Walsh was himself the fruit of street preaching, and he, during his short, but useful life, spent much time in preaching to the Irish peasantry in their native tongue, and thousands of these, through his instrumentality, were converted to God.

Another of those eminent missionaries, was the Rev. Charles Graham, a native of the county of Sligo. Mr. Graham had beeen educated in the Church of England, but feeling a consciousness of inward depravity, he attempted to find through the instrumentality of the "Church," that peace which his soul panted after. Being disappointed here, he went to a Catholic mass meeting, where there happened to be a funeral service at the time. He learned that the person who was about to be buried had been a poor man, had lost all his cattle by disease, and that through the persuasion of his neighbors, the priest had taken up a collection of five pounds, to assist him in his distress; but asking the priest for the collection next day, the latter said to him, "I made no collection for you; but for myself." The poor man, enraged at such monstrous injustice, swore solemnly that he never would bow his knee before the priest again. This poor man soon after died, and when dying, the hard-hearted priest refused to administer to him the last rites of his religion. He was, however, prevailed upon to attend to the funeral, at which time Mr. Graham was present. The address of the priest on this occasion, was, "This man's soul is in hell, for he did not pay the rent of his soul for the last three years; and you will all be damned likewise, if you do not pay the rent of your souls regularly." These facts, and this address, convinced Mr. Graham that he must seek for light somewhere else, than in the Roman Church. Shortly after, he providentially became acquainted with the preaching and doctrine of the Methodists, and through their instructions, he was soon led to the fountain of salvation.

Mr. Graham's first sermon was preached in the streets of the village of Milltown, where he was an entire stranger. Not knowing where to find a lodging for the night, he inquired of a lad if he knew any one in that town who had the Bible, and read it. "O yes," said the lad, "the clerk of the

Church." Mr. Graham rode up to the door, and told him he had come to find lodging with one who read the Bible. The man was confounded. "I read the Bible, sir! no indeed, I never read it, except what I read at Church, on Sunday." He, however, invited Mr. Graham to stay with him, and through the advice of the good missionary, he resolved henceforth to read the Bible, and subsequently became a valuable member of the Methodist Society which was formed in that place. Through the instrumentality of Mr. Graham, many persons of note and respectability were converted to the pure doctrines of the Gospel, from popery and error.

Another missionary of great usefulness, but of entirely different mould from Walsh, Graham, or Ouseley, was Bartholomew Campbell, a simple and uncultivated child of nature, who added to his natural simplicity a degree of strangeness and uncouthness, at once amusing and ludicrous. Campbell had been a Roman Catholic, but becoming burdened on account of sin, and not knowing what to do, he went to the priest, who enjoined penance and pronounced absolution, but still he found no peace to his mind. His mental distress increasing, he went to other priests, but still "hell lay open before him." At length he went a pilgrimage of forty miles, to St. Patrick's Purgatory, at Lough Derg, where he supposed all sin might be remitted, and having gone through with all the prescribed penances, paid all the necessary fees, received absolution from the resident priest, he fondly hoped that peace of mind would be secured; but alas, all these things were found to be unavailing. He returned to the priest with disappointment, and told him of the continued anguish of his spirit. "Did not I give you absolution?" said the priest "*You did, father.*" "And do you deny the authority of the Church?" "*By no means, but my soul is in misery; what shall I do?*" "Do! why go to bed and sleep." "*Sleep! no, father, perhaps I might awake in hell!*" The priest, exasperated at his stubbornness, as he supposed, threatened to horsewhip him; and poor Campbell went to a retired spot, and despairing to find mercy anywhere else, he with groans and tears, called aloud for Christ to have mercy on him, and *He* who said, "Come unto me, all ye that labor and are heavy laden," gave the poor pilgrim "rest," and his soul was filled with joy unspeakable. He at once returned to the priest, and told what great things the Lord had done for his soul. "O, father," said he, "I am happy, I have found the cure." The ghostly "father," thinking him mad, again threatened him with the horsewhip. Campbell ran to a number of his fellow-pilgrims, exhorting them to turn from these vanities, and come directly to Christ, who would give them the *cure* and the *jewel*. After his return home, he became extremely anxious for the salvation of his wife, and believing that there was truly some virtue in a pilgrimage to Lough Derg, he insisted on her going there. His horse was attached to the cart, and a bed placed upon the latter; and on the bed, Campbell, his wife, and two children took their seats, and started for the Lough. But Mrs. Campbell did not there find the *cure* and the *jewel*, found by her husband, for the reason that she had not as yet felt her need of them. Shortly after, Campbell related to a priest in the neighborhood, what he had experienced at the Lough. The priest was affected even to tears, but charged Campbell not to say a word to the people on the subject. "Father," said he in reply, "they will all go to hell; and you will go thither with them, if you hide the *cure* from them." The priest, however, reiterated his admonitions. Soon after, the priest was celebrating mass in an old burial ground, and when he had concluded, Campbell stepped up to him and said, "Father, you are to christen a *bairn* in the village, go, and leave the people to me. The dead souls, you see, are standing over the dead bodies; and I hope the Lord will awaken the uppermost." "Take care," said the priest, "what you do; make no disturbance, I charge you." After the priest left, Campbell began to exhort the people, and with so much effect, that the ignorant multitude wept and fell on their knees, crying for mercy so loudly, that the noise was heard in the village. The priest hearing it, came running back. "You rascal," said the latter, to Campbell, "do you oppose the Church?" "No, father, I have found the Church." "You villain, begone," said the now infuriated shepherd, at the same time striking Campbell over the head with a horse-whip. Poor Campbell had yet a portion of the "old Adam" in him, and scarcely knowing what he did, gave the priest a push, who falling over a grave, brought his feet higher than his head. So sudden was the transition from loud lamentation on account of sin, to anger and resentment at seeing *God's holy praste* sticking his heels up in the air, that a general Irish *melee* was the result, and Campbell was obliged to fly for his life. This unfortunate affair brought poor Campbell into great darkness, in which he remained until he met with some Methodists, who understood his case, and led him back to the fountain for the removal of guilt. He soon after regained his peace of mind, and became a useful member and missionary among the Methodists in Ireland.

Mr. Campbell subsequently became a great admirer of Dr. Coke, and whenever it was announced that the latter was about to pay a visit to the country, Campbell would mount his old white horse and ride off to meet the doctor, and accompany him to the various places of worship whither he was going. His appearance on such occasions, was sufficiently ludicrous to create a smile in the countenance of the most taciturn and serious observers, especially when viewed in contrast with the more grave and respectable appearance of the doctor, who, knowing the man, was not disposed to find fault with his uncouth, yet well-meant attentions.

We have thus far allowed ourselves to digress from the chief subject of the chapter, for the purpose of showing the instruments which God was employing to bring many of the Irish to a knowledge of the truth.

About the time in which Mr. Ouseley joined the Methodist Conference, a deep and extensive rebellion took place in Ireland, known as the "Irish Rebellion." It has been supposed by many, that the only object which the rebels had in view, was the deliverance of Ireland from the unjust rule of the British government. The history of the proceedings of the rebels will, no doubt, convince the impartial reader that this was by no means the only object, if indeed it was the chief object. The only rational ground of belief is, that the rebellion was designed to exterminate the hated name of *Protestant* from the island; and the subsequent cruelties practised upon the unoffending Protestants, by the bigoted and blood-thirsty papists, all prove that their object was *popery* more than *liberty*—an alliance with the pope more than liberation from England. The history of that period is one of bloodshed, and the most diabolical cruelties inflicted upon unoffending men, women, and even children, that the historian of any nation has ever been called upon to record. It is true, there were a few Protestants at first leagued with the papists in their efforts to throw off their allegiance to the crown of Great Britain, but these were the dupes of the paid agents of popery, and as soon as they discovered the *real* intentions of the papists, and especially when they saw their fellow-protestants by thousands, murdered in cold blood before their eyes, they could no longer remain the dupes of designing men, but at once forsook the ranks of the rebels, and extinguished the flame of rebellion in the northern portion of the island.

In the year 1799, Mr. Ouseley's name first appeared on the minutes of the Conference. This, it will be perceived, was at a time when that ill-fated country had just passed through the scorching ordeal alluded to in the preceding paragraph—a time when the religious and political elements were still in commotion. The field of labor assigned to Mr. Ouseley and his associate missionaries, Rev. Messrs. M'Quigg and Graham, was not limited by any territorial bounds except the rolling sea around the island. They were emphatically missionaries at large, but *Irish* missionaries, appointed under the auspices of the adventurous Coke, to labor for the good, not of a single parish or circuit, but for the good of Ireland.

The success of these missionaries during the first year of their labors under the authority of the Conference was such, that the next Conference added to the number, by the appointment of Mr. Bell. Messrs. M'Quigg and Bell travelled through the provinces of Connaught and Leinster, while the other two travelled and preached more at large. Their favorite places for preaching, were the streets and markets; and the mighty power of God accompanied their word with such unction, that young and old frequently fell prostrate in the most public places of resort. Among the subjects of revival under their instrumentality, were two young men who had met to fight a duel, but were prevented by means of a wall falling on one of the spectators, which crushed him to death. A short time after, both these young men were converted, and walked for years together in the ways of religion and virtue. Nor was the success of the missionaries confined to the conversion of nominal Protestants, but hundreds, yea, thousands of the Catholic population were converted, not only to protestantism, but to Christianity—being born from above. But we are not to suppose that Satan could see his kingdom thus falling, without making a strong effort through his agents to stop the progress of the work by persecution and other means of like character. Mobs were resorted to, by persons of the baser sort, as a laudable way of stopping the mouths of God's messengers. Stones, dirt, &c., were at times freely discharged at them, but "none of those things moved them;" they still went on their way rejoicing.

At the Conference of 1802, Mr. Ouseley was again appointed, in connection with Mr. Graham, to the Irish mission. Their field of labor was the provinces of Leinster, Munster, and Ulster, embracing the districts where the rebellion had raged most fiercely a year or two previously. Even here, their word was attended with power, and many of the rebels were the subjects of converting grace. Many are the pleasing incidents related in connection with their labors in this part of the work, but our limits will not allow us to transcribe them. At the Conferences of 1803 and 1804, they were, for the sixth time, appointed to labor together, their field of labor gradually becoming smaller each year, as laborers increased in numbers; and it is worthy of note, that in Ireland, the only influential opposers to the Methodists were the Roman priests, who saw their crafts were in danger, while the clergy and dignitaries of the Episcopal Church were generally favorable to the labors of the missionaries, and while civil officers of high repute, afforded them all the protection in their power. How different from the conduct generally of like classes in England. In 1805, Mr. Ouseley was appointed to labor with Rev. Wm. Hamilton, as his colleague. The former while preaching one Sabbath day in the streets of Carlow, where he found hundreds of country laborers who were in town looking for employment, with their reaping hooks or sickles over their shoulders, was rushed upon by a number of these persons who were evidently determined to destroy him; and had it not been for a gentleman who opened his door and dragged Mr. Ouseley into his house, they no doubt would have succeeded in their purpose.

During the year following the Conference of 1806, Mr. Ouseley appears to have labored mostly in the district of country, round and about Dublin. On one occasion he visited the town of Drogheda, which has always been noted for the swarm of beggars, who daily infest its streets. Mr. Ouseley, desirous of doing this neglected class some good, if possible, gave notice that he would preach to them on the morning of his departure from the town. In obedience to the call, a vast multitude of beggars collected together, who stood next the preacher, besides hundreds of others drawn together by the novelty of the occasion. Mr. Ouseley took for his text the history of the rich man and Lazarus, and not only did the beggars weep, but those who came as spectators merely, were greatly affected. Mr. Ouseley retired, bearing with him the blessings of the poor creatures, for whose special benefit he had labored.

At the next Conference, Mr. Ouseley directed his attention to the region round about his own native province. In this region of country, he was very successful in his labors. He not only knew how to give "the trumpet a certain sound" when preaching, but he always had a seasonable word of advice for every person, whether high or low, rich or poor, Protestant or Catholic. Coming up one day in summer to where some men were cutting peat, he inquired, "What are you doing, boys?" "We are cutting turf," was the reply. "Sure you don't require them this fine weather?" "No, sir, we don't want them now; but we will want them in the cold days of winter out here, and in the long nights." "And, ye fools, won't it be time enough to cut them when ye want them? Let winter provide for itself." "O, *muisha*, sir, it will be too late then." Mr. Ouseley's moral may be inferred from the above.

While Mr. O. was in Dublin on one occasion, he had a call from a gentleman of note, to visit a certain noble lord residing there. The gentleman was a pious man, and had a great anxiety for the spiritual welfare of his noble friend. He had made several attempts to prevail on clergymen of the establishment to speak with his friend on the subject of salvation, and although he once obtained a promise to that effect from one of the clergy, yet all who had been spoken to, were evidently afraid of his lordship. At last he thought of Mr. Ouseley's being in town; "I'll tell you *what*," said he to himself, "I'll go to Gideon; he's in town; *he'll* go with me." He accordingly went with his carriage after Mr. Ouseley, who willingly consented to go with him to the mansion of his lordship. After the usual compliments, Mr. Ouseley in the most plain, yet respectful manner, urged upon his lordship's attention the importance of being prepared for eternity. "Mr. Ouseley," replied his lordship, "public business must be attended to, and we have no time for these things." Mr. O. replied, "But, my lord, we must have time to die, and we should be prepared for that inevitable event." "And what am I to do, Mr. Ouseley?" "There is the New Testament, it contains the will of the Lord Jesus Christ, and tells you what you are to do, my lord." "But, Mr. Ouseley, there are many things in that book which I can understand, and that I admire. I must confess, however, there are other things I cannot agree with." "Ah! my lord, that will never do. What if your lordship had a case submitted to you by an individual, for an opinion; and after your opinion had been drawn up with the utmost care, and legal accuracy, he would say, 'Why, my lord, there is part of this I like pretty well, but with other parts I cannot agree,' what would you say, my lord?" "Ah! I perceive your meaning: we must receive the *whole* as a revelation from God." "Exactly so, my lord. Take up that book; believe what it says; and *do* what it commands, and you will, my lord, be prepared by His mercy, for the hour of death, and for that day, when the great Judge shall appear." The nobleman expressed his gratitude to Mr. Ouseley for his kindness and frankness, and invited him and his friend to dinner, which invitation they accepted, but during the repast,

Mr. O. would in the most faithful manner, call his lordship's attention to the "one thing needful," and that, too, in a way in which he was not accustomed to listen to gospel truth.

Great trouble and agitation prevailed during the years 1806–7, throughout the province where Mr. Ouseley was at that period laboring. A body of men, called "*Threshers,*" infested the country, who organized themselves into a band of freebooters, for the ostensible purpose of putting an end to the tithing system, and to reduce the dues or fees of the Romish priests. They committed many ravages upon the property of the peaceable inhabitants of the country, crying vengeance on the priests and ministers, so that those who had heretofore gladly received the missionaries, and especially Mr. Ouseley, were now afraid to open their houses for their reception. Mr. O. however, was nothing daunted, but urged his way along from place to place, and wherever he met a company of the *Threshers*, he preached plainly to them, and in return they not only respected him, but even threatened vengeance against any Roman priest who would molest him.

In one place, where ten or twelve Roman Catholics had been converted, and had joined the Methodist Society, the priest, who was a great drunkard, came among them and greatly terrified the people who came to hear Mr. O. by threatening to curse them, and make the very hair fall off from their head, and when dying would not give them the *seal of Christ* (the ointment of extreme unction), and then, said he, "what will you do?" Mr. Ouseley preached them a sermon on false prophets, and one cried out in Irish, "O, the priest—the priest, why is he hindering us from all this comfort and sweetness?" The next morning, Mr. O. preached again in the same place to a large congregation, where a number of conversions took place. First a Romish woman cried for mercy, and soon was praising God aloud; then a Protestant young woman was converted; then a Romanist; then a Protestant again, until half a dozen or more in the course of a few minutes were converted, and praised God from a full heart. "O," said one in Irish, "God is dealing finely, and fairly, for he is giving us one about of each sort." "O," said some of the converted Romanists, "the priest may talk, and that is all he'll have for it."

In 1808, Mr. Ouseley and Mr. Hamilton visited the county of Clare. The latter, in describing some of the scenes through which they passed, remarks, "Such a year of persecution I never had. Cruel mockings are nothing, and showers of stones and dirt, are but play; but bloodshed and battery are no joke. Last Christmas we were waylaid, and robbed of our books. Mr. Ouseley was hurt, and lost his hat in the affray, and he had to ride seven miles without one. I thought we should never leave the spot. It happened near Eyre-court on the Shannon. We had preached there that day, and had a battle with the priest and his people. The priest beat my horse greatly, and the people dragged him down on the street, and I on his back, but a soldier got me into the barrack-yard. Ouseley was hurt there too. The soldiers then got to arms, loaded their pieces, fixed their bayonets, marched out before us, and formed a square about us both in the street, until we preached to the market people. They then put us safe out of town; but never thought that our persecutors had got out before us, and lay concealed until we came up, and then sur-sounded us with horrid shoutings, as if Scullabogue barn had been on fire. At another time a big priest and I were in holds with each other, as he was going to pull Mr. Ouseley down. I could easily have injured him, for he was very drunk."

During the next year, Mr. O. preached on the Galway and Clare mission, with Rev. Wm. Rutledge for a colleague. The following incident is related in reference to a village frequently visited by Mr. Ouseley. A class had been formed, but a gang of desperadoes were determined to break up the meetings. One evening they resolved to attend a class-meeting, and to effect their purpose they selected their leader to enter the room before meeting commenced, so that at the proper time, he might open the door for the rest of the gang. The members, knowing the character of the intruder, suspected mischief, but said nothing to him. At length the meeting opened by singing. The intruder said to himself, "This is very *purty;* I'll not disturb them." Prayer was offered: "I'll let them alone till they have done their prayers." They began to speak; "I'd like to hear what they have to say," said Pat. The leader of the class went all round, and while they were speaking, God's Spirit began to operate on the heart of the wicked man. At length the class-leader spoke to him, and said: "My good man, have you any knowledge of the things of which we have been speaking? Did you ever feel yourself a sinner before God, and that you deserved forever to be excluded from his presence?" The poor man began to weep, and cried out in the bitterness of his soul: "Lord have mercy upon me! What shall I do? I am a wicked sinner!" The state of poor *Pat's* mind was unexpected to the members of the little class. Prayer, fervent and effectual, was immediately offered in his behalf, and he soon became a subject of the converting grace of God, and afterward was found a zealous advocate of the "truth as it is in Jesus." While the class was praying for the conversion of the weeping penitent, his comrades without were waiting with the utmost impatience for the opening of the door; and not knowing what was going on within in reference to their companion, they kept walking back and forth, frequently saying: "The devil's among the *Swaddlers.*"

In such a manner was God often pleased to manifest his power in the subjugation of the depraved heart to his will and authority; thus causing "the wrath of man to praise him," while "the remainder of wrath" he was pleased to "restrain."

At the Conference of 1810, Mr. Ouseley was reappointed to the Galway and Clare mission, having two young men appointed as his helpers or assistants in the work. One of these describes a scene of which he was a witness, which serves to show the ignorance and superstition of the Irish papists, for whose special benefit these missions had been instituted. While passing a place of religious resort, called Kilmacduagh, he saw men and women in the most indecent manner, walking on their bare knees over rough gravel and stones, the blood streaming from their lacerated limbs; while gazing on the scene with horror and pity, he was approached by the spiritual superintendent or guide, who offered to escort him over the place. After being shown all the curiosities, the missionary inquired why the people were exposing and cutting themselves in that dreadful manner. "O, for penance; for the benefit of their souls," replied the guide. "What is the cause of so much of that tree yonder, being cut away?" "I'll tell you: the saint of this place, Macduagh, travelled round the world on his knees till he came to a place below there; and there a girdle which he had round him, fell off; there was a tree standing there, which received such virtue, that a piece of it would preserve from sickness and accident, and if thrown into a house on fire, would put it out." "And where is that tree now?" "O, it's all cut away." "Did it then transfer its efficacy to the one which they are now cutting away?" "When the first was all gone, why, they began at the other. Do, sir, take a piece of it with you; it will keep you from all harm; nothing can ever happen to you while you have it about you; nor can any house be burned where it is." "Thank you, I shall not mind it now. You seem so very well acquainted with these performances, I suppose you have frequently engaged in them yourself; have you?" "Not as often as I ought, for myself; but I have often to perform penance for other people." "How is that?" "Why, when any of them are sick, or their children sick, they make a vow to the saint, that if they recover, they will go through so many rounds here; then, when they don't like to go through them themselves, they get me to perform their vows for them." "Do they not pay you, for thus performing their vows for them?" "O yes; if they didn't, there would be no virtue in the thing at all." During this dialogue, the guide uttered several oaths and curses, and on the missionary expressing his want of confidence in such a wretched system of religious penance, "Ah! you are not Irish," said the guide. "Indeed I am," said the missionary; "I have never been in England." "If you are not English, you belong to them, so you do," retorted the guide.

Mr. Ouseley continued his indefatigable labor for the benefit of his benighted and degraded countrymen, penetrating the most remote and lonely districts of country, going frequently without food and shelter; and exposing himself to the reproach of the ignorant and degraded Catholics, that he "might win them to Christ;" and such was his earnestness and zeal, that he never was satisfied, unless during every meeting, and under every sermon, souls were converted to God. Nor did he neglect his studies, amidst his multifarious travels and missionary duties. While riding on horseback, he generally had his Greek testament in his hand, or a Latin, English, or Irish book, from which he would store his mind with an increase of useful knowledge, while going from place to place. Wherever he stopped also, if only for a moment, he had words of instruction and counsel for the unconverted. On one occasion, he stopped at a stream to water his horse, and seeing a young lady standing in the door of a neighboring house, he went toward her, took her by the hand, spoke to her about her soul, and prayed that the blessing of God might rest upon her. About two years afterward, being invited to preach in that neighborhood, he was kindly asked by a young man, to go home with him to his house. Mr. Ouseley did so; the lady of the house received him in the most affectionate manner, and then related to him that she was the same person whom he had addressed as above stated; that the few words of counsel and instruction then given, led her to Christ; that she was now married to the young man who had invited him home, and that her husband was a class-leader.

In 1811, Mr. Ouseley was again appointed to the Galway and Clare mission, and his labors and those of his colleagues, having been greatly blessed, it became necessary to erect a number of chapels for the accommodation of the societies formed by them. All classes were solicited to aid in the erection of these chapels, and not only the Protestant gentry and clergy contributed freely for the purpose, but strange as it may seem, many of the Roman Catholic priests and gentlemen, greatly aided in the work by donations and recommendations to their people to assist. On one occasion, one of Mr. Ouseley's colleagues—Mr. O'Reilly—applied to the Roman parish priest, of Nenagh, for a subscription for the Nenagh Methodist Chapel. Upon being informed of the object of the visit, the kind-hearted priest said, "Indeed, *asthore*, I will give you a guinea on account of your name." "I could give you the money now, but I want to see you again," continued he. Mr. O'Reilly called again, and the guinea was immediately paid, the priest, at the same time, desiring him to lend him some Methodist books, for, said he, I want to form a judgment for myself of your religion. One of this priest's parishioners, a lady of great respectability, had been awakened under Methodist preaching, which fact gave great offence to the priest's coadjutor. The latter came to the priest, and said, "There now—what will you do? your whole parish are going after the Swaddlers. There is Mrs.

K——, the most respectable woman in your flock, gone too." "And what would you have me to do?" said the priest. "Denounce her from the altar," was the reply. "*Muisha*, then, I'll not denounce her, or any one else; let the decent woman go where she likes."

About this time, a Father Thayer, a Roman priest from America, arrogantly challenged the whole Protestant literati to answer his arguments in favor of Romanism. Mr. Ouseley took up the gauntlet, and in the most masterly manner, drove his antagonist from the ground, which so mortified the American champion of popery, that giving way to his disappointment and chagrin, he shortly after died in Limerick, a victim to his own folly, in arousing the most able man in Ireland, to a defence of Protestantism. This controversy gave rise to Mr. Ouseley's great work, entitled "Old Christianity, against Papal Novelties," a work which does honor to the land of his birth.

As an instance of his controversial powers, we will relate the following incident. Being in company one evening with a Romish priest, named Glin, the latter abruptly attacked Mr. O. on doctrinal subjects. Mr. Ouseley at once raised objections to the popish doctrines of extreme unction, transubstantiation, &c. In relation to the former, the priest inquired, "O, my dear sir, was it not taught by St. James as having been instituted by Jesus Christ?" Mr. O. replied, "No, sir; you are aware that in order to its being a sacrament, it should have been *instituted* by Christ; and so much was the Council of Trent at a loss, that three hundred bishops, with the pope at their head, could not find a single word of our Lord to sanction its institution. Lest you might suppose me arguing unfairly, I'll quote the words of the Trent Council for you." He then quoted verbatim the words of the Council, and proved thereby, that extreme unction is not a sacrament of Jesus Christ. He next spoke on the subject of half-communion and the real presence, and so confounded the poor priest, who was indeed a man of considerable argumentative powers, that the latter exclaimed, "O, my dear sir, if you were to see all the books that I saw, when I was at college in France, on that one subject"—the real presence—"you would be afraid to speak a word upon it all the days of your life." Mr. O. rejoined, "My dear sir, there are some things a child may know as well as an archbishop; for instance, how many panes of glass there are in that window." "Poh!" said the priest, "that's a physical fact; any one can tell that." "Is it not equally a physical fact, that John the Baptist was not the son of the Virgin Mary?" "Very true indeed, sir," replied the priest. "Why is he not her son?" inquired Mr. O. "Because John the Baptist was never born of the Virgin Mary," said the priest. "Could any man that had never been born of her, ever become her son?" "Certainly not," replied the priest. "Could any *thing* that never was born of her, ever become her son?" "Indeed, I think not," said the unsuspecting priest. "I have you now, my good fellow," exclaimed Mr. Ouseley; "can the corn which grew last year, ground by the miller, baked by the baker, and consecrated by the priest, by any power of God or man, ever become the son of the Virgin Mary?" "O," said Father Glin, "all things are possible to God." "No," retorted Mr. O., "all things are not possible to God, for it is impossible for God to lie, or work a self-contradiction, which would be necessarily involved in the doctrine of your Church; and how can any rational being believe, that the accidents to which the host may be liable, can happen to the Son of God? It can be carried away by the wind, and totally disappear; be devoured by an animal, a mouse or a cat; a spider can be drowned in the cup; it can be frozen, fall on the ground, be vomited by the priest, piously swallowed up again, licked up with the tongue; and the wine can, if poisoned, be poured on linen or tow, dried, then be burned, and the ashes buried in holy ground. Now, sir, permit me to ask, can you believe the doctrine of your own Church? Can any man in his senses believe that any of the above occurrences take place in regard to the true Christ?" The priest was confounded, and said, "True enough, sir; a great many people think that all things are possible to God, but he could not make this stick in my hand without two ends to it, nor make two hills without a valley between them." Thus he acknowledged himself vanquished, and wisely gave up the contest. On a subsequent visit to the gentleman's house where the above conversation took place, the priest said: "These Methodist preachers are queer fellows; I declare, I did not think they were such men." "But what do you think of your own argument, Father Glin?" said one to him. "If it were not for the price of bread," he replied, "I would never celebrate mass again as long as I live."

Mr. Ouseley, however, had worse foes to contend with than the arguments of Romish priests. A Romish Irish mob is the most formidable foe, and the most ferocious enemy that any person can meet, by night or by day. A tribe of North American Indians are not half so much to be dreaded by the unfortunate being who comes in contact with them, as the Irish mob, especially where whiskey is plenty, and *shillelahs* are numerous. On the next day but one after the above conversation took place, as Mr. O. was passing through Loughrea, he suddenly stopped his horse, and said to his companion, "I feel as if the atmosphere was crowded with devils; we'll be attacked in town;" and sure enough, scarcely had they made their appearance in the main street, than the crowd who were in attendance at the market, as soon as they discovered the "swaddlers," set up a most fiendish yell, as though all hell had broken loose, and the inhabitants of the pit of darkness had appeared, to re-act on earth the horrid tragedies of the world of woe. Abuse and execrations of the most awful kind were heaped upon them, and all kinds of missiles were flung with the utmost fury at their heads. Mr. O., however, was protected by the soldiery of the place, and after running through the most imminent danger, he providentially with his companion, Mr. O'Reilly, escaped unhurt. But time would fail to relate all the providential escapes of Mr. Ouseley, from the wrath of an ignorant populace, who were generally instigated to their deeds of hostility by the presence and commands of their spiritual advisers.

At the Irish Conference of 1813, Dr. Coke presided for the last time. He was on the eve of departing for India. Mr. Ouseley volunteered his services to accompany the Doctor, and though the former pleaded with tears in his eyes, for liberty to go, and the latter urged the Conference to grant leave, yet in the opinion of his brethren, his services could not be spared from the Irish missions, and he was reluctantly compelled to remain at home. At this Conference, he was appointed to the counties of Antrim and Londonderry, where he labored for several years with great success. Not being required, however, by the Conference, to confine his labors to those counties, he visited different parts of the kingdom, meeting in some places with respectful treatment, and in others narrowly escaping with his life, from the violence of the popish mobs. In the course of his travels, while on this mission, he was the instrument of the conversion of a very devout Romanist, by the name of Rorke. This man, while under conviction, went to several priests, to inquire what he should do to be saved. One told him to "Go to Lough Derg;" another, "Go to Lady's Island;" and another, "Receive the Lord's body." "Do you think," said Rorke to the latter, "you can make the Lord's body for me?" "I have that power, Philip; can you doubt it?" "Please your reverence," said Rorke, "I have two little hens, but no cow; now if you can turn them into two milch cows for my children, to give us milk, I shall believe then that you have the power you say." "Get agone, get agone," said the priest, and left him to find consolation the best way he could.

In the farther relation given of the biography of Mr. Ouseley, it would be pleasant to relate his frequent conversations with Roman priests, or other champions of popery who fancied themselves competent to defend its absurdities; a few of these only, we can give. On one occasion, a young Romanist who had just completed his studies in Maynooth College, and who was in the habit of assailing Protestant gentlemen, manifested a great desire to meet Mr. Ouseley in controversy. An opportunity soon offered at the house of a Protestant, where there was a large company present. After dinner, the Romanist introduced his favorite theme, and soon the conversation turned on the subject of transubstantiation, the Romanist asserting that Jesus Christ converted the bread into his own body. "Did not our blessed Lord eat of that bread, and drink of that cup, after the consecration?" asked Mr. Ouseley. "Yes," was the reply. "And do you think that he ate himself?" "I believe he did," replied the young man. "Then," retorted Mr. Ouseley, "his *own head* was in his *own mouth*, as were his feet and his whole body, and so a part is greater than the whole! And yet his feet were on the ground!!" The company present laughed immoderately at the absurd idea, and the young collegian acknowledged himself vanquished.

On another occasion he fell in with a young woman who was a bigoted Romanist, although otherwise a very interesting and intelligent person. She said she would rather be damned than become a Protestant. Mr. Ouseley hearing of her sought her out, and said to her, "Biddy, would you not rather have one half-hour's conversation with Jesus Christ, who is to judge you, than if all the clergy on earth—pope, priests, preachers, &c., were to talk to you till doomsday?"

"Surely, I would," she replied. "But had he so conversed with you, would you not be afraid of forgetting any part of it; and would you not on your knees beg of him to give it to you in writing?" "Certainly, I would." "Now if he gave you that writing, would you not put it in your very bosom, and read it night and day, and prefer it to all the teachers on earth, nor part with it on any account whatever?" "All this is true, sir: I most certainly would not part with it." "Then, Biddy, you have this very thing in this house,—the New Testament. For if Jesus Christ were now to come, having given the Gospel in infinite perfection (and the Protestant and Roman Catholic Testaments are in substance the same), he would in no wise alter the Gospel. Hence you have only to read and obey it, and all shall be well. But there is a practice in your religion which Christ never taught: that is private confession." He then explained the Scripture in relation to the woman accused of wickedness, and showed that when brought to the Saviour he said, "Neither do I condemn thee; go and sin no more." "You see, Biddy," said Mr. O., "Christ did not confess her, nor lay penance on her. Now had he found an apostle confessing the woman, and laying penance on her contrary to his example, what would become of such an apostle, unless he promised never to do so again? Or, if he met you, my child, going to such confession, and should say to you, 'Did I ever teach you the like: and are you going to tell the world I was wrong?' What would you answer? surely you would say, 'Lord, I will never go to confession again.'" The result of this conversation was, that "Biddy" never went to confession again, but became a faithful and worthy member of the Methodist Society, notwithstanding the priest's bitter opposition to her; and through her means, her parents were both subsequently converted and also united with the Methodists.

While travelling in the county of Wexford, he rode into a

town on the Sabbath for the purpose of preaching, and as is customary in Ireland, after mass large numbers of the Catholic congregation were engaged near the Roman Chapel in playing ball, gambling, drinking, &c. Mr. Ouseley with holy indignation, went immediately to the priest, and said: "Are not you, sir, the pastor of Christ's flock?" "Indeed, I am, sir," replied the priest. "Then why do you not turn out the unruly ones, according to the command of Christ our Lord?" "Lord help me," said the priest, "if I turn out these, I'll have none at all." "Better for you to have none at all, or have only three, and have such a church as Christ and his apostles founded, than have the whole countryside of such fellows." "True for you, sir; but Lord have mercy on us, what shall we do for the bit of bread?" Mr. O. then referred to the impious lives of some of the popes, and showed the absurdity of considering them as the head of Christ's true flock. "True enough for you," said the priest, "there's their lives on the table there." After Mr. O. withdrew, the priest's coadjutor came in and said: "So you have had that heresiarch Ouseley here." The priest replied, "Get you gone, sir; Mr. Ouseley is a gentleman and a scholar, sir; what you are not. You dare not open your mouth, sir, if he were present." It is worthy of record, that when this priest (who evidently loved Ouseley), was breathing his last he cried out: "O Mr. Ouseley! Mr. Ouseley!"

We have thus given a few specimens of Mr. Ouseley's conversational powers, and of the good effects which seemed to follow his personal labors in this direction. We might fill the space allotted to this chapter with various other anecdotes and incidents as connected with his long and useful life.

From the Conference of 1813, to the close of his life in 1839, Mr. Ouseley continued in his work of laboring for the salvation of his countrymen. He not only visited all parts of Ireland repeatedly, but made frequent visits to England and

Scotland for the same purpose, and in each of those kingdoms he preached to overwhelming congregations. Dnring his days and hours of sickness, his mind was always active, and many valuable thoughts dropped from his pen during his seasons of confinement to his room. Letters, strictures, reviews, discussions, &c., owed their existence to his leisure hours while sick. After a long and useful life he closed his earthly career in the city of Dublin, on the 14th day of May, in the year 1839. His remains were deposited in Mount Jerome Cemetery, Harold's Cross. Mr. Ouseley's last sickness was of about three weeks' duration, and during this time he was perfectly resigned to the will of heaven. His last words were: "I have no fear of death; the Spirit of God sustains; God is my support." May our "last end, be like his."

CHAPTER IX.

BISHOP ASBURY.

FRANCIS ASBURY, the subject of the following sketch, was born in the parish of Harrodsworth, about four miles from Birmingham, England, on the 20th or 21st of August, 1745. His parents, though belonging to the humbler class of English society, were honest and industrious, and were able to procure a comfortable maintenance for themselves and family. They had but two children, a son and daughter, and as the latter died while in infancy, Francis was left as the only child of his parents. At an early age, he was sent to school, where he remained till about thirteen years of age. Having received rather rough treatment from his teacher, he at the above age, preferred leaving school and learning a trade, at which he continued till he was nearly twenty years of age.

Soon after his apprenticeship commenced, he was awakened to a sense of his sinfulness by nature, through the conversation and prayers of a pious man, with whom he became associated. The effect of such awakening, was, that he immediately began to pray morning and evening, and not relishing the cold formal sermons of his own parish minister, he visited other parish churches for the purpose of listening to men who were more evangelical and zealous in the cause of Jesus Christ. Shortly after his awakening, he heard of the Methodists, and on inquiring of his mother, who, where, and what they were, she directed him to a person, who would take him to Wednesbury to see them. On repairing thither, he found that the Methodists were not "the Church," but to him something better. The people seemed devout,—men and women kneeling down and saying: "Amen!" Then singing hymns! And stranger still the preacher had no prayer-book, and yet prayed wonderfully! He took his text, and preached, and yet had no sermon-book! This was all new and wonderful to Francis, who never had seen it in this fashion before. The preacher talked about confidence, assurance, &c. &c., to all of which Francis was a stranger, and led him still further to see his lost condition while out of Christ, and prompted him to seek earnestly for pardon at the hand of God.

Shortly after this, while engaged with a companion in praying, in his father's barn, the Lord pardoned his sins, and justified his soul. He soon felt it to be his duty, young as he was, in age and experience, to hold meetings for reading and prayer. He also ventured occasionally to exhort the people to repentance, and some professed to find peace in believing through his instrumentality. He subsequently became a local preacher in the Wesleyan connection, which relation he sustained nearly five years, when, at the age of twenty-one, he gave himself wholly to the work of the ministry under the direction of Mr. Wesley. After officiating about five years more as a travelling preacher in England, when a call having been made by Mr. Wesley, at the Bristol Conference in August, 1771, for laborers to volunteer for the American continent, Mr. Asbury at once offered himself for the work, and was accepted. At the close of Conference he hastened home to inform his parents of his design, and although he had one of the most tender mothers, she interposed no obstacles in his way, but freely gave him up to the cause of God and of universal Methodism.

Having formed, while a local and travelling preacher, an extensive acquaintance among the good people of Staffordshire,

Warwickshire, and Gloucestershire, had felt it his duty also to visit them before his departure. Many of these friends wondered at the moral heroism of the young man, who could thus consent to leave his "happy home and happy country, far in distant lands to dwell," but none opposed him in his undertaking, no doubt believing that it was a call of Providence. Having thus made a flying visit to different parts of England, he returned to Bristol in the latter part of August, where he found Mr. Richard Wright—who had also been appointed to America—awaiting his arrival, that they might sail together. So very little money had Mr. Asbury laid up during his ministerial labors in England, that when he arrived in Bristol he had not a penny of money in his pocket; but the Lord soon opened the hearts of his friends, who supplied him with comfortable clothing, and ten pounds in money

On the 2d day of September, Mr. Asbury and his colleague, Mr. Wright, set sail from a port near Bristol, and after finding himself on the wide expansive ocean, the former began strictly to examine his motives in going to America. He inquires: "Whither am I going? To the new world. What to do? To gain honor? No; if I know my own heart. To get money? No, I am going to live to God, and bring others so to do. In America, there has been a work of God: some moving first among the Friends, but in time it declined: likewise by the Presbyterians, but among them also it declined. The people God owns in England are the Methodists. The doctrines they preach, and the discipline they enforce are, I believe, the purest of any people now in the world. The Lord has greatly blessed these doctrines and this discipline in the three kingdoms; they must, therefore, be pleasing to him. If God does not acknowledge me in America, I will soon return to England. I know my views are upright now—may they never be otherwise!"

After a pleasant voyage of five weeks, the two missionaries

landed in Philadelphia, and were cordially received by the people, as also by Mr. Pilmore, who was then stationed in that city. After spending a few days with them, Mr. Asbury left for the city of New York, where he arrived on the 12th of November, and on the next day preached in John-street church, from the text, "*I determined not to know anything among you, save Jesus Christ, and him crucified.*" In New York he found Mr. Boardman, the colleague of Mr. Pilmore, and was as kindly received by the former as by the latter.

Hitherto, the labors of Messrs. Pilmore and Boardman—who, previously to the arrival of Mr. Asbury, were the only Methodist missionaries in America—had been confined almost exclusively to the cities of New York and Philadelphia. The number of Methodists in New York at this time, was three hundred; in Philadelphia, two hundred and fifty; and a few in Maryland, gathered under the labors of Mr. Robert Strawbridge, a local preacher, the whole amounting to about six hundred souls. Mr. Asbury resolved, however, not to confine his labors to the city, but to make excursions into the country places, for the purpose of preaching Christ to the inhabitants. Accordingly, he soon after made excursions to West Farms, and Westchester, as also to Rye, New Rochelle, and Staten Island, and in all these places he was hailed as the messenger of God, and had great success among the people, although sometimes called to suffer persecution among the rabble.

In December, 1772, Mr. Asbury went into Kent County, in Maryland. On one occasion, before preaching, a minister of the English Church came to him, desiring to know who he was, and whether he was licensed. Mr. A. told him his name, and that he was regularly licensed as a Methodist preacher. The minister began to speak great swelling words, and said he had authority over the people, and was charged with the care of their souls. He said also, that Mr. Asbury could not, and should not preach: and if he attempted it, he should proceed against him according to law. Mr. A. gave him to understand that he had come to Maryland for the express purpose of preaching, and preach he would; he further asked the reverend gentleman if he had authority to bind the consciences of the people, or if he was a justice of the peace? The clergyman replied, by accusing him of making a schism. Mr. A. retorted by saying, that he did not draw people from the church. The minister said that he kept people from their work. Mr. A. inquired if fairs and horse-races did not hinder them from their work? and informed the gentleman that he had come to help, instead of to hinder him from doing good to the people. "I did not hire you for an assistant, nor do I want your help," replied the clergyman. Mr. A. rejoined by saying, that if there were no swearers or other sinners, he was sufficient. "But what do you come for?" asked the minister. "To turn sinners to God," said Mr. A. "But cannot I do that, as well as you?" Mr. A. replied, by stating that he, Mr. A., had authority from God to preach the gospel. The clergyman laughed him in the face, and said, "You are a fine fellow, indeed!" Mr. Asbury, not to be intimidated by such clerical insolence, began to preach, and call on the people to repent, and turn from all their transgressions, so that iniquity should not prove their ruin. The poor parson could only give vent to his rage, by cautioning the people against coming to hear Mr. Asbury. But in spite of all such treatment, the people came out to hear the word, and many of them received it into good and honest hearts.

From the above circumstance, the reader can perceive the manner in which Mr. Asbury and his colleagues in the missionary work, were received by those who would monopolize the cure of souls, and who claimed to be, by divine right, in the succession from the apostles; but all these things moved not Mr. Asbury, who in the midst of opposition kept steadily onward in the pursuance of his great work of saving souls.

In October, 1772, Mr. Asbury received a letter from Mr. Wesley, appointing him as the General Assistant, or Superintendent of all the preachers and Societies in America, and requiring a strict attention to all the rules of the Society, both as it regarded preachers and people. As yet, no annual Conference had been held, but the interchange of preachers appears to have been determined upon by mutual consent, at the quarterly meeting conferences, which at that time were but three or four in number. At one of these meetings, held in Maryland, Dec. 23d, 1772, the preachers were regularly assigned their respective fields of labor, by Mr. Asbury, himself remaining in Baltimore, and occasionally extending his visits to the regions round about, everywhere being received as the messenger of God, and everywhere "making full proof of his ministry."

In June, 1773, Messrs. Rankin and Shadford arrived in Philadelphia, from England, having been sent over by Mr. Wesley to reinforce the small number of preachers in America. As Mr. Rankin was Mr. Asbury's senior, both in age and ministerial standing, it seemed good to Mr. Wesley to appoint the former in the place of Mr. Asbury, to the office of General Assistant, and giving him power also to call the preachers together in an annual Conference. Accordingly, on the 4th day of July, 1773, the first regular Conference ever held in America, met in the city of Philadelphia. It was composed of ten preachers, and the number in the Societies are reported to have been 1160. At this Conference, Mr. Asbury was re-appointed to Baltimore, where he labored efficiently, extending as opportunity offered, his travels into other portions of Maryland. During this year, he assisted in the erection of a Methodist church in Baltimore, since known by the name of Light-street Church. In 1774, Mr. Asbury was appointed to New York and Philadelphia cities, in connection with Mr. Rankin, each of them being required to change alternately, once in three months. It appears, however, from Mr. Asbury's journal, that he was not confined to those two places during this year, but that he travelled extensively in all the region of country around those cities, preaching the Gospel and raising Societies in different parts of the wide field. His labors, in fact, were so extensive, that he seriously injured his health, and was for a length of time confined to his bed. In 1775, he was appointed to Norfolk, Va., where he found about thirty persons only in Society, without any place of worship, except an old shattered playhouse. He, however, persuaded the "feeble few" to attempt the erection of a church, which they finally succeeded in doing.

It appears by reference to Asbury's journal, that a difference of opinion obtained between him and Mr. Rankin, in relation to the proper administration of discipline. The latter gentleman was not only a strict, but a severe disciplinarian, so much so, that his appointment by Mr. Wesley, as General Superintendent, did not give very great satisfaction to either the preachers or people. Mr. Asbury was also a strict enforcer of the rules of discipline, but without that severity which characterized the administration of Mr. Rankin. Hence these gentlemen had their particular friends and adherents, and although Mr. Asbury does not appear to have interfered with the proper administration of discipline by Mr. Rankin, the latter could not but perceive that the affections of the preachers and people were placed more fully on Mr. Asbury than on himself. The knowledge of this fact led Mr. Rankin to suppose that Mr. A. might have used undue means to supplant him in the affections of the people, if not to remove him from his official position as General Assistant. In accordance, therefore, with these surmisings—and they were nothing more, having no other foundation than jealousy to build upon—Mr. Rankin wrote to Mr. Wesley, and in some manner not precisely known, misrepresented Mr. Asbury's conduct and motives, to the father of Methodism. These misrepresentations appear, for the time being, to have had the desired effect on Mr. Wesley's mind; so much so, as to lead him to desire Mr. Asbury's return to England, and in reference to his expected return, he writes to Mr. R., saying: "I doubt not but brother Asbury and you will part friends. I shall hope to see him at Conference (in England). He is quite an upright man. I apprehend he will go through his work more cheerfully when he is within a little distance from me." From this, it appears that Mr. A. had been desired to return immediately, as the letter is dated May 19th, 1775, and the English Conference would assemble in about two months thereafter, at which time Mr. Wesley hoped to see him. Mr. Asbury, however, did not return, and we find Mr. Wesley, in a letter dated July 28, 1775, "rejoicing over honest Francis Asbury, and hoping he will no more enter into temptation."

Shortly after this correspondence, the ever memorable war of the Revolution began, which rendered the situation of some of the leading preachers unpleasant in the extreme. This was particularly the case with Messrs. Rankin and Asbury, the former of whom, soon after the issuing of the Declaration of Independence, July 4, 1776, resolved to return to England. He, however, deferred his departure until September, 1777. Mr. Asbury resolved, however, to remain true to the cause of American Methodism, and "not to depart from the work on any consideration." In thus resolving, Mr. Asbury placed himself in imminent peril, arising from the fact that one of the preachers—an Englishman by the name of Rodda—had so far forgotten his calling as a minister of the Gospel, as to become a warm partisan and friend of royalty, and was even detected in reading the King's proclamation while discharging his duties on his circuit. This one circumstance was sufficient to awaken jealousy in regard to the political integrity of other Methodist preachers, and particularly of those from England: hence they were not even permitted to preach in many places, and Mr. Asbury, who was always exceedingly guarded in reference to his expressions of political preference, was, at the beginning of hostilities, fined five pounds at or near Baltimore, for no other crime than preaching the Gospel. Still, however, he kept on discharging his duty as a minister of the Lord Jesus Christ.

At this time, it was enacted by the several State Legislative Assemblies, that the oath of allegiance to the State authorities should be taken by all the inhabitants residing within their respective jurisdictions. Mr. Asbury had no objection to the oath of allegiance, but had conscientious scruples about taking the one prescribed by the State of Maryland, in which State he was then residing. In consequence of this refusal, Mr. Asbury was threatened with imprisonment as a "tory," and was obliged to retire into the State of Delaware, where he found a quiet and pleasant asylum at the residence of Judge White, a man of great influence in that State, and where he remained in a state of partial concealment for nearly a year, until the height of the political tempest had passed away. But even here, Mr. Asbury did not pass his time in idleness; for although he could not with propriety address a public congregation on the Sabbath, yet he would visit from house to house, and was probably instrumental in doing as much good as he possibly could have done by more public labors. While in this state of seclusion, the Conference of 1779 met at the house of Judge White, and as Mr. Rankin had left for England, and no successor had been appointed as yet by Mr. Wesley, the Conference, by vote, chose Mr. Asbury as the General Assistant, which station he afterward filled by the appointment of Mr. Wesley himself, in 1782. During the next year (1783), peace was declared between Great Britain and her hitherto rebellious colonies in America;

and after a long and severe struggle, the independence of these United States was secured, and acknowledged; and strange as it may appear to many, the cause of Methodism, instead of having become defunct during the din and confusion of war, and by the departure of some of the preachers and the imprisonment of others, the Society had increased during the struggle, from 3,148 members, to 14,986. The number of preachers had also increased, so that in 1783, there were no less than eighty-three appointed by Mr. Asbury, to different fields of labor.

The year 1784, forms a new era in the history of American Methodism. Hitherto the Methodists had been regarded as members of the Church of England, but now it became necessary to acquire an organization of their own, especially as the Church of England had lost its ecclesiastical jurisdiction over its churches in America, and these latter had not as yet acquired an independent existence. The consequence was, that there were very few ordained Episcopal clergymen in America, and the majority of those who were ordained, were by no means qualified, either by grace or morality, to administer the ordinances of the Church—even if they had been willing to do so—to the Methodists. Besides, not a single Methodist preacher in America had been ordained, and thus the fifteen thousand members, and the fifty or sixty thousand adherents of Methodism, with their families, were deprived of the administration of the ordinances of the Church, particularly Christian baptism. True, a few of the preachers in the more southern portions of the United States had, without ordination, ventured in view of the seeming necessities of the case, to administer the ordinances of baptism and the Lord's Supper; but these administrations, by Mr. Asbury, Mr. Wesley, and the great body of the American preachers, were held to be irregular, and were consequently abandoned. Meanwhile, constant applications were being made for relief, to Mr. Wesley, as the acknowledged father of Methodism; and he, after due deliberation and prayer, set apart Dr. Coke as a Bishop, and gave him authority to proceed to America and organize the Societies in that country into an Episcopal Church, and also to ordain Mr. Asbury as Joint Superintendent, or Bishop of the same. Accordingly, Dr. Coke, in compliance with his instructions, proceeded at once to America, and on the 25th day of December, 1784, organized the Methodist Societies into the Methodist Episcopal Church in the United States, and ordained Mr. Asbury first as deacon, then as elder or presbyter, and finally as a superintendent, or bishop.

Does the bigot, or the stickler for the exploded dogma of apostolic succession, inquire if Mr. Wesley had authority to confer Episcopal consecration on Dr. Coke? We answer, he had; first, because he was as truly a scriptural bishop as any man in England; and secondly, because he was *more* than a bishop—he was in a high sense an *apostle*, and gave greater evidence of his call to the apostleship, than the Bishop of London ever gave of his call to the Episcopacy. Wherein, we ask, did John Wesley fail to show the true signs of an apostle? Was an apostle sent and commissioned by Jesus Christ to teach all nations, baptizing them, &c.? And did not Mr. Wesley receive such a commission? Did an apostle give evidence of the divinity of his call by the success attending his labors? And did not Wesley the same? Let the *seventy thousand* Methodists in Great Britain, besides the thousands in America, and in other portions of the earth, at the time of his decease, answer this question. If success is to be considered as an element in the evidence of a divine call to the apostleship, surely Mr. Wesley, more than any one man since the apostles' time, has furnished such proof of an extraordinary call; and had he never been ordained by the English Episcopacy, yet had the same success attended his labors, we should not have hesitated to acknowledge his authority as a divinely commissioned legate of the skies. But aside from these considerations, Mr. Wesley was in duty bound to provide the word of life and the ordinances of the Gospel for these poor sheep in the wilderness, for whose souls none of the ecclesiastical dignitaries of the Church of England seemed to care.

It was under these circumstances, that Mr. Asbury was set apart to the episcopacy,—an event which more than any other conspired to the permanent establishment and success of Methodism in America. Before we proceed in our narrative of events as connected with the biography of Bishop Asbury, it may be proper to observe that, although Mr. Wesley ordained Dr. Coke to the episcopacy, and ordered the ordination of Mr. Asbury to the same office, yet he did not design the application of the term *bishop*, to these newly created *episcopoi*. The term preferred, and employed by Mr. Wesley, was the simple one of *superintendent*. This term was selected in preference to the other, because of the enormous abuses which had existed in the Church, in connection with the title bishop. Besides, the name itself was associated in Mr. Wesley's mind with all the grandeur and pomposity of modern prelates, and for this latter reason he strongly objected to its use among his preachers, as applied to any one of their brethren; and for the same reason he disapproved of the employment of the term *priest* or *presbyter*, as applied to an ordained elder in the Methodist Church; as also of the use of the term *college*, when applied to a literary institution of the highest grade, preferring as he did, the more modest and unassuming appellation of *school*.

We deem it necessary to make these remarks preparatory to the introduction of a letter, written by Mr. Wesley, to Bishop Asbury, in the year 1788, after the title bishop began to be generally employed by the preachers, in their addresses to the bishops. The letter referred to, was dated London, Sept. 20, 1788, and contains the following words, which we give as an extract:—"But in one point, my dear brother, I am a little afraid both you and the doctor differ from me. I study to be *little;* you study to be *great:* I *creep;* you *strut* along. I found a *school;* you a *college!* Nay, and call it after your own names. O, beware! Do not seek to be *something.* Let me be nothing, and Christ be all in all.

"One instance of this, your *greatness*, has given me great concern. How can you, how dare you suffer yourself to be called a *bishop?* I shudder and start at the very thought! Men may call me a knave or a fool, a rascal, a scoundrel, and I am content; but they shall never, by my consent, call me a bishop. For my sake, for God's sake, for Christ's sake, put a full end to this."

We have thus given, in Mr. Wesley's own words, his objection to the use of the title bishop, by Mr. Asbury, or Dr. Coke; and these words afford sufficient evidence that Mr. Wesley, while he disapproved of the name *bishop*, was not opposed to the office itself. Whatever fears may have disposed Mr. Wesley to oppose the assumption of the title, yet the history of the Church since that period, and especially the history of the worthy men who have since then filled the episcopal chair, prove the falsity of these fears, and the propriety of adopting the title.

After his consecration to the episcopacy, Bishop Asbury began a series of labors and travels which have rendered his name immortal, and which have fully entitled him to the appellation of *Apostle of American Methodism.* He first directed his attention to the founding of a Methodist College. Being joined, in this important enterprise, by Dr. Coke, they soon succeeded in collecting a sufficient amount by subscriptions and donations, to warrant the erection of a noble brick edifice, one hundred and eight feet long by forty wide, in the town of Abingdon, Va., about twenty-five miles from Baltimore. In December, 1787, the college was solemnly dedicated by Bishop Asbury, to the service of God, and of religious knowledge. In ten years afterward, the college was destroyed by fire. A second college was secured in the city of Baltimore, but like the former, it soon perished in the flames. Mr. Asbury, although the friend of sound education, appears to have become discouraged about making any further attempts to secure the erection of collegiate edifices.

In 1788, Bishop Asbury crossed the Alleghany Mountains, and as an illustration of the mode in which this modern bishop "*strutted*" through the world, we will give his own account of his journey: "We had to cross the Alleghany Mountains again, at a bad passage. Our course lay over mountains, and through valleys, and the mud and mire was such as might scarcely be expected in December. We came to an old forsaken habitation in Tygers Valley: here our horses grazed while we boiled our meat: midnight brought us up at Jones', after riding forty, or perhaps fifty miles. The old man, our host, was kind enough to wake us up at four o'clock in the morning. We journeyed on, through devious, lonely wilds, where no food might be found except what grew in the woods, or was carried with us. We met with two women, who were going to see their friends, and to attend the quarterly meeting at Clarksburgh. Near midnight we stopped at A——'s, who hissed his dogs at us: but the women were determined to go to quarterly meeting, so we went in. Our supper was wasted. Brothers Phœbus and Cook took to the woods; old —— gave up his bed to the women. I lay along the floor on a few deer-skins, with the fleas. That night our poor horses got no corn; and the next morning they had to swim across the Monongahela; after a twenty miles' ride, we came to Clarksburgh, and man and beast were so outdone, that it took us ten hours to accomplish it. * * * My mind has been severely tried under the great fatigue endured both by myself and horse. O, how glad I should be of a plain, clean plank to lie on, as preferable to most of the beds; and where the beds are in a bad state, the floors are worse."

In 1789, George Washington was elected the first President of the United States of America, and while Congress was in session, in the city of New York, a congratulatory address was prepared by order of the New York Conference, for presentation to President Washington. The duty of its presentation, and the reception of the President's reply, devolved on Bishop Asbury, who was very politely received by the President, and to whom a complimentary reply was given. The estimation in which the Father and savior of his country was held by Bishop Asbury, may be inferred from the following language, which he used on hearing of Washington's death, in 1799: "I am disposed to lose sight of all but Washington. Matchless man! At all times he acknowledged the providence of God; and never was he ashamed of his Redeemer. We believe he died not fearing death," &c.

In 1791, Bishop Asbury visited New England for the first time, and opened his mission in the city of New Haven, Conn. His appointment to preach was published in the city papers, and although many of the literati came to hear him, yet no one invited him to their homes; and although he attended the chapel of Yale College, in time of prayers, no one invited him to visit the interior of the college, although some of the faculty were present who had heard him preach. This cold treatment induced him to say that if the opportunity ever should occur, he would "requite their behavior, by treating them as friends, brethren, and gentlemen." "The difficulty," he adds, "I met with in New Haven, for lodging, and for a place to hold meeting, made me feel and know the worth of Methodists more than ever." Bishop Asbury subsequently visited Boston, where his reception was as cold as at New

Haven, and he remarks, in reference to it, "I have done with Boston until we can obtain a lodging, a house to preach in, and some to join us." Such was the cold-hearted Christianity of New England Calvinism, in those days of tithes and state support. Were Bishop Asbury now alive, and were he to visit either New Haven or Boston, he would find that a mighty change had taken place since his first visit to New England, not only in the localities named, but in all the towns and villages through which he passed. He would find that the seed then sown by him and his fellow-laborers in the vineyard of Christ, had indeed taken deep root, and germinated, and fructified, so that not only "thirty" or "sixty," but even "an hundred fold" has been brought forth in that cold and sterile soil. The following remarkable passage occurs in his Journal after having made the above visit. In reference to the "standing order," as they were then called, he says: "I am inclined to think the eastern church will find this saying hold true in regard to the Methodists, '*I will provoke you to jealousy by a people that were no people: and by a foolish nation I will anger you.*' They have trodden upon the Quakers, the Episcopalians, the Baptists,—see now, if the Methodists do not work their way." This almost prophetic language has been literally fulfilled; the Methodists have "*worked their way*" in spite of all opposition.

It would be pleasing no doubt to the reader, to follow Bishop Asbury in his various journeys over the American continent, but our limits will only allow us to state in reference to this point, that he was constantly active, always on the move from place to place; like the apocalyptic angel he flew "through the midst of heaven, having the everlasting gospel to preach," to the inhabitants of earth. As a further illustration of his peculiar trials and privations, however, we may be allowed to give a few incidents. While travelling in the south, he relates as follows: "Having rode in pain twenty-four miles, we came to O.'s tavern, and were glad to take what came to hand. Four miles forward we came to Home's Ford, upon Catawba River, where we could neither get a canoe, nor guide. We entered the water in an improper place, and were soon among the rocks and the whirlpools. My head swam, and my horse was affrighted. The water was up to my knees, and it was with difficulty we retreated to the same shore. We then called to a man on the other side, who came and piloted us across, for which I paid him well. My horse being afraid to take the water a second time, brother Gibson crossed, and sent me his, and our guide took mine across. We went on, but our troubles were not at an end; night came on, and it was very dark. It rained heavily, with powerful lightning and thunder. We could not find the path that turned out to Connell's. In this situation we continued till midnight or past. At last we found a path which we followed until we came to dear old father Harper's plantation; we made for the house and called; he answered, but wondered who it could be; he inquired whence we came; I told him we would tell him when we came in; for it was raining so powerfully that we had not much time to talk. When I came dripping into the house, he cried, '*God bless your soul, is it brother Asbury? Wife, get up.*'"

As a further illustration of the extent of his travels on horseback, he remarks on one occasion: "From the best judgment I can form, the distance I have travelled is as follows:—from Baltimore to Charleston, S.C., one thousand miles; thence up the State of South Carolina, two hundred miles; from the centre to the west of Georgia, two hundred miles; through North Carolina, one hundred miles; through the State of Tennessee, one hundred miles; through the west of Virginia, three hundred miles; through Pennsylvania, and the west of Maryland, and down to Baltimore, four hundred miles." Thus making in a single tour on horseback, through rivers and swamps, over hills and mountains, preaching almost every day, lodging in log-cabins, or on the cold ground, a journey of two thousand three hundred miles, in a few months' time! On another occasion he writes, that he travelled "six hundred miles with an inflammatory fever and a fixed pain in" his "breast." These facts are sufficient to show the self-sacrificing spirit of the apostolic Asbury, while they should put to blush the assertions of those who have accused him of being a man greedy of honor.

In consequence of Bishop Asbury's severe labors, his health became so seriously affected that at the General Conference of 1800, he meditated a resignation of the office of bishop, and with this design, actually wrote a letter to that effect to be laid before the Conference. The Conference, however, after the matter was presented, passed resolutions approbatory of his course as a bishop, and earnestly entreating him to continue his services to the Church in that capacity, as far as his strength would permit. The entreaty of the Conference thus made, had the effect of inducing him to relinquish his design of resigning his office for the present, and as Dr. Coke was under the necessity of spending the greater portion of his time in Europe, and consequently could render but partial assistance in the episcopal work, the Conference elected the Rev. Richard Whatcoat as the colleague of Bishop Asbury. Mr. Whatcoat had been selected for this office by Mr. Wesley himself, at the same time that Dr. Coke and Mr. Asbury were appointed, but as the state of the work did not demand three bishops, his election to the office was deferred until the time above referred to.

After the adjournment of the General Conference of 1800, Mr. Asbury continued, through much bodily affliction, to travel far and near, presiding in the Conference, and visiting all portions of the work, preaching the Gospel of the kingdom to the poor on the frontiers of the country, as well as to the rich in the populous cities of the land. In referring to these labors he remarks in his journal: "Why should a living man complain? But to be three months together on the frontiers when generally you have but one room and fire-place, and half a dozen of folks about you, strangers perhaps, and their families, certainly (and they are not usually small in these plentiful new countries) making a crowd,—and this is not all—for here you *may* meditate if you *can;* and here you *must* preach, read, write, pray, sing, talk, eat, drink, and sleep, or fly into the woods. Well! I have pains in my body—which are very afflictive when I ride, but I cheer myself with songs in the night." During the year 1802, he rode about four thousand miles, mostly on horseback, through snow and rain, but God was always present to cheer and comfort him.

At the General Conference of 1804, Bishops Coke, Asbury, and Whatcoat were all present, and presided alternately over the deliberations of the Conference. Two years subsequently, Bishop Whatcoat died at the residence of Governor Bassett, in the State of Delaware, in the seventy-first year of his age. The decease of Bishop Whatcoat left Bishop Asbury virtually alone in the episcopal work, Dr. Coke's presence in Europe being still requested by the English Conference; so that during the year 1807, Bishop Asbury was under the necessity of presiding in the seven Conferences of the Church, and of travelling six thousand miles in ten months, in order to do it. During these travels, he was frequently under the necessity of lodging, and eating in taverns, but it is worthy of record, that whatever might be the character of the house where he stopped, if only to eat a meal, or feed his weary beast, he made it a point always to ask the privilege of praying with the family before he left them; which permission was seldom if ever refused.

At the General Conference of 1808, Bishop Asbury was the only bishop present. The Conference, however, elected the

Rev. Wm. M'Kendree as an episcopal colleague to fill the place vacated by the death of Bishop Whatcoat. Bishop M'Kendree being comparatively young and robust, rendered valuable assistance to his aged colleague, which the latter appreciated, and in proper terms acknowledged from time to time. The two bishops generally rode during the first year of M'Kendree's episcopate together, that the senior might introduce the junior member of the episcopacy, to the respective Conferences, as also to the people in every part of their extended diocese. In reference to their travels together, Mr. Asbury remarks on one occasion, "My flesh sinks under labor. We are riding in a poor thirty-dollar chaise in partnership, two bishops of us, but it must be confessed it tallies well with the weight of our purses. What bishops! Well—but we have great news, and we have great times, and each Western, Southern, and Virginia Conference will have one thousand souls truly converted to God. Is not this an equivalent for a light purse? And are we not well paid for starving and toil? Yes, glory to God!" That the purses of these bishops were "light," may be inferred from the fact, that their salary was eighty dollars a year, and their travelling expenses eleven, or a trifle over *twenty cents a day!* Whatever might have been their motives for enduring the hardships incident to the discharge of their episcopal functions, no one we think can justly accuse them of being prompted by a desire to grow rich.

In the year 1811, Bishop Asbury visited Upper Canada, which at that period, and until 1828, was embraced within the jurisdiction of the American General Conference, and was consequently under the supervision of the Bishops of the Methodist Episcopal Church. Passing through the Indian village of St. Regis, he crossed the St. Lawrence to Cornwall, and for the first time in forty years, stood again under the flag of his native country. In reference to his feelings on this interesting occasion, he remarks: "My strong affection for the people of the United States, came with strange power upon me, when I was crossing the line. Why should I have such new feelings in Canada?" These "feelings," were no doubt occasioned by the operations of his memory, bringing vividly before the mind, the days of his youth, his country, his parents, his early associates, his troubles during the war of the Revolution, and especially the mighty changes which had been wrought since his emigration to America, not only in the civil condition of his adopted country, but in the condition of that branch of the Church of Christ, of which he was the acknowledged head, and of which, in an important sense, he had been the apostle. The good bishop passed along up the northern shore of the St. Lawrence, stopping frequently and preaching to the people on his way. After visiting Kingston, and other important places in Canada, he recrossed to Sackett's Harbor in an open boat, having a "*tremendous passage*," as he informs us in his journal. After landing in the United States, he proceeded to meet the Genesee Annual Conference, in Paris, Oneida County, New York, from which place in company with Bishop M'Kendree, he proceeded on a tour through New York, Pennsylvania, Ohio, Kentucky, Tennessee, and other southern states of the Union, travelling some sixteen hundred miles, over rough roads, and through other hindrances in about two months.

In 1812, the first Delegated General Conference, assembled in the city of New York, Bishops Asbury and M'Kendree being present. Soon after the adjournment of the Conference, war was declared against Great Britain by the United States, and although this war was exceedingly detrimental to the interests of pure religion, it did not prevent Bishop Asbury from pursuing his customary labor for the benefit of souls. It is true, when he heard of war being declared, his soul was cast down within him, while he reflected on the miseries that must necessarily ensue; he, however, felt it his duty as an American citizen and bishop, to pray earnestly for the success of the arms of his adopted country,—declaring publicly on the floor of an Annual Conference, that he who at such a time refused to pray for his country, deserved not the name of a Christian, or Christian minister. This last remark was made with reference to the fact, that there was a faction in the Eastern States, who not only opposed the war, but even refused to pray for their rulers on that account. Bishop Asbury, during the year 1812, presided over nine Conferences, was present at ten camp-meetings, and travelled six thousand miles; but although his labors were severe, so much so, as almost entirely to prostrate his physical system, and render it necessary for his friends to lift him into his carriage, he exclaims, "O, let us not complain, when we think of the suffering wounded, and dying of the hostile armies! If we suffer, what shall comfort us? Let us see,—Ohio will give us six thousand for her increase of members in one new district." So that amid the ravages of war, the bishop's heart was consoled with the reflection that God was reviving his work.

In 1814, Bishop Asbury was seized with a severe attack of inflammatory fever, in New Jersey, so that his life for some time was despaired of by his friends and physicians. He, however, suddenly recovered strength sufficient to go out. In reference to his partial recovery of strength, he says: "I would not be loved to death, and so came down from my sick room, and took to the road, weak enough. Attentions constant, and kindness unceasing, have pursued me to this place. I look back upon a martyr's life of toil and privation, and pain; and I am ready for a martyr's death. The purity of my intentions—my diligence in the labors to which God has been pleased to call me—the unknown sufferings I have endured —What are all these? The merit, atonement, and righteousness of Christ alone, make my plea."

The friends in Philadelphia, in consequence of the bishop's infirmity, made him a present of a light four-wheeled carriage, and in four days after, we find this extraordinary man in Pittsburgh, across the Alleghany Mountains, having urged his way through swamps, rough roads, mountainous passes, &c., in order to get there. From this time until 1816, Bishop Asbury continued to discharge his episcopal duties as much as his wasted strength would allow, flying from place to place, with almost rail-road speed, until at length the wheels of life began to move more slowly, and the veteran bishop was admonished that his work on earth was nearly finished.

On the 24th of March, 1816, he reached the city of Richmond, Virginia, at which place he preached his last sermon, from these words: "For he will finish his work, and cut it short in righteousness: because a short work will the Lord make upon the earth." This sermon was preached by the venerable and apostolic man while seated upon a table in the pulpit, having been carried from his carriage to the sacred desk. After sermon, he was assisted to his carriage, and pursued his way to Spottsylvania, Va., where he put up at the house of his old and valued friend, Mr. George Arnold, where he finally died on the 31st day of March, 1816, in the 71st year of his age, and the 55th of his ministry. He died in great peace, and raised both his hands in token that Jesus Christ was precious to him in the hour and moment of dissolving nature.

His remains were interred in the family burying ground of Mr. Arnold, but by order of the next General Conference, which assembled in Baltimore on the first day of May following, they were disinterred, and removed to Baltimore, where they were finally deposited under the recess of the pulpit of the Eutaw-street Church, in a vault prepared for the purpose.

Thus died Francis Asbury, and thus was a weeping Church left to mourn the departure from earth of their father and beloved senior Bishop. It is scarcely necessary, after what has been said, to attempt a description of Bishop Asbury's character. Let it suffice to say, that he was emphatically a CHRISTIAN—a man of deep religious experience; that he was also a divinely appointed CHRISTIAN MINISTER, giving the most indubitable evidence of this fact, by the success attending his labors. He was also an example of benevolence and true Christian charity. His entire effects, after his decease, were found to be worth only about two thousand dollars, which he left to the Book Concern, for the benefit of the worn-out preachers, widows, and orphans. He was temperate in all things, and remarkably plain and modest in his apparel. His arduous labors have been referred to; during the forty-five years of his ministry in America, it has been estimated that he preached no less than sixteen thousand five hundred sermons, besides his lectures, exhortations, &c. &c. He also must have travelled not less than two hundred and seventy thousand miles, or about eleven times the circumference of the earth! He probably also presided in not less than two hundred and twenty annual Conferences, and ordained not less than four thousand persons to the office of the ministry, besides tens of thousands who were admitted by him to the Church, by the rite of baptism.

Bishop Asbury was a good preacher; but perhaps his greatness never appeared to better advantage than when presiding in the annual or general Conferences of the Church; and yet with all his excellencies, it is not to be taken for granted that Bishop Asbury had no defects. He probably had many, but they were defects arising solely from the weakness of human judgment, and not from any moral deficiency, or badness of heart. He was never married, assigning as a reason, that before his elevation to the episcopacy his time was so much occupied in regard to the duties of his sacred calling as to afford no opportunity to attend to matrimonial affairs; and after being elected Superintendent, he thought it would be nothing less than wicked to enter into a matrimonial alliance with any lady, from whom he must be separated eleven months in every year. Hence he chose to remain single, and like Paul the apostle, give all his time and talents to the Church of God, which indeed were freely given and abundantly blessed to the good of God's Israel. Bishop Asbury "*rests from his labors, and his works do follow him.*"

CHAPTER X.

BISHOP WHATCOAT.

COMPARATIVELY little is known of this holy man, as no extended account of his life and labors has ever been written; a circumstance that is deeply to be regretted, the more especially as the subject of this chapter was so intimately connected with the organization of the Methodist Episcopal Church in the United States. It is, however, less surprising that the life of Bishop Whatcoat has not been given to the Methodist public, when we consider that the same is true of his venerable colleague, Bishop Asbury, who, were it not for the public documents of an ecclesiastical nature, in relation to which he bore so conspicuous a position, and which have been happily preserved from oblivion and destruction; and more especially for his journal, which has been providentially preserved, but little would have been known of that great man. The fault, however—if fault there is—of not having a written history of these early fathers of Methodism, does not rest on the shoulders of their sons in the gospel, some of whom have done what they could to rescue their names and memory from oblivion. To no person more than to Dr. Nathan Bangs, is the Church indebted for an attempt of this character, and it is justly due to this voluminous writer and ecclesiastical historian to say, that had it not been for his unwearied efforts to bring to light facts which otherwise would have been entirely forgotten among the transactions of the past, the little that we now know in reference to some of the burning and shining lights of Methodism, would be entirely unknown to the present or succeeding generations. In the preparation of this short chapter, therefore, we are obliged to acknowledge our indebtedness to the "History of the Methodist Episcopal Church," for the principal facts found therein.

Richard Whatcoat was born in England, in the year 1736, and being brought up in the "nurture and admonition of the Lord," was saved from those habits of vice and sin, into which many of the youth plunge thoughtlessly and heedlessly. At the age of twenty-two years, he was converted to God, and received the witness of his adoption into the family of God; and as the result of such conversion, he began immediately to bring forth the "fruits of the Spirit," and to live, not only "a sober and righteous," but a "godly life." He appears to have connected himself with the Methodists soon after his conversion, and labored for some time as one of Mr. Wesley's local preachers. In 1769, he joined the travelling connection in England, and labored for a period of fifteen years, as a faithful minister of the Lord Jesus Christ, under the direction of Mr. Wesley. During this period, he made full proof of his ministry, and by his zeal and fidelity rendered himself useful and acceptable as a preacher, wherever he was known.

In the year 1784, the Macedonian cry was heard from the western shore of the Atlantic, saying, "Come over and help us." This cry was made by the thousands of Methodists in America, who were like sheep without a shepherd, having, indeed, to some extent, the preaching of the Gospel among them, but from various causes alluded to in a preceding chapter, were deprived of the ordinances of baptism, and the Lord's Supper. The request was made to Mr. Wesley, that he would adopt some measures for the relief of his American children. After proper consultation, Mr. Wesley resolved on sending a partial supply of ministers, and Mr. Whatcoat, who, although he was past the meridian of life, had all the zeal and missionary fire of youth, at once volunteered his services for that distant field of labor; and dear to him as was his own native land, and thrice dear as were the thousands of friends he must leave behind him, he nobly resolved to forsake all for the sake of preaching the gospel to the poor.

As before stated, Mr. Whatcoat, previous to his embarkation for America, was solemnly set apart by presbyterial ordination, performed by Messrs. Wesley, Coke, and Creighton, presbyters of the Church of England, to the office of an elder in the Church of God, and in the month of September, 1784, left the shores of England, and landed in the City of New York, in company with Dr. Coke, on the 3d of November, in the same year. After landing in New York, Mr. Whatcoat, accompanied by the doctor, proceeded to Philadelphia, and from thence to the State of Delaware, and on the 15th of the same month, they met Mr. Asbury, at Barratt's Chapel, in that State, where Dr. Coke apprized the latter of the provision made by Mr. Wesley, for the organization of an independent Methodist Episcopal Church. In reference to this meeting, Mr. Asbury says, in his Journal, "Sunday, 15. I came to Barratt's Chapel. Here, to my great joy, I met those dear men of God, Dr. Coke and Richard Whatcoat. We were greatly comforted together. The doctor preached on *Christ our wisdom, righteousness, sanctification, and redemption.* Having had no opportunity of conversing with them before public worship, I was greatly surprised to see Brother Whatcoat assist, by taking the cup, in the administration of the Sacrament. I was shocked when first informed of the intention of these, my brethren, in coming to this country; it may be of God. My answer then was, "If the preachers unanimously choose me, I shall not act in the capacity I have hitherto done, by Mr. Wesley's appointment. The design of organizing the Methodists into an independent Episcopal

Church, was opened to the preachers present, and it was agreed to call a General Conference, to meet at Baltimore the ensuing Christmas; as also that Brother Garrettson go off to Virginia to give notice thereof to the brethren in the South." The surprise manifested by Mr. Asbury, at seeing Mr. Whatcoat assist in administering the Lord's Supper, by "taking the cup" and passing it, arose from the fact that he (Mr. Asbury) had not as yet been informed that Mr. Wesley had ordained any of his preachers, and knowing that Mr. Whatcoat had always been considered simply as a *preacher*, without ordination, he wondered greatly why he should assist in a work which belonged to ordained ministers alone; but when informed of what Mr. Wesley had done, and of what he intended to be done for his Societies in America, Mr. Asbury's "surprise" no doubt quickly fled, and he heartily acquiesced in what appeared to be the indications of divine providence in relation to his church in America. The extraordinary Conference, called as above, met in Baltimore, at the time appointed. There were at this period, eighty-three preachers in the travelling connection in America, and out of this number sixty were present, which, considering the brief notice given of the calling of the same, shows the unanimity with which Mr. Wesley's proposition was received, and the relief sent accepted.

At this Conference, Mr. Whatcoat was present, and although we know but little of his acts during the session of the same, he no doubt cheerfully acquiesced in the proceedings of his American brethren, with the utmost cordiality and pleasure, and after the session had closed, he went to the field of labor assigned him by his superiors in office, and continued to labor for many years, as a faithful servant of the Church, and as a devoted minister of Christ. During the most of the time intervening between the organization of the church and that of his being elected bishop, Mr. Whatcoat labored as a presiding elder, or assistant to the bishops of the church ; and as in these days, the field of a presiding elder's labors was very extensive, embracing entire States, we may well imagine that Mr. Whatcoat's office was no sinecure, whatever the honor might be, and that the salary, sixty-four dollars per annum, was not sufficiently great to be tempting. To those who live at the present day, it may be a matter of wonder how such men as Asbury, Whatcoat, and M'Kendree could be satisfied with the paltry sum of sixty-four dollars, as an annual salary ; and the only reason we can assign for the fact is, that the Societies being weak, and the members few, and poor, it was thought by the preachers themselves, to be as much as could be raised for their support ; another reason might be found in the fact that expenses were not as great in these days as at the present. Then preachers and people were contented to be clothed in the coarsest garb ; while at the present day, the people not only array themselves in clothing of better materials, but expect the preachers to do so likewise. In fact, were a minister of the present day to clothe himself as our forefathers did, he would be considered quite eccentric, and his usefulness would no doubt be greatly impaired.

Besides, the necessary expenses and outlays in the early days of Methodism, were not equal by one half what they now are, for example : in the article of books alone ; then, if a Methodist preacher had a Bible, hymn-book, and discipline, with a copy of Wesley's sermons, and a few other books, he was fully equipped for the moral warfare ; but at the present, a minister of the Methodist Church who would confine himself to these, would be considered as a perfect ignoramus. It is expected and required of him, that he keep pace with the improvements of the age in which he lives, and not only must he avail himself of the knowledge afforded by reading and studying the Word of God, and the discipline of the Church, but he must as a matter of necessity, keep pace with his hearers in regard to literature and science of every description. But to do so, he must have books and periodicals, and these cannot be obtained without money.* Another consideration is, that the most of the early preachers, including the bishops, were unmarried. Such was the demand for their continual services at different points of the work, that they were constantly on the move, and as in the case of Bishop Asbury, they did not think it morally right to win the affections of any lady, knowing that they could enjoy her society but a few weeks in the course of the year. Besides, they felt that they could more exclusively devote themselves to the work of the ministry, if they remained free from the burdens and cares of a family: hence, their expenses were comparatively small, and as they had no board bill to pay, they could as well afford to live on sixty-four dollars a year, as their successors can on five times that amount. Still it is evident, that no men possessed of as much enterprise and knowledge as they, would have for the sake of the paltry sum alluded to, forsaken home and kindred, and consented to become strangers and pilgrims in the most emphatic sense. Neither could they have been desirous of securing the applause of men; for a very short experience must have taught the most of them that worldly honor and esteem was not to be found by serving in the ranks of the Methodist itinerancy of those days. Still they were actuated by motives, and these motives were begotten in the heart by the spirit of grace; they were impelled to act, and this impulsion was the effect of God's love shed abroad in their hearts; they had an ambition, but it was the ambition of doing good—a desire to save men from the wrath to come;

* During the first year of the author's itinerancy, in 1836, his entire receipts for the year were sixty-seven dollars; and out of this, he had to clothe himself, provide travelling equipage, and pay more than twenty dollars for text books, whereby he might gain the necessary amount of knowledge required by his Conference during that year.

and to secure the salvation of their fellow-men, they "counted not their lives dear, so that they might finish their course with joy, and the ministry which they had received of the Lord Jesus, to testify the gospel of the grace of God." But let us return to the subject of the chapter.

At the General Conference of 1800, it became necessary to release Dr. Coke partially from his engagements to the American Church, at the urgent solicitation of the British Conference, who earnestly desired his services as the superintendent of various missions, and as the President of the Irish Conference. In consenting to the partial release of the Doctor, it became necessary in view of Bishop Asbury's infirm health, to elect an additional bishop. Much discussion was had previous to the election, in relation to the powers of the new bishop, some contending that he should be considered only as the assistant of Bishop Asbury. It was, however, resolved by the majority, that the bishop to be elected and consecrated, should be equal in power and authority with the senior bishop already in office.

After the above point was settled to the satisfaction of all parties, the next important question to be settled was in relation to the person who should be selected for the office. There were two candidates in the field—Mr. Whatcoat and Rev. Jesse Lee, each of whom had his friends, and both of whom had peculiar qualifications for the office of a bishop in the Church of God. Mr. Whatcoat was an Englishman, an old and valued minister; one too, who had been designated three years previously, by Mr. Wesley himself, as a proper person to be selected as a bishop of the Methodist Episcopal Church, and who had even requested his election to that office. On the other hand, Mr. Lee was an American by birth, and a favorite among the preachers; his talents also were of a more popular character, and commanded for him the respect and esteem of all who were acquainted with him.

On balloting for a bishop, it was found on the first count, that there was a tie between them, each having received an equal number of votes. On the second ballot being counted, there were found fifty-nine votes for Mr. Whatcoat, and fifty-five for Mr. Lee, whereupon the former was declared to be duly elected. On the 18th of May, he was publicly consecrated to the episcopal office by the imposition of the hands of Bishops Coke and Asbury, assisted by some of the elders present.

After the adjournment of the General Conference of 1800, Bishop Whatcoat labored efficiently and successfully as a bishop of the Church, and made full proof of his ministry in this new and important relation. He greatly assisted the senior bishop in the discharge of his onerous and responsible duties, and as long as his health would allow him to do so, he travelled extensively over the continent. At the General Conference of 1804, he was present, and assisted Bishops Coke and Asbury in presiding over the deliberations of the body, but his health was greatly impaired, and in 1806, it was thought necessary by Bishop Asbury to recommend the calling of a special General Conference in May, 1807, for the purpose of strengthening the episcopacy, as Bishop Whatcoat was supposed to be near his end. Each of the Annual Conferences promptly recommended the same, except the Virginia Conference, of which Rev. Jesse Lee was an influential member, which refused to concur in the recommendation; and in consequence of this refusal, the special session could not be called, as the plan proposed required the concurrence of *all* the Annual Conferences, in order to call a special session.

While the proposal to call a special General Conference, was being presented to each of the annual Conferences, Bishop Whatcoat departed this life at the residence of ex-governor Bassett, in the State of Delaware, on the 5th day of July,

1806, after an illness of thirteen weeks, during which time his bodily sufferings were of the most excruciating character. But in the midst of them all, he possessed his soul in perfect patience, and expressed from time to time his firm trust and confidence in Jesus Christ his Saviour, and even amidst the agonies of dissolving human nature, became a "conqueror; yea, more than conqueror, through Him that loved him." Thus died the venerable Bishop Whatcoat in the seventy-first year of his age, and in the thirty-seventh year of his ministry, and sixth of his episcopate.

Shortly after his death, Bishop Asbury visited the place of his sepulture, at the Wesleyan Chapel, in Dover, Del., and preached his funeral sermon from the words: "But thou hast fully known my doctrine, manner of life, purpose, faith, long-suffering, charity, patience." 2 Tim. iii. 10. In the course of this sermon, Bishop Asbury remarked as follows: "I have known Richard Whatcoat, from the time I was fourteen years of age to sixty-two years most intimately, and have tried him most accurately in respect to the soundness of his faith. On the doctrines of human depravity, the complete and general atonement of Jesus Christ, the insufficiency of either moral or ceremonial righteousness for justification in opposition to faith alone in the merit and righteousness of Christ, and the doctrine of regeneration and sanctification. I have also known his manner of life at all times and places, before the people as a Christian, and a minister; his long-suffering, for he was a man of great affliction, both of body and mind, having been exercised with severe diseases, and great labors." Bishop Asbury declared that such was his unabated charity, his ardent love to God and man, his patience and resignation amid the unavoidable ills of life, that he always exemplified the tempers and conduct of a most devoted servant of God, and of an exemplary Christian minister.

The following remarks are from Dr. Bangs: "As he lived

for God alone, and had assiduously consecrated all his time and powers to the service of his Church, so he had neither time nor inclination to 'lay up treasures upon earth,'—hence it is stated that he died with less property than was sufficient to defray the expenses of his funeral. He could therefore say, more in truth than most of the pretended successors of St. Peter, who is claimed by some as the first link in the episcopal succession, 'Silver and gold have I none, but such as I have' —'my soul and body's powers,' I cheerfully consecrate to the service of God and man. These remarks of themselves sufficiently indicate the character of the deceased, without saying anything more; yet it may be proper to add, that though we do not claim for him deep erudition, nor extensive science, he was profoundly learned in the sacred Scriptures, thoroughly acquainted with Wesleyan theology, and well versed in all the varying systems of divinity with which the Christian world has been loaded, and could therefore 'rightly divide the word of truth, giving to every one his portion of meat in due season.' For gravity of deportment, meekness of spirit, deadness to the world, and deep devotion to God, perhaps he was not excelled, if indeed equalled by any of his contemporaries or successors. 'Sober without sadness, and cheerful without levity,' says the record of his death, he was equally removed from the severe austerity of the gloomy monk, and the lightness of the facetious and empty-brained witling. His words were weighed in the balance of the sanctuary, and when uttered either in the way of rebuke, admonition, or instruction, they were calculated to 'minister grace to the hearer.' It is said, that on a particular occasion, when in company with Bishop Asbury, the latter was complaining loudly of the perpetual annoyance of so much useless company, —Bishop Whatcoat with great modesty and meekness, mildly remarked, 'O bishop, how much worse should we feel, were we entirely neglected.' The former bowed an acquiescence to the remark, and acknowledged his obligations to his amiable colleague, for the seasonableness of the reproof, but much more for the manner in which it was administered,—an occurrence alike creditable to them both.

"His preaching is said to have been generally attended with a remarkable *unction from the Holy One.* Hence those who sat under his word, if they were believers in Christ, felt it good to be there, for his doctrine distilled as the dew upon the tender herb, and as the rain upon the mown grass. One who had heard him, remarked, that though he could not follow him in all his researches—intimating that he went beyond his depth in some of his thoughts—yet he felt that he was listening to a messenger of God, not only from the solemnity of his manner, but also from the 'refreshing, from the presence of the Lord,' which so manifestly accompanied his word. The softness of his persuasions, won upon the affections of the heart, while the rich flow of gospel truth which dropped from his lips enlightened the understanding.

"Such was Bishop Whatcoat. And while we justly attribute to him those qualities which constitute an 'able minister of the New Testament,' we present as the distinguishing trait of his character, a meekness and modesty of spirit which, united with a simplicity of intention, and gravity of deportment, commended him to all as a pattern worthy of their imitation. So dear is he in the recollection of those who from personal intercourse, best know and appreciate his worth, that I have heard many say, that they would give much, could they possess themselves of a correct resemblance of him upon canvass. But as he has left no such likeness of himself behind, we must be content with offering this feeble tribute of respect to his memory, and then strive to imitate his virtues, that we may at last see him as he is, and unite with him in ascribing 'honor and dominion to him that sitteth upon the throne, and to the Lamb forever.'"

It is probably owing to Bishop Whatcoat's extreme meekness and modesty, that so little is now known of the peculiar and interesting incidents of his life. Had he kept a journal, as did his friend and colleague, Bishop Asbury, many interesting items might have been preserved for the benefit of future generations. Still sufficient is known of him to immortalize his memory, and to impress the mind of every Methodist at least, who reads this feeble sketch, with a sense of the true greatness of the man.

"The righteous shall be held in everlasting remembrance."

CHAPTER XI.

REV. JESSE LEE.

THE subject of this chapter, sometimes denominated the apostle of New England Methodism, was born in Prince George County, Virginia, in the year 1758. His forefathers came from England soon after the first settlement of Virginia, and his parents were respectable members of the Church of England, and they dedicated their children to God in baptism, while in a state of infancy, according to the rites and ceremonies of the Church of which they were members.

At a proper age, Jesse was sent to school under the instruction of a God-fearing teacher, who took pains to improve his pupils, morally as well as intellectually; hence the morning service of the Church was performed regularly on the Wednesday and Friday of every week. Besides, the scholars were taught the Catechism of the Church, which was attended with good results, especially in Jesse's case, who, when he felt an inclination to do something wrong, would stop at the recollection of the lessons taught in his Catechism, and refrain from the commission of the act. His father also seconded the efforts of the teacher in the enforcement of morality, and their united labors were not in vain, as young Lee was never known to indulge in those degrading vices which many of his associates delighted to indulge in. He never uttered a profane expression but once, for which he afterward felt heartily sorry.

But although young Lee was moral and circumspect in his outward walk like all other men, he had "an evil heart of unbelief;" a heart opposed to the requirements of God and the spirituality of the Gospel. When he was fourteen years of age, his father, who had hitherto trusted in external ordinances for salvation, was led to see the necessity of "being born from above" before he became fit for the "Kingdom of God:" he accordingly sought, and obtained the forgiveness of sins, and having, in the fulness of his heart, declared to his wife "what the Lord had done for his soul," she too was led to embrace the Saviour, and become a spiritual "worshipper of the Father." The conversion of his parents produced a powerful effect on the mind of Jesse; his conviction for sin became pungent, and fearing one morning, that he would drop into hell, he was constrained to cry aloud for mercy, and soon the Lord appeared for his relief, so that young Lee could exclaim with the Prophet, "O Lord, I will praise thee; though thou wast angry with me, thine anger is turned away, and thou comfortest me."

In the year 1774, when Jesse was about sixteen years of age, Mr. Robert Williams, a Wesleyan preacher, visited that part of Virginia where Jesse's parents resided. They soon became attached to the first Methodist Society formed in that vicinity, and Jesse, stimulated by their example, united also with the Society. From this time forward, Mr. Lee's house became a regular preaching place, and a home for the weary itinerant, and like Obed-edom of old, the Lord blessed him abundantly in basket and in store, because the "ark of the Lord rested there." The year 1775 was distinguished by a great revival of religion in Virginia, and during this revival Jesse Lee, although but seventeen years of age, felt an impression that it was his duty to labor personally for the salvation of souls, and he had an ample field for the improvement of his talents and the exercise of his Christian graces.

About this period he left his father's house, for the purpose of residing with a bereaved relative in North Carolina. Here he was appointed a class-leader by the preacher in charge of the circuit, and from this time forward, he frequently exhorted at class-meetings, prayer-meetings, &c., and would sometimes hold meetings for the purpose of giving the "word of exhortation," and on the 17th of November, 1779, he preached his first sermon at a place called the "Old Barn," his text being, "Behold what manner of love the Father hath bestowed upon us, that we should be called the sons of God!" &c.

Mr. Lee served the Church for some time, in the capacity of a local preacher, while he pursued the task of cultivating the soil, as the means of gaining a livelihood, but while pursuing his peaceful avocations, and spending all his spare time in preaching the Gospel of the Prince of Peace, he was drafted to serve in the army, the United States being then engaged in the war of the Revolution. Mr. Lee, though a friend to his country, and a well-wisher to the cause of liberty, had imbibed the idea that it was wrong for him, as a Christian, to bear arms or to kill any of his fellow-creatures. He determined however to join the army, and to trust in the Lord for deliverance from the necessity of taking life. On the 29th of July, 1780, he arrived at the encampment, and shortly after was called on parade. The sergeant soon went round with the muskets, and offered one to Mr. Lee, but he refused to take it; the lieutenant then brought him one, but he still refused to take it. The lieutenant threatened him with the guard-house, and went to see the colonel, and coming back set the gun down against him. Mr. Lee told him he might as well take the gun away, or it would fall, the officer then placed him under guard. After a while the colonel came, and taking Mr. Lee aside, began to converse with him in relation to the propriety of bearing arms, but his reasons were not sufficiently cogent to make any change in Mr. Lee's mind, so that he left him in the care of the guard. After dark, Mr. Lee told the guard that they must have prayers before they went to rest, and finding a Baptist under guard, he asked him to pray. After prayer, Mr. Lee told the soldiers and others, that if they would attend in the morning, he would pray with them. The soldiers brought straw for him to lie on, and offered him their blankets and great-coats for covering, so that he slept quite soundly. The next morning being Sabbath, some hundreds of people flocked together at the sound of Mr. Lee's singing, and they joining with him, the surrounding plantation echoed with the songs of Zion. After singing they had a season of prayer, and many of the poor soldiers wept.

After prayer, a tavern-keeper came out and talked with Mr. Lee, and informed him, that while in bed he heard him praying, that he could not refrain from tears, and had come to see if he would be willing to preach to the people. Mr. Lee consented, provided the Colonel's permission could be obtained. This was granted, but before preaching, the Colonel came and took Mr. Lee out to talk with him again, on the subject of bearing arms. The latter informed the Colonel that he was a friend to his country, but that he could not kill a man and preserve a good conscience, and that he was willing to do anything while in the army, but fight. Whereupon the Colonel kindly gave him the charge of a baggage-wagon, so that he might be relieved from the necessity of fighting, and then released him from confinement, telling him that he might stand on a bench by the Colonel's tent, and preach. While preaching, many of the officers and soldiers were very much affected, and at the close of the preaching, some of the gentlemen present went about with their hats for the purpose of making a collection of money for the preacher, which Mr. Lee no sooner saw, than he peremptorily requested them to desist, thinking that if the people could afford to sit and hear him, he could afford to stand and preach to them. It was not customary in those days for local preachers to receive any remuneration for their services.

Mr. Lee moved with the army from place to place, improving every opportunity of preaching to the soldiers. After being some months with the army, the Colonel appointed Mr. Lee sergeant of the pioneers, a birth with which he was well suited. After remaining a few weeks longer in the army, the Commanding General gave him an honorable discharge from further service, and he, with a glad heart, took his journey homeward, and soon had the satisfaction of meeting with his friends, from whom he had been separated for three months and a half.

In 1782, Mr. Lee, having attended the Virginia Conference, was appointed in connection with Mr. Drumgoole to form a new circuit. On their way to their appointed field of labor, they stopped at the house of a Quaker, and asked permission to tarry for the night. "If you choose to get down," said the honest Friend, "I will not turn thee away." This blunt reply rather confounded the young itinerant, as not knowing whether he would be welcome or not, but as it was night and no time for ceremony, they dismounted and tried to make themselves as much at home as possible, and they soon found that the Quaker, blunt as he was, was by no means lacking in true benevolence and charity. Before retiring to rest, the guests begged the privilege of attending family prayers. "If you have a mind to pray, I will leave the room," and suiting the action to the words, he retired, and left them to attend to their devotions in their own way. Mr. Lee labored as a travelling preacher during a part of this year, and at the next session of the Conference, was received on trial, and was appointed to Caswell circuit, North Carolina.

The following year (1784), Mr. Lee was appointed to Salisbury circuit, where his labors were greatly blessed to the good of the people. In the month of December, he received an official note, informing him of the arrival of Dr. Coke, and Messrs. Whatcoat and Vasey, and requesting his attendance at Baltimore on the 25th of the same month ; but as he was five hundred miles from the seat of Conference, and had only twelve days' notice, he considered it impossible with his poor state of health, and the unfavorable state of the roads at that season of the year, to attend, so that he remained on his circuit. Soon after the organization of the Church, and the election and consecration of Mr. Asbury to the Superintendency of the Church, Mr. Lee had the privilege of meeting the latter at one of his appointments. Just before the commencement of the service, Bishop Asbury appeared with his black robe, cossack, and band, and as it was a novel sight to see a Methodist arrayed in canonicals, Mr. Lee felt deeply grieved at what he considered an innovation upon the plainness and simplicity of Methodism, and he stoutly opposed the practice. He did not allow his zeal for plainness to destroy his affection for the bishop, but at the request of the latter, became for a time his travelling companion, and accompanied him as far south as Charleston, S. C.

In 1787, Mr. Lee was appointed to Baltimore City circuit, an appointment of great importance, and which he filled with great acceptability and success, preaching not only in the churches and school-houses, but on the commons, in the markets, and wherever he could find a congregation. In the spring of 1788, he visited his native place in Virginia, where a remarkable revival of religion had been in progress for some time. Respecting this revival, Mr. Lee says in his journal: "I surely have cause to bless and praise God, that I came to Virginia this spring to see my old friends. But such a change in any people I never saw.—They told me instances of persons, who were quite careless in the morning, and perhaps laughing at religion, but going to meeting they were cut to the heart, and dropped down as if dead; and after lying awhile, some perhaps for hours, and others not so long, have leaped up and praised God from a sense of his forgiving love; and it has been quite common for Christians, when they have been much comforted, to praise God aloud; and while in an ecstacy of joy, have gone to the wicked and taken hold of them, and exhorted them with tears to seek the Lord. Others have gone to their wicked relations—parents to their children, children to their parents, the husband to the wife, and the wife to the husband, and wept over them and prayed for them till the power of God has laid hold of them, and they have been made subjects of converting grace. So mightily has the Lord blessed the labors of his people in this place."

At the Conference of 1788, Mr. Lee was strongly solicited by Bishop Asbury and others, to receive ordination, but such was his humility and his view of the sacredness and awfulness of the holy office, that he refused to take the same upon him, at least for the time being. He, however, received an appointment to Flanders circuit, where he labored with untiring perseverance for the upbuilding of Messiah's kingdom.

But we must now introduce Mr. Lee to a new field of labor, where he is destined to plant the banners of Methodism on the soil of the pilgrims, and to carry, what appeared to many in that day to be a new gospel, among the staid inhabitants of New England; a work which has gained for Jesse Lee the by no means inappropriate appellation of Apostle of New England Methodism. In 1789, Mr. Lee attended the Conference in New York city, and received an appointment to Stamford circuit, in the State of Connecticut. The circumstances which led to his appointment as a Methodist preacher among the New Englanders, appear to have been providential. As early as 1785, Mr. Lee, while travelling with Bishop Asbury to Charleston, S. C.,* had occasion to call on a merchant by the way, whose clerk was a native of New England. Mr. Lee learned much from this young man in relation to the religious condition of his native land, and instantly entertained a desire to go and preach the doctrines of a free and full salvation to that people, and the desire thus begotten in his mind continued for the term of four years, until at length he was gratified by an appointment among them.

At the period now referred to, there were no less than two hundred Methodist travelling preachers, and forty-three thousand Methodist members in the United States; and yet strange to tell, there was not a single Methodist preacher, nor a single Methodist Society in all New England! It is true, that Rev. Mr. Black, a Wesleyan preacher, and Rev. Cornelius Cook, had preached in different parts of New England, but without having been stationed there by the authority of the Conference. The reason for this apparent neglect of the Methodists to cultivate this ground hitherto, may be found in the fact that New England was well supplied with preaching, and with preachers. Indeed, Congregationalism was both established and supported by law, although at the time of which we speak, it is an admitted fact, that the Churches of New England had in a great measure lost the life and power of godliness, and many of them had fallen into the meshes of cold-hearted Socinianism, with an evident leaning toward Rationalism. Another reason may be found in the fact, that the religious sentiments of the people of New England were so perfectly antagonistic to the principles and doctrines of Methodism, that the advocates and promulgators of the latter were looked upon as the worst kind of heretics;

* Mr. Stevens, in his "Memorials of Methodism," says this transpired in 1775; but this is evidently an error, as Mr. Asbury was not ordained till 1784.

and hence, notwithstanding the acknowledged lukewarmness and heterodoxy of many of the New England Churches, no friendly voice was ever heard saying to the followers of Wesley, "Come over and help us."

It was under these circumstances that Jesse Lee was commissioned to unfurl the banners of Methodism within the strongholds of bigotry and dead formality; and on the 11th of June, he set foot upon the soil of Connecticut. His first sermon was preached in the town of Norwalk, where he found a few who were willing to inquire, "whether these things were so," of which he had spoken. As the circumstances connected with this, his first sermon in New England are interesting, we will quote his own words: "June 17th, at 4 o'clock, I arrived in Norwalk, and went to one Mr. Rogers, where one of our friends had asked the liberty for me to preach. When I came, Mrs. R. told me her husband was from home, and was not willing for me to preach in his house. I told her we would hold meeting in the road, rather than give any uneasiness. We proposed speaking in an old house that stood just by, but she was not willing. I then spoke to an old lady about speaking in her orchard, but she would not consent, but said we would tread the grass down. So the other friend went and gave notice to some of the people, and they soon began to collect, and we went to the road where we had an apple-tree to shade us. When the woman saw that I was determined to preach, she said I might preach in the old house, but I told her it would be better to remain where we were. So I began on the side of the road, with about twenty hearers. After singing and prayer, I preached on John iii. 7, '*Ye must be born again.*' I felt happy that we were favored with so comfortable a place. Most part of the congregation paid particular attention to what I said, and two or three women seemed to hang down their heads as if they understood something of the New Birth.

After preaching, I told the people that I intended to be with them again in two weeks, and if any of them would open their houses to receive me, I should be glad, and if they were not willing, we would meet at the same place; some of them came and desired that I should meet at the town-house the next time; so I gave consent. Who knows but I shall yet have a place in this town where I may lay my head?

"Thursday, 18th, I rode about sixteen miles to Fairfield, and put up at Mr. Penfield's tavern, near the court-house, and soon told who I was, and what was my errand; the woman of the house asked me a few questions, and in a little time wished to know if I had a liberal education. I told her I had just education enough to carry me through the country. I got a man to go with me to see the two principal men of the town, in order to get permission to preach in the court-house; the first said he had no objection, the other said he was very willing. However, he asked me if I had a liberal education. I told him I had nothing to boast of, though I had education enough to carry me through the country; then I went to the court-house, and desired the schoolmaster to send word by his scholars that I was to preach at six o'clock; he said he would, but did not think that many would attend. I waited till after the time, and no one came; at last I went and opened the door and sat down. At length the schoolmaster and three or four women came; I began to sing, and in a little time thirty or forty collected; then I preached on Rom. vi. 23. I felt a good deal of satisfaction in speaking. My soul was happy in the Lord; and I could not but bless God that he gave me to feel for the souls of those that heard me. The people were very solemn toward the end of the sermon, and several of them afterward expressed, in my hearing, their great satisfaction in hearing the discourse. After Mrs. Penfield came back to the tavern, she pressed me much to call the next day, and preach at her sister's, who, she said, was much engaged in religion, and would be much pleased with my manner of preaching. This appeared to me to be an opening of the Lord: so I told her I would. I stayed all night, and prayed with the family, who were very kind, and would not charge me anything, but asked me to call again."

Mr. Lee had now fully opened his mission in New England, and he continued going from place to place, preaching the gospel of peace to the inhabitants of those lands. On the 4th of July we find him at Stratford, Conn., where he put up at a tavern, and then went to the man who kept the key of the town-house, and obtained his consent to preach therein. The man told him he did not know much about the Methodists, they might be like the New-Lights. Mr. Lee in reply, said he did not know much about the New-Lights, but some people thought that the Methodists resembled them in their preaching. "Well," said the man, "if you are like them, I would not wish to have anything to do with you." Mr. Lee inquired what objections he had to the New-Lights. "Why," replied the man, "they went on like madmen; there was one Davenport that would preach, and hollo, and beat the pulpit with both hands, and cry out 'Come away, come away to the Lord Jesus Christ. Why don't you come to the Lord?' till he would foam at the mouth, and sometimes continued it, till the congregation would be praying in companies about the house." "For my part," said Mr. Lee, "I wished that the like work was among the people again." Mr. Lee accordingly preached in the town-house, and was hospitably entertained by the people.

During the summer and autumn of 1789, Mr. Lee visited a large number of places in Connecticut and Rhode Island, and the snows and frosts of a New England winter did not deter him from discharging the duties of his mission. Under date of February 6th, 1790, Mr. Lee states: "I rode to Putney. After meeting, an old man came and spoke to me, and asked me why I did not go into the back settlements and preach to the people that were not favored with the Gospel as they were in Putney; I told him my call was to sinners, and that I found many of them wherever I went. I then asked him if all the people in the neighborhood were converted? He said they had the means; I asked him if any of them (the standing order I suppose is meant) preached in Putney? He said no; but they preached near enough for all to go and hear. I told him he put me in mind of the dog in the manger, who would not eat the hay himself, nor suffer the ox to eat it; they would not come to the place to preach, and were not willing that I should; at which many present could not refrain from laughing heartily. He said, 'a busybody about other men's matters,' according to the original, was one that preached in another's parish without his consent. I told him the words might be well applied to him in *meddling* himself with my preaching. He still insisted on the necessity of my going where there was no regular preaching, and where the people were suffering for want of it. I told him if he thought that some one ought to go to the new settled parts of the country, that he was the very man to go. He said he was too old; I replied, that a person was never too old to do good. We then parted, and he bid me adieu. When I came away, I asked what old gentleman that was; they told me that it was Mr. Birdseye—a worn-out priest, that preaches once in a while, and was but little admired among the people. I wist not that he was a priest, and no wonder that the people laughed when I compared him to the dog in the manger."

During the spring of 1790, Mr. Lee visited different parts of Massachusetts, Vermont, and New Hampshire; and in the following summer directed his course to the city of Boston, praying that in this place he might have some fruit also. The following account of his introducing the Gospel as preached by him and his co-laborers, taken from "Steven's Memorials," will, no doubt, be interesting to the reader. "In the centre of Boston Common still stands a gigantic elm—the crowning ornament of its beautiful scenery. On a fine summer afternoon in July, 1790, a man of middle age, of a serene but shrewd countenance, and dressed in a style of simplicity which might have been taken for the guise of a Quaker, took his stand upon a table beneath the branches of that venerable tree. Four persons approached, and gazed upon him with surprise, while he sung a hymn. It was sung by his solitary voice; at its conclusion he knelt down upon the table, and stretching forth his hands, prayed with a fervor and unction, so unwonted in the cool and minute petitions of the Puritan pulpits, that it attracted the groups of promenaders who had come to spend an evening hour in the shady walks, and by the time he rose from his knees, they were streaming in processions from the different points of the Common toward him. While he opened his small Bible and preached to them without 'notes,' but with the demonstration of the Spirit and of power, the multitude grew into a dense mass, three thousand strong, eagerly catching every utterance of the singular stranger, and some of them receiving his message into 'honest and good hearts.' One who heard him at, or about this time, says: 'When he stood up in the open air and began to sing, I knew not what it meant. I drew near, however, to listen, and thought the prayer was the best I had ever heard. He then read his text, and began, in a sententious manner, to address his remarks to the understanding and consciences of the people; and I thought all who were present must be constrained to say, 'It is good for us to be here.' All the while the people were gathering, he continued this mode of address, and presented us with such a variety of beautiful images, that I thought he must have been at infinite pains to crowd so many pretty things into his memory. But when he entered upon the subject matter of his text, it was with such an easy, natural flow of expression, and in such a tone of voice, that I could not refrain from weeping; and many others were affected in the same way. When he was done, and we had an opportunity of expressing our views to each other, it was agreed that such a man had not visited New England since the days of Whitefield. I heard him again, and thought I could follow him to the ends of the earth.'"

It is proper to remark, that before preaching on the Common, he had endeavored to find some house where he might deliver his message, but he conld get none to encourage him in his endeavors to do so; none would put themselves to the trouble of finding a place for him, and knowing that the Common was the only spot where he could find a pulpit, he repaired there, as above graphically described. On the following day he left Boston, and passing through Salem where he preached, he went to Newbury-port, and called on Mr. Murray, the Presbyterian minister of the place. When Mr. Murray found that he belonged to Mr. Wesley's party—in distinction from the Whitefieldian Methodists—he very politely offered to treat Mr. Lee as a gentleman, and as a Christian, but not as a preacher, assigning as a reason that he had recently been informed by letter that a preacher of the Wesleyan party, had lately been up the Connecticut River, and had held meetings in four different places in one day. Mr. Lee candidly acknowledged that he was the guilty man; and as he could not secure Mr. Murray's pulpit, he was thankful at having the privilege of preaching in the court-house.

After making a short tour to New Hampshire and other places, he returned to Boston, where he not only preached on the Common, but in a private house, and also in a Baptist Church, and on the next Sabbath preached again on the Common, to a congregation of five thousand people. He thus pursued his way from place to place, preaching day and night wherever he found an opening, so that during this Conference year he travelled several thousand miles, visited six States, and the greater part of the large towns, and villages of New England. In reference to these labors he says: "In most places I have met with a much kinder reception than I could have expected, among persons holding principles so different from mine: but yet I have been much opposed and have been under the disagreeable necessity of spending much of my time in talking on controverted points, sometimes in public and ofttimes in private. When I was opposed, if I discovered an inclination to wave the discourse, they would immediately conclude that my principles were so bad, that I was afraid to let them be known; and if I were silent, it would all go for truth. For these reasons I have been led to debate the matter with the principal part of those who have spoken to me with a calm spirit."

Mr. Lee attended the Conference of 1790, in New York, and was appointed to Boston, as his field of labor for the ensuing year. He also consented to receive ordination, and was privately ordained deacon, by Bishop Asbury, and on the day following, was publicly ordained elder. After the adjournment of Conference, he proceeded immediately to his appointed field of labor, and arrived on Saturday the 13th of November. Not being able to secure a place wherein to preach the next day, he went to hear a Universalist but was not much edified. During the next week he had great and heavy trials. He took much pains to get a house to preach in, but all in vain. A few friends also tried, but with no better success. As the weather was cold and wet, the Common was out of the question; but Sabbath after Sabbath, and week after week passed away, and Mr. Lee found no place wherein to invite a congregation. On the 30th of November, a gentleman went with him to the High Sheriff, for the purpose of obtaining the use of the court-house. The latter informed him, that the clerk of the Court had the disposing of the house, and that he must apply to him. So they went to the clerk, but he very abruptly refused, and after hearing him talk awhile, Mr. Lee left him, more discouraged than ever. On the following Thursday, a friend went to, and told him that he had used every possible means to get a particular school-house for him to preach in, but had at last received a positive denial. Being thus shut out of the metropolis of New England, he on the 13th of December, left the city and went to Lynn, about twelve miles distant, where he was hospitably received, and where he spent about a week in preaching, visiting, &c., and where he felt greatly encouraged. He then returned to Boston, where everything appeared as dark and forbidding as before. He was obliged to get a new boarding-place, and when he had settled his bill for former board, he had but two shillings and a penny (34 cents) left, and this he would not have had, if a person a few days previously, had not purchased a pamphlet that he kept for his own use, and in this manner enabled him to discharge his bill. As it was, Mr. Lee felt thankful that he had the means to discharge his pecuniary obligations, and said, "If I can always have two shillings by me, beside paying all I owe, I think I shall be satisfied."

Notwithstanding all these discouragements, Mr. Lee lingered around Boston until he had an opportunity of delivering his message in a private house, and his word took effect on the hearts of some, who were brought to feel the force of divine truth. From the relation of the above facts, the reader may judge of the impediments and obstacles that were placed in the way of the introduction of Methodism into New England, and especially into the city of Boston, which has since become so famous for its Methodist Churches and congregations, and where in the year 1852, the General Conference of the Methodist Episcopal Church is destined to hold its quadrennial session. What a change has thus been wrought by the mighty power of God! The remainder of this Conference year Mr. Lee spent in Boston, Lynn, Marblehead, and various other places.

At the Conference of 1791, Mr. Lee was appointed presiding elder of the New England district, and that the reader may judge of the success of his former labors in this rather unpromising field, it is proper to observe that his district embraced *six circuits*, with *eleven circuit preachers*, all raised principally through the labors of this indomitable pioneer. During this year he travelled many hundreds of miles, preached three hundred and twenty-one sermons, gave twenty-four public exhortations, and read twenty-one authors, comprising over five thousand pages, besides his daily Bible reading!

At the Conference of 1792, he was appointed presiding elder over a small district, comprising only four circuits, another elder having been appointed to a portion of his former extensive charge; and such had been the growth of Methodism in New England since the time of Mr. Lee's first visit, that in 1793, an annual Conference was held in Lynn on the first of August. At this latter Conference, the subject of this chapter was appointed to the Province of Maine, a place at that period very far removed from the influences of Methodism, there being no circuit formed nearer to it than two hundred miles distant. It was also nearly destitute of the ministry of other churches, the country being new and very sparsely populated, and the most of the inhabitants being comparatively poor. This appointment would no doubt have been somewhat trying to the faith and patience of some ex-presiding elders, but Jesse Lee had a willing heart to go to any place where souls stood in need of salvation. So bidding adieu to his warm-hearted Methodist brethren in Lynn, he commenced his lonely journey for that distant field. The people generally received him gladly, and he was instrumental during the year, in doing much good in different portions of the province. At the next Conference, he was appointed to New Hampshire district, where he also labored efficiently and successfully, and on the 21st of June, 1794, had the satisfaction of preaching a dedication sermon in a new church, in Readfield, being the first Methodist Church in the Province of Maine.

A few weeks later, Mr. Lee had the still greater satisfaction of laying the corner-stone of the first Methodist Church in the city of Boston. A small Society had been formed here in 1790, and for five years Mr. Lee had been endeavoring to promote its interests and to erect, if possible, a place of worship; at length, on the 8th of August, the few brethren ventured to begin the important enterprise, and the corner-stone was laid by Mr. Lee with all due solemnities. Mr. Lee at this time remained several weeks in the city, and although the Methodists were now in possession of a "hired house," wherein to worship, yet as it would accommodate comparatively but few hearers, resorted again to the Common. Having thus "set things in order" in Boston, he again set out to superintend the interests of his extensive district. In Provincetown, he stopped and preached twice for the encouragement of the Society. In this place, the little band of Methodists had resolved to build a church, to prevent which, a town-meeting had been called, which voted that the Methodists should not be allowed to have a house of worship in that town! Notwithstanding the decree of the town, the Society resolved to proceed in the erection of the building. Accordingly, the materials were collected, but a company of daring spirits, led on by the chief men in the town, went one night and removed the materials to another place, constructed the effigy of a Methodist, and tarred and feathered it. Mr. Lee went to see the ruins, and felt confident that God would yet "cause the wrath of man to praise him" in that town.

For several years Mr. Lee filled the important office of presiding elder in the Eastern States, and in 1797 was appointed by Bishop Asbury to preside over the deliberations of the New England Conference, at its session in Wilbraham, Mass., the latter being unable to attend on account of indisposition. The bishop also required him, after Conference, to proceed on a tour to Georgia, Kentucky, and other southern States, for the purpose of assisting him in his episcopal duties, which directions Mr. Lee cheerfully obeyed; and at the General Conference of 1797, was requested by that body to fill Bishop Asbury's appointments until the next spring. After completing this tour, he returned again to the north, attended several Conferences with Bishop Asbury, and then proceeded southward again, and thus he continued for several years to be the travelling companion and assistant of the venerable bishop.

At the General Conference of 1800, it became necessary to elect an additional bishop, especially as Dr. Coke would be absent from Europe but a short time, at any given period, and as Bishop Asbury had become quite infirm by age and severe trial. When the election was made, there were but two candidates in the field, Messrs. Whatcoat and Lee (see life of Bishop Whatcoat), and although all other circumstances being equal, Mr. Lee would no doubt have been the choice of a large majority of the preachers, yet in obedience to the formerly expressed wishes of Mr. Wesley, and in deference to the age and experience of Mr. Whatcoat, the latter by a few votes in the majority was duly elected Bishop of the Church. From intimations given by Bishop Asbury to Mr. Lee, the latter inferred that the preachers would generally vote for him, in case an additional bishop was made; and as there appeared to be considerable spirit among Mr. Whatcoat's friends in relation to the matter, and a few words dropped prejudicial to the claims and qualifications of Mr.

Lee, the latter felt deeply disappointed at the result, and no doubt was wounded somewhat in his feelings. What added to this honest grief, was a report which had been circulated by some person unknown, to prevent his election, to the effect that Bishop Asbury had said that brother Lee had imposed on him and on the connection for a length of time, and that the bishop "would have got rid of him long ago, if he could." When this report reached Mr. Lee's ears, he went directly to Bishop Asbury, who, according to the expectation of Mr. Lee, at once contradicted the false statement, and expressed an earnest desire that Mr. Lee should continue to act as his assistant, and as soon as possible, the worthy bishop made the same statement in open Conference. Thus it is, that the best of men are made the subjects of calumny and reproach, and thus Mr. Lee lost an election to the highest office in the Church, to which he was justly entitled, and which no doubt would have been awarded him, had it not been for the above false report. We are not, however, to infer that Mr. Lee "desired the office of a bishop" merely for the sake of the honor which such an office would confer upon him. From the known humility of the man, and his perfect antipathy to everything like worldly display, such a conclusion would at once be unreasonable and absurd. If he was ambitious in this respect, it was such an ambition as aimed solely at the good of the Church, and the salvation of mankind; and if disappointed in his expectations, it was a disappointment arising from a mistaken view of the feelings of the preachers towards him. Mr. Lee had many warm friends among the preachers; he knew not that he had any enemies; nor had he just reason to conclude that those who voted for the successful candidate were such, nor that in preferring another candidate, they lacked confidence in his piety, integrity, or ability.

Although disappointed, however, for the moment, he did not allow his personal feelings to dampen his ardor in the cause of his Divine Master. Indeed we may infer that his chagrin was but momentary, as in his journal he states, "We never had as good a General Conference before; we had the greatest speaking, and the greatest union of affections that we had ever had on a like occasion." A few days after the adjournment of the General Conference, Bishops Asbury and Whatcoat appointed Mr. Lee to act as an assistant to the bishops at the yearly Conferences, and informing him that he was at liberty to make his own appointments, South or East, as might suit his convenience. He, however, preferred taking a single circuit, and after having made a tour through the New England States, he went to New York city, where he labored and preached until the next spring, when he returned to Virginia, and was appointed presiding elder of the South District, and for several years in succession, he filled several important places in the southern section of the work.

In 1808, he once more visited the northern Conferences, and while in Newport, Rhode Island, he, for the first time in his life, heard the bell in a Methodist Church ring to call the people to meeting; he took no exceptions to the bell, but he warmly protests against the square pews in the church, by which a portion of the congregation were obliged to sit with their backs toward the preacher. He also objected to the sale of the pews, and the promiscuous sitting of men and women together, but notwithstanding these prejudices, he preached and found that God could bless his word, even in a pewed church! He then went to Boston, where the Methodists had erected a large church in addition to the old one. He preached in both, but felt the most freedom in the "old meeting-house," and although the new one was large and elegant, he did not like it because it was pewed. After having visited his old friends in New England, in different places, and having rejoiced, wept, and prayed with them, and preached to them, he again turned his course toward the South.

In 1809, Mr. Lee published a History of the Methodists in America, and thus had the honor of being the first Methodist historian on this side of the Atlantic. Being in the vicinity of Washington, D. C., superintending the publication of this work, he was elected Chaplain of the House of Representatives, a post which he filled with credit to himself and the Church of which he was a minister, and with great acceptability to the members of Congress, as may be inferred from the fact of his re-election to the same office at the next session of that honorable body, and also at the sessions of 1811, 1812, and 1813. In 1814 he was chosen Chaplain of the Senate, which post he also filled with distinguished honor. But, although thus repeatedly called to officiate to the nation's representatives, Mr. Lee never forgot that he was a Methodist preacher, and hence in the interims of the sessions of Congress, he filled such places as were assigned him by the authorities of the Church, his last appointment being at Annapolis, the capital of Maryland.

In August, 1816, Mr. Lee attended a camp-meeting on the eastern shore of Maryland, where he preached twice, the text for the latter sermon being 2 Peter iii. 18, "*But grow in grace.*" He preached a most fervid and glowing discourse, which proved to be his last one, as in the evening of the same day he was seized with a severe chill, which gave place to fever. On the following day he was removed to Hillsboro', where he was received into the house of a Mr. Sellers, where he lingered until the 12th of the following month. On the day before his death, his soul was so overwhelmed with the love of God, that he was constrained to cry out, "Glory! glory! glory! hallelujah! Jesus reigns!" Almost his last words were, "Give my respects to Bishop M'Kendree, and tell him that I die in love with all the preachers; that I love him, and that he lives in my heart," and on the 12th day of September, 1816, Jesse Lee's triumphant spirit

"Passed through the crystal ports of light,
And seized eternal youth."

He died in the fifty-ninth year of his age, and thirty-sixth of his itinerant ministry, beloved and regretted by a large circle of friends in all parts of the American continent.

A few observations on the character of Mr. Lee, will close this chapter. From the incidents already related in the life and labors of Mr. Lee, none can doubt his piety, or the deep and fervent desire which he possessed to glorify God, and benefit his fellow-men. On no other principle can we account for his multifarious labors, and self-denying efforts to do good. As we have seen, he obtained a clear evidence of his acceptance with God, and the love of God and of man was the ruling passion of his after-life.

As a preacher, Mr. Lee was far above mediocrity; for fervency and zeal in his pulpit efforts, he probably had no superior in those days of primitive simplicity and fervor; and in addition to his zeal, he possessed the happy art of clothing his thoughts in rich and appropriate language. But what gave him the greatest success as a preacher was the manifest sincerity of the man, combined with a soul full of pathos and tenderness which frequently displayed itself through flowing tears, which by the sympathy of our nature would as frequently produce an impression on the hearts, and draw tears from the eyes of others. In this respect if in no other, he was one of nature's orators, a preacher whose chief characteristic was the power of eloquence which pleased not so much the ear, as it affected and subdued the heart.

To profound learning, Mr. Lee never laid any claim; as he frequently said, *he had just education enough to carry him through the world.* We are not, however, to understand that he was an ignorant man in the common acceptation of the term. A person who was familiar with the doctrines and precepts of the word of God, as was the subject of our sketch, cannot be an ignorant man. One who has travelled as much, preached as frequently, and observed men and actions as long as did Jesse Lee, cannot in the nature of things be a mere ignoramus; true, he might not have had that knowledge of the classics which would no doubt have made him still more extensively useful and brilliant as a minister of the Gospel, but he did possess that knowledge, without which all other acquirements are vain—a knowledge of sin forgiven, and of the way and plan of salvation. But in addition to this, he had a respectable amount of knowledge as it relates to the more common branches of science. Of this fact his published works afford abundant evidence; and the fact also that he was chosen for six successive sessions of Congress to the important and dignified station of Chaplain, proves that he was not a mere novice, or destitute of the necessary qualifications for a minister of Jesus Christ.

It is proper to look at him also, in another aspect—as the pioneer of New England Methodism—and it is in this relation, that he sustained to the revival of religion in the Eastern States, under the instrumentality of Methodist doctrines, and Methodist preachers, that Jesse Lee appears in all his moral grandeur and true greatness. In these northern regions, far from friends and home, he single-handed wages war with the religious formality and bigotry of the New England Churches, and it is greatly owing to his indefatigable labors and indomitable perseverance, that the Eastern States are indebted, not only for what of Methodism they now possess, but in a great measure for that spiritual Christianity which now dwells so largely in the bosom of other evangelical Churches in New England; and we cannot repress the utterance of our thoughts when we say it is our candid belief, that had Jesse Lee visited those States a half-century sooner than he did, there would at the time of his actual labors among that people, have been less formality, less Unitarianism, less latent infidelity; and had his labors been bestowed a half-century *later*, instead of what we now find of genuine piety, and orthodoxy of sentiment, a dark cloud of skepticism, and Unitarian rationalism, with a much larger *quantum* of Universalism, would have brooded over the rocky shores of New England. Jesse Lee, like the apocalyptic angel, flying from town to town, and from State to State, preaching the doctrines of repentance and faith, was in an important sense the apostle of New England. But here our reflections must end.

CHAPTER XII.

REV. BENJAMIN ABBOTT.

Benjamin Abbott was born on Long Island, N. Y., in the year 1732. But little is known in regard to his early life, as he did not embrace the religion of the Saviour, until he was forty years of age. His father dying while Benjamin was a lad, and having made provision in his will, that his sons should be put out to learn trades, the subject of this chapter was indented as an apprentice to a hatter, in Philadelphia, where he soon fell into bad company, and became addicted to card-playing, cock-fighting, and many other evil practices. Leaving his master before the expiration of his apprenticeship, he went to New Jersey, and labored on a farm with one of his brothers. Soon after this he married, but the domestic relation, instead of having the effect of drawing him into the paths of virtue, only seemed to rekindle the desire for vicious indulgence. So that he continued to live in rebellion against God, drinking, fighting, swearing, gambling, and attending fairs and other places of public resort, for the purpose of meeting with those of his own disposition, and sinful habits. In a word, he was what even the world would call, a *very wicked man*, and the only redeeming trait in his character at that time, appears to have been a disposition to treat his family kindly, and provide for them comfortably, a trait not often found in the case of the hardened inebriate.

Yet during this wild career of wickedness and sin, Abbott

was not without a respect for religion. He even attended church, and professed to be a Presbyterian in sentiment, and was often convicted of his sins and wickedness, by the Spirit of God which spoke in thunder tones to his guilty conscience, and alarmed him of his danger and his doom. Often did he make promises of amendment, and as often did he forget to fulfil them. When he was about thirty-three years of age, he had a dream of being carried to hell, where the devils put him into a vice, and tormented him till his body was all covered with blood: he was then hurried into another apartment, where he was pierced by the stings of scorpions, and as fast as he would pull one out, another would strike him; he was next introduced to a lake of fire, into which the devils were throwing the souls of men and women. Two regiments of devils were moving through the chambers of the damned, blowing up the flames, and when it came his turn to be thrown in, one devil took him by the head, another by the feet, and while in the act of throwing him in, he awoke, and found it was a dream. We make mention of this dream not because of its singularity, but as a specimen of the horrors which haunt the pillow of the wretched inebriate. The effect of such terrible and awful visions of the night,—which appeared as realities to him,—was such, that he would promise solemnly to amend his ways; but, alas, poor man, he had not as yet learned the necessity of seeking divine aid in so doing; thus he lived until he was forty years of age, a miserable sinner, being "without hope, and without God in the world," tormented by day and by night, and yet in his ignorance, not knowing precisely how to escape from his apparently hopeless condition.

One Sabbath-day his wife attended a Methodist meeting, a few miles distant from their place of residence. On her return, Abbott asked her how she liked the preacher. She answered that he was as great a preacher as she ever heard in her life, and persuaded her husband to go and hear for himself. Accordingly, on the next Sabbath, Mr. Abbott went and heard a sermon from the text, "*Come unto me all ye that labor, and are heavy laden, and I will give you rest.*" Says Mr. Abbott in relation to the services, "The preacher was much engaged, and the people were crying all through the house; this greatly surprised me, for I never had seen the like before. The sermon made no impression on me; but when he came to the application, he said, 'It may be, that some of you may think that there is neither God, nor devils, nor hell, only a guilty conscience; and indeed, my friends, that is bad enough. But I assure you that there is both heaven and hell, God and devils.'" Mr. Abbott now remembered his dreams, and his misspent life, and all his sins were brought vividly before his mind, and he returned home under the influence of deep conviction, but still was ignorant of the way of salvation.

Soon after this, the preacher went to preach in the neighborhood where Mr. Abbott resided, and as Methodist preaching was a new thing, many went out to hear him; he preached with power, and the word took such hold of Mr. Abbott, that it "shook every joint in his body," and he cried aloud for mercy. When the sermon was ended, the people flocked around the preacher and began to dispute on doctrines; as for Abbott, they said he was going mad. He returned home in great distress of mind, and having been brought up under the teachings of Calvinism, and believing in the doctrines of election and reprobation, he concluded that he was a reprobate, and that he must be damned, do what he would. From this time onward, his burden of sin increased, and he was tempted to commit suicide, and no doubt would have done so, had it not been for the reflection that the torment of the damned is still more insupportable than the upbraiding of a guilty conscience; at length, after suffering the most intense anguish of spirit, and having been properly instructed in relation to the way of salvation by faith, he ventured his all on Jesus Christ, and found rest to his soul on the 12th day of October, 1772. "My heart," he says, "felt as light as a bird, being relieved of that load of guilt which before had bowed down my spirits, and my body felt as active as when I was eighteen, so that the outward and inward man were both animated." "I arose and called up the family, and took down the Testament, and the first place I opened to, was the ninth chapter of Acts, where Saul breathed out threatenings and slaughter against the Church or disciples of the Lord, and if I had had a congregation I could have preached, but having none but my own family, I expounded the chapter and exhorted them, and then sang and prayed. After breakfast, I told my wife that I must go and tell the neighbors what the Lord had done for my soul. The first place I went to, the man and his wife were both professors of religion and members of the Baptist Church; I expected they knew what these things were, and would rejoice with me; but to my great surprise, when I related my experience, and told what God had done for my soul, it appeared as strange to them as if I had claimed possession of Old England, and called it all my own. I then set out to Jacob Elwell's mill, about two miles off, where I expected to meet with divers persons, and to have an opportunity to exhort them, and tell them what I had found. On my way there, I exhorted all I met with to turn to God. When I got to the mill, while I was telling them my experience, and exhorting them to flee from the wrath to come, some laughed, and others cried, and some thought I had gone distracted. Before night, a report was spread all through the neighborhood that I was raving mad; at evening I returned home, and asked my wife about her conviction and conversion, expecting, as she professed religion, that she knew what heart religion was; but to my astonishment, I found she never had experienced a change of heart. She had been awakened when young, under a sermon of Mr. Hunter, a Presbyterian minister, which brought her to prayer, but in progress of time it wore off again. About seven years after that, as a brother of hers was sitting under a fence, watching for deer, another man who was also hunting, about sunset, seeing his head through the fence, and taking it to be a fox, shot and killed him; this unfortunate affair gave her another alarm, which brought her again to prayer; but this also wore off in a short time, and she lived in neglect of that duty until after we were married and had three children; at which time the measles came into the family, and under her afflictions and distress, she covenanted with God to be more religious: from which time she became a praying woman, and joined the Presbyterian Church, and was looked upon as a very religious person, although she rested short of conversion, and remained a stranger to the new birth. I told her that she had no religion, and was nothing more than a strict Pharisee; this gave her displeasure, and she asked me if none had religion but those who knew it? I told her no, not one; for all who had it, must know it.* Next day she went to her minister, to know what he thought of it. He told her she was right, for people might be good Christians and know nothing about what I insisted on; and advised her not to mind me, for I was expecting to be saved by my works. This gave her a momentary satisfaction, and home she came quite strong, and attacked me, and related what her minister had said;

* The author feels it his duty to dissent from the doctrine here taught. He believes that every child of God *may* know that his sins are forgiven; but he is also convinced that some may be the children of God, and through the influence of improper religious instruction, may not have so "full an assurance of faith" as to be able conscientiously to say, that they know they are converted.

she also brought a book which he had sent me, entitled Bellamey's New Divinity, in which he insisted upon conversion before conviction, and faith before repentance. I read it about half through, and found him a rigid predestinarian. His doctrine of decrees, and unconditional election, and reprobation, so confused my mind, that I threw it by, determined to read no more in it, as my own experience clearly proved to me that the doctrines it contained were false. Next day, my wife carried the book back. I desired her to tell the minister from me, that it was full of lies, which Scripture and experience both proved. He sent for me to come and see him; accordingly, the day following I went and dined with him; after dinner, he requested all the family to withdraw from the dining-room; they did so, and he and I were left alone. He then told me he understood that God had done great things for me; whereupon, I related my conviction and my conversion; he paid a strict attention until I had done, and then told me that I was under strong delusions of the devil. He got a book out of his library for me to read; as he handed it to me, the Lord showed me by the voice of his Spirit that the book was not fit for me. However, I disobeyed the Divine impression, and took it at the minister's request; I returned home and felt a temptation to doubt, and called to mind my various sins, but none of them condemned me. I then thought upon a particular sin, which I concluded would condemn me; but in a moment I felt an evidence that that sin was forgiven as though separate from all the rest that ever I had committed; but recollecting the minister had told me 'I was under strong delusions of the devil,' it was suggested to my mind, it may be he is right; I went a little out of the road and kneeled down, and prayed to God if I was deceived to undeceive me, and the Lord said to me, 'Why do you doubt? Is not Christ all-sufficient? Is he not able? Have you not felt his blood applied?' I then sprang upon my feet and cried out, Not all the devils in hell, nor all the predestinarians on earth, shall make me doubt; for I knew that I was converted: at that instant I was filled with unspeakable raptures of joy."

We have given these lengthy extracts for the purpose of showing the exercises of Mr. Abbott's mind, after having obtained the "adoption of a son," and for the purpose of showing the power of grace in "converting such a sinner from the errors of his ways." Having at length gained the victory over his doubts and temptations, in reference to his being truly converted, the next important question to be decided by him, was in relation to the Church he should join. He accordingly commenced reading the different Confessions of Faith, Articles of Religion, &c., of the various Churches, and then read the Bible from beginning to end, with reference to the same subject. His natural feelings would have prompted him to join some other Church than the Methodists, but after delaying the matter for some six months after his conversion, and while one day meditating prayerfully upon the subject, he exclaimed, "*I am a Methodist! I am a Methodist!*" He then returned home resolving to be such, although he knew that persecution and reproach would be poured upon him from every quarter. In a few days after, he joined the Methodists, and his wife being happily converted to God, she united with them also, and in the course of three months after his wife's conversion, six of their children were also converted to God; a small class was formed in the neighborhood, and Mr. Abbott was appointed Leader.

One day being invited to dine at the house of a friend, Mr. Abbott on sitting down to the table proposed asking a blessing upon the food; as soon as he began, two workmen present began to laugh. This was too much for Abbott to endure in silence; he consequently rose and began to exhort them in a very rough manner, thundering out hell and damnation against them, with tears in his eyes. This broke up the dinner, and neither of them ate anything at that time.

Mr. Abbott soon became a man "full of faith and the Holy Ghost," and his neighbors when sick, would send for "Old Abbott," to pray with them; and soon he received an impression, that it was his duty to preach the Gospel; and as in those days, there was not that degree of formality observed, as at the present day, in reference to allowing men to preach who thought themselves called to the work, he appears to have begun preaching before he was called by the voice of the Church, but evidently not before he had received a call from God. His first effort at preaching was on the occasion of a funeral which he had been requested to attend. As soon as it became noised abroad that Mr. Abbott had become a preacher, he received frequent invitations to hold meetings in different neighborhoods. While at one of his appointments the following occurrence took place: Mr. Abbott was preaching with great zeal and power, and in the course of his remarks, said, "'For aught I know, there may be a murderer in this congregation! Immediately a lusty man attempted to go out, but when he got to the door he bawled out, and stretched out both his arms and ran backward, as though some one had been pressing on him to take his life, and he endeavoring to defend himself from the attack, until he got to the far side of the room, and then fell backward against the wall, crying out bitterly, that he was the murderer, for he had killed a man about fifteen years before!" The man lay in great anguish of soul, while Mr. Abbott having recovered himself from his surprise and astonishment, resumed his discourse. The man finally recovered himself, and went away into parts unknown, and was never seen, nor heard from afterwards.

Shortly after the above occurrence, the war of the Revolution commenced, and in some parts of the country, the name *Methodist*, was considered as synonymous with *Tory*. This arose from the imprudence of a few of the English Wesleyan Missionaries, who believing it to be their duty to "fear God and honor the king," were not sufficiently guarded in their expressions in reference to the politics of the day; hence, many of the Methodist preachers and members were looked upon with suspicion, and became the subjects of bitter persecution and reproach. This was the case with Mr. Abbott, who because he was a Methodist, became exposed to the sneers and scoffs of the wicked and profane, who under the pretence of patriotism, aimed a blow at vital Christianity, and godly sincerity; but Mr. Abbott frequently called to mind the words of the Saviour, "The servant is not greater than his Lord," and he resolved to preach and labor for his divine Master even though he should die for it.

On a certain evening after having preached, Mr. Abbott was accosted by a minister who was present, who asked him if he was a Wesleyan. Mr. Abbott replied in the affirmative Then said the minister, "You deny the perseverance of the saints." "God forbid," replied Mr. Abbott, "for none can be saved unless they persevere to the end." "But you believe in the possibility of falling from grace?" Mr. Abbott said yes; on which the minister abruptly gave him the lie; but Mr. Abbott appealed to the testimony of Scripture on this point, and requested the minister to explain a passage in Ezek. iii. 20, 21, but the minister refused. His elder being present, said he ought to explain the passage, but instead of doing so, he became passionate, and said he was brought up at college, and certainly knew about these things, but that Abbott was a fool, and that he could cut such a fellow's throat; then turning to his elder, he said, "If there was a dog's head on your shoulders, I would cut it off: Do not you know the articles of your own church? I will teach you better." Mr. Abbott told him that the curse of God was upon all such watchmen as he was, who did not warn the people against sin. The minister replied, that he could cut such a fellow's throat, and that it made his blood boil to hear the perseverance of the saints denied. Mr. Abbott desired him to explain the passage; but all the reply he received, was: "You are a fool, you know nothing at all. I was brought up at college, and I will have you before your betters."

At another time, in the same town, while he was preaching to a crowded house, a mob of soldiers came rushing in with guns and fixed bayonets, and while the rest surrounded the door, one went up to him and presented his gun, as though he would run him through. While the soldier was piercing with his bayonet, Mr. Abbott kept wielding the "sword of the Spirit"—the word of God, proclaiming the terrors of the law in a loud voice, which finally made the assailant quail before him, and retreat to the door. His comrades tried to urge him back, but he refused to cope any longer with a man who was so evidently armed with the "whole armor of God." Mr. Abbott was then allowed to finish his discourse in peace. At his next appointment there, he found one hundred men under arms. When he began to preach they grounded their arms and listened to him in a quiet and orderly manner. Mr. Abbott, about this time, also was drafted to serve in the militia, but as he could not make it appear right for him to fight with, and kill his fellow-men, he was excused by paying a sum of money sufficient to furnish a substitute.

At one of his appointments, the Lord made bare his arm so that many fell to the floor; their cries were great, and sinners sprang to the doors and windows, and fell one upon another in getting out: five jumped out at a window, one person called out to Mr. Abbott that he was a devil. A young man cried to a magistrate present to command the peace, but the magistrate answered that it was the power of God. Another person, with tears in his eyes, entreated the people to hold their peace, to which an old woman replied, "They cannot hold their peace, unless you cut out their tongues." At another place, shortly after, while he was preaching, a lady fell to the floor; Mr. Abbott asked the people what they thought of it, and if they did not think it was of the devil. "If it is," said he, "when she comes to, she will curse and swear, but if it is of God, she will praise him." When she "came to" she praised the Lord with a loud voice.

Mr. Abbott had the happy art of always being able to give a word of advice in season, which frequently like bread cast upon the waters, was found after many days; an instance of this kind he relates in his autobiography.

"I set out for quarterly meeting, and on my way I stopped to get my horse shod, and went to a house where I found an old woman spinning, and asked her for a drink of water; she gave it to me. I said to her, You have given me drink to refresh my body, I will strive to give you the waters of life, by persuading you to make application to Jesus Christ. After telling her the terrors of the law, and the promises of the Gospel, I asked leave to pray, which she granted. Three years after, as I was on my way to a quarterly meeting, I met with about twenty persons who were on their way to the same meeting. As soon as they saw me, a woman from among them ran to me and said, 'How do you do, my father?' I asked her how she came to know me? She answered, 'I will soon convince you, I have cause to know you: do you not remember asking me for a drink of water, and that you set before me the plan of salvation, and went to prayer with me? You had not been gone half an hour before I expected to be in hell every moment. I cried to God mightily without any intermission, until he set my soul at liberty: therefore, I will call you my spiritual father.'"

While Mr. Abbott was thus instrumental as a Christian of doing good to individuals, he by no means neglected the spiritual welfare of communities; hence we find him urging the people where he occasionally labored to the work of building a house for the Lord. In a place called Penns-Neck, he had for four years tried to prevail upon the inhabitants to erect a church, during which period they were obliged to meet in a grove, when the weather permitted; at length growing weary of their tardiness, he agreed with a carpenter to build one, who went on to the spot at the time appointed. Mr. Abbott told him he had no timber for the building, and therefore he must go begging. He accordingly went to a neighbor and said, "We are going to build a house for God, what will you give towards it?" "Two sticks of timber for sills." He then went to a Quaker widow, and obtained two sticks more. He went to another person, who gave him timber enough to complete the house. He then told others that they must draw the materials, and in four days the latter were all on the spot. In a week more the frame was raised, and in six weeks the job was completed, and Mr. Abbott begged the money to pay the carpenter. The consequence of the erection of this house was the "moralizing and Christianizing" of the whole neighborhood.

The following extracts will no doubt be found interesting by the reader:—"Next day I set out for my appointment, but being a stranger, I stopped at a house to inquire the way, and the man told me he was just going to that place, for there was to be a Methodist preacher there that day; and our preacher, said he, is to be there to trap him in his discourse, and if you will wait a few minutes until a neighbor of mine comes, I will go with you. In a few minutes the man came, who, it seems, was a constable. So we set off, and they soon fell into conversation about the preacher, having no idea of my being the man, as I never wore black, or any kind of garb that indicated my being a preacher, and so I rode unsuspected. The constable being a very profane man, he swore by all the gods he had, good and bad, that he would lose his right arm from his body if the Methodist preacher did not go to jail that day. When we arrived at the place appointed, I saw about two hundred horses hitched. I also hitched mine, and retired into the woods, where I prayed, and covenanted with God, upon my knees, that if he stood by me in this emergency, I would be more for him through grace than ever I had been. I then arose and went to my horse with a perfect resignation to the will of God, whether to death or to jail. I took my saddle-bags and went to the house ; the man took me into a private room, and desired I would preach in favor of the war, as I was in a Presbyterian settlement. I replied I should preach as God should direct me. He appeared very uneasy, and left me, and just before preaching he came in again, and renewed his request, that I would preach up for war ; I replied as before, and then followed him out among the people, where he made proclamation as follows :—Gentlemen, this house is my own, and no gentleman shall be interrupted in my house in time of his discourse, but after he has done you may do as you please. Thank God, said I, softly, that I have liberty once more to warn sinners before I die. I then took my stand, and the house was so crowded no one could sit down. Some hundreds were round about the door. I stood about two or three feet from the constable who had sworn so bitterly. When he saw that I was the man that he had so abused on the way, with so many threats and oaths, his countenance fell, and he turned pale. I gave out a hymn, but no one offered to sing ; I sung four lines, and kneeled down and prayed. When I arose I preached with great liberty. I felt such power from God rest upon me that I was above the fear of either men or devils, not regarding whether death or jail should be my lot. Looking forward, I saw a decent-looking man trembling, and tears flowed in abundance, which I soon discovered was the case with many others. After preaching, I told them I expected they wanted to know by what authority I had come into that country to preach. I then told them my conviction and conversion, the place of my nativity and place of residence; also my call to the ministry, and that seven years I had labored in God's vineyard; that I spent my own money, and found and wore my own clothes, and that it was the love that I had for their precious souls for whom Christ died, that had induced me to come among them at the risk of my life; and then exhorted them to fly to Jesus, the ark of safety—that all things were ready—to seek, and they should find, to knock, and it should be opened unto them. By this time the people were generally melted into tears. I then concluded, and told them on that day two weeks they might expect preaching again. I mounted my horse and set out with a friendly Quaker for a pilot. We had not rode above fifty yards when I heard one hallooing after us. I looked back and saw about fifty running after us. I then concluded that to jail I must go. We stopped, and when they came up, I crave your name, said one—I told him, and so we parted. He was a justice of the peace, and was the person that I had taken notice of in time of preaching, and observed him to be in great anxiety of mind. No one offered me any violence; but they committed the next preacher on that day two weeks, to the common jail."

The following extract, though somewhat lengthy, is both instructing and amusing: "Next day we went to our appointment, where the congregation was chiefly Germans, and a well-behaved people. Here the Lord wrought wonders, divers fell to the floor, and several found peace. I lost both the power of my body and use of my speech, and cried out in a strange manner. The people also cried aloud; here I thought I should frighten them, being in a strange country and among a people of a strange language; but glory to God, it had a contrary effect, for they continued all night in prayer.

"Next morning, I set out with about twenty others for my

appointment, where we found a large congregation. When I came to my application, the power of the Lord came in such a manner, that the people fell all about the house, and their cries might be heard afar off. This alarmed the wicked, who sprang for the doors in such haste, that they fell one over another in heaps. The cry of mourners was so great, I thought to give out a hymn to drown the noise, and desired one of our English friends to raise it, but as soon as he began to sing, the power of the Lord struck him and he pitched under the table, and there lay like a dead man. I gave it out again, and asked another to raise it : as soon as he attempted, he fell also. I then made the third attempt, and the power of God came upon me in such a manner, that I cried out, and was amazed. I then saw that I was fighting against God, and did not attempt to sing again. Mr. Boehm, the owner of the house, and a preacher among the Germans, cried out, 'I never saw God in this way before.' I replied, this is a Pentecost, father. 'Yes, be sure,' said he, clapping his hands, 'a Pentecost, be sure!' Prayer was all through the house, up stairs and down. I desired Mr. Boehm to go to prayer; he did so, and five or six of us did the same. A watchnight having been appointed for that evening, and seeing no prospect of this meeting being over, although it had begun at eleven o'clock, I told Boehm that we had best quietly withdraw from the meeting-house. When we had got out of the door, a young man came out and laid hold on the fence to support himself from falling, and then cried amain for God to have mercy on him. 'To be sure,' said Mr. B., '*I never saw God in this way before.*' We exhorted him to look to God and not to give up the struggle, and God would bless him before he left the place. I took the old gentleman by the arm, and we walked quietly to the house to get some dinner. About five o'clock, a person came from the preaching house, requesting that I would go there immediately, for there was a person dying. We went without delay. I went up stairs, and there lay several about the floor, some crying for mercy, and others praising God. I then went into the preaching-room, and there they lay about the floor in like manner. I then went to see the person said to be dying; she lay gasping. I kneeled down to pray, but it was instantly given me that God had converted her soul, and therefore instead of praying for deliverance, I gave God thanks that he had delivered her, and immediately she arose and praised God for what he had done for her soul."

"We set out with about forty friends, to the next appointment. The people being gathered, after singing and prayer, I began to preach, and God laid to his helping hand; many cried aloud for mercy. One young man being powerfully wrought upon, retired up stairs, and there thumped about upon the floor, so that Mr. B. was afraid that he would be injured in body. '*To be sure*,' said he, '*I never saw God in this way before*.' I told him there was no danger, he was in the hands of a merciful God. In a few minutes after, attempting to come down stairs, he fell from the top to the bottom, and hallooed aloud, 'The devil is in the chamber! the devil is in the chamber!' which greatly alarmed all the people. This brought a great damp over my spirits, for I thought if I had raised the devil, I might as well go home again. However, after a little space, I bid some of the dear people go up stairs and see if the devil was there: several went up to see what the matter was, and there they found a man rolling, groaning, and crying to God for mercy; they returned, and told us how matters stood."

"Next day, at my appointment, we had a crowded house, and the Lord laid to his helping hand; divers fell to the floor, and several cried aloud for mercy. After preaching, an old Presbyterian gentleman attacked me, and told me it was all the work of the devil—that God was a God of order—and this was perfect confusion. Well, said I, if this be the work of the devil, the people, many of whom then lay on the floor as dead men, when they come to, they will curse and swear and rage like devils; but if it be of God, their notes will be changed. Soon after, one of them came to, and he began to praise God with a loud voice; and soon another, and so on, until divers of them bore testimony for Jesus. Hark! hark! said I to my old opponent—brother, do you hear them? this is not the language of hell, but the language of Canaan. I then appointed prayer-meeting at a friend's house, in the neighborhood. After the people had gathered, I saw my old opponent among them. I gave out a hymn, and brother S. went to prayer, and after him myself. I had spoken but a few words, before brother S. fell to the floor, and soon after him every soul in the house, except myself and my old Presbyterian opponent and two others. I arose, and gave an exhortation, and the two men fell—one as if he had been shot; and then there was every soul down in the house, except myself and my old opponent. He began immediately to dispute the point, telling me it was all delusion and the work of the devil. I told him to stand still and see the salvation of the Lord. As they came to, they all praised God, and not one soul but what professed either to have received justification or sanctification, eight of whom professed the latter. I then replied, hark! is this the language of hell? Here your eyes have seen the salvation of the Lord.—Time called us away to our next appointment, which was about seven miles distant. Here we met with my old Presbyterian opponent again; on seeing him, I was sorry, for I concluded that we should have some disputing again. I fixed my eyes on him, and cried mightily to God that if one man fell that day, it might be him. As I was preaching, I heard several cry out, 'Water! water! the man is fainting!' I looked round, and saw it was my old opponent, trembling like Belshazzar: I told them to let him alone, and look to themselves, for that it was the power of God that had arrested him. They let him go, and down he fell on the floor, struggled awhile, and then lay as one dead. When I finished my discourse, and dismissed the people, in order to meet the class, I desired some of our friends to carry him out, as he was in our way: they did so, and laid him on a bed in a back room. After class, I went in to see my old opponent; he had just come to, and was sitting on the bed. Now, thought I, is this the work of the devil, or not? but said nothing to him, nor he to me.

"Next morning we went to our appointment, where we had a large congregation. Looking round, I saw my old Presbyterian friend again. This was nine miles distant from my former appointment. I felt great freedom in speaking: a woman began to shake in a powerful manner, and three or four cried out 'Water! water!' I told them that it was the power of God that had fallen on her, so they let her go, and down she fell on the floor. I bid them to look to themselves, and went on with my discourse; some wept, some sighed, and some groaned. When I dismissed the people, not one offered to go. I then desired some one to speak to them, and brother C. arose and said, 'You stand amazed at the power of God, and well you may,' and gave a smart exhortation. By this time I had gathered a little strength, and gave them an exhortation; they wept all through the house. I then said, For God's sake, if any can speak for God, say on; for I can speak no more. Who should arise but my old Presbyterian opponent, and began with informing them that he was not one of this sect, that he had been with me four days, and that he never had seen the power of God in this way before; and added, It is the power of God! and gave a warm exhortation for about three quarters of an hour. I then dismissed the people.

It would no doubt be interesting, to multiply extracts as

found in the life of this "Son of thunder," but our limits oblige us to hasten with the narrative of his labors in a more summary manner. After laboring as a local preacher for upward of sixteen years, he felt it his duty to join the travelling connection, which he did in 1789, at the Conference held in Trenton, New Jersey, in April of that year, and was appointed to Dutchess circuit, in the State of New York. The circuit was new, and he found but a few converted souls on it. He, however, began to preach the doctrine of Bible holiness, and although the people mostly belonged to other churches, yet the Lord graciously owned his word, and rendered his labors a blessing to the people. In 1790, Mr. Abbott was elected to the office of a deacon, and in 1793 was admitted to the office of an elder, and he labored in his holy vocation until the year 1795, when on account of ill health, he was obliged to retire from the itinerant field, and was never able to resume his duties as a travelling minister.

Mr. Abbott's last appointment was Cecil circuit, in the State of Maryland, where he proved himself to be the same holy man that he had been for the previous twenty years. On the 3d of February, 1795, he was seized with a violent ague, which was followed by scorching fever, and pain in his side. The doctor being called, pronounced his case hopeless, and gave him up as a dead man. He, however, revived, and was able to walk and ride out, and even to attend Church, and visit his friends. The winter of 1795–6, was spent by him in Philadelphia. An instance of his fidelity in reproving sin occurred in the spring of this year. At a funeral sermon which was preached on the occasion of the death of a pious lady, Mr. Abbott was able to be present, and at the close of the sermon, he rose and gave an exhortation. Seeing a gentleman present who had once been a fellow-laborer with him in the gospel, but who had wickedly departed from his God, Mr. Abbott felt it his duty to address his exhortation particularly to him, and called to mind the many happy hours they had spent together in the service of God. The gentleman received the advice given, as an affront, and thought himself ill-used. On Mr. Abbott's being informed of the manner in which his well-meaning effort had been received, he simply said, "Why if I were able to take my horse and go and see him, I should not have made use of that opportunity; but as I am not able to go and see him, I was convinced that if I let that opportunity pass, I should never have another; and I thought it was my duty to speak as I did: therefore I leave the event with God. I am sure that it cannot hurt him, or do him any injury; for a man that is posting in the broad way to damnation, cannot be easily worsted. O! I have seen the time that we have rejoiced together as fellow-laborers in Christ, and it grieves my soul to see that the devil has got the advantage of him!" The final result of Mr. Abbott's plainness was, that at the next quarterly meeting after his death, the gentleman alluded to rose in the love-feast, and declared that God had healed all his backslidings, and that he had made Father Abbott the instrument of his restoration to the favor of God.

About the first of June, Mr. Abbott was able to attend another funeral, at which the officiating clergyman in the course of his remarks said, that, "Death is the king of terrors, and that he makes cowards of us all." After sermon, Mr. Abbott took occasion to converse with the minister, and dissent from the doctrine taught in the above quotation. "For," said he, "perfect love casteth out fear;" "and for my part," said he, "I can call God to witness that death is no terror to me! I am ready to meet my God, if it were now!"

On the 12th of August, he being very feeble, said to a brother who came to see him, "Brother F. I am going to die, and to-morrow you must go to Philadelphia for Brother M'Cluskey, to come and preach my funeral sermon:" to which the brother replied, "Father Abbott, you may continue some time yet, as the time of your death is uncertain." "No," said Mr. Abbott, "I shall die before you would get back from Philadelphia, unless you travel in the night." The brother replied, "It will not answer to go before your decease." "Why," rejoined Mr. Abbott, "I shall die, and I do not wish my body kept until it is offensive: you know the weather is warm, and the distance is considerable." "That is true," replied the brother, "but if I were to go to Philadelphia for brother M'Cluskey to preach your funeral sermon and you not dead, the friends would laugh at me, and he would not come." "Ah!" said he, "it may be so; I never thought of that; perhaps it will be best to stay till I am dead."

On the day but one, following the above conversation, this eminently useful servant of God breathed his last. The last sentence which he intelligibly articulated was, "Glory to God! I see heaven sweetly opened before me!" After this, he frequently repeated single words as "*See!—See!—Glory!—Glory!*" &c., in the meanwhile clapping his emaciated hands together, until nature became exhausted, and he ceased at once to work and live. He died in Salem, New Jersey, on the 14th of August, 1796, in the sixty-fifth year of his age, and twenty-third of his ministry. He was buried according to his oft-repeated desire, in the Methodist burial-ground in Salem. His funeral being attended by a large concourse of his fellow-citizens, and by Christian ministers of different denominations.

Thus lived, and thus died, Benjamin Abbott, "a brand plucked from the burning—a man who had wasted forty years of his life in sin and vice, and yet, who, through the mercy of God in Christ Jesus, became as eminent for piety and usefulness in the Church of God, as he before had been notorious for wickedness and folly. It is scarcely necessary to add many remarks in relation to the character of Mr. Abbott as a preacher of the Gospel, after having given the lengthy extracts which are found in this chapter. Suffice it to say that for burning, zeal and power in the pulpit, he probably never had a superior in the Methodist Church. In regard to education, Mr. Abbott was probably behind the most of the preachers of that day, but what he lacked in knowledge he made up in power, and the influence he exerted over the minds of a congregation was truly wonderful, and the more so in view of his want of education. The great secret of his success, however, may be traced to his depth of piety; for being one of those persons to whom "the Lord had forgiven much," he felt it his duty to "love much" in return, and hence his burning desire for the salvation of souls. It is barely possible that Mr. Abbott was too much of a zealot—that he suffered things to be carried too far in some of his meetings, although we would by no means affirm this; for who can limit the power of God, or who place bounds to the operations of his grace? It is much easier to cry "confusion" and "disorder," than to define the precise limit at which confusion begins and order ends. Were our modern *lovers of order* to undertake the task of stating how far the apostles and disciples were orderly or otherwise on the day of Pentecost; they would find it a more onerous task than simply to find fault with the exhibitions of God's power in latter days, especially under the labors of Abbott:

"Peace to his ashes."

CHAPTER XIII.

BISHOP M'KENDREE.

William M'Kendree was born in King William County, State of Virginia, on the sixth day of July, 1757. His parents were reputable, and appear to have been communicants of the English Church, in which William was educated. Of his early life we know but little, as no biography of this eminent man has as yet been given to the Church. Of one thing, however, we are assured: that he lived to the age of thirty years before he became the subject of converting grace. At the latter age, under the ministry of the Rev. John Easter, who travelled on the circuit near where he lived, he was awakened to a sense of his lost condition as a sinner, and was led to seek for pardon and reconciliation through the atoning blood of our Lord Jesus Christ. Nor did he seek in vain; peace and pardon were granted him in answer to the prayer of faith, and his soul became unspeakably happy while "filled with the fulness of God."

This happy change took place in the year 1787, and being possessed of an ardent love for souls, he was led almost immediately after his conversion to sigh for the salvation of his unconverted neighbors and friends. His desire for their salvation led him to improve upon the talents committed to his care by the "master of the vineyard," and soon he became a preacher of that faith which had so recently changed his "darkness into light." The year after his conversion he offered himself to the Virginia Conference of the Methodist Episcopal Church as a travelling preacher, and was by that body received on trial, and appointed to a circuit. He had not been long engaged in the ministry before he manifested talents of a very high order. In the year 1792, some opposition was manifested by a few of the preachers, to the power of the bishops in stationing them without an appeal to the Conference. The opposition was led by a highly popular preacher, by the name of James O'Kelly, who served as a presiding elder in the State of Virginia. Mr. O'Kelly introduced a resolution to the Conference of 1792, the design of which was to secure to every preacher who thought himself injured, an appeal to the Conference with liberty to state his objections, and if the Conference approved of his objections, require the bishop to appoint him to another circuit. The resolution thus presented elicited very strong debate, which lasted three days, but which was finally lost by a large majority. The failure of the effort to secure the passage of the resolution so operated upon the mind of the mover, that he, with some others, withdrew from the Church, and organized a separate organization, with the name of "Republican Methodists."

Mr. M'Kendree participated more or less in the discussion, and favored the views of Mr. O'Kelly and his party; and although he did not, like the leader of the movement, withdraw from the Church, he nevertheless was so much disappointed at the failure of the proposed measure, that he refused to take an appointment at that Conference. After the adjournment, however, he took pains to examine more critically, the true nature of the measure which had been proposed with so much warmth, and defeated by so large a majority of his brethren, and became convinced of his error, and of the propriety of the course pursued by the Conference. Accordingly, at the request of Bishop Asbury, he again entered the travelling field, and took an appointment, and was stationed in Norfolk,

Va. The examination of the subject alluded to above, convinced him that the only way to preserve the itinerancy of Methodism unimpaired, was to continue in the hands of the bishop the sole power of appointment, and in these views he continued till the end of his life.

In 1796, Mr. M'Kendree was appointed to the charge of an important district in the Virginia Conference as a presiding elder, and at the expiration of three years of faithful and successful service, was removed to the Baltimore district, where he presided one year with equal fidelity and success. In 1800 he was selected by Bishops Asbury and Whatcoat to take charge of a Western district, which required fifteen hundred miles travel quarterly, to go around it. He entered upon this field of labor with great zeal, and had the satisfaction of knowing that his labors were not in vain in the Lord.

It was while Mr. M'Kendree was stationed on this district, that camp-meetings were instituted, and no sooner did he become acquainted with their utility, than he at once with all the vigor of a deeply anxious mind, and an ever-burning desire for the salvation of souls, labored heartily in these precious means of grace; and through his instrumentality thousands in that particular part of the work were no doubt converted to God. Such was his success as a preacher, that his fame became known all over the land, and his "praise was in all the Churches."

At the General Conference of 1808, it became necessary to elect a bishop to fill the vacancy occcasioned by the decease of Bishop Whatcoat. To most of the senior members of the Conference Mr. M'Kendree was personally known, and to them he appeared as the most fitting person to fill that important office. Many of the younger members, however, were entirely unacquainted with him, except by reputation. Being called upon to preach before the Conference on Sabbath morning, his sermon was so powerful, that both old and young looked upon him as the man for the office. Accordingly on the next day, when a balloting for a new bishop was ordered, it was found that out of one hundred and twenty-eight votes cast, ninety-five were for Mr. M'Kendree, who was therefore declared to be duly elected, and on the 17th of May was consecrated by Bishop Asbury and other elders of the Church.

A new field was now opened before Bishop M'Kendree, and after the adjournment of the Conference, as already stated in the Life of Bishop Asbury, the latter took him with him for the purpose of introducing him to all the Conferences, and also to the brethren in different parts of the land. It will, however, be unnecessary to repeat the history given in the preceding chapter, where the labors of the two men of God are spoken of in connection: we will therefore pass to the General Conference of 1812. This was the first delegated General Conference of the Methodist Episcopal Church, and is remarkable also, as the first Conference at which either of the bishops had presented a written address. After the opening of this venerable body in due form, Bishop M'Kendree over his own signature, presented to the Conference the following document.

"*To the General Conference of the Methodist Episcopal Church, now assembled in the city of New York.*

"Dear Brethren: My relation to you and the Connection in general, seems in my opinion to make it necessary, that I should address you in some way, by which you may get possession of some information, perhaps not otherwise to be obtained by many of you.

"It is now four years since by your appointment, it became my duty jointly to superintend our extensive and very important charge. With anxious solicitude and good wishes, I have looked forward to this General Conference. The appointed time is come, and the Lord has graciously permitted us to meet according to appointment, for which I hope we are prepared jointly, to praise and adore his goodness.

"Upon examination, you will find the work of the Lord is prospering in our hands. Our important charge has greatly increased since the last General Conference: we have had an increase of nearly forty thousand members. At present we have about one hundred and ninety thousand members, upward of two thousand local, and about seven hundred travelling preachers in our Connection, and these widely scattered over seventeen States, besides the Canadas, and several territorial settlements.

"Thus situated, it must be expected in the present state of things, that the counsel and direction of your united wisdom, will be necessary to preserve the harmony and peace of the body, as well as co-operation of the travelling and local ministry, in carrying on the blessed work of reformation, which the Lord has been pleased to effect through our instrumentality. To deserve the confidence of the local ministry and membership, as well as to retain confidence in ourselves, and in each other, is undoubtedly our duty; and if we consider that those who are to confide in us are a collection from all classes and descriptions, from all countries of which the nation is composed, promiscuously scattered over this vast continent—men who were originally of different education, manners, habits, and opinions, we shall see the difficulty, as well as the importance of this part of our charge.

"In order to enjoy the comforts of peace and union among us, we must 'love one another;' but this cannot abide where confidence does not exist; and purity of intention, manifested by proper actions, is the very foundation and support of confidence; thus 'united, we stand:' each member is a support to the body, and the body supports each member; but if confidence fails, love will grow cold, peace will be broken, and 'divided we fall.' It therefore becomes this body, which by its example is to move the passions and direct the course of thousands of ministers, and tens of thousands of members, to pay strict attention to the simplicity of gospel manners, and to do everything as in the immediate presence of God. If we consider the nature of our business, and the influence of civil governments and political measures, it will hardly be expected that every individual in so large a body as you form, will continually be sufficiently and strictly evangelical in all cases; it is therefore hoped in cases of failure, that the wisdom and firmness of your united prudence as a body, will counteract evil effects, by a well-ordered and prudent disapprobation and better example. Church and State should never be assimilated.

"Connected as I am, with you and the Connection in general, I feel it my duty to submit to your consideration the appointment of the Genesee Conference; and perhaps it may be for the general good, if in your wisdom you should think proper to take into consideration a division of the work in the western country, and a proper arrangement of the work in general; and the magnitude and extent of the work which the Lord has graciously pleased to prosper in our hands, may make it proper for you to inquire if the work is sufficiently within the oversight of the Superintendency, and to make such arrangement and provision as your wisdom may approve. I would also suggest the necessity of keeping in view, not only the travelling, but the relation and situation of our local brethren; and to pursue that plan which may render the whole most useful; and it may also be proper to bring into view any unfinished business (if any) which we had under consideration at our last General Conference. Hitherto, as a body, we have been preserved by our well-digested system of rules, which are as sinews to the body, and form the bonds of our union. But it is evident both from Scripture and experience that men, even good men, may depart from first principles, and the best of rules; it may therefore be proper for you to pay some attention to the administration, to know the state both of the travelling and local ministry, as it relates to doctrine, discipline, and practice.

"Before I conclude, permit me, my dear brother, to express a few thoughts concerning the view I have of the relation in which I stand connected with this body. It is only by virtue of a delegated power from the General Conference, that I hold the reins of government. I consider myself bound by virtue of the same authority, to exercise discipline in perfect conformity to the rules of the Church, to the best of my ability and judgment. I consider myself justly accountable, not for the system of government, but for my administration; and ought therefore to be ready to answer to the General Conference for past conduct, and be willing to receive information and advice to perfect future operations; and I wish my brethren to feel themselves perfectly easy and at liberty. (—To give advice, &c.)

"I shall take the liberty here, to present my grateful acknowledgments for the high degree of confidence which my beloved brethren have placed in me, and especially the able counsel and seasonable support afforded by many, which has, I believe, with the divine aid, preserved and supported me. Dear brethren, such are the effects of our high responsibility, connected with a consciousness of the insufficiency of my talents for so great a work, that I move with trembling. Your eyes, and the eyes of the Lord are upon me for good. We shall rejoice together to see the armies of Israel wisely conducted in all their ranks, carrying the triumphs of the Redeemer's kingdom to the ends of the earth; and the Lord will rejoice to make his ministers a flame of fire. In you I have all confidence, and on you I depend for aid, and above all I trust in divine aid. Influenced by these considerations, and with my situation in full view, I cannot entertain a thought of bearing such awful accountability longer than I am persuaded my services are useful to the Church of God, and feel a confidence of being aided by your counsel and support, which is with you to give in any way or form you may judge proper. And while I join with you, my dear brethren, in pure gospel simplicity to commit and recommend ourselves, and our several charges to the special care of the Great Head of the Church, I remain with sentiments of love and confidence, your servant in the Gospel of Christ,

"WILLIAM M'KENDREE.

"New York, May 5th, 1812."

We have thus given at full length the first episcopal message, or opening address, made by a bishop of the Methodist Episcopal Church, to the General Conference of that Church. Why Bishop Asbury did not unite in the presentation of the address, we have not the means of knowing. It was evidently, however, not because he dissented from the doctrines contained, or the views expressed in the same; for after the address had been read and referred to appropriate committees Bishop Asbury rose and addressed the Conference extemporaneously, through Bishop M'Kendree, who occupied the chair, and recommended a consideration of the same, or similar points, alluded to in the written address.

The address thus quoted, serves to throw light upon the character of good Bishop M'Kendree; and to understand some portions of it, it is necessary to observe that the ground which the bishop found it necessary to take on the presiding elder question—alluded to on a previous page—after he had become convinced of his former errors in that respect, subjected him to no small amount of prejudice during some periods of his episcopal administration. Because he had changed his opinions on the subject, and found it necessary as an honest man, to act in accordance with those opinions.

it was thought by some, that he was ambitious, and was actuated by a love of power. These suspicions and prejudices rendered it rather a hard task, especially in some of the northern Conferences, where the O'Kelly doctrines were more generally embraced, to please some of the preachers in relation to the appointments they received from the bishop; but he, conscious of his integrity in the matter, and being satisfied that the existing policy was the only safe one for the Church to pursue, continued to discharge the duties imposed upon him by the General Conference, while he held himself responsible for the manner of their performance to the body from which he had received the authority to discharge the same. Hence the bishop in this address states that he holds himself "justly accountable, not for the *system* of government, but for his administration," and that he was "ready to answer to the General Conference for past conduct, &c." It should, however, be recorded to the honor of the bishop's memory, that whatever asperities may have existed in relation to the matter alluded to, time has removed any prejudices that may have arisen from the subject; while the history of the Church since that period, has proved the correctness of the bishop's views, and of the policy advocated by him and endorsed by the General Conference.

It may be proper in this connection to speak somewhat more at large of the ministerial character of Bishop M'Kendree, and in doing so, would avail ourselves of the remarks found in Bangs's "History of the Methodist Episcopal Church," to which work we are mainly indebted for all that is written in regard to the biography of Bishop M'Kendree. On page 197, Dr. Bangs, in speaking of the bishop's character, says:

"1. Bishop M'Kendree gave unequivocal evidence of deep piety, and of a mind and heart thoroughly imbued with gospel truth. This evidence is found in his entire life, in his words, and actions.

"2. Having devoted the early days of his ministry chiefly to the new countries west of the Alleghanies, he had neither the time nor the means of acquiring much information from the study of books, though it was evident that he had stored his understanding with a variety of the most useful branches of knowledge for a minister of Jesus Christ. Had he been favored with the opportunity of a thorough education in his youth, and pursued the path of science in after years, he might have shone in the galaxy of literature and science; for he had an understanding sufficiently strong and acute to enable him to grapple with any subject within the range of human intellect, and equal to the acquirement of any branch of human knowledge.

"This was evident to all who were intimate with him, and could duly appreciate his worth. His mind indeed was capable of the nicest distinctions of the most critical researches and of the widest expansion. How often did he, by a well-timed and pointed remark, unravel the sophistry of the sciolist and confound the pedantic pretender to wisdom and science! As if by a sudden inspiration of thought, he would make a ray of light flash upon a subject, and thereby render that clear and intelligible which before was obscure and perplexed. It was once remarked by a preacher of no mean attainments, who was on intimate terms with the bishop, that he had often felt himself mortified and chagrined when endeavoring to let him into the secret of something of importance, he found that the bishop was already in possession of the facts in the case, and could therefore give more information than the other could impart.

"His constant intercourse with all sorts of company in his various peregrinations through the country, enabled him to treasure up much useful knowledge from actual observation, and to suit himself with an admirable adaptation to the variety of classes and circumstances of the people with whom he came in contact. This also gave him a clear insight into the human character, and a comprehensive view of that character in all its variety of shades and distinctions. And though he did not 'affect the gentleman' by an apish imitation of the fopperies of fashion, he was easy and polite in his manners, while he at all times maintained the dignity and gravity of the Christian minister. His perfect knowledge of the human character enabled him to wield with good effect the weapon of truth, and to apply it with admirable facility and exactness to the various cases which came up for consideration.

"3. As a preacher of the Gospel, he was plain and pointed, and his sermons consisted chiefly in explaining and enforcing experimental and practical godliness. Though possessed of a mind extremely acute, which, had he been trained to metaphysical researches, would have been competent to the most abstruse subjects, yet he seldom entertained an audience with dry and monotonous disquisitions, but entered directly into the heart, laid open the secret springs of human action, and applied the truths of God's Word to the understanding and conscience with powerful effect.

"There was indeed a great variety in the character of his sermons. Though he seldom failed to 'make out what he took in hand,' yet he sometimes sunk rather below mediocrity, while at other times he soared and expanded, and astonished you with irradiations of light, and with the power and eloquence with which he delivered the tremendous truths of God. On these occasions, assisted, as he most evidently was, by the Holy Spirit, he would carry you away with him on the eagle wings of truth, and then having gently seated you on its firm foundation, melt you into the tenderest emotions by the sweet and gentle accents of affectionate entreaty, which poured from his lips in the most pathetic streams of gospel simplicity, truth, and love.

"It was a sermon of this character which he preached before the General Conference in 1808, a few days previous to his election to the episcopal office, and which no doubt contributed much to his elevation to that station, more especially by securing the votes of those who were not personally acquainted with him. To give as fair a representation of this sermon and its effects as I am able, I will simply relate what passed in my own mind on that occasion.

"It was the first General Conference I had ever attended, and the name of William M'Kendree was unknown to me, and I believe also to many other junior members of the Conference. He was appointed to preach in the Light-street Church on Sabbath morning. The house was crowded with people in every part, above and below, eager to hear the stranger, and among others, most of the members of the General Conference were present, besides a number of colored people who occupied a second gallery in the front end of the church. Bishop M'Kendree entered the pulpit at the hour for commencing the services, clothed in very coarse and homely garments, which he had worn in the woods of the west; and after singing, he kneeled in prayer. As was often the case with him when he commenced his prayer, he seemed to falter in his speech, clipping some of his words at the end, and hanging upon a syllable as if it were difficult for him to pronounce the word. I looked at him, not without some feelings of distrust, thinking to myself, 'I wonder what awkward backwoodsman they have put into the pulpit this morning, to disgrace us with his mawkish manners and uncouth phraseology?' This feeling of distrust did not forsake me until some minutes after he had commenced his text, which contained the following words:—'For the hurt of the daughter of my people am I hurt; I am black; astonishment hath taken hold on me. Is there no balm in Gilead; is there no physician there? Why then is not the health of the daughter of my people recovered?'—Jer. viii. 21, 22.

"His introduction appeared tame, his sentences broken and disjointed, and his elocution very defective. He at length introduced his main subject, which was to show the spiritual disease of the Jewish Church, and of the human family generally; and then he entered upon his second proposition, which was to analyze the feelings which such a state of things awakened in the souls of God's faithful ambassadors; but when he came to speak of the blessed effects upon the heart, of the balm which God had provided for the 'healing of the nations,' he seemed to enter fully into the element in which his soul delighted to move and have its being, and he soon carried the whole congregation away with him into the regions of experimental religion.

"Remarking upon the objections which some would make to the expression of the feeling realized by a person fully restored to health by an application of the 'sovereign balm for every wound,' he referred to the shouts of applause so often heard upon our national jubilee in commemoration of our emancipation from political thraldom, and then said, 'How much more cause has an immortal soul to rejoice and give glory to God for its spiritual deliverance from the bondage of sin!' This was spoken with such emphasis, with a soul overflowing with the most hallowed and exalted feelings, that it was like the sudden bursting of a cloud surcharged with water, and the congregation was instantly overwhelmed with a shower of divine grace from the upper world. At first, sudden shrieks, as of persons in distress, were heard in different parts of the house; then shouts of praise, and in every direction sobs, and groans, and eyes overflowing with tears, while many were prostrated upon the floor, or lay helpless on the seats. A very large athletic-looking preacher who was sitting by my side, suddenly fell upon his seat, as if pierced by a bullet; and I felt my heart melting under sensations which I could not well resist.

"After this sudden shower, the clouds were disparted, and the sun of righteousness shone out most serenely and delightfully, producing upon all present a consciousness of the divine approbation; and when the preacher descended from the pulpit, all were filled with admiration of his talents, and were ready to magnify the grace of God in him, as a chosen messenger of good tidings to the lost, saying in their hearts, '*This is the man whom God delights to honor.*' 'This sermon,' Bishop Asbury was heard to exclaim, 'will make him a bishop.'

"This was a mighty effort, without any effort at all—for all seemed artless, simple, plain, and energetic, without any attempt at display or studied design to produce effect. An attempt, therefore, to imitate it would be a greater failure than has been my essay to describe it; and it would unquestionably lower the man's character who should hazard the attempt, unless when under the influence of corresponding feelings and circumstances.

"It has been already remarked, that he sometimes fell below himself, when his mind appeared to be barren and unfruitful. Though this was the case, yet he always exhibited the powers of a 'master-workman,' even when those powers seemed to be cramped apparently for want of some internal energy to put them in vigorous motion, and make them play with ease and effect. But what added much to the force of the truths which he uttered was his commanding appearance, the gravity of his demeanor, the sprightliness of his manners, the fire which shot from an eye which bespoke kindness and intelligence, and the natural gracefulness of his action in the pulpit. His voice was clear and musical, and the words which dropped from his lips fell upon the ear with delight, producing a harmony between the outward voice and the inward sensation.

"His rhetoric was faulty. Either from an impediment in-his speech, or from a habit induced from early usage as before hinted, he would sometimes hang upon an unaccented syllable, as in the use of the word *continually*, on the penultima he would rest thus, *al–ly*, as if unable to add the final syllable to the word. At other times he would clip a word in the middle, or end, and leave it half enounced, probably from some imperfection in the organs of speech. These, however, are little things, like black specks in a diamond, which set off its beauties by contrast, and were lost sight of, whenever he entered into his subject as he generally did, as to make you forget everything but the truth he uttered, and the God he proclaimed.

"There was also, at times, the appearance of affectation in his manner, and the modulation of his voice, which detracted so far as was apparent, from the reverence one wishes to feel for an ambassador of the Most High. Those, however, who may have observed this defect—and it certainly is a great defect, wherever it is discovered—may have misjudged, and taken that for art, which arose mostly from the variety of emotions produced by the ebbings and flowings of a full heart, and the several aspects of the subjects occupying the speaker's mind and tongue.

"But whatever defects, the eye of candid criticism might detect in Bishop M'Kendree as a public speaker, or as a sermonizer, judging from the rules of strict propriety, take him all in all, as a preacher of righteousness, sent of God to instruct mankind in the pure and sublime doctrines of the Gospel, he was a star of the first magnitude, and as such he diffused the hallowing and mellowing light of divine truth all around him, wherever he went, and whenever he preached. In the West especially, whence he returned surrounded with a halo of glory, which had been gathering around his character for several years, in the midst of the shakings and tremblings produced by the camp and other meetings, thousands could say, that his preaching was not with the enticing words of man's wisdom, 'but in power and in much assurance, and in the Holy Ghost.' Nor were his labors in the pulpit unappreciated in the Atlantic States, after he had passed through them, in the character of a general superintendent, and had an opportunity to show himself to his brethren, 'as a workman that needed not to be ashamed.' His zeal rose with the dignity of his subject, and his mind expanded as he ranged through the spacious and prolific field of theological truth, while he chained and charmed his hearers with the melody of his voice, and penetrated their hearts by the energy with which he spoke in the name of God, and the directness of his appeals to the understanding and conscience. Such was Bishop M'Kendree in the pulpit.

"4. He was an ardent friend and active promoter of all the institutions of the Church. When the Missionary Society was formed, he entered immediately into its spirit and design, gave it his hearty support, and defended its objects both by word of mouth, and by his pen, as well as by liberal contributions. And after our aboriginal missions were begun, with so much success, he visited them personally, preached to the nations, and held interviews with the chiefs and counsellors with a view to obviate difficulties, and promote their welfare in every way within his power.

"5. Let us now view him as a ruler in the Church. As has been already seen, he constantly set an example to his brethren in the ministry of unreserved devotion to the cause in which he was engaged, and of indefatigable labor so long as his strength would sustain him in the pursuit of good. This enabled him to silence the clamors of such as might be tempted to believe that in the exercise of the executive powers as the president of a Conference, he was guilty of laying burdens upon others, which he was unwilling to bear himself; and the writer of this article had frequent opportunities during the five years in which he held the office of presiding elder under Bishop M'Kendree's administration, as well as at other times, to watch his proceedings, and though sometimes so placed, as to have strong temptations to find just cause of censure, yet truth compels me to say, that I believe he was always actuated by the purest motives and an enlightened desire, to act impartially in all cases which came before him for decision. Whatever partialities he might feel for one, in preference to another, arising out of personal friendship or otherwise, there is good reason to believe, that he never willingly allowed these things to bias his judgment in the execution of his trust, or in the distribution of the preachers to their several stations and tasks. And who that understands anything of the complicated machinery of Methodism, but must know the extreme delicacy and perplexing difficulty of fixing so many men, some old and infirm, some young and inexperienced, others of mature age, judgment, knowledge, and influence in their several stations, so as to meet as nearly and justly as may be the claims of all, and not disappoint the expectations of any either among preachers or people! Such a man must be more than mortal. And hence the assiduity with which a conscientious bishop, must needs apply himself to the difficult task, even to satisfy the dictates of his own judgment.

"As a general superintendent, therefore, Bishop M'Kendree was wise and discreet, pure and energetic, infusing into the general system of the itinerancy life and activity, and setting such an example to all, both preachers and people, as to acquire and maintain their affection and confidence.

"6. Viewed as a man of God, he had many excellencies, and but few defects. He was naturally, as all men of genius are, of a warm temperament, his passions were easily moved, and he sometimes manifested a severity in his disposition and expressions, which detracted from the general amiableness and dignity of his character, and sometimes wounded the feelings of his friends. Yet with these strong feelings to grapple with, self-knowledge was so deep, and grace predominated so powerfully, that he generally *possessed his soul in patience*, and even in the midst of conflicting sentiments and arguments, he had that perfect command of himself, or control over his feelings, that he seldom betrayed anything inconsistent with the Christian bishop, evincing a philosophic gravity which indicated a soul calm and serene, while the storm might be raging around him."

"7. When compared with Bishop Asbury, in the performance of his official duties in consecrating men to the ministry, the contrast was obvious. Though equally fervent and at times manifesting much more of the 'unction of the Holy One,' yet he fell much below his venerable predecessor in the dignity and solemnity of his manners, and in the authoritative manner in which he administered the holy ordinance. Equally impressed, however, with the imposing obligations of the sacred office and of its mighty responsibilities, he neglected no convenient opportunity to impress both the one and the other, upon all who took upon themselves the vows of their God. And sometimes under the impulse of a sudden inspiration, he would offer up to God a fervent intercession for blessings to rest upon them and their labors, and conclude with a short and pithy admonition or exhortation suited to the occasion.

"8. In presiding in the Conferences, impartiality guided his decisions, and he introduced a more orderly manner of doing business, than had heretofore characterized their proceedings. Bishop Asbury used to say, as an apology for the desultory manner in which he sometimes allowed the affairs of a Conference to be conducted, 'I was with you in weakness, and at first I had to be president, secretary, and almost everything; but now the days of your childhood are passed, you have a president who has grown up in the midst of you, and who therefore understands your wants; let him, therefore, lead you forth as men of mature age, under the dictation of those rules of order you may mutually devise for your regulation.' In conformity with this patriarchal counsel, under the advisement of Bishop M'Kendree, a set of by-laws were introduced and adopted, for the more orderly manner of conducting the business of an annual Conference. This wise arrangement prevented the appearance of arbitrary power on the one hand, and the irregularities of independent action on the other.

"In the exercise of his prerogatives as president of the Conferences, he was sometimes called upon to check the forwardness of some, to correct the wanderings of others, as well as to encourage all to a just and diligent performance of their respective duties. In administering admonition or rebuke, he sometimes did it with the keenness of a razor, and yet seemingly with the mildness of a dove. I remember on a certain occasion, a young preacher of more confidence than prudence, who had left some small business to become an itinerant, was boasting of the great sacrifices he had made for the cause, when Bishop M'Kendree checked him by asking in his peculiarly soft and mild manner, 'Brother, have you made greater sacrifices than St. Paul resolved to do, when he said, *If meat make my brother to offend, I will eat no more meat while the world standeth?* Or than those who said, *We have left all for thy sake?*' I need not say that a sense of shame sat on the countenance of this vain boaster.

"But however mild and yielding he might appear in his general administration, there were times in which he thought the circumstances called for it, when he could show all the firmness of a despot, without any of his haughty and domineering feelings. A debate once arose in the New York Conference, respecting electing a man to elder's orders, who had been a travelling deacon only one year, because he had travelled for several years in connection with the Wesleyan Conference in England, and he was finally elected. In the course of the debate, one of the speakers averse to the proposed election, pleaded that if elected, the presiding bishop would be compelled to assume the character of a pope, and refuse to ordain him. After the question was decided, the bishop arose and informed the Conference in mild, but firm tones, that with all his respect for the decision of the Conference, he must decline to ordain the brother; 'but,' said he, 'in doing this, I deny the imputation that I assume the character of the pope, for I act according to your laws, by which I am forbidden to consecrate a person to the office of an elder, until he shall have travelled two years as a deacon, unless in case of missionaries, and this brother does not appear in the character of a missionary. Were I, therefore, to ordain him according to your vote, I might be impeached at the next General Conference for an unconstitutional act, for which I could offer no reasonable excuse. Hence, it is not an assumption of unauthorized power in imitation of the pope of Rome, in defiance of law and order, by which I refuse to comply with your request, but it is a deference I feel for constitutional law, made and sanctioned by yourselves, and from the infraction of which, I am bound by my office alike to protect both you and myself. Repeal your law, and make a different regulation, and I will bow to it with all readiness; but while the law exists, I am bound to obey it, and see that it is obeyed by others.'

"This sensible appeal induced the Conference to reconsider its vote, and the motion to elect was withdrawn. Thus the good sense of the bishop, united with such a commendable firmness, saved both him and the Conference from perpetrating an unconstitutional act."

Having thus given a description of Bishop M'Kendree's

character in these lengthy extracts, we will proceed to trace his history in brief terms, from the Conference of 1812 until the close of his useful life.

During the interim of the General Conference of 1812–1816, the duties and labors of the episcopacy devolved chiefly on Bishop M'Kendree, on account of the infirm health of his beloved and venerable colleague, and who, before the time had arrived for the session of 1816, had quietly left this world of cares. At the request of the General Conference, and at the re-interment of the senior bishop, Bishop M'Kendree delivered a funeral oration, in which he did ample justice to the memory of that great man. The death of the latter, left the Church with but one bishop, until the election of Bishops George and Roberts, on the 14th of May, 1816. The addition of these two vigorous ministers to the episcopacy, was a great relief to Bishop M'Kendree, whose health was becoming quite enfeebled by his multifarious labors. But notwithstanding his weakness of body, he continued to travel over the continent, and preside in the Conferences as usual.

At the General Conference of 1820, the three bishops were present, two of whom presided alternately, Bishop M'Kendree having informed the Conference that the state of his health was such, that he could not preside. The Conference deeply sympathized with the venerable bishop in his bodily afflictions, and passed the following resolutions :

"1. *Resolved*, That it is the wish and desire of this General Conference that Bishop M'Kendree, during his afflictions and debility, should travel in such directions, or remain in such places, as he may judge most conducive to his own health and comfort ; and that he be accordingly, at the close of the Conference, respectfully and affectionately requested so to do.

"2. That whenever Bishop M'Kendree shall think himself able, it is the desire of this Conference that he should continue, so far as health will permit, the exercise of his episcopal functions and superintending care.

"3. That the committee appointed by the last General Conference, to make provision for the families of the bishops, are hereby continued, and that the same committee be directed to take into consideration Bishop M'Kendree's health, and to provide for defraying any extra expenses, which in their judgment, his afflictions may make requisite."

The sympathy of the Conference thus expressed, afforded great consolation to the afflicted bishop, and drew from him acknowledgments of the warmest gratitude, for the kindness manifested toward him. Notwithstanding his release from active labor, the bishop attended as many of the Conferences as he possibly could, and rendered himself especially useful in the missionary department of the work. At the General Conference of 1824, Bishop M'Kendree was present, and opened the session by religious services, a duty which always devolves on the senior Superintendent, if present. His health was so far improved as to enable him to preside in connection with the other bishops during the session, but in view of his age and infirmities, the resolutions of the former General Conference in relation to him, were substantially re-adopted, while for the same reason, and the continued extension of the work and the increase of Conferences, two other bishops—Soule and Hedding—were added to the episcopacy, and were consecrated by Bishop M'Kendree to their high and holy office. At the General Conference of 1828, Bishop M'Kendree was also present, and likewise at the Conference of 1832, which was the last ever attended by him, as previous to the session of 1836, he was called to his reward.

Bishop M'Kendree never fully recovered his health, so as to do effective service, after the General Conference of 1816; but he lingered along in this vale of tears, travelling, preaching, presiding, &c., as much as his health and strength would allow him to do, until the year 1835, when he was released by the "Great Shepherd and Bishop of Souls," from his labors on earth. At the session of 1832, just alluded to, being in great feebleness of body, and being sensible that he never would meet in General Conference again, he, on the day before the final adjournment of that body, arose from his seat, and, with his head silvered over and bleached by age, and a countenance full of love, and his hands leaning upon the top of his staff like the patriarch of old, he with faltering lips, and his eyes full of tears, gave his last address to them, and said like the apostle John, "My brethren and children, love one another. Let all things be done without strife or vain glory, and strive to keep the unity of the spirit in the bonds of peace;" and, then spreading forth his trembling hands, and lifting his still weeping eyes toward heaven, he pronounced upon them the apostolic benediction, and took his final farewell. Bishop M'Kendree's last sermon was preached in Nashville, Tennessee, on the 23d of November, 1834. On the 5th of March following, this truly apostolic bishop breathed his last. His dying words were: "*All is well for time or for eternity. I live by faith in the Son of God. For me to live is Christ, to die is gain.*"

"Not a cloud doth arise to darken my skies,
Or hide for a moment my Lord from my eyes."

In this peaceful and triumphant state, the weary pilgrim closed his eyes on all things terrestial, after a toilsome journey of seventy-eight years through this vale of tears.

"Farewell, my friends, adieu, adieu,
I can no longer stay with you;
My glittering crown appears in view.
All is well! All is well!

"Bright angels are from glory come,
They're round my bed, they're in my room;
They wait to waft my spirit home.
All is well! All is well!"

CHAPTER XIV.

BISHOP GEORGE.

ENOCH GEORGE was born in Lancaster county, State of Virginia, in the year 1767 or '68. It appears that his mother died while he was quite young, thus leaving him at an age when he mostly needed a mother's care and a mother's instructions. Young Enoch, however, realized the truth of the declaration of the holy psalmist, at least in part, when he says, "When father and mother forsake me, the Lord will take me up." While he was thus deprived of a mother, it fell to the lot of an elder sister to act the parts both of sister and mother, to the youthful orphan. During the minority of Enoch, his father removed from Virginia to the State of North Carolina, and it was while residing in this State, that he was awakened to a sense of his lost and ruined condition as a sinner before God. These convictions of sin came upon him through the instrumentality of the Methodist ministry, when he was in his eighteenth or nineteenth year. Young as he was, he felt that he was not too young to be a sinner against God, that he was not too young to die, and that if he died without being converted to God, he must be damned forever. This conviction led him to seek for the remission of sins, through the blood of the atonement: and after having struggled for liberty, he at length obtained forgiveness at the hand of God, through our Lord Jesus Christ. The forgiveness thus extended to him, was not of that nature which some teach it to be—a visitation, or infliction of the whole penalty of the law on the head of the offender, and then an overlooking of the guilt, without reference to the sacrifice upon the cross—to the atonement made by Jesus Christ—but a remission of the penal consequences of transgression, so that the hitherto condemned culprit could exclaim, "Lord! I am damned; but thou hast died," or more appropriately in the words of Scripture, "Therefore being justified by faith (not by punishment), we have peace with God through our Lord Jesus Christ."

After Enoch's conversion, he was soon called upon, to

——"Tell to sinners round,
What a dear Saviour he had found,"

and not only to tell what the Lord had done for his soul, but to pray for those who were still out of the ark of safety, and to exhort them publicly to be reconciled to God. It is true, he did not rush thoughtlessly and heedlessly into the vineyard of the Lord, without waiting for a call from the Master of the vineyard, and it was after a great sacrifice of feeling, that he consented to become a preacher of the gospel. He had received at different times, impressions that it was his duty to go out and devote his entire time and talents to the service of the Church; he had listened to the voice of the Spirit saying, "Go preach," and after laboring in vain to suppress these impressions in regard to duty, and feeling that a "woe" would be pronounced against him, if he "preached not the gospel;" he at length said, "Here I am, Lord; send me," and he entered at once upon the work, but with much diffidence and distrust of his own abilities, yet looking to the "Master of the vineyard," for grace and strength to enable him to discharge the duties of his holy vocation, in a manner acceptable to God and profitable to his fellow-creatures.

After having accepted the call of God and of his Church, to labor as a herald of salvation, and having received a "license" or certificate of his call by the latter, he travelled for a short time on a circuit in connection with the Rev. Philip Cox, and was then sent by Bishop Asbury to assist the Rev. Daniel Asbury in forming a circuit, on the head-waters of Catawba, and Broad Rivers. Having made "full proof of his call to the ministry," while laboring upon these circuits, he was at the next session of the Conference, received on trial, and appointed to labor on the Pamlico circuit, where he remained for a single year, and at the next session of the Conference in 1791, was appointed to the Caswell circuit, where he also remained one year. After having thus travelled two years, and having given further proof of the divinity of his call, he was admitted into full connection with the Conference, and was ordained a deacon in the Church of God, in 1792, by Bishop Asbury. He then received an appointment to Guilford circuit, and the following year, 1793, was appointed to Broad River where he had previously labored. At the close of the latter year, he was ordained elder in the Church, and stationed on the Great Pee Dee circuit. In 1795, he was stationed in Edisto circuit, with instructions to labor three months in Charleston, South Carolina. In 1796, and '97, he filled the office of presiding elder, and gave general satisfaction to both preachers and people, as also to the appointing power of the Church, by the manner in which he discharged the important and laborious duties of the presiding eldership.

In 1798, Mr. George's health partially failed, and supposing the northern climate would best agree with his constitution, he travelled as far north as New York. After two years spent in a northern locality, his health was measurably restored, and he resumed his labors in the southern section of the work. In 1800, he was appointed presiding elder of Potomac district in the Baltimore Conference, but before the close of the year, on account of his arduous labors, his health again failed, and becoming somewhat discouraged about the probability of being able to render himself useful as a travelling minister, he thought best to apply for a location in 1801, which the Conference granted, and he again entered the local ranks. After a partial respite of two years, from the toils and cares of the itinerancy, his health again rallied, so that he ventured in 1803, to re-enter the travelling connection, and was appointed to Frederick circuit. In 1804, he was appointed to the presiding eldership of Baltimore district, and in 1805, to that of the Alexandria district, in the District of Columbia. In 1807, he received an appointment to Georgetown, D. C.; in the following year to Frederick circuit; in 1809, to Montgomery circuit, and in 1810, to Baltimore circuit. In 1811, he was re-appointed presiding elder of the Potomac district, where he labored most efficiently during the constitutional term of office—four years—and at the expiration of that term, was further honored with the charge of Georgetown district.

It is a matter of regret that so little is known of the labors and history of Mr. George, previous to the year 1816, and it is also to be deplored, that subsequent to that time no authentic records have been kept, so that the Church might now be favored with incidents connected with the private life and public labors of this truly great man. Such has been the paucity of materials from which to furnish even a brief history of the life and labors of Bishops M'Kendree and George, that the author, after surveying them, concluded to let them pass without any attempt to write a separate chapter for these worthy men, but knowing that in a work of this character, the reader might expect at least a brief account of all the deceased bishops of the Church; and that the virtues and sacrifices of these men of God demanded that their names should be perpetuated; and believing that the reader will readily forgive the comparative brevity of these articles, in view of the impossibility of furnishing a correct account to any considerable length, without the aid of *materiel*, the author has concluded to give the reader the benefit of all the light he can find on the subject, hoping that the day is not far distant when an extended biography of the bishops of the Methodist Episcopal Church, will be given to the Methodist public.*

Mr. George was elected a delegate by the Baltimore Annual Conference, to the General Conference of 1816, which latter body assembled on the first of May, in the city of Baltimore. The first thing which seemed to arrest the attention of the delegates on their meeting together, was the absence of their beloved senior bishop Asbury—who had a short time previously *departed* this life. His absence, and the knowledge of his death, and that the Conference would never again see his face on earth, and have the advantage of his long experience in conducting the affairs of the Church, and in presiding over their deliberations, spread a melancholy gloom over the house, and caused the members to feel that there was a vacancy in the episcopacy which no man could possibly fill with all that acceptability and talent which had characterized the episcopal labors of the now-sainted Asbury. As Bishop M'Kendree was the only surviving bishop, it became necessary at an early stage of the session, to fill the episcopal bench by the election and consecration of two additional bishops. Accordingly the Committee on the episcopacy reported that in their opinion "the superintendency in consequence of the ever to be lamented death of our venerable father, Bishop Asbury, and the im-

* Since this chapter was commenced, the author has seen an advertisement in the Christian Advocate and Journal, New York, calling for materials of the above description, to aid in the compilation of the Lives of Bishops' M'Kendree and George. The author sincerely hopes the call will be a successful one.

paired state of the health of Bishop M'Kendree, and the increasing extent of the work, is such as to require immediate and adequate strengthening," and they further recommended the appointment of "two additional bishops."

After the adoption of the report of the Committee, the Conference proceeded on the 14th day of May, to the serious and awfully responsible duty of electing two persons to the episcopacy; and notwithstanding the many brilliant names that might have been presented as candidates for the honors of the episcopate, the choice of the Conference fell on Enoch George, and on Robert R. Roberts, the former having fifty-seven, and the latter fifty-five votes, out of one hundred and six that were cast on the occasion—fifty-four votes in either case being necessary to a choice. After their election, they were solemnly set apart to their sacred office by the imposition of the hands of Bishop M'Kendree, who was assisted in the service by a few of the elders present.

After his election and consecration to the episcopacy, Bishop George began to discharge all the duties devolving on him as a servant of the Church, with that diligence and zeal which has always been characteristic of the Methodist episcopacy in America. The entire work was so laid out by the three bishops, that each one during the intervals of the General Conference, might visit once, or oftener, every Conference in the Connection, thus preventing the possibility of a resemblance in their fields of labor, to a diocesan episcopacy. They considered themselves as bishops of the whole Church, and not of any particular portion thereof; hence their *diocess*, if it might be called such, comprehended the whole of the United States and its territory, and rendered it necessary for them to travel the whole length and breadth of the land. Wherever Bishop George went, he diffused the spirit of piety among the people, and of ministerial zeal and fidelity among the preachers, and in his hands, as well as in those of his colleagues, the government of the Church was administered with all due faithfulness, the Conferences being punctually attended, and the union, peace, stability and prosperity of the Church being very generally promoted in all its borders.

At the General Conference of 1820, the three bishops were present, but on account of the feeble health of the senior bishop—M'Kendree, the labor of presiding over the deliberations of the Conference, devolved mostly on Bishops George and Roberts, both of whom in a verbal address, called the attention of the Conference to various subjects of public interest, and especially to the state of our Church in Canada, which had suffered very materially from the war of 1812–'15. As all intercourse between the States and the Canadas was suspended during the continuance of the war, the Methodists in those Provinces were but partially supplied with preachers from the American Conferences; and the British Conference, anxious to supply the Methodists who were subject to the British government, with preaching and the ordinances, sent various missionaries to Upper and Lower Canada. Many of the Methodists in these provinces, however, were ardently attached to the Methodist Episcopal Church in the United States, and were not at all pleased with the appointment of English missionaries among them; while others of the Canadian Methodists, not only preferred the English missionaries, but insisted on their remaining to the exclusion of the American ministers. This state of things begat mutual jealousies and mistrust among the members in Canada, and at the General Conference of 1820, the subject came formally before that body, by the address of the bishops just adverted to, and then by means of memorials, petitions, remonstrances, &c., from the adherents of the American preachers. After a long and patient consideration of the whole matter, the Conference solemnly, and with great unanimity, resolved that it was "the duty of the bishops of the Methodist Episcopal Church to continue their episcopal charge over our Societies in the Canadas, all except Quebec." The Conference also ordered an address to be sent to the brethren in Canada, in which mention is made of a "letter sent by Bishop George to the British Conference, containing a full development of the affairs of Canada."

It would appear from this address, that Bishop George had been corresponding with the British Conference on the subject of the existing Canadian difficulties during the interim of the General Conference, but as no direct and conclusive reply had been received, he thought it necessary to present the matter, as before stated, to the consideration of the latter body. It may be proper to state in this connection, that the Rev. John, afterward Bishop Emory, was at the Conference of 1820, appointed a delegate or representative to the British Conference in England, with full power to adjust all existing difficulties between the two bodies, arising out of the Canadian affairs, and that he happily succeeded in so doing to the perfect and lasting satisfaction of all parties interested in the matter.

Nothing worthy of special notice appears to have taken place in the life or history of Bishop George during the interval between the General Conferences of 1820–'4. His time was wholly occupied in attending to the duties of his station and the interests of the Church. At the session of 1824, he was present in connection with Bishops M'Kendree and Roberts, and as during the preceding four years the work had gradually extended itself, so as to require additional strength in the episcopal board, it was at this General Conference, resolved, that two additional bishops be elected and consecrated, and the choice fell on the Rev. Joshua Soule and Rev. Elijah Hedding, who, on the 27th of May, 1824, at 12 o'clock M., were solemnly consecrated to the office of bishops, by the bishops then present, the senior bishop officiating.

After the adjournment of the General Conference, Bishop

George, accompanied by Bishop Hedding, paid a visit to the brethren in Canada, and presided over the deliberations of the Canada Annual Conference, which held its session in Hallowell, U. C. A desire had been growing, for a few of the past years, on the part of some of the Canadian preachers, headed by a member of the Canada Conference, named Ryan, for the establishment of an independent Church organization in Canada, with power to appoint a bishop of their own selection, who should reside among them. A petition to this effect had been presented to the General Conference of 1824, signed by a portion of the Canadian preachers; but as the General Conference did not consider that it had constitutional power to grant the prayer of the petitioners, a resolution was passed whereby a separate Conference was erected in Canada, to continue under the superintendence of the bishops of the Methodist Episcopal Church. This decision of the General Conference by no means suited the ambitious views of Ryan and his associates, by whom a Conference, consisting mostly of local preachers, was organized previous to the assembling of the Canada Conference, which had recently been formed by the action of the General Conference. It was under these circumstances, that Bishops George and Hedding met the Canada Conference at its first session, and through their laudable endeavors and explanations, peace was measurably restored among the brethren, and things continued as they had been, until the next session of the General Conference in 1828, when the Canada brethren were authorized, if they preferred it, to constitute themselves into an independent body, which act was consummated by them at their ensuing session.

At the General Conference of 1828, a long and affectionate address to the Wesleyan Conference in England, signed by Bishop George, as the President of the body, was adopted, and subsequently sent by the Rev. Wm. Capers, who was appointed delegate to the British Conference. As this address contains much information in relation to the state of the Church at that time, we will copy it for the benefit of the reader.

"*Address of the General Conference of the Methodist Episcopal Church, to the Wesleyan Methodist Conference.*

"Beloved Fathers and Brethren: Having by the mercy of our God brought the present session of our General Conference near to a close, we avail ourselves of this opportunity, to convey to you our Christian salutations. Our beloved brother, the Rev. William Capers, whom we have elected as our representative to your Conference, will more fully explain to you the state of our affairs, the strong affection we have to you as our elder brethren, and our fervent desire to preserve with you the bond of peace and the unity of the spirit.

"Our present session, though laborious, and involving various and important points vitally connected with the interests of our Church, and of Christianity generally, has been marked with general harmony of feeling, and mutual good-will; and we humbly trust it will tend to strengthen the bond of union among ourselves, more fully to combine our strength, to concentrate and harmonize our views and affections, and to give a new impulse to the great work in which we are engaged.

"To stimulate us to diligence in this most sacred of all causes, the bright example of your persevering efforts in the cause of God, is placed before us. Deriving our doctrines from the same great fountain of truth, the Holy Scriptures, and admitting the same medium of interpretation, the venerable Wesley and his coadjutors, and we humbly hope, pursuing the same great objects, the present and future salvation of souls, we desire ever to cultivate with you the closest bond of union and Christian fellowship. Under the influence of these views and feelings, we have rejoiced in your prosperity and witnessed with unmingled pleasure, the extension of your work, particularly in your missionary department.

"With you also, we have our portion of afflictions. Through the disaffection of some, and the honest, though as we think, mistaken zeal of others, in some parts of our extended work, the harmony of our people has been disturbed, and principles to us novel in their character, and deleterious in their influence on the excellent system we have received from our fathers, have been industriously circulated. Though we may not flatter ourselves that these unhappy excitements are fully terminated, yet we presume to hope that the decided and almost unanimous expression of disapprobation to such proceedings by this General Conference, and among our preachers and people generally, will greatly weaken the disaffection, and tend to correct the errors of the wandering, as well as to confirm and strengthen the hand of all who desire to cleave to the Lord, 'in one faith, one baptism, and one hope of our calling.'

"Since our last session we have witnessed with joy and gratitude an unusual effusion of the Holy Spirit. Revivals of religion have been numerous and extensive in almost every part of our continent. Upward of sixty-nine thousand have been added to our Church during the past four years, and the work is still extending. Stretching our lines over so large a continent, many parts of our work, particularly in the new settlements, require great personal sacrifices to carry to them the blessings of our ministry, and much diligence and patient perseverance to preserve our beloved people in the unity of the faith. For these great objects *we* are not sufficient—'our sufficiency is of God! But having devoted ourselves exclusively to this work, and confiding in the strength and goodness of Him, whose we are, and whom we profess to serve in the fellowship of the Gospel, we hope not to faint in the day of trial, but to persevere in conveying the glad tidings of peace to the destitute inhabitants of our land, until every part of it shall break forth into singing, and hail with joy the coming of the Lord.

"Cheered with this prospect, we are endeavoring to strengthen each other in the Lord. And the happy results of our missionary labors, both among the frontier settlements of our white population and the Indian tribes, particularly the latter, are pleasing indications of the Divine approbation. It does indeed seem as if the set time had come to favor these lost tribes of our wildernesses, and to bring them into the fold of Christ. These natives, hitherto 'peeled and scattered' in the United States and territories, as well as in Upper Canada, are bowing to the yoke of Christ with astonishing alacrity, and thus giving evidence that his grace is sufficient to convert even the heart of a savage, and to transform him to the gentleness of Christ. On this subject, however, we need not enlarge, but refer you to our periodical works—the extensive circulation of which, among our people, gives increased impulse to the work, carrying information cheering and delightful to many thousands, of the efficacy and triumph of redeeming mercy,—and to our beloved brother and representative, the bearer of this address, who will more particularly tell you, 'face to face,' how much we rejoice to be co-workers with you in the extensive field of labor, and to witness such evident tokens of the Divine goodness to our fallen world.

"Recollecting the Christian deportment, the ministerial gravity and dignity, and what is more endearing to us, the brotherly affection of your late delegate to our Conference, the Rev. Richard Reece, and his amiable companion, the Rev. John Hannah, both of whom have left a sweet savor behind them, we take much pleasure in giving to you this renewed assurance of our unabated attachment to those doctrines and that discipline, by which both you and we are distinguished; to set our seal to the maxim that 'the Wesleyan

Methodists are one throughout the world;' and also our desire that the intercourse between us, by the mutual exchange of delegates, may be kept up and continued; and that as a means of our edification and comfort, we shall be happy to receive whomsoever you may appoint to visit us at our next session.

"With sentiments of unfeigned respect and Christian affection, we are, dear brethren, one with you in the fellowship of Jesus Christ.

"Signed in behalf of the General Conference of the Methodist Episcopal Church, held at Pittsburgh, (Pa.,) May, 1828.

"ENOCH GEORGE, *President*.

"MARTIN RUTER, *Secretary*."

At the General Conference of 1828, at which the above document was prepared, Bishop George was present, and assisted his episcopal colleagues in the discharge of their official duties. Nothing calling for special remark, otherwise occurred, at this session of the body, if we may except the important fact, that it was the last session of the General Conference that Bishop George ever attended; he having on the 23d of the ensuing August, died at Staunton, Virginia, in the sixty-first year of his age, and in the thirty-eighth year of his ministry. His last words were: "Glory to God!"

Bishop George was a man greatly and deservedly beloved by all who knew him, and as might be supposed, his death was severely felt and deeply lamented, throughout the length and breadth of our Zion Much might be said relative to his character and conduct as a Christian and Christian minister. A few words, however, on this point, must suffice. Dr. Bangs, who was personally acquainted with him, thus describes him:

"That which distinguished Bishop George among his fellows, was the warmth of his zeal and the quickness of his movements. This, no doubt, arose from the depth of his piety. He seemed, indeed, to live and walk with God. This was evident from the uniformity of his devotions, as well as from his general deportment, both before the public, and in his more private intercourse with his friends. He always rose early in the morning, and if circumstances permitted, would spend the morning before breakfast in a solitary walk in the field, for meditation and private devotion ; and in these lonely rambles, he delighted in the contemplation of the Deity as he is seen in his works and ways, and in holding communion with him in praise and prayer.

"He was naturally eloquent, and his eloquence was all natural. He never sought to embellish his subjects with artificial tinsels of pulpit oratory, substituted by some, for those overflowings of the heart, which proceed from being filled and fired with the truth which the lips utter. Hence his 'preaching was not with the enticing words of mans' wisdom,' but it was in 'demonstration and power,' and 'with much assurance in the Holy Ghost.' He was more distinguished, however, for affecting the heart and moving the passions, than for enlightening the understanding and informing the judgment. Whenever, therefore, you saw him begin to rub his eyes with his fingers, as if wiping thence the gushing tear, you might expect a pouring forth of those streams of gospel truth, generally of that declamatory or hortatory character which were calculated to move the hearer to weep or shout, according to his predominant feeling And he seldom concluded a sermon without greatly moving his audience in either of these ways, because he was first moved himself by those sacred and heavenly emotions which were evidently produced by the energetic workings of the Holy Spirit.

"Viewing him, therefore, simply as an ambassador of God, sent peculiarly to awaken the conscience of the sinner, and to alarm or strengthen the faith of the believer, and quicken him in the divine life, he was most eminently qualified for his great work. In addition to the holy pathos with which he breathed out the 'words of truth and soberness,' his voice was exceedingly musical, shrill, and clear, his action natural and expressive of the feelings of his heart, and all calculated to impress the hearer with the solemn truths which fell from his lips. If, however, we may judge him by other tests of a pulpit orator, we should detect some defects. In education he was quite deficient, and his general reading was very limited. For this lack of acquired knowledge, he might be considered as furnishing more than a substitute, in the pointedness of his appeals, and the manner in which he fortified all his positions by direct appeals to the sacred Scriptures. And if he dealt in detached sentences, instead of following a consecutive order and arrangement of argumentation, he was abundantly compensated in the blessed effects which he saw produced in the hearts of those who heard him, and knew how to appreciate the value of a sermon more from its unction than its argument. His premises were found where every minister of Christ should find them—in the Bible; and his conclusions were then drawn without much regard to logical arrangement, and certainly without any circumlocution, direct and with a force it was hardly possible to resist. And from the earnestness of his manner, some have entirely mistaken his object and his motives. Beholding the emotions which were very generally produced in the pious part of his hearers, sometimes expressed in loud shouts of praise, those who were mere outward court worshippers, or uninterested hearers, have retired from the sanctuary under a conviction that Bishop George was acting the part of a mountebank, speaking for the purpose of gaining shouts of applause. A sad mistake this. He ascended the pulpit, not as a stage player mounts the stage, but as an ambassador of Christ, commissioned to declare his counsel unto the people, and to negotiate a

'Peace 'twixt earth and heaven.'

And in the fulfilment of this commission, he did not trifle with the awful realities of time and eternity, but poured forth from a full heart the solemn truths of God, in a manner which penetrated the conscience and drew forth the confession, by sobs and shouts, that God was with him of a truth.

"Such was Bishop George in the pulpit. In the chair of the Conference he was less acceptable. Though he was always intent on accomplishing the greatest amount of good, by the best possible means, he often defeated his purpose by the haste with which he endeavored to despatch the business. His manner, also, was sometimes abrupt and undignified, and of course did not always command that respect which every conscientious mind would wish to feel, and pay to a superior. Nor were his decisions always made with that wisdom and deliberation, needful to produce a conviction of their correctness in all cases. He appeared, therefore, to much greater advantage in the pulpit, than in the chair of the Conference; and had he lived and died simply as an itinerant Methodist preacher, he had commanded more respect, than was felt for him as a general superintendent of the Church. These defects, however, detract nothing from his natural worth, nor render him less worthy of affection as a Christian bishop, or as a man deeply and seriously devoted to the best interests of the human family;—for who is perfect in every respect?

"But in whatever light we view him, he will long be remembered with affection, as one of the early pioneers, in the ranks of the itinerancy, as an indefatigable laborer in the Lord's vineyard, who won many sinners to Christ, and was always a sun of consolation to God's believing people.

"The warmth of his affections won him many friends, and the affability of his manners endeared him to them as a brother beloved, who might be approached at all times, with a cheerful confidence.

"His death was sudden and unexpected. Its announcement, therefore, spread a temporary gloom over the Methodist community. But death did not find him unprepared. He met this 'last enemy' not only with meek submission, but with a holy triumph, and a well-grounded hope of eternal life. As the words, 'Glory to God!' had often fell from his lips in the pulpit, so in his last moments, in full view of the invisible world, he shouted forth the praise of God, and no doubt went to the shades of bliss and immortality."

Thus far the historiographer of the Methodist Episcopal Church, in relation to the character of Bishop George; and from the account thus candidly, and as we have no doubt, impartially given, we learn that the most eminent men are not above criticism, and that, however perfect a man may be in many respects, yet absolute perfection cannot be predicated of any mortal even in his "best estate." Bishop George, however, with all his imperfections, was undeniably a great man, and what is of still more importance, he was a *holy* man. Let his name and memory, therefore, be honored by succeeding generations; for "*the memory of the just is blessed.*"

We cannot close this brief account of the life and death of Bishop George, without giving the following tribute of respect to his memory, written by the late lamented Dr. Fisk, president of the Wesleyan University at Middletown, Conn. It was originally written in a lady's Album, and was afterward inserted in the Christian Advocate and Journal.

"BISHOP GEORGE.

"Bishop George has gone to heaven. He left this world for glory on the 23d of August last; and from the known tendency of his soul heavenward, and his joyous haste to be gone, there can be little doubt but his chariot of fire reached the place of its destination speedily; and the triumphant saint has long ere this, taken his seat with the heavenly company. And since he is gone, the owner of this, to whom I am a stranger, will pardon me if, upon one of her pages, I register my affectionate remembrance of a man, whom I both loved and admired, and at the report of whose death, my heart has been made sick. I loved him, for he was a man of God, devoted to the Church with all his soul and strength; I loved him, for his was an affectionate heart, and he was my friend. But the servant of God, the servant of the Church, and my friend, is dead. I admired him—not for his learning, for he was not a learned man; but Nature had done much for him. She had fashioned his soul after an enlarged model, and had given it an original cast and an independent bearing; into the heart she had instilled the sweetening influences of a tender sympathy, and infused into the soul, the fire of a spirit-stirring zeal, sustained by a vigorous and untiring energy; but to finish his character, grace came in, and renewed the whole man; and the Spirit anointed him to preach the gospel; and the Church consecrated him to be one of her bishops. He superintended with dignity and faithfulness; he preached the gospel with the Holy Ghost *sent down from heaven.* The unction that attended his word, was not merely like the consecrating oil that ran down Aaron's beard, but it was like the anointing of the Spirit that penetrates the heart. He preached with his soul full of glory; no wonder then, that his dying words were, '*I am going! and that's enough! glory! glory!*' Yes, thou triumphant Spirit, *that is enough.* 'May I die the death of the righteous, and may my last end be like his.'"

CHAPTER XV.

REV. BISHOP ROBERTS.

Robert Richford Roberts was born August 2d, 1778, in Frederick County, Maryland. His father was a respectable farmer, and was a zealous member of the Church of England, and a soldier of the Revolution. Robert R. was put to school when between four and five years of age, and before he was seven years old, he was able to read the Bible quite intelligibly. He was baptized in infancy according to the usages of the Church of England, and when older was taught the Catechism of the Church, and was while but a boy, the subject of deep religious impressions, although his parents were not at that time experimentally pious, but rested in the outward form of religion.

When young Roberts was about seven years of age, his father removed to Westmoreland County, Pennsylvania, where the inhabitants were mostly Presbyterians, and as the elder Roberts entertained a dislike for any kind of worship, that was not of "the Church," he seldom worshipped with them. Three years after his removal to Pennsylvania, the neighborhood where he resided was visited by Methodist preachers, but he would not hear them, believing them to be false prophets. At length Mrs. Roberts was constrained to go, and took young Robert R. with her. She was powerfully convicted under the sermon, but on account of the wishes of her husband, she refrained from going to hear them again for a length of time. The other members of the family, however, continued to attend from time to time, and a quarterly-meeting being held in the neighborhood, the elder son, John, was prevailed upon by his sisters to attend the love-feast, and bring back an account of what might transpire there. On his return, they were all curiosity to know what he had seen and heard, and to their astonishment he told them, he believed the Methodists were a good people. This reply was strange to young Robert R., who had heretofore heard his brother say very severe things against that people.

Soon after this, one of his sisters being under conviction, retired to the woods to pray; young Robert overheard her asking God to pardon her sins, and he wondered very much, what enormous sin she could have committed, to affect her thus deeply. Soon after this, he learned, that three of his sisters had united with the Methodist Church, and that his elder sister, Sarah, had actually prayed in public! Such was the effect of this young lady's prayers and zeal, in the cause of Christ, that shortly, others of the children, together with the father and mother, joined the "sect everywhere spoken against," and the house of the elder Roberts became a regular preaching place, and a home for the preachers. When Robert R. was about fourteen years of age, he obtained the evidence of his acceptance with God, and soon after joined the Methodist Episcopal Church. He also commenced attending school again, a privilege he had not enjoyed since he left Maryland.

In the spring of 1796, young Roberts being nearly eighteen years of age, in company with four other young men, left his father's house and went to Shenango, now Mercer County, Pa. The Legislature of Pennsylvania had passed an act granting four hundred acres of land to actual settlers under certain conditions. Robert R. and one of his brothers thinking this to be a good offer, concluded to comply with the conditions prescribed, and thus secure a home and independence. They travelled on foot, and carried their provisions in knapsacks upon their backs. They, however, caught plenty of wild game by the way, which added greatly to their necessarily scanty store. In the meantime, his brother and another of his associates becoming discouraged with the prospect before them, returned home, but Robert and two others kept on their way, until they arrived at a place where the land suited them, and where they resolved to make a location. Here they fell in with two other young men, who were also looking for land, and the five resolved to keep together, and form a settlement in the wilderness. They cut logs, built a cabin, covering it with chestnut bark, and deadened a few trees. Soon, however, their provisions ran out, and Mr. Roberts had no money to purchase any more; one of his associates, however, lent him some, and they had to go twenty miles to obtain a supply, and when obtained were obliged to carry it on their backs the same distance. The price which they paid for provisions and seed for their ground, was high compared with present prices; corn was two dollars per bushel, and potatoes three dollars! The crops of the succeeding summer came in very scantily, the corn being mostly destroyed by squirrels. Mr. Roberts, accordingly, made up his mind to return home, and assist in harvesting. When he arrived at the paternal mansion, his parents and friends were greatly rejoiced to see him, fearing before his arrival that he was dead.

In the spring of 1797, Mr. Roberts in company with two of his brothers, and six other persons, started once more for Shenango. Here they remained for some time, clearing land, planting corn, &c. His brothers, however, soon returned home, designing ultimately to settle on the lands near Robert's location. After their departure, so greatly was our young pioneer distressed for provisions, that he actually subsisted for three weeks on squirrels and salt! until his brothers returned again, in company with his father and one of his sisters, who brought with them four horses laden with provisions, and four cows. Robert R. and his sister determined to spend the winter in the settlement, which they accordingly did very comfortably, he spending his time mostly in hunting, and meeting with some providential escapes from the fury of wild beasts, that he wounded without instantly killing, and she being in more or less dread of the Indians, who wandered through the forest. In the spring of 1798, Mr. Roberts was joined by his father, brothers, and another sister, all of whom had come to settle permanently in the new country.

About this time, Mr. Roberts having gone to procure more provisions, was on the way entertained at the house of a local preacher, and in the neighborhood a meeting was held. After a sermon by the local preacher—Mr. Gurwell—the latter called on Mr. Roberts to say something by way of exhortation, to the people. He accordingly made the attempt, and delivered a brief address fraught with pathos and good sense, which betokened the future greatness of the young backwoodsman. This was his first effort at public speaking.

About the middle of April, Mr. Roberts and his younger brother started for their old place of residence, for the purpose of conveying to Shenango a part of the family, which had been left behind. Among these last, was his maternal grandfather, Mr. Richford, an old gentleman ninety-three years of age. As the only mode of conveyance was by horseback, it was extremely difficult for the old man to pursue the journey, as streams of considerable width and depth had to be forded. To add to the difficulty of the undertaking, the old grandfather being in his dotage, was somewhat peevish and fretful, and not a little stubborn, as well as fearful. However, by dint of stratagem and perseverance, they succeeded in getting the old man along, at the expense of an occasional wetting.

Our emigrants were ten days on the journey, and lay out every night, there being no taverns or dwelling-houses the whole distance. Robert R. carried bags of flour and other provisions, over streams, by walking on the trunks of fallen trees. Nancy Roberts drove three cows and two pigs, carrying an axe on her shoulder, and walking all the way. Sarah walked also the entire distance, carrying a spinning-wheel on her shoulder. Another sister, Sophia, sometimes rode behind the pack, on one of the horses, and sometimes walked.

The removal of the Roberts family to Shenango, was the means of introducing Methodism into that hitherto wilderness country, so that in the summer of 1798, a Society was formed by local preachers who had also emigrated to that region. Robert R. was appointed leader of the class, and made himself useful in holding prayer-meetings, &c. In the meantime, the country was becoming rapidly inhabited by emigrants from older places, so that there were religious meetings frequently held among them by local preachers, who were sometimes assisted by Mr. Roberts. In the winter of 1799, Robert R. went to his former place of residence, with a large quantity of furs, amounting in value to about one hundred and fifty dollars, the proceeds of his hunting during the former part of the winter. Before his return home, he was married to Miss Elizabeth Oldham, of York County, Pa., and shortly after their marriage, they took up their line of march for Shenango; Mrs. Roberts, the new-made bride, riding on a pack-horse, and with the bridegroom being obliged to remain out all night in the woods, with snow on the ground, and the weather being severely cold, it being the beginning of February. To add to the dreariness of their situation, Lewis Roberts, who had charge of the horses carrying the provision for the journey, had proceeded somewhat in the advance, and Robert and his bride having been overtaken by the darkness of the evening before coming up with him, were compelled to lie down on their snowy bed dinnerless and supperless, having eaten nothing since early in the morning. Sleep was of course out of the question, especially as a pack of hungry wolves began to howl around most lustily. "Robert," exclaimed the bride, "they will certainly eat us up before morning." "No, Betsy," replied the courageous bridegroom, "they will be afraid to approach us; and if they do, this half burned stick, with its red blaze, will terrify them, so that they will never face it to assault us." In the morning, they resumed their journey, and overtook Lewis, who had found shelter in an inhabited hut during the night, and through the good providence of God, they in due time all arrived home in safety; and the new-married couple took up their residence in a small log hut, without a window to let in the light and keep out the cold, without a chair, or bedstead, or table, except those made in the rudest possible manner, but where they found that contentment and true happiness, which are so frequently found wanting in the splendid mansions of the great.

In the summer of 1800, Robert R. received a license to exhort. Previously to this time, his mind had been greatly exercised in regard to his being called of God to preach the Gospel, but determining, if possible, to disobey the call, he had thus far lived without any attempt to discharge the duties which he felt were imposed upon him, and tried to persuade himself that God would release him from the discharge of ministerial duties, because he viewed himself to be totally unqualified for the work; but so thought not his friends and neighbors, who, knowing his talents, and being acquainted with his consistent daily deportment as a Christian, were persuaded that there was a work for him to do. He, however, continued to stifle his convictions, and the warm and earnest entreaties of his friends, until at length he became very unhappy and uneasy in his mind, so much so, that he was obliged for the sake of recovering his lost peace, to make an attempt to preach, let the consequences be what they might, although he was almost certain that he would utterly fail in the attempt. He accordingly preached from the text, "O, Lord, revive thy work," and the Society were so much pleased with his first effort, that they immediately recommended him to the Quarterly Conference as a suitable person to preach the Gospel. As the quarterly meeting for his own circuit was passed, he was advised by the preacher in charge, to repair to another quarterly meeting on an adjacent circuit, with his recommendation. Having now fully resolved to offer his services to the Church, not only as a preacher, but as an itinerant, he complied with the advice, and being furnished with a letter from the preacher in charge, to the Quarterly Conference of Ohio circuit, he rather reluctantly, because of his being a stranger, attended the quarterly meeting of the above circuit, and received a license to preach, and a recommendation to join the Baltimore Annual Conference.

After receiving his license and recommendation, he returned home to make preparation for the itinerant field, although he was quite doubtful whether the Annual Conference would receive him, especially as he was a married man, and as but few married men in those days, were received into the travelling connection. He was, however, received, and appointed to Carlisle circuit, Pa. As soon as he received information of his appointment, he distributed the most of his household utensils among his neighbors and relatives, and with two horses, one for himself, and the other for his wife, with their clothes, and bedclothes packed on the saddles, they started for their field of labor. Carlisle circuit, at that period, embraced about thirty appointments, to be filled once in four weeks. Before he had completed his third round on the circuit, he lost both his horses, and was also attacked with small-pox and measles. While under the influence of the latter disease, the family, in whose house he happened to be taken sick, were very kind to him, and kept him warm, and gave him nothing but warm drinks. One night, however, while the family were all asleep, he went to the pump, and took a copious draught of cold water, being very thirsty. He returned to bed, fell asleep, awoke in a perspiration, and found himself materially better, and soon recovered so as to resume his labors on the circuit.

Mr. Roberts soon gave evidence of more than ordinary abilities as a preacher, so that his congregations, especially in York, Pa., were composed of the *élite* of the village, but such was his diffidence that this circumstance only seemed to embarrass him. On one occasion, seeing the large number of fashionable people who were flocking to the Church, he hesitated about entering, and actually withdrew to a private place, where he remained until such time as he supposed the congregation would have grown impatient, and many of them have left the house. In this, however, he was disappointed, as they all remained till he made his appearance. He made no apology, but trusting in God, went on with his discourse, and his effort, on that occasion, was spoken of with so much admiration, that it only served to increase the size of his congregation in future.

By the kindness of friends, a horse was purchased for him, and at the Conference of 1803, he was appointed to Montgomery circuit, Maryland, where he labored with great success, as the junior preacher, during a part of the year, and as the preacher in charge during the latter portion of the same. At the Conference of 1804, Mr. Roberts was admitted into full connection, and ordained deacon by Bishop Asbury. He was appointed to Frederick circuit, as the field for his labors during the ensuing Conference year, and being in the vicinity of Baltimore during the session of the General Conference, he attended the latter body as a spectator, but after being permitted to be present for two days, the Conference ordered close doors, by which means he and other spectators were shut out, a circumstance which disappointed him not a little; he consequently returned to the circuit, of which he had the charge, and pursued his accustomed rounds, his wife, the meanwhile, living in an upper room, and supporting herself by her own industry. The circuit embraced the place of his birth, and on his first going to the spot he visited an aged aunt, who, like his father, before his conversion, was a high-toned Episcopalian. She at first warmly received her nephew, but on learning that he was a Methodist preacher, she changed her demeanor towards him, and gave him to understand that she did not like "*turncoats*." He replied, good-naturedly, that he never had a coat, until he got among the Methodists. She soon allowed natural affection to overcome her denominational bigotry, and extended to him a cordial welcome.

Harper's Ferry was included in the list of his appointments, but for the first two or three times of visiting the place, he found no congregation to preach to, and was about giving up the place in despair. At length, the lady, at whose house he stopped, resorted to a novel expedient to collect a congregation for the young preacher: She appointed a quilting party at her house, and invited a large number of the ladies to attend. Mr. Roberts, without knowing anything of the expedient, happened there on his regular round, and found the house full of ladies, busily engaged in making two bed-quilts. Soon after he made his appearance, the lady of the house proposed preaching, which was assented to by him and the company. He accordingly preached to them, and they were so well pleased with the discourse, that ever after, there was no want of a congregation in that place. In the fall of the year 1804, Mr. Roberts made a visit to his friends in Shenango, and leaving his wife among them to spend the winter, he returned to his circuit, where he spent the remainder of the year with profit to himself and others.

At the Conference of 1805, he was appointed to Shenango circuit, an appointment which, though it did not embrace the neighborhood where his friends lived, brought him much nearer to them. While on this circuit, he called one day on a Presbyterian family, to get his horse fed; the ladies of the house supposing him to be a minister, were very desirous to know whether he was a Presbyterian or a Seceder, but without giving them any direct answer, they took it for granted, that he was a Presbyterian. The lady and her daughter took occasion to say some bitter things against the Methodists, but he let them pass without any opposing remarks. Being invited to stay to dinner, he did so, and after dinner, when about to leave, the lady requested him to stay over the Sabbath, and attend Church, as the minister would be very glad to see him. He informed her that he could not stay, as he had an appointment himself. She then wished to know if he was seeking a call from a congregation. He replied that he already had congregations; to which she answered, that she had never heard of any one by the name of Roberts having a congregation in that part of the country. She wished to know where his congregation was, and he, in reply, gave her a list of his appointments on his extensive charge, at which tho good lady expressed great surprise. He then remarked, that he was one of those people of whom she had spoken so reproachfully, a short time before. "Not a Methodist!" she exclaimed, with astonishment. "Yes," he replied. "Well, no person could have taken you for one," said the good lady. She, however, invited him to call again, and ever after, treated him with the greatest respect and attention.

Through the kindness of his presiding elder, Mr. Roberts at the second quarterly meeting, received an appointment which embraced his former place of residence, and where his land was situated. Having a little spare time, he superintended the erection of a mill, on a stream near his residence, the object of which was to supply the wants of his family from its proceeds, as his receipts from the circuits did not pay his expenses. This, however, proved a detriment to his usefulness, so much so, that he ever after regretted having had anything to do with the mill, and strongly advised all preachers never to leave the word of God, to serve tables, as they would be losers in the end.

At the next Conference of 1806, Mr. Roberts was ordained elder, by Bishop Asbury, and was returned to Erie circuit, the field of his former labors near home. It, however, embraced all that territory now included in the Erie Conference, except that part which lies in the State of New York, and required six weeks to go round it. While going to an appointment one evening, he was by an accident on the road, unavoidably belated and overtaken by the darkness of night, and as there was no road, or even path to guide him, he was forced to seek shelter in a log-cabin, where he found the children and furniture all besmeared with bear's grease, so that he hesitated about stopping. He, however, felt obliged to take shelter somewhere, and as he was cordially welcomed to the best the house afforded, he concluded, notwithstanding the filthiness of the place, to tarry for the night. He was informed by his hostess, that she had no bread in the house, nor anything to make any of; she, however, cooked a large supply of fat bear's meat and potatoes, which she hospitably placed before him, on a slab table. Though extremely hungry, Mr. Roberts did not relish his supper, and ate but little. As there was no regular bed in the house, they furnished him with a small quantity of straw, which was spread on the floor before the fire. On this he lay, his feet toward the fire, having his saddle-bags for a pillow, and his great-coat for his covering. As the night was cold, he slept but little, and after having taken his breakfast of bear's meat in the morning, and having baptized several of the children, he proceeded joyfully on his way.

While on Erie circuit, Mr. Roberts was invited to attend a meeting to be held in a Methodist house, where a Seceder minister was to deliver a sermon, for the purpose of convincing the Methodists of their error in maintaining that Jesus Christ died for the whole human family. The text was, "Contend earnestly for the faith once delivered to the saints," and the propositions advanced, were: 1. That Christ did not die for all the sins of all men; for then all men must be saved. 2. That he did not die for some of the sins of all men; for none could be saved. 3. That he died for all the sins of some men; for some only would be saved. When he had concluded his discourse of four hours' length, Mr. Roberts begged the privilege of replying, which was granted. He took hold of the arguments advanced with such masterly powers for a few minutes, that the Seceder, seeing himself likely to be worsted in the contest, withdrew from the house, leaving Mr. Roberts the master of the field. The effect produced was such, that many of the seceders were ever after among his most attentive hearers, notwithstanding the avowed wishes of their minister to the contrary.

At the Conference of 1807, Mr. Roberts was appointed to Pittsburg (Pa.) circuit, and at the succeeding Conference of 1808, was stationed at the West Wheeling circuit. As the General Conference sat this year, and as all travelling elders were at that period *ex-officio* members of that body, he felt it to be his duty to attend, although after having paid his moving expenses to his new circuit, he had but a single half-dollar left, wherewith to bear his expenses on the journey of three hundred miles. He, however, borrowed a half-dollar of his colleague, but such was his economy, and the kindness of friends on the road, that when he arrived in Baltimore, he had five cents of the dollar left. While at the Conference,

Mr. Roberts was appointed to preach in the Light-street Church, and supposing that the members of that Church were somewhat tinctured with pride, he delivered a severe sermon on the subject. His own clothing was coarse, and had been much worn. A few days after having preached the sermon, he was waited on at his room by a tailor, who took his measurement for some new articles of apparel, which were soon finished, and presented to him by some friend unknown. So much was his sermon liked by the members of the Light-street Church, that they petitioned Bishop Asbury to station Mr. Roberts over them as their pastor; accordingly in the latter part of the summer, he was officially requested by the bishop to leave West Wheeling, and proceed immediately to Baltimore, but such was his diffidence, that he hesitated to comply, nor was it until he had received a second peremptory letter, and had been strongly advised by his faithful wife to a compliance with the bishop's request, that he consented to go. He accordingly, with a few dollars in his pocket, and with a couple of horses for himself and wife to ride on the journey, started for his new appointment, having recourse during the day to his saddle-bags, for supplies of bread and cheese, and stopping with their acquaintances over-night. He spent the remainder of the Conference year very pleasantly, and at the next Conference of 1809, was re-appointed to the Baltimore station. In 1810, he was stationed at Fells Point, and in 1811, in Alexandria, D. C., where he was so greatly esteemed by people of different denominations, that he frequently exchanged pulpits with the resident clergymen of the place, especially the Protestant Episcopal minister In 1812, he was stationed in Georgetown, D. C., and while here, had an introduction, in a formal manner, to Mr. Madison, President of the United States. His reserve, and dignified mien, so far attracted the attention of the President, that the latter expressed a desire to form an acquaintance with him in a more private and informal manner. He accordingly, some time after, made the President and his lady a private visit, and after a delightful and profitable interview, it was terminated by a solemn season of prayer.

During the years 1813 and '14, Mr. Roberts was stationed in the city of Philadelphia, a place which has always secured the services of the most able ministers of the Church. While a resident of Philadelphia, he made a visit to Indiana, to which State his brother Lewis had removed. On his journey, he stopped at Orleans, where was a company of United States soldiers stationed. He found the latter engaged in target-shooting, and as Mr. Roberts appeared to take some interest in the exercise, they invited him to try his skill at the rifle, which he did, and fairly surpassed the whole company in the correctness of his aim, which proved, as might be expected, a matter of astonishment to the soldiers, who acknowledged themselves beaten in the use of their own favorite weapon, by a Philadelphia clergyman. We mention this circumstance, to show that Mr. Roberts, although elevated to a dignified position in society, and whose acquaintance was sought for by the great and honorable of the land, did not feel himself so far above his more humble fellows, as to refuse to take an interest in their innocent diversions and useful pastimes. In 1815, Mr. Roberts was appointed presiding elder of Schuylkill district, which then embraced within its bounds Philadelphia and vicinity. At the Philadelphia Conference of 1816, in consequence of the recent death of Bishop Asbury, and the indisposition of Bishop M'Kendree, it became necessary to elect a president of the body, from among the presiding elders, and although Mr. Roberts was the youngest presiding elder in the Conference, yet he was chosen president by a large majority of votes, an evidence of the confidence placed in him by his brethren who knew him best.

As the Philadelphia Conference sat in the latter part of

April, and the General Conference was to sit on the 1st of May following, there happened to be present at the session of the former, a large number of delegates from the north, and east, on their way to Baltimore. Those delegates could not fail to discover the ease and dignity, with which Mr. Roberts discharged the duties of President; and as it would be necessary to elect one or two additional bishops, at the General Conference, their minds appear to have unanimously centred on him as one of the candidates; accordingly, on the 14th of May, when the votes for bishops were counted, it was found that Enoch George, and Robert R. Roberts, had each a majority of all the votes, and they were, consequently, declared to be duly elected Bishops of the Methodist Episcopal Church. After his election, and previously to his consecration, he had serious misgivings about the propriety of accepting the important office, to which he had been elected, honestly supposing that his brethren had overrated his abilities. He even proposed to some of his confidential friends, a desire to resign the office by declining consecration; these friends, however, who were no doubt better judges of his qualifications for the office of a bishop, than he was himself, persuaded him to be obedient to the call of God and his Church, to which he finally consented, and on the 17th of May, 1816, he was duly consecrated by the only surviving bishop,—M'Kendree—the latter being assisted by some of the senior elders present.

On Bishop Roberts' return to Philadelphia, from General Conference, his wife inquired what he designed to do with her, in regard to a place of residence, &c. He replied, that she might remain in Philadelphia, or anywhere east of the Alleghany Mountains, or she might reside on their land in Shenango, or travel with him as she chose. The former course she thought would be too expensive, the latter, too inconvenient; she accordingly elected, to reside in the small cabin which he had erected with his own hands, twenty years previously. She even sighed for that independence incident to a western life. They accordingly started for their old home, the friends in Baltimore having in the meantime, in the kindest manner, procured for him the carriage and travelling trunk of the deceased Bishop Asbury. In crossing the mountains, they found a piece of new-made road, where the mud was very deep. Mrs. Roberts, and their little nephew—George Roberts, who was with them—had to alight and walk to the summit of a hill. Meanwhile, the horses and carriage got fast in the mud, and the bishop literally was obliged to "put side and shoulder to the wheel," in order to extricate himself. The clerical fashion in those times, was long-boots, long-stockings, and breeches. His attempts to relieve the carriage from the mud, had besmeared him from head to foot, the mud running over the tops of his boots. As he gained the ascent his wife who had turned round awaiting his arrival, when she saw his be-smattered appearance, could not repress a laugh, while she exclaimed, "You are a pretty-looking bishop now." At length they arrived at their journey's end, and leaving his beloved wife among his friends, he proceeded to the discharge of his episcopal duties in attending the Conferences, &c.

After completing his visitation of the Annual Conferences, he repaired to Shenango, where he spent the greater part of the winter, not forgetting, occasionally, to spend a day in hunting. In the fall of 1817, he again visited Indiana, in company with his wife. It was while on a journey to visit one of the Southern Conferences, that the occurrence took place which gave rise to the widely circulated story, of "Bishop George, and the young Preacher,"—a story which has been published in most of the periodicals in the United States. The accounts concerning the incident, are very contradictory, and grossly exaggerated. The true hero of the tale was Bishop Roberts, and not Bishop George, as currently reported; and although the former frequently spoke of the occurrence, he never would reveal the name of the young man who figured so largely in the affair. As the story is of some length, and is probably remembered by most of our readers, and as no authentic written version is now in existence, we will not transcribe it to our pages. Suffice it to say, that such an occurrence did take place, and that the thoughtless young preacher, who unknowingly slighted his bishop, and permitted him to go to bed supperless, was afterwards heartily ashamed of his conduct, and became a useful and eminent man among his brethren.

Sometimes, when Bishop Roberts was on his way to visit the Conferences, he was obliged to take his lodgings on the cold ground. One night he thus slept on the ground, holding while asleep, his horse by the bridle, to prevent his straying; and at another time while pursuing a new route through the Genesee Flats, he subsisted for three days on strawberries. The reasons for such exposure and want, was not because he had no friends, or because the country could not have afforded him food and shelter, but because of his extreme diffidence and natural independence of spirit, which induced him rather to suffer, than to ask a favor of any person. In this regard, we think the good bishop was blameworthy, for he should have remembered, that there is a blessing in giving, as well as in receiving, and that in depriving his friends of the opportunity of giving, he was in fact injuring them, more than he would have done by an opposite course.

In 1819, Bishop Roberts removed his residence from Shenango, to Lawrence County, Indiana; his object in doing so, was to be near his brother Lewis, to whom he was ardently attached; and as he liked the country better than he did that of his former location, and was obliged to support himself in part by agriculture, his salary being only the meagre sum of two hundred dollars per annum,—he thought he could spend a portion of his time in laboring with his hands, and thus administer to his own necessities. In his removal, he was accompanied by three of his nephews, and a niece. In his journey, which took several weeks, he scarcely ever put up at a private house, but at a tavern, and it was scarcely ever known, who, or what he was, till after his departure. When Sunday arrived, he would attend some place of worship near, taking a retired seat in some part of the house, without informing any person who he was. At length they arrived at the new episcopal residence, in Indiana, consisting at first of a cabin or hut, made of unhewn logs, clapboard roof, and being without chimney, door, window, floor, or loft. Their provisions, which they carried with them, were by this time exhausted, and they had to make their supper on roasted potatoes. These were placed in a row on one of the *sleepers* of the cabin, and the good bishop devoutly asked a blessing on the meal, and after having partaken of the same, returned thanks to the Giver of all good. After supper, his young niece retired to one corner of the cabin, in rather a disconsolate mood, and stated to her cousins, that she did not see why uncle should ask a blessing, and return thanks for a supper of nothing else in the world, but roasted potatoes. For bedsteads, they placed some unhewed sticks across the sleepers, and on them made their beds. After retiring, the wolves began to howl, and as there was no door to prevent their entrance, the young niece became exceedingly terrified; but the tender-hearted uncle assured her, that the large fire would sufficiently intimidate the ravenous animals, to prevent a very near approach, and being thus assured she finally fell asleep, while the wolves thought it best to keep at a respectful distance.

After a good night's rest, the bishop and his nephews went to work to make their rude dwelling as comfortable as possible. For this purpose, the logs were smoothed with an adze, a floor was laid, chimney raised, and hearth laid, so that it became quite a respectable dwelling for one of its kind. After having completed the house, the bishop, with his nephews, cleared three acres of land, eating their breakfast before day, and in the evening their time was spent in making rude articles of furniture for the dwelling. During the winter, ten acres of land were cleared and fenced, so that it was ready for sowing and planting in the spring. As they needed a cow, the bishop had to borrow twenty dollars, wherewith to purchase one; and to procure wheat and corn, he had to sell one of his four horses. As the nearest mill was eighteen miles distant, and it required a great loss of time to get grinding done, they pounded their corn in a trough made for the purpose, and used it in the form of hominy.

In the spring, Bishop Roberts left home to attend the Annual Conferences. The following interesting anecdote is related of him in one of his journeys:

"Early in the year 1819, Bishop Roberts, on his way from Pennsylvania to the Conference in the South, arrived on Sabbath morning, in Fincastle, the county seat of Botetourt County, Va. Having no acquaintance in the place, he called at a public house, and took breakfast. On making inquiry in relation to the arrangements for the Sabbath, he was told that there was but one meeting-house in the town, and that the Rev. Wm. Cravens, a Methodist minister, had to preach there at 10 o'clock, and also the Rev. Mr. Logan, a Presbyterian minister, at 11 of the same day. At the sound of the bell, the bishop went to the church, and took his seat among the hearers. According to arrangement, Mr. Cravens preached, and Mr. Logan followed. The Rev. Edward Mitchell, a Methodist minister, who lived a few miles south-west of the place, was called upon to close. When the congregation was dismissed, Mr. Roberts inquired of Mr. Mitchell, how far he lived from the town, and in what direction. Being politely answered, he then said to Mr. Mitchell, if he would wait until he could get his horse from the house at which he had put up, he would go along with him. To this, Mr. Mitchell readily consented. As they left the town, Mr. Mitchell, who was fond of conversation, and always desirous of giving it a religious turn, commenced talking about the preaching they had heard. Mr. Cravens having insisted on the doctrine of restitution, he wished to know of the stranger, what was his opinion of it. Mr. Roberts stated that he did not object to the doctrine in the least. Mr. Mitchell still wishing to turn the subject to the best advantage with the stranger, said, very pointedly, it was one thing to consent to the truth, and another to practise upon it. Mr. Roberts discovering that he was not suspected, was willing that Mr. Mitchell should give what direction to the conversation he might think proper, and modestly replied, with his usual peculiarity to such questions as were proposed to him. When they arrived at Mr. Mitchell's residence, Mr. M. said to him, 'There is the stable, and the hay, and corn, and my rule is, that all who come to see me, must wait on themselves.' To this, the stranger raised no objections, and put up his horse. When he had done, the dinner was ready. Mr. Mitchell, as was his custom, asked a blessing, and when seated, resumed the conversation, and took the liberty of inquiring of the stranger where he was from, and to what place he was going. On these questions being answered, he was next asked what was his name. To which the bishop replied, 'My name is Roberts.' 'Any relation to Robert R. Roberts, one of our bishops?' asked Mr. Mitchell. 'My name is Robert R. Roberts,' said the stranger. At this, Mr. Mitchell involuntarily dropped his knife and fork, and gazed a moment speechless at his visitor, and all at once the thought struck him, that his appearance, conversation, and general deportment, were those of a minister of the Gospel, and it was a matter of astonishment to him, that he had not thought of his being a clergyman before.

"Mr. Mitchell, after having composed himself a little, asked the bishop why he had not made himself known to them when he first entered the town, and preached for them. To which the bishop replied, that it was his intention so to have done: he had travelled rapidly, the day before, in order to enjoy the holy day of rest among them, but on learning the arrangements that had been made, and also that Mr. Cravens, like himself, was a stranger, and had only stopped to spend the Sabbath day there, he thought it best to attend the house of God as an humble hearer of the word of life, and thus have the privilege of worshipping with the people of that strange land, in the capacity of a private Christian."

From the above, it will be seen that the bishop was always averse to the act of proclaiming who he was, on his arrival at any place. The following extract, being the substance of a narration given by Bishop Roberts to Bishop Morris, will serve further to illustrate his course in this respect.

"Bishop Roberts, once travelling on horseback, along a road with which he was unacquainted, inquired for a quiet house of entertainment, where he might spend the night, and on recommendation, went to one without knowing the character of the man that kept it, but who he subsequently learned was a local preacher of his own denomination. He obtained leave to stay all night, and supper was provided for him. Shortly after which, the landlord lit a candle, placed it in the lantern, and when about going out of the house, said to the bishop, 'If you wish to retire before we return, you can take a bed in the adjoining room; we are going to a meeting.'

"*Bishop.*—'What sort of a meeting is it?'

"*Landlord.*—'It is what we Methodists call a class-meeting.'

"*B.*—'I should like to go along, if it would not be intruding.'

"*L.*—'No intrusion at all. We allow serious persons to

attend class-meetings a few times without becoming members, if they wish.'

"They proceeded together to the meeting, which was well attended. The class-leader was a young man of much zeal, and little experience. After speaking to all the members, he came to the bishop, when the following conversation ensued:

"*Leader*. 'Well, stranger, have you any desire to serve the Lord, and get to heaven?'

"*B*. 'I have such a desire.'

"*L*. 'How long have you had this desire?'

"*B*. 'I cannot say precisely how long now, but for many years.'

"*L*. 'Well, do you think, old gentleman, that you know anything about the enjoyment of experimental religion?'

"*B*. 'Yes, brother, I trust I do know, and have known a long time what experimental religion is, though I acknowledge I have not been as faithful as I should have been, and consequently have not made that progress in religion which it was my privilege to have made. Still, I have a good hope in the mercy of God, through Christ, that I shall be saved in heaven at last.'

"The leader closed the exercise himself, in the usual way, and the bishop returned with his host in silence. After they had been seated a short time, a small table was placed in the room, with a Bible and hymn-book. The landlord, after deep study, looked at the Bible, then at the bishop, and again seemed to be in a deep study. After a few more side glances, he rose and started towards the table, then stopped, cleared his throat, and went to the door and spit; then turned again toward the table, but finally stopped and said to the bishop, 'Old gentleman, you appear to be a man that knows something of religion; it is our practice here to have family worship; perhaps you would be willing to read and pray with us?'

"*B*. 'I have no objection, brother, if you wish it.'

"He proceeded to read, sing, and pray in his own impressive manner. The landlord then took a candle, and showed him his room; and started out, got to the door, and stopped, turned round, hesitated, and finally remarked, 'Old gentleman, if it would be no offence, I would like to know your name.'

"*B.* 'No offence at all, brother, my name is Robert R. Roberts.'

"When the bishop related this anecdote to the writer, he added, 'And they paid me well for telling my name; for they detained me two days, and made me preach several times.' I wished him to tell me how the young class-leader looked about the close of his first sermon, but he declined making any comments."

In 1825, several ministers on their way to Conference, called at Bishop Roberts' residence. One of them—Mr. Randall—being an Englishman, and recently from that country, had a great desire to see a bishop of the Methodist Church, as also his residence; no doubt expecting to behold some of the splendor attached to the prelacy of England, but he found only a dwelling of the most humble pretensions. The bishop was not in the house when they arrived, but the visitors were told that he was out in the grass lot. The Englishman, impatient to see him, could not wait until he came in, but went out to catch a glimpse of him, if possible. One of the preachers pointed to the bishop in the lot, but the Englishman remarked that he saw no bishop there. "Look in the grass lot," said the other. He looked again, and said, "I see a man there, but no bishop." "But that is certainly the bishop," replied his companion. "No! no!" rejoined he, "that cannot be, for the man is in his shirt sleeves." Soon the bishop came up, and the remarks which had been made were related to him, which he seemed to relish with great pleasure.

From the time of his election to the episcopacy, to that of

his death, Bishop Roberts made his annual visits to the Conferences with punctuality, and always presided with dignity, and to the entire satisfaction of the preachers. Nor was it alone in the Conferences, and by the preachers, that he was beloved and respected. The people in every place where he appeared, admired the simplicity of his manners, and the humility of his deportment. In a certain town, a violent opposer of the Methodist Episcopal Church once thought it his duty to declaim publicly against the Methodist bishops, and represented them as going about the country in a style of magnificence and splendor. As his remarks were generally believed, a corresponding degree of prejudice was created in the minds of the people against the bishops and the Church, and a seceding church was formed in the place, which was likely to *eat up* the old one. A few weeks after, Bishop Roberts providentially passed through the place, and when it was announced that he would preach, a general curiosity was excited to see and hear the pompous prelate, as they supposed him to be. The house was filled to overflowing, and at the appointed hour, the *prelate* appeared, arrayed in an old faded calico robe, or loose gown, and all his other apparel of the coarsest kind; and when the good old bishop preached in his artless, winning way, he won the hearts of the entire congregation, so that the current immediately set in, in an opposite direction, and the seceders soon gave up their new Church, and returned in a body to their old home.

Bishop Roberts' labors during the last years of his life, were arduous and unremitting. In the spring of 1842, he set out to visit the Indian Missions, west of the Arkansas and Missouri, purposing also to visit those on the Upper Mississippi; and this, too, when his health was very feeble. The hardships endured by the old man and his travelling companion, had we space to notice them, would prove that the office of a Methodist bishop is by no means a sinecure, but we must forbear. One little incident connected with this visit to the wilds of the West, we will notice. While in the neighborhood of Fort Leavenworth, the bishop and his companion stopped at an Indian trading house, and requested accommodations for the night. The trader was unwilling to accommodate them, not knowing who they were. They offered to take up with fire and shelter merely, but all entreaty was unavailing. At last, the bishop's companion turned to him and said, "*Bishop*, what is to be done?" "Why, we must get some fire and camp out," replied the latter. The word *bishop*, had a powerful effect on the Frenchman's ears, for he immediately said, "O, by no means, gentlemen, you shall be very welcome to stay;" and stay they did, and found comfortable entertainment for the night. The gentleman who accompanied the bishop, after finding out the value of the title *bishop*, never failed to use it in every case of subsequent emergency, and found it always paid all expenses.

In compensation for these laborious services, the bishop, as we have seen elsewhere, received the annual allowance of two hundred dollars! In addition, however, to the above, the General Conference, in view of the necessary family expenses of the married bishops, authorized the book agents at New York, to make them an annual allowance for table expenses. From 1816 to 1819, no such allowance was received, for some cause, by Bishop Roberts; so that for the first three years of his episcopate, two hundred dollars was the sum total of his receipts. From 1819 to 1832, he received two hundred dollars additional, for table expenses, making his annual receipts four hundred dollars; and at no time during his life, did they exceed six hundred, all told. Now, when it is known that bishops are expected to be examples of hospitality and benevolence, and that the occasions for the exercise of these traits of character are very frequent, it is truly a matter of astonishment, how on the one hand, they could give liberally, and on the other, find means to do so. The true secret is to be found in the rigid economy of those self-denying men, and their companions in life.

Bishop Roberts for many years, was subject to an asthmatic complaint, which become increased by the cold weather of the winter of 1842–3. He was finally prostrated upon the bed of disease, and on the 26th of March, 1843, he closed his eyes in death, at his residence in Indiana. His remains were interred within the precincts and solitude of his own farm, where they remained for several months, but at length, by vote of the Indiana Conference, they were disinterred, and conveyed to Greencastle, Ia., for final interment, where they were deposited in a beautiful spot near the buildings of the Indiana University. Baltimore, Louisville, and Cincinnati, all begged the privilege of removing his remains to their respective localities, but it was, perhaps, more fitting that they should remain in the State where he had so long resided, and that the University to which he had bequeathed all his disposable property, should have the honor of receiving his remains, and giving to them a place of sepulture. His end was peaceful, and his last breathings were those of prayer. Thus died Robert R. Roberts, in the sixty-fifth year of his age, the forty-first of his travelling ministry, and the twenty-seventh of his episcopate.

A brief description of his person and character will close this chapter. Physically, Bishop Roberts was comely in his person ; his height, five feet ten inches ; his frame, heavy and inclined to corpulency ; his features, large, but not gross ; his eye blue, and noticeable for its calmness ; his manners totally unaffected, and the very pattern of true simplicity. Mentally considered, Bishop Roberts was a man of more than ordinary talents ; his mind was penetrating, his judgment sound, and his memory wonderfully retentive. As a preacher, he may have had his superiors for power, and what is usually called eloquence; but for clearness of thought, simplicity of style, and above all, the divine unction which attended the word, he had few, if any, equals. In regard to piety, which embraces all the elements of Christian duty and feeling, he was above suspicion. No greater eulogy need be given him, than that he was emphatically a good man, a good *minister*, and a good BISHOP. "For" him "to live," was "Christ; to die" was "gain."

JOHN EMORY

CHAPTER XVI.

BISHOP EMORY.

In the Christian ministry have always been found men of diversified talents and acquirements. Some have possessed a gigantic intellect, with a refined and polished education, which having smoothed the natural unevenness of their character, has left nothing but the pure diamond to glitter and enlighten the world. Others, with the same strength of mind, the same vigor of understanding, the same capacity for knowledge, are, for lack of opportunity, left like the diamond in its rough and unpolished state, which although it may not dazzle so much, is nevertheless as purely a diamond as the other. It must be admitted also, that men, and especially ministers, differ very much in their natural, as well as acquired abilities; while some are persons of only moderate strength of mind, others, are perfect intellectual giants; but each one is necessary to the progress of truth, and each is requisite to fill the important station designed for him in the arrangements of divine providence. The apostles of our Lord differed in strength of understanding, as well as in acquired abilities; one had the learning and refinement of Paul, another the zeal and ardor of Peter, while a third had the love and superior piety of John; and all these "diversities of gifts" were bestowed for the express purpose of meeting the diversified views and feelings of men, that the whole body of Christ might be edified, not only by a "diversity of operations" but by a "difference of administrations."

In a preceding chapter, we have seen Bishop George as a diamond dug from the earth, but retaining in part, its unpolished surface, arising from obscurity, and becoming an acknowledged leader and superintendent of the largest protestant denomination of Christians in the United States. As the subject of the present chapter, we are called to the contemplation of a man filling the same important office, and yet entirely dissimilar in many respects, from the subject of the former; a man, who to strength of understanding, added the advantages of education and the polished refinement of the Christian gentleman.

John Emory was a native of the State of Maryland, and was born in the year 1788. He was, at an early age, carefully instructed in the rudiments of education, and as he was designed by his parents for the profession of law, they directed his course of study with direct reference to their design; and young John was by no means backward in applying his mind to the pursuit of knowledge, intending, no doubt, at some future day, to act a conspicuous part at the bar, as well as in the councils of the nation. Up to the age of seventeen, he lived, as the majority of youths do, "without God, and without hope in the world," but at the latter age, through the instrumentality of the Methodists, he was powerfully convinced of sin, and led to consecrate himself, with all his talents and acquirements, to the service of God. As the result of such unreserved consecration, he soon obtained the forgiveness of sin, as also the "witness of the Spirit," to bear witness with his spirit, that he was a child of God and an heir of heaven.

Shortly after young Emory's conversion, he felt himself called to cast in his lot with the Methodists, and after having taken this important step, he felt an impression that it was his duty to forsake the study of law, and devote himself to the work of the ministry. Young Emory was not the only one who received an impression of his duty in that respect; for as the Spirit of God in its operations upon the mind of the candidate, and upon the minds of the members of his Church harmonizes in pointing out the way of duty, so in Mr. Emory's case, the Church with which he had connected himself, soon discovered that God had a work for him to do; consequently, he soon received license to exhort, and preach; and in the year 1810, when in his twenty-second year, he entered the travelling ministry, by being received on trial in the Philadelphia Annual Conference of the Methodist Episcopal Church. It is comparatively unimportant what particular circuits he travelled during his novitiate; suffice it to say, that he made full proof of his call to the ministry, and in due course of time was honorably received into full connection with the Conference, and ordained first a deacon, and subsequently an elder in the Church of God, having, in the meanwhile, filled the various stations assigned him by his senior brethren, with great credit to himself, and honor to the Church.

In the year 1816, although but an elder for two years, and consequently one of the younger members of the Conference, and being but twenty-eight years of age, such was the confidence reposed in him by his brethren, that they elected him as a delegate to the General Conference, which assembled that year in the city of Baltimore. While met with his brethren in the highest council of the Church, he displayed talents of no ordinary kind, and it was a knowledge of the possession of these talents combined with an elevated tone of piety, which induced the General Conference itself to bestow upon him some of the highest honors, and invest him with some of the gravest responsibilities which it had power to confer upon the ministers of the Church.

In the year 1820, he was by the Baltimore Conference, of which he had become a member, again elected to a seat in the General Conference, and a further mark of honor was conferred upon him, by the General Conference, in selecting him as its representative to the British Wesleyan Conference in England. At this period, important questions relating to the Methodists in the Provinces of Canada, were being agitated between the British and American Methodists. Methodism was planted in Canada, principally by the labors of ministers of the Methodist Episcopal Church in the United States, and the Societies raised up in different parts of the two provinces, had been supplied with preachers from the latter Church, until the war of 1812–15, during the existence of which, it was both inconvenient and unsafe for American ministers to cross the boundary line. Hence, the British Conference considered it a duty to send missionaries to different parts of the provinces, who occupied the various fields of labor assigned them, until the cessation of hostilities. When peace ensued, and all barriers to passing and repassing were removed, a large portion of the Societies desired to be supplied again with the word of life, and the ordinances of religion from their former pastors and ministers; while another portion desired a continuance of the labors of the English Missionaries among them. And as the bishops of the American Church did not possess sufficient authority to withdraw their jurisdiction from the Societies in Canada, it became necessary for them to appoint preachers to places hitherto occupied by them, but now occupied by the preachers of the English Connection. This state of things led to considerable confusion and agitation, in the localities alluded to, and a correspondence ensued, in relation to existing difficulties, between the bishops of the American Church, and the missionary committee of the English Conference.

The Rev. Messrs. Black and Bennett were appointed by the Wesleyan Conference, as delegates to the General Conference of the Methodist Episcopal Church, to adjust if possible the existing difficulties between the two bodies, and a long and friendly letter was received from the former body, an extract of which relating to these difficulties, we will give to the reader: "To preserve a good mutual understanding and the unity of the Spirit, and as far as possible, a co-operation in promoting the good work of the Lord, we feel it our duty to state to you, a subject of local difference which to us has been painful, and which we feel a delicacy in stating, but to which we are compelled from the necessity of the case, that the word of the Lord be not hindered. In consequence of application being made to the British Conference, from the Society at Montreal, a missionary was sent to that place, and received as the messenger of the gospel of peace; but we are sorry to learn, that some misunderstanding has taken place between brothers Strong and Williams, our missionaries, and brother Ryan, your presiding elder for Lower Canada. From the former, we have received a statement of their proceedings, and from the latter, a letter of complaint. We have also received a letter from Brother Bennett, the chairman of the Nova Scotia district, who has visited Montreal, &c., and reported to us his proceedings. Upon a review of the whole, and from the most serious and deliberate consideration, we are led to conclude that considering the relative situation of the inhabitants of Montreal, and of Canada to this country, and particularly, as a principal part of the people appear to be in favor of our missionaries, it would be for their peace and comfort, and the furtherance of the Gospel, for our brethren to occupy those stations, especially the former, and to which we conceive we have a claim, as a considerable part of the money for building the Chapel and house, was raised in this country. We trust our American brethren will see the propriety of complying with our wishes in respect to these places; not to mention their political relation to this country, which however is not of little importance, for we are conscious that their general habits and preferences, are in favor of English preachers, being more congenial to their views and feelings, which should certainly be consulted, and will tend to facilitate the success of the Gospel, and their spiritual prosperity. As your, and our object is, mutually to diffuse the knowledge of Him whose kingdom is not of this world, and by every possible means to promote the immortal interests of men, let us not contend,—we have one Master, even Christ—but give place to each other, that the word of the Lord may have free course, run and be glorified. We cannot but hope that from the contiguity of the labors of the brethren belonging to the two Conferences, the spirit of lenity and love will be promoted, and by this measure a more perfect reciprocal intercourse established. As you have kindly invited our esteemed brethren Messrs. Black and Bennett, to take a seat in your Conference, we have directed them to pay you a visit at Baltimore, for this purpose, and to amicably arrange and settle this business, whom we trust you will receive as our representatives and as brethren."

The document from which the above extract is taken, was signed in behalf of the Wesleyan Mission Committee, in London, by Rev. Messrs. Wood, Benson, and Buckley, and after having been read to the General Conference was referred to a special committee, who presented a report which was adopted. As this report will serve to throw additional light on the subject of Mr. Emory's visit to England, we beg leave to transfer it to our pages.

"The Committee appointed by the General Conference to confer with Messrs. Black and Bennett, delegates appointed by the London Methodist Missionary Society, to represent the British Connection in this Conference, and if possible to make an amicable adjustment of certain differences between our Church, and the British Connection, relative to Upper and Lower Canada, beg leave to submit the following report, viz.:—

"1. Your Committee have had several friendly interviews with the above-mentioned delegates on those subjects, and they are happy to state, that there appears to be an earnest desire to have all existing difficulties terminated, to the peace and mutual satisfaction of both parties, and to perpetuate the Christian union and good understanding which have hitherto existed.

"2. It appears from written communications, as well as from verbal testimony, that unhappy dissensions have taken place in Montreal, between certain missionaries, sent (at the request of a few official members of the Society in that place, in time of the last war) by the London Missionary Society, and some American preachers, which have terminated in the division of that Society.

"3. Although the late hostilities between the two countries, separated for some time those provinces from the immediate superintendency of the Methodist Episcopal Church in America, yet all the circuits (except Quebec) were as regularly supplied as circumstances would admit of, with American preachers.

"4. It furthermore appears, from written and verbal communications, that it is the desire of the great majority of the people in Upper and Lower Canada, to be supplied as heretofore, with preachers from the United States.

"5. In the two provinces, there are twelve circuits, and one station (Montreal), which have eleven meeting-houses, which have been hitherto supplied by American preachers.

"These things being duly considered, together with the contiguity of those provinces to the western and northern parts of the United States, your committee respectfully submit the following resolutions:—

"*Resolved*, By the delegates of the Annual Conference of the Methodist Episcopal Church, in General Conference assembled,

"1. That we cannot consistently with our duty to the Societies of our charge in the Canadas, give up any part of them, or any of our chapels in those provinces, to the superintendence of the British Connection.

"2. That a respectful letter be addressed to the London Methodist Missionary Society, explaining the reasons for the above resolution."

In accordance with the second resolution, a respectful and friendly letter was sent to the Wesleyan Missionary Committee, giving the reasons which led to the adoption of the first resolution, and requesting that the preachers in each Connection in Canada, might be permitted to occupy and labor in their respective fields, without molestation from each other. Whatever disposition might have existed on the part of the General Conference, or the Wesleyan Missionary Committee, to heal existing difficulties, it was found much easier to recommend peace and mutual forbearance, than it was to heal the breach which had been made in certain localities, particularly in Montreal and Kingston; hence, for a number of years subsequent to the General Conference of 1816, two parties were found in those localities, and in Montreal, both British and American preachers were regularly stationed over the Society (or more properly Societies) in that city, until the local feeling became so excited, as to be intolerable; and the same state of things existed to a greater or less extent in several parts of Upper Canada.

At the General Conference of 1820, the subject again came before that body, by numerous memorials and complaints, from the several Societies in Upper Canada, protesting in the strongest terms against the interference of the British missionaries, and praying for a continued supply of the word of life and the ordinances of the Gospel, from the United States. Whereupon, the General Conference adopted a resolution, instructing the bishops to continue their superintendence over all the Societies in the Canadas, excepting Quebec. They then made provision for the appointment of a delegate to the British Conference, to negotiate in regard to the existing difficulties, and effect if possible an amicable arrangement. Mr. Emory, as before stated, was the person selected to proceed to England on this important mission. He accordingly sailed for Europe in the month of July following, and was cordially received by the British Conference, as the messenger of peace.

After having opened his commission, an arrangement was happily effected in relation to hitherto existing difficulties. A series of resolutions was accordingly adopted by the Conference, to which Mr. Emory, as the representative of the American Connection, cheerfully assented. The substance of these resolutions is as follows :—

1. That as American and British Methodists are but one body, it is inconsistent with such unity, to have different Societies and congregations in the same towns and villages.

2. That this principle govern the two Conferences in their adjustment of disputes.

3. That the most effectual mode of carrying this rule into effect, is for the American brethren exclusively to occupy Upper Canada, and the British missionaries Lower Canada.

4. That should any place on either side of the boundary line, be destitute of religious help, then either body, with the consent of the General Conference, or Canada District Meeting, may appoint preachers to such destitute settlements.

5. That each party be bound to supply all places left vacant by the other, under the agreement made, with preachers, &c.

6. That the English Mission Committee address a letter to all the members in Upper Canada, informing them of the arrangement, and requesting them to transfer their membership to the Methodist Episcopal Church.

7. That the bishops of the American Church direct a simi-

lar letter to the members in Lower Canada, making a similar request, to place themselves under the care of the British missionaries.

In addition to the plan of agreement entered into between the British Conference and Mr. Emory, as the representative of the American Church, for the settlement of difficulties, several other resolutions were adopted by the former, as expressive of their good feeling toward, and desire for a closer union with their transatlantic brethren. In these resolutions, they commend the American Church for its zeal and efficiency, and expressed a desire for a continued interchange of delegates; they strongly express their high approbation of the selection of Mr. Emory as the representative to their body; that there should be a regular exchange of ministers, magazines, missionary reports, and notices, and all new original works published by the European and American Methodists, from their respective book-rooms.

Mr. Emory, having discharged the duties assigned him by his brethren, soon after returned home, and having made his report of the success of his mission, returned to his appropriate work of preaching the Gospel, and was cordially welcomed back to his former field of labor.

In accordance with the resolutions adopted in England, the Wesleyan Missionary Committee in London on the 20th of August, 1820, addressed a letter of instructions to their missionaries in Upper and Lower Canada, replete with sentiments of kindness and affection, and in which honorable mention is made of Mr. Emory, and exhorting them to carry out the provisions of the resolutions in the same temper and spirit, with which they were mutually agreed upon. A letter referring to the same matter, was also addressed on the 20th of October following, by Bishop M'Kendree to the members, official members, and trustees, in Lower Canada, in which they are advised to place themselves and their chapels, under the care of the English missionaries. "This communication to you," says the venerable bishop, "we confess is not made without pain; not from any want of affection for our British brethren, but from the recollection of those tender and endearing ties, which have bound us to you. But a necessity is laid upon us.—It is a peace-offering—No other consideration could have induced us to consent to the measure. Forgive, therefore, our seeming to give you up. We do not give you up in heart, in affection, in kind regards, in prayers."

The result of these pacific measures, was that all matters of an unpleasant nature as existing between the two bodies, were at once removed, and ever since that period, nothing but friendship and good-feeling have existed between the British and American Methodists, a state of things, for which both parties are greatly indebted to the Christian urbanity and dignity of Mr. Emory.

In 1824, Mr. Emory was elected assistant-agent of the Book Concern in New York, an office which he filled to the entire satisfaction of the General Conference, and, indeed, of the whole Church, and one which demands more than ordinary business qualifications, on the part of the person filling it. After having served the Church in the above capacity for four years, he was elected by the General Conference, as the principal agent of the Concern, and although his physical strength during this period, would not allow him to perform all that active service in the department, which he would have been glad to have rendered, yet by his judicious counsels, and wise arrangements, he continued to manage its interests, and promote its prosperity in a manner truly praiseworthy.

It was during the period in which he sustained the office of assistant-agent, that Mr. Emory found it necessary to enter the lists of controversy, and do battle for the cause of truth and righteousness. The occasion which called for the use of his pen as a polemic writer, was one in which the well-being of the Church was at stake, and in which a combined effort was being made to subvert the constitution of the Church; and as a necessary result, to destroy its efficiency and success: we allude to the efforts of the "Reformers," who commenced their operations as early as the year 1824, by the presentation of memorials and petitions, from lay members and local preachers to the General Conference, praying that body to grant them "the right," as they termed it, of a voice in the legislative department of the Church; in other words to admit of lay representation in the General Conference. The General Conference knowing, that however proper a system of lay delegation might be for other branches of the Christian Church, yet it must effectually destroy the itinerancy of the Methodist Episcopal Church if permitted, saw fit to declare against the expediency of the measure proposed. This refusal to grant the prayers of the memorialists, at once awakened the deadliest hostility not only to the government of the Church, but to its chief officers, and leading men. A paper was accordingly established in the city of Baltimore, which had now become the head-quarters of the malcontents,—bearing the imposing title of "Mutual Rights," and advocating in the strongest and most belligerent manner possible, the necessity of lay representation. Not content with the publication of this periodical, the disaffected formed themselves into what they called "Union Societies," for the express purpose of overthrowing the government of the Church.

In this work, the "Reformers" were led on by Rev. Nicholas Snethen, who had formerly been an influential travelling preacher, but who having *located*, had taken up his residence near Baltimore, and who by personal addresses, and by articles in the "Mutual Rights," and "Wesleyan Repository,"—another reform paper,—had in the grossest terms, condemned the existing policy of the Church. In the meanwhile, the

Rev. Alexander M'Caine, a popular travelling minister, volunteered his services in aid of the cause of reform, and published a pamphlet entitled the "History and Mystery of Methodist Episcopacy," in which he attempted to prove, that unfair and dishonorable measures had been pursued in the organization of the Methodist Episcopal Church; that Mr. Wesley never designed the establishment of a Methodist Episcopacy in America; and as a matter of consequence, the episcopacy of Methodism is spurious; and Coke, Asbury, and other fathers of the Church, who assisted in its organization, were designing and corrupt men.

As the most of these worthy men were in their graves, such an outrageous attack upon their memory, aroused the spirits of their sons in the gospel, many of whom had stood aloof from the controversy, but who could not remain at rest, and see the well-earned fame of the fathers of Methodism, sacrificed on the altar of reform. As already intimated, Mr. Emory stepped forth in honor of the memory of the dead, and in the year 1827, published "A Defence of 'Our Fathers;' and of the original organization of the Methodist Episcopal Church, against the Rev. Alexander M'Caine and others; with historical and critical notices of early American Methodism." As a brief analysis of a portion of the contents of this work, may be both interesting and profitable to the reader, we will invite attention to a few sections.

In the preface, Mr. Emory says: "The work here presented to the reader, is not a party work. It is an attempt to wipe off the foul stains, which have been cast on us by the aspersion of our founders. If Mr. M'Caine's book be true, it is impossible that any Methodist who is a real friend of the Church, and of our fathers, can otherwise than feel himself disgraced. To such, a satisfactory refutation of it, cannot fail to be acceptable. Whatever may be the claims of the respective questions of ecclesiastical polity agitated among us, let them stand on their own basis. To attempt to promote any of them by personal attacks on the dead, is an unworthy resort; and with the judicious and reflecting, can only be regarded as indicating a deficiency of better arguments."

The body of the work contains nineteen sections. In the first section, Mr. Emory treats of the true nature of episcopacy, and shows, that many of the most celebrated archbishops and bishops of the Church of England taught the doctrine, that episcopacy is by no means necessary to the existence and perpetuity of the Church of Christ, and that nineteen twentieths of all the episcopalians in Great Britain and the United States, agree with the above in sentiment. He quotes largely from Stillingfleet's "Irenicum" to prove that Christ established no particular form of Church government, but that each individual branch of the Church of Christ, may select such form as is best designed to promote its interests. In the second section, Mr. Emory proves that Bishop White, the father of American Episcopalianism, and bishop of the Protestant Episcopal Church in Pennsylvania, held the same opinions precisely as did Bishop Stillingfleet. Section third, embraces Mr. Wesley's opinion, which coincides with the foregoing.

Section fourth is occupied with a consideration of the origin and nature of ministerial ordination, and he herein shows, that Mr. Wesley discarded the idea of episcopal ordination as understood by high Churchmen. In section fifth, Mr. Emory takes up the ordination of Dr. Coke by Mr. Wesley, and quotes some objections from Mr. M'Caine's book, thus: "If," says Mr. M'Caine, "Mr. Wesley ordained Dr. Coke a bishop in the common acceptation of the term, then did he create a Church officer greater than himself, and of consequence he brought himself into subjection to Dr. Coke, by making the doctor his superior." Again, "If the doctor was constituted a bishop, he was raised to a rank above a presbyter, and invested with superior powers. In that case, he that was sent, was greater than he that sent him,"—"then Mr. Wesley, who was only a presbyter, and consequently inferior to a bishop, assumed the prerogative to send his superior to do a work in his name, which he himself could not do;" and again,—"If the doctor, by the imposition of Mr. Wesley's hands, is created a bishop, then the objection of the Bishop of Norwich lies in full force in 'the greater is blessed of the less.'"

In reply to these objections, Mr. Emory says: "We have already seen what Mr. M'Caine represents to be the 'common acceptation, of the term bishop (which by the way we have shown, is *not* the common acceptation), viz.: an order of ministers distinct from presbyters by *divine appointment*, to whom the power of ordination is reserved by the *same appointment*, and is the chief mark of their distinction;—and in whom, as successors of the apostles, is vested the exclusive right of granting the divine commission to execute the ministerial office.—Now, *if* Mr. Wesley ordained Dr. Coke in no such sense;—*if* he pretended to no such thing;—*if* neither our bishops, nor the Methodist Episcopal Church have ever pretended to any such thing;—what then? Why then it follows, that all the smart sayings on this transaction, which have been repeated, and copied from my Lord Bishop of Norwich, down to Mr. M'Caine, are wholly wide of the mark, and are shaken both from Mr. Wesley and us, as the lion shakes to air, the mists shed on his mane.—If Mr. Wesley's position be true, that bishops and presbyters are the same order, the Bishop of Norwich should have first overthrown this position, if he could, to have established his own.

"But," says Mr. M'Caine, "as Mr. Wesley and Dr. Coke were of the same order,—the doctor had the same clerical right to ordain Mr. Wesley a bishop, as Mr. Wesley had to ordain the doctor."—As good a *clerical* right;—Mr. M'Caine seems to have felt here, that his argument was lame. He knows well that the true question is not as to the mere clerical power of ordination abstractly; but whether in the circumstances then existing, as to acknowledged jurisdiction, and the exigency of the times, Dr. Coke had as good a right to ordain, and send Mr. Wesley to superintend the American Methodists, as Mr. Wesley had to summon a council and to ordain and send him."

Mr. Emory then proceeds to give a brief but comprehensive account of the history of the organization of the Methodist Episcopal Church, and proves, most conclusively, that the fathers of Episcopal Methodism went no farther than they were fully authorized to do by the exigences of the case, and the express authority of Mr. Wesley; and triumphantly vindicates their memory from the slanderous charges preferred against them by their sons in the ministry.

The sixth section is occupied with a consideration of Dr. Coke's letter to Bishop White, in which the former proposed a plan of union for the Methodists and Episcopalians in America, and to secure which he expresses his belief, that the generality of the preachers would not refuse to receive reordination at the hands of an Episcopalian bishop. From this expression of belief, on the part of the doctor, Mr. M'Caine inferred, that the doctor had doubts about the validity of his own consecration, and of the ordination of those preachers admitted by him to holy orders. But Mr. Emory shows that such an inference is perfectly irrational, and completely disarms his antagonist at that point.

In section seventh, Mr. Emory proves from the "Prayer Book" prepared by Mr. Wesley, for the American Methodists, in 1784, and in which a form of ordination for three distinct officers is found, that such form of ordination would not have been recommended by Mr. Wesley, unless he had designed the organization of an Episcopal Church. Section eighth is in reference to the "Prayer Book of 1786;" and in this section, Mr. Emory asks the following important questions ;—the reader bearing in mind the fact, that Mr. M'Caine claimed that Dr. Coke had violated, or at least superseded his instructions in organizing the Methodist Societies into an Episcopal Church.

"1. If Dr. Coke and Mr. Asbury were conscious that they had been guilty of duplicity, imposition, and fraud, or of violating Mr. Wesley's instructions in the organization of the *Methodist Episcopal Church*, is it probable that they would immediately after, have printed and published the Minutes with this title, and with an explicit statement of what had been done, and thus have exposed their acts in the face of Mr. Wesley, and of the world? Is it probable that Dr. Coke, particularly, who had the Minutes printed, would have done this, knowing that he was so soon to return to England?

"2. Is it not rationally presumable, that a copy of these Minutes had reached Mr. Wesley in the interval between their publication in the middle of January, and the last of July of that year, before the close of the British Conference?

"3. Is it not at least certain, that Mr. Wesley must have felt sufficient interest in this matter, to have required from Dr. Coke a particular account of what had been done in America?

"4. Is it not presumable, that Dr. Coke carried with him a copy of the printed Minutes?

"5. Is it not presumable, that Mr. Wesley would have inquired of him whether minutes were not taken, knowing our custom to take minutes at all our Conferences, and also have requested to see them?

"6. Could Dr. Coke have declined to show them, or have concealed from Mr. Wesley what had been done, without the grossest duplicity and positive falsehood?

"7. Is it probable that Dr. Coke was not only so knavish, but so stupid as to hazard his reputation, character, standing, and even his salvation, thus cheaply and foolishly, when he must have anticipated with certainty that Mr. Wesley would, at some future time, obtain a knowledge of what had been done, if he did not then?

"8. If Dr. Coke could have been guilty of such baseness, is it not probable that Mr. Wesley would have received information of it from some quarter; at least before his death; which did not take place till nearly six years afterwards?

"9. If Mr. Wesley had ever discovered that Dr. Coke had so grossly betrayed his trust, and imposed both on him and on us, could he have continued afterwards so highly to esteem and honor him as he notoriously did, even to the day of his death?"

Mr. Emory then proceeds to show that from 1785 to 1791, Dr. Coke was regularly employed by Mr. Wesley, in places of the greatest trust and responsibility, such as being appointed to the London circuit, to the presidency of the Irish Conference, &c., and at his death, appointed him the chairman, or *first* member of four important trusteeships. After making these statements, and asking a few more important questions, Mr. Emory again inquires, "Where is the evidence, that he ever objected to the title of the Church, or to the terms 'episcopal,' or 'episcopacy?'" "Where is the evidence, that he ever protested or remonstrated against either of these, or against our adoption of the 'episcopal' form of Church government, under the direction of superintendents, elders, and deacons?"

In the above manner, Mr. Emory triumphantly refutes the flimsy objection that Mr. Wesley did not design an episcopal form of government for the Methodists in America, and in the next (ninth) section of his book, he notices the oft-quoted letter of Mr. Wesley to Bishop Asbury, and as completely overcomes his opponent at this point, as at any previous one. Did our limits allow, we would be glad to give the substance of the greater part of the admirable work which we have noticed thus far. Suffice it to say, that the arguments advanced were deemed conclusive by the great body of the Methodists, and that the work rapidly passed through various editions, and procured lasting honor for the author, as a man of deep critical acumen, and laborious research.

At the close of Mr. Emory's constitutional term of office in the Book Concern, he was elected bishop of the Church by the General Conference of 1832, and was consecrated by the laying on of the hands of Bishops M'Kendree, Roberts, Soule, and Hedding. After his elevation to the episcopacy, Bishop Emory entered at once upon the discharge of his important duties with such a degree of zeal, and yet with all that deliberation which might have been expected from a man of his eminent abilities; and thus during his earthly stay, he continued to give proof of his fitness for the highest, and most awfully responsible office that exists in the Church of God. Although but a young man, comparatively, and many years of usefulness and efficiency were expected from him, yet his career was suddenly cut short, by a sudden and unexpected accident.

On the morning of the 16th of December, 1835, he arose from his bed in the enjoyment of usual health. After attending to his religious duties, he left his home, which was near the city of Baltimore, for the purpose of attending to some episcopal duties in the latter place. While pursuing his journey leisurely, his horse, which was attached to a light carriage, became frightened and unmanageable. The bishop was thrown with violent force from his carriage, and received a severe wound on his head. He was immediately deprived of his senses, and although all the aid which could be derived from medical attendance was speedily secured, yet death had marked him for its prey, and at seven o'clock on the evening of the same day, he breathed his last,

"And ceased at once, to work and live."

The only word uttered by him between the moment of his fall and that of his death, was, "Amen!" in answer to one of the many prayers offered up in his behalf.

Thus died Bishop John Emory, D.D., in the forty-eighth year of his age, the twenty-sixth of his ministry, and fourth of his episcopate, leaving not only a large circle of friends to mourn their loss, but a Church to bewail the sudden departure of one of her beloved bishops. Never in the history of that Church, of which the deceased was so bright an ornament, had one of her chief pastors been called so suddenly and unexpectedly away; and never before, was such unfeigned sorrow felt at the removal of one of the leading spirits of the age, than on the occasion of this good man's death.

We have, perhaps, sufficiently sketched the leading traits in Bishop Emory's character, to show what manner of man he was; but little, therefore, need be said in reference to the same. A few general remarks will close this chapter.

1. Bishop Emory was emphatically a good man. From the hour of his conversion to God, until the time of his death, he invariably gave evidence that his heart was renewed by divine grace, and the evidence thus furnished arose from his consistent holy life,—a blameless conversation, and a deportment which seemed to say, "follow me as I follow Christ."

2. His qualifications for a minister and a bishop, were of a high order. He possessed a sound judgment, and a discriminating mind, with a thorough education; all these qualifications, rendered him peculiarly fitted for the duties of the sacred office. We have seen specimens of his logical acumen, and controversial tact in the extracts given from his "Defence of our Fathers;" and his business tact may be inferred from the manner in which he acquitted himself as the representative of the Church to the British Conference, as also while agent of the Book Concern. His writings display great clearness and force, as well as great originality.

3. As a preacher, he was far above mediocrity. He always evinced a correctness of taste in the selection of his subjects, and in his manner of treating them; and although he was a careful, and critical analyzer of the several points which might be under consideration, yet his pulpit efforts were far from being dry, or uninteresting to the less informed hearer. All, whether learned or unlearned, listened with deep interest to whatever proceeded from his mouth.

4. Bishop Emory was a man of great humility. Although elevated at different times by the suffrages of his brethren, to the most honorable positions in the Church, yet he had very little confidence in his own powers of mind, and as a matter of consequence, he never felt himself above his more humble brethren, but on all occasions of importance, was in the habit of consulting his friends in reference to the propriety of any measure which he thought best to pursue; and he was always ready to listen to everything which might be urged against any favorite project, before he finally made up his mind in relation thereto.

5. Bishop Emory was a useful man. True, he had not preached as many sermons, or travelled as many thousands of miles as his worthy colleagues in the Episcopacy, nor of many of his less noted brethren, in the ministry, but his life, from the time of his entering into the ministry, was spent in doing good. Eternity alone will disclose the actual amount of good performed by him, and although he died under circumstances which rendered it impossible for him to bear testimony in the dying hour, to the power and efficacy of that gospel which he preached to others, no doubt can exist, but he has received from the Master of the vineyard, the welcome plaudit, "Well done, good and faithful servant—enter into the joys of thy Lord."

CHAPTER XVII.

REV. WILLBUR FISK, D.D.

WILLBUR FISK was born at Brattleborough, Vermont, August 31st, 1792. He was a descendant of the New England puritans, and his parents, who were decidedly pious, gave their son a religious education, which no doubt prepared him in a measure, for the important stations he was afterwards called in the providence of God to fill.

His father, Judge Fisk, was a man of sterling integrity, and after having removed to the county of Caledonia, in the northern section of the State of Vermont, he was called to fill various important offices. For seventeen years at intervals, he was a member of the State legislature. He also filled the office of Chief-justice of the County, for many years.

Notwithstanding Willbur's early religious education, and his freedom from the grossest sins, yet he manifested at an early age, the natural corruption of the human heart, which frequently displayed itself in fits of anger and passion. At the age of eleven years, however, he became the subject of powerful religious impressions, and from the force of conviction was led to look to Jesus Christ as the sinner's friend, and by the exercise of faith in Him, as his redeemer and personal Saviour, he soon obtained the forgiveness of sin, and the possession of a renewed heart. His conversion to God was clear and convincing, not only to himself, but to his friends; and he shortly afterward united with the Methodist Episcopal Church as a probationer.

In consequence of his father's removal into a part of the State of Vermont, where educational advantages were not at that time as extensive as they are now, Willbur was not favored with the early training at school, which would have been desirable. From the age of seven to that of sixteen, he only attended school two or three years, a circumstance which he ever after regretted. But although deprived of the advantages of a public school, his time was by no means entirely wasted, as he was very fond of reading; and while at his work, assisting his father in the cultivation of his farm, he employed many a spare moment in perusing works of science. His thirst for knowledge, at length, became so intense, as to unfit him for his usual employment, and to render him dissatisfied with his situation as a cultivator of the soil. In the winter of 1808–9, when he was about sixteen years of age, his father sent him for three months to the county grammar-school at Peacham, where he applied himself closely to the elementary principles of language, and the mathematics. At the end of the quarter, he returned to assist his father, where he remained until the autumn of 1810, when he again spent six weeks in the grammar-school, and then took charge of a district school for the winter.

His advantages at the grammar-school, only served to increase his thirst for knowledge; and although his father's circumstances, through the reverses of fortune, would not allow him much aid, yet he nobly, and resolutely resolved, that with his own unaided efforts, he would acquire a collegiate education. Accordingly, in May 1811, he commenced the study of Latin grammar, and in a little over a year, he fitted himself for admission to the University of Vermont, located in Burlington, which he entered as a Sophomore in August, 1812, where he pursued his studies with unwearied diligence, until the University course of instruction was suspended by the war of 1812–15, a division of the northern army having taken possession of the University buildings as a barracks! But although driven from the halls ef science in Burlington, he was grateful that there existed other literary institutions, where he might complete his course. He, accordingly, went to Middlebury for the purpose of entering the College, but while conversing with the president of the institution, the latter spoke somewhat derogatorily of the University from which Fisk came, which so wounded the feelings of our young student, that with indignation he turned away, and entered Brown University, at Providence, Rhode Island, in the summer of 1814, and where he graduated with distinguished honor in August, 1815.

Mr. Fisk was now in his twenty-third year, and it became necessary for him to choose a profession. In early life, his parents had hoped that he might be a minister of the Gospel, and his own thoughts were evidently in that direction when he first attended the grammar-school; but during his stay at Peacham, he lost a sense of the divine favor, and knowing that God would not select a backslider to preach the gospel to others, he, after many severe conflicts with his conscience, instead of resolving to return to his "father's house" like the prodigal of old, and then await further developments and providential indications, entered upon the study of law, in the office of the Hon. Isaac Fletcher, in Lyndon, the place of his father's residence. While in this office, he applied himself most assiduously to his legal studies, and gave promise of attaining singular eminence as a lawyer and a statesman. But while aiming after worldly honors and emoluments, his pious parents were weeping in secret over his religious declension; and his father, on one occasion, said to him, that he had a secret hope, that Willbur's religious emotions would be enkindled anew, and that he would feel that *woe*, spoken of by

St. Paul, *if he preached not the Gospel;* and his pious mother afterward said, "While Willbur was aiming at becoming a distinguished statesman, I was all the time praying, that he might be made a minister." Thus Mr. Fisk, for a while pursued his thorny path, vexed on the one hand, by the clamors of his judgment, and the prayers and entreaties of his parents, and on the other, by the flattering allurements of wealth and fame.

After having pursued the study of law for some time, a highly flattering offer was made him, by a gentleman near Baltimore, Maryland, of the situation of private tutor, which offer he gladly embraced, as the most ready and honorable way of replenishing his scanty purse, which had become well-nigh exhausted by the expenses incurred in securing his education. While engaged in his office of tutor, he received all the attention and respect which he could have desired, and in return, gave all due diligence to the work of instructing his pupils; but while in the midst of usefulness, he was prostrated by a severe attack of hemorrhage of the lungs, and by the advice of his physicians, he hurried home to the paternal mansion. While at Burlington, Vermont, on his way home, he was seized with another severe attack, and the benevolent inn-keeper, at whose house he lay sick, was distressed at the thought of a young gentleman dying at his house, away from his friends, without ascertaining before he died, whether he felt himself prepared for the solemn event. The tavern-keeper was not a professor of religion, and the unusual circumstance of being asked about his spiritual state by a man whose business would naturally lead him to think of anything else but the preparation of the soul for death, led Mr. Fisk to search his heart; and he felt doubly reproved by the fact, that one who ought to have been his pupil, had become his spiritual adviser.

God, who is rich in mercy, did not suffer Mr. Fisk to die

at that time, but raised him up, and enabled him to return home, in company with his affectionate father, who, hearing of his son's dangerous illness, hastened to Burlington, and had the pleasure of seeing him partially restored to health. In the meanwhile, Lyndon, the place of his father's residence, was being favored with a glorious outpouring of the Spirit, and several of Mr. Fisk's personal friends were the subjects of the work. Under these circumstances, and those just related, it is not wonderful that his former impressions returned; but before he could regain the favor of God, he was obliged to seek it "carefully, and with tears," nor did he long seek in vain. Soon, the love of God was shed abroad in his heart, and to the surprise and delight of the pious portion of community, he arose one Sabbath evening, and declared what God had done for his soul. He also confessed his derelictions from the path of duty, and stated his resolution henceforth to be wholly on the "Lord's side." The effect on the assembly was electric, as he spoke with intense emotion, and all felt an interest in him as a young gentleman of prepossessing appearance, and of highly gifted powers of mind.

As soon as Mr. Fisk was restored to his heavenly Father's favor, he began to exert himself for the spiritual good of others, by attending religious meetings, and leading the inquiring mind into the path of duty and safety, and he soon began to feel a renewal of his convictions in relation to his duty of preaching the gospel. But here, a question of importance had to be settled, viz.—the branch of the Church, to whose service he should especially devote his time and talents. His judgment and theological views inclined him to the ministry of the Church, in whose bosom he had been reared, and through whose instrumentality he had been reclaimed from his wanderings; but on the other hand, his temporal advantage, his ease and emoluments, his honor and reputation, all pointed to some other Church. Nor were these all; his old

College friends, when they heard of his inclination to be a *Methodist preacher*, were perfectly astounded, and raised a violent outcry against it, and one of them, in writing to Mr. Fisk, accounts for this inclination, on the principle that the latter would "rather rule in hell, than serve in heaven." But another, and still more serious obstacle, was found in the circumstance, that while at College, he had formed the acquaintance of Miss Peck, a young lady of superior intelligence, who was a member of the Protestant Episcopal Church. This acquaintance ripened into mutual attachment, and even to a promise of marriage at some future time. But neither party, at this period, anticipated the fact of his ever becoming a Methodist preacher. Under these circumstances, Mr. Fisk had too much honor, and too much respect for the cherished object of his affections to involve her in embarrassment on account of his course, without consulting her feelings on the subject. Hence, in a letter to her, he says: "When you gave me an undivided heart, you knew not to whom you gave it. If my health is restored, I expect I shall try, by the assistance of Heaven, to preach the Gospel. I know not what denomination I shall commence preaching among, but think, most probably, among the Methodists. If I am convinced that among this people I shall be most in the way of my duty, with them I shall continue; for though I could have a much better living with almost any other denomination, yet I am determined to do my duty, at the loss of all things." In another letter, in which he alludes to Miss Peck's denominational scruples as a barrier to their union, he says: "I should love you less if you felt differently. You must certainly act conscientiously. Those who come together from interest or passion, make out to get along, I know not how, without being united in principle. But we must act differently. My friend may differ from me in principle and in form; yet if his heart is right, I can still love him. I can give the right hand of fellowship to my Christian neighbor, though we belong to different Churches; but I wish the partner of my bosom, not only to worship the same God with me, but to kneel at the same altar." In further corresponding with this lady, he learned that she had three prominent objections to Methodist theology. These related to the doctrines of final perseverance, Christian perfection, and human depravity; and in reply, he says: "I must frankly tell you, that with my present views, if I am a minister of the Gospel, I must preach the doctrines of holiness of heart, and the danger of falling from grace properly explained and understood."

From these extracts, it will be seen that Mr. Fisk had a number of inducements of a worldly and selfish character, to incline him to the ministry of some other Church than that of the Methodists. Besides, a college-bred Methodist minister, was a thing unknown in America, since the days of Dr. Coke, and if he cast in his lot with the Methodist preachers of the age, he must expect to bear his share of reproach on account of the ignorance—so called—of the Methodist ministry.

After weighing these, and other considerations, in his own mind, his judgment and piety led him to make the necessary sacrifices, and devote himself to the work of a Methodist itinerant preacher. His health having in the meantime greatly improved, he began, as all Methodist preachers do at their setting out in the ministry, to "exhort;" that is, to hold meetings for prayer and exhortations; and after having given suitable evidence during a few months' trial as an exhorter, he was, on the 14th of March, 1818, licensed to preach as a local preacher. His first sermon was delivered in the town where he had been reared, and his text on that occasion was, "Who is sufficient for these things?" and the congregation were greatly surprised at the clear and important views which he presented. With his splendid qualifications as a pulpit orator, Mr. Fisk rose still higher in the estimation of the public, and as a matter which might have been expected under the circumstances, received from time to time many flattering encomiums upon his talents and success. His parents, although highly gratified, were fearful of the result which so much praise would have on the mind of their son. Hence his good old mother, for the purpose of preventing self-adulation as much as possible, would name some defect in his discourses; and so repeatedly and incessantly did she do so, that there was positive danger of her believing that her Willbur, after all, was but a slender preacher. This danger, however, was averted by the following amusing circumstance. One day she received a letter from one of her sisters, informing her that a son of the latter had become a preacher, and expressing a wish that Mrs. Fisk could hear him, as she thought he was an excellent preacher. When Mrs. Fisk had read this paragraph, she placed the letter in her lap, and while she raised her spectacles from her eyes, she exclaimed: "Sister B—— has never heard MY SON!"

Soon after having received license to preach, Mr. Fisk was employed by the presiding elder to labor on Craftsbury circuit, a place about twenty-five miles from home. His preaching in the village of Craftsbury, was at first in a private house, and then in the court-house. While here, his labors were greatly blessed; so much so, that one of the bigoted disciples of Calvin was led to exclaim in view of his success: "That Fisk has been about here, and has undone in a few months, all that our minister has done in twelve years." While here, he narrowly escaped death by the hand of an insane person. A lady, at whose house he often stayed, was subject to frequent fits of derangement. During one of these fits, she rushed upon him with a large sharp-pointed knife in her hand, and tearing open his vest, she placed the sharp point to his breast, exclaiming, "You must die. You talk so much of heaven, I am going to send you there; for you are too good to live." Mr. Fisk, without quailing, looked her steadily in the eye, when, after pausing for a moment, she removed the knife and said, "You are fit to live, or die. We want such men on earth, so I will let you live a little longer."

In the summer of 1818, Mr. Fisk joined the Annual Conference, as a probationer, and was sent back to Craftsbury circuit, where he endured sufferings of various kinds, from the rigor of the climate, and his necessary exposure to all kinds of weather; but he labored for God and for souls, and he was cheered with the reflection that his reward was in heaven. At the New England Conference of 1819, Mr. Fisk was sent to Charlestown, Mass. This appointment was a trying one to him, as the Society was small, and embarrassed with debt; but he trusted in the Lord, and his labors were greatly successful, and his congregations large and respectable. While stationed in Charlestown, he attended a camp-meeting on Cape Cod, where he experienced the blessing of "perfect love," which more fully prepared him for the work of the ministry.

At the Conference of 1820, Mr. Fisk was admitted into full connection and ordained a deacon, and by the appointing power was re-appointed to Charlestown; and during the summer, he attended the Commencement of Brown University, and took his degree of Master of Arts. During his second year in Charlestown, Mr. Fisk was the subject of bitter persecution, which he endured with hardiness, as a good soldier. He also suffered much from his old complaint, hemorrhage of the lungs, which so entirely prostrated him, that his physicians gave him up; but his brethren of different denominations of Christians in Charlestown and Boston, believing that "the prayer of faith shall save the sick," cried mightily to God for his recovery, and the disease was graciously rebuked, so that he partially recovered his health, and was able by easy stages to reach his father's house in a few weeks, where he was obliged to remain partially inactive, and to refrain from preaching altogether, for more than a year. He spent much of his time, however, in riding on horseback, and visiting different places, and in holding correspondence with his long list of friends.

At the New England Conference of 1822, Mr. Fisk was ordained elder, and placed upon the superannuated list, but was requested by the Conference, as far as his health would allow, to act as agent for the Newmarket Academy, the only Methodist institution, at that time, in New England. For the purpose of ascertaining whether anything could be done to renovate the institution, which had been dragging out a feeble existence for a few years past, he visited the place of its location, and learning from its leading supporters and managers that the same policy was designed to be pursued which had kept it in its feeble state, he declined having anything to do as an agent for the institution. In a conversation with Miss Peck, subsequently, in relation to the matter, he said, "But if the Lord spare my life, and will give me influence, with his blessing, the Methodist Church shall not want academies nor colleges." After making this remark, and having left the room, a gentleman who heard the remark, said, "Mr. Fisk, if he live, will be a president or a bishop; and with his humility, how bright will be his example!"

During his excursions this year, taken for the benefit of his health, he visited his relatives in Brattleborough, his native town, and was invited to preach on the Sabbath in the Congregational Church. As yet, no Methodists had preached in town, but the inhabitants with one consent considered Methodism as heretical in the extreme. Mr. Fisk preached with his usual felicity of manner, and as few of the congregation knew the stranger, or that he was a Methodist preacher, his sermon was greatly admired. One old lady who thought the "doctrines" of Methodism to be those "of devils," was particularly loud in her expressions of admiration, when her son informed her of her mistake, by saying, "Well, mother, you have heard a Methodist preacher at last, and *you have lived through it.*" The old lady was thunderstruck! but had been too loud in her professions of admiration, to retract anything she had said in favor of the sermon. A gentleman who was similarly caught, backed out by saying, "Well, well, well, if that be Methodism, I wish we had more of it."

Toward the close of the Conference year, Mr. Fisk was united in marriage to Miss Peck, after a courtship of seven years. The union of these two highly gifted and intelligent persons, was followed by the most happy consequences to both parties. At the session of the Conference, Mr. Fisk was present, and took an effective relation. When the subject of the Newmarket Academy came up for consideration, the presiding bishop said to Mr. Fisk, "Why have you not solicited funds for the academy?" "Because, sir, my conscience would not let me," replied Mr. Fisk. "Must the Conference then be governed by *your* conscience?" inquired the bishop. "No, sir," rejoined Mr. Fisk, "I do not wish the Conference to be governed by my conscience, but *I* must be; neither do I wish to control the Conference in any way; but if after examining the school for themselves, the Conference see fit to place it on a different footing, it shall have my utmost exertion."

At the preceding Conference, Mr. Fisk had been requested to preach a sermon on the doctrine of Future Punishment, which request he complied with at the present session. Such was the estimation in which this discourse was held, that the students of Brown University, many of whom were present, —the Conference session being held in Providence—requested a copy for publication. The Conference also passed a resolution unanimously requesting its publication, and it has since passed through numerous editions in this country and in England, and is considered an unanswerable argument against the no-future-punishment theory.

At this Conference, Mr. Fisk was appointed presiding elder of the Vermont district, which comprised at that time the whole of Vermont, east of the Green Mountains. He went to his field of labor in the spirit of his divine Master, and faithfully and successfully discharged the duties of his office, and in a short time the flame of revival began to burn in various parts of his extensive district. In the fall of this year, he brought his lady home to his father's house, and on their journey homeward, they stopped after nightfall at a comfortable-looking farm-house, in the State of New Hampshire, and Mr. Fisk inquired of the old lady who opened the door, if they would entertain strangers. "Yes," replied she, "if you have any religion." "If we have not," said Mr. Fisk, "perhaps you can help us to some." "O, then, come in, come in, with all my heart," replied the hospitable dame. In the morning before parting, Mr. Fisk led the devotions of the family, and when her guests left, the lady of the house followed them to the door exclaiming, "God bless thee, thou blessed of the Lord, continue faithful, and God will hold thee in his right hand."

Mr. Fisk was a delegate to the General Conference of 1824, which assembled in Baltimore, but such was the tiresome and perplexing nature of the business, which occupied his attention while here, that in writing to a friend in Vermont (Hon. B. F. Deming), he says, "I am tired of *this* business, and long to be back again to my work. A camp-meeting is a Heaven compared with a General Conference." Such was his ardor of mind and desire to be constantly employed in the work of winning souls to Christ.

During the two succeeding years of 1824 and 1825, Mr. Fisk was re-appointed presiding elder of Vermont district, and while here it fell to his lot, by the choice of his fellow-citizens in Randolph, where he now resided, to welcome the celebrated General Lafayette—who was then making his northern tour—to the hospitalities of the village, which he did in a short, but appropriate speech, which drew tears from the eyes of the old veteran, especially when Mr. Fisk in the most beautiful language alluded to the "glorious triumph of the Church of the First-born in Heaven."

But we must now introduce Mr. Fisk to the reader in his connection with the literary institutions of the Church. Thus far, since the calamities which befell the Cokesbury College by its repeated destruction by fire, but little had been done to establish literary institutions under the auspices of the Methodist Episcopal Church. As before stated, an academy had been opened at Newmarket, New Hampshire, but such was its state, that the noble-minded Fisk refused to have anything to do with it, unless means were taken to establish it on a different foundation. Accordingly, a committee consisting of Rev. Messrs. Hedding, Lindsey, and Fisk, was appointed at the New England Conference of 1823, to examine into its state, and adopt such measures in reference to it, as they judged most proper. About this time the good people of Wilbraham, Mass., offered the Committee to erect suitable buildings for the purpose of an academy, and pledged themselves to sustain it, if located at that place. The offer was accepted, and one gentleman of Boston, Amos Binney, Esq., generously gave ten thousand dollars for the object.—A charter was obtained from the legislature of Massachusetts, and in November of 1825, the institution was opened by an address from Mr. Fisk, who at the next meeting of the trustees, was elected principal of the academy. As he was still presiding elder on Vermont district, it was not until May, 1826, that he removed to Wilbraham and commenced the active duties of principal. The institution opened with only seven scholars, the number, however, increased to thirty during the term, and the next year, seventy-five were in attendance, while a few years afterwards, several hundreds were found frequenting its halls. The institution shared during the year 1826, in a glorious revival of religion, in which many of the students were brought to the knowledge of the truth as it is in Jesus. Such revivals were frequent during Mr. Fisk's connection with the institution, and resulted in the conversion of many precious souls.

At the session of the legislature of Vermont in 1825, Mr. Fisk was selected to preach the Election sermon at its next session, which he did on the 12th of October, 1826. The sermon, as is usual, was published by the act of the legislature, and although a larger number of copies than usual were ordered to be printed, a second edition was speedily called for. After the delivery of the sermon, Mr. Fisk was elected Chaplain to the legislature, a post which he filled with distinguished honor and acceptability, and when the legislature adjourned he returned to his duties at Wilbraham.

Mr. Fisk was chosen delegate to the General Conference of 1828, which assembled in Pittsburgh, Pa. On his way thither, he visited that wonder of nature, the falls of Niagara. Mr. Fisk gazed upon the stupendous scene, with feelings of awe and devotion. "It seemed to me," he subsequently remarked, "like an image of eternity, and in its rolling, tumbling, foaming, sparkling billows, its resistless currents, its eddying whirlpools, its all-engulfing, all-overwhelming torrents, it appeared a striking image of those fiery steeps, and rolling billows, and noisy caverns, where the spirits of the lost are tossed in ceaseless terror." A utilitarian gentleman, who formed one of the company, taking another view of the subject, exclaimed, "I suppose, if all the worlds that compose this vast universe, were so united by cogs, as to turn each other, here is water-power enough to move the whole!" What an idea! At the opening of the Conference, Mr. Fisk was appointed Chairman of the committee on Education. He prepared a very able report on the subject, and recommended the establishment of several institutions of a collegiate character. The report and resolutions were adopted, and their publication served to give additional impulse to the cause of education in the Methodist Church. On the adjournment of the Conference, he returned to Wilbraham, and resumed his duties as principal.

An amusing incident occurred in the latter part of 1828, arising out of his connection with the academy, which is worth relating. A clergyman in a town adjoining Wilbraham, sent a letter to Mr. Fisk, in which he bitterly com plained that a certain student in the academy—a licensed exhorter—had been endeavoring to proselyte two young persons of his charge; and assigns as a reason for addressing Mr. Fisk on the subject, the supposition that the students were sent out to the villages round about, at the discretion, and under the direction of Mr. Fisk. To this rather singular complaint from such a respectable source, Mr. Fisk replied, that he was both pained and grieved at such proceedings on the part of the young student, and that he had preferred charges against such student for his conduct, and stating that he should expect the clergyman to appear at the time and place of trial, and substantiate the charge preferred. This course of procedure was entirely unexpected by the latter, who forthwith sent a letter of apology, and stating that he had been a trifle too positive, that the facts were only reported to him by others, &c. &c., and informing Mr. Fisk that it would be "quite inconvenient to attend." In this manner the clergyman was glad to back out of the dilemma, in which he found himself so unexpectedly, yet somewhat ceremoniously placed.

In January, 1829, Mr. Fisk was chosen to preach the "Election Sermon," before the Senate of Massachusetts. He also received many flattering proposals for honorable situations in different parts of the country. He was strongly solicited to allow himself to be a candidate for the presidency of the Vermont University, as also to become agent of the American Bible Society. In 1829, he was appointed agent of the Society for the Observance of the Sabbath, with a salary of one thousand dollars per annum, and travelling expenses. He was also, during the same year, elected president of La Grange College, Ala., and about the same time, was elected to a professorship in the University of Alabama, with a salary of two thousand dollars. He was also at the preceding Canada Conference, elected bishop of the Methodist Episcopal Church in Canada. But to all these tempting offers, Mr. Fisk was obliged to return answers of declinature, not because he thought himself insufficient to fill the offices alluded to, nor because he could not render himself useful, as well as honorable, in those situations, but because to accept, to use his own words, "Would build up Willbur Fisk, but it would not build up Methodism." The fact is, his interests had now become so closely identified with the educational interests of New England Methodism, that to forsake his present situation, he felt would be doing the Church an injury, while he well knew that to retain the same, it must be at the sacrifice of ease, honor, and emoluments; for it should be remembered, that at the time of his connection with the Wilbraham Academy, he had only the scanty support of a Methodist travelling preacher, a salary not greater than that secured by many a common laborer, while at the same time he was doing the work of *three men!* Such was Willbur Fisk, in his early connection with the literary institutions of the Methodist Episcopal Church, and such were the sacrifices which he made to secure their prosperity.

In 1829, Mr. Fisk received from Augusta College, in Kentucky, the title of D.D. At first he resolved not to accept it, but before he could make a formal refusal of the honor, his friends having immediately and so generally applied the title to him, it was beyond his power to prevent its future application.

About this period, many noble minds in the nation were becoming aroused to the ravages of intemperance, and its consequent evils. Societies had been organized in different places for the promotion of temperance. Mr., now Dr. Fisk, entered heart and soul into the work of reform, and although many of his brethren in the Church and the ministry, stood aloof from the enterprise, on the ground that the Church was all the temperance society that was necessary, and although the Christian Advocate and Journal, the official organ of the Church, took a decided stand against him, yet he continued to battle for the good cause; and perhaps it is not saying too much, to ascribe to him the honor of having elevated the cause to its present high and commanding position in the Church, more than any other single person ever connected with it.

Through the persevering efforts of Dr. Fisk and others, the cause of education in the Methodist Church was swiftly on the advance. Already had two Methodist Colleges been established, one in Kentucky, and another in Pennsylvania. In 1829, the New York Conference took measures to establish a college of high grade, somewhere in the north. The New England Conference was invited to join in the enterprise, and after having received several flattering offers from different localities, the joint committee of these two Conferences selected Middletown, Conn., as the site for the establishment of the Wesleyan University, the inhabitants of that place having generously presented the committee with thirty thousand dollars worth of property, besides an additional local subscription of eighteen thousand dollars.

In 1830, Dr. Fisk was elected the first president of the Wesleyan University, a situation which he filled with great honor to himself and the Church, as long as he lived. As the institution did not open for the reception of students until September, 1831, Dr. Fisk spent a portion of his time, in the meanwhile, in soliciting funds for the University, and in awaking a general interest in its favor, both among preachers and people. His inaugural address delivered at the opening, was a splendid production, and so greatly was it admired by some of the leading men in the nation, that it at once raised the literary character of the institution; and many young gentlemen sought admission to its classic halls, knowing that under the presidency of such a man as Fisk, the University must flourish and become justly popular.

In 1832, Dr. Fisk was again a member of the General Conference, and during its session he served as chairman of several important committees, and bore a conspicuous part in the numerous important discussions which arose in that reverend and venerable body. After his return to Middletown, he devoted himself as usual, to the interests of the University, but not to these alone, for we find him zealously engaged in the promotion of every good work, and especially that of temperance, having become one of its ablest defenders, and one of its acknowledged champions. He also took a deep interest in the cause of missions, and was, in fact, one of the originators of the Liberia and Oregon missions of the Methodist Episcopal Church.

Dr. Fisk found it necessary also, about these times, to do battle for the truth in opposition to the various phases and dogmas of New England Calvinism. He had some time previously, at the request of certain distinguished civilians, preached a sermon on the subject of predestination. The sermon being published, and being confessedly an able refutation of the doctrine as generally held, and preached by Calvinistic divines, awakened a host of able opponents among the doctors of divinity, and other less-noted ministers. Hence, for several years, in pamphlets, periodicals, &c., the controversy was carried on with spirit, yet with Christian courtesy, so far as Dr. Fisk was concerned, and various publications left as the result of this controversy, stamp the doctor as a man of gigantic intellect, and superior power of mind.

In 1835, the great abolitionist excitement began to rage with intensity in the Methodist Episcopal Church, and although Dr. Fisk, from the beginning, designed to have little or nothing to do in the matter, yet he was by force of circumstances, drawn into the heated controversies of the day, on that exciting subject. He disapproved strongly of the proceedings of the *ultraists*, as they were called, and espoused the *conservative* side of the question. In this position he was fortunate enough to have the principal leading men of the Church agree with him in his views, but unfortunate in having a large majority of his own Conference—the New England—opposed to his particular views in this respect. However, a difference of views in regard to the best means to promote the abolition of slavery, did not detract from the general respect and esteem entertained for him by his brethren, as is evident from the fact that at the very height of the anti-slavery storm, they elected him in 1835, to a seat in the next General Conference; but as the entire delegation, save himself, were obviously elected with reference to their views on this subject, he felt himself under the necessity of declining the honor conferred, by resigning his seat in the General Conference.

In September, 1835, he received the degree of doctor of divinity from his Alma Mater, the Brown University, an honor, which he no doubt appreciated more than the one from another University previously bestowed, because of his former connection with the first-named institution.

On account of Dr. Fisk's numerous labors, his health became seriously impaired, and in the fall of 1835, having received a commission from the Joint Board of the Wesleyan University, to visit Europe for his health, and the advancement of the interests of the institution, he set sail on the 8th of September, accompanied by Mrs. Fisk, and a young gentleman connected with the University, for Liverpool, where they, in due season arrived, and proceeding from thence to London, were affectionately received by the Rev. Richard Reeve, President of the British Conference. Dr. Fisk and party remained in London until November, when they proceeded to Paris, where he formed an agreeable acquaintance with many pious friends. From Paris they proceeded slowly to Rome, where they spent the Passion Week, and witnessed all the absurdities and fooleries of the Romish Church. Our travellers remained in Italy during the winter, visiting different places, and although Dr. Fisk lay dangerously ill for awhile, yet the Lord spared his valuable life, and enabled him to return to London in the early part of the summer of 1836.

After his return to London, he found an agreeable home in the family of Rev. Dr. Alder, and he spent a number of weeks in visiting the different places of note, and also the Universities of Oxford and Cambridge. In the meanwhile the American General Conference had held its session in May, 1836, in Cincinnati, O., and had appointed Dr. Fisk as their delegate to the British Wesleyan Conference, in Birmingham, which held its session in July and August of the same year. Dr. Fisk had also, at the same General Conference, been elected to the responsible office of bishop, thus receiving the highest ecclesiastical honors which the Church could confer on him, during his absence in a foreign land.

About the time of his arrival at the seat of the Birmingham Conference, a strong effort was made, by some of the leading English abolitionists, to prejudice the public mind against him, on account of his former position on the subject of American slavery; and a document had even been sent to the British Conference, signed by a number of the ultraists in New England, which was well adapted to create a prejudice against the doctor. The British Conference, however, had too much magnanimity to pay much attention to these outbursts of party feeling, and they extended to the doctor a very cordial welcome as the representative of American Methodism.

After the Conference adjourned, Dr. Fisk and lady visited the principal cities of England, Scotland, and Ireland, and in the month of October following, took passage in the same ship which carried them to Europe, and which safely landed them in New York, on the 23d of November, and soon after he made his way to Middletown, where he was joyously received by the faculty and students of the University, as well as by the citizens generally. It may be proper in this connection to state, that at the request of many persons, Dr. Fisk published an account of his travels in Europe, a work which has been well received, and generally appreciated.

After Dr. Fisk's return to America, he was strongly solicited, by many of his friends, to take upon him the office and work of a bishop, by consenting to be consecrated in due form; but with his usual modesty, he declined the honor, assigning, among other reasons, his want of physical strength to endure the labors of the office, and pleading his engagements to the University. He accordingly remained at the head of that institution, using all his powers to promote its prosperity, until the time of his last sickness.

During the fall and winter of 1838, Dr. Fisk's health began to decline rapidly, so that it became evident to himself and others, that his days on earth were rapidly numbering. Yet during his long and painful illness, he preserved the utmost composure of mind, and maintained to the very last, his anxiety for the welfare of the University. When informed by the council of physicians, that he could not tarry much longer, he said to the senior Professor, "There are a few things I should like to see done before taken from this world; but what am I, that I should have a hand in those things? There is the poor University; but I hope you will stand by it, and that God will bless it." His conversation from this time, till he died, was heavenly and divine. His sick chamber was a perfect paradise. The next to the last sentence he uttered, was, "Yes; glorious hope!" and his last words were addressed to his affectionate wife, who took his hand and inquired if he knew her, he replying, "Yes, love; yes.'

At ten o'clock in the forenoon of the 22d day of February, 1839, the pure and lovely spirit of the dying Fisk, took its departure for the heaven of purity and loveliness; and as he was lovely in life, so in death, his appearance was singularly lovely, too much so seemingly, to be consigned to the coldness and dampness of the grave; but the grave is no respecter of persons, and the earthly remains of Willbur Fisk now repose under the green sod of the college cemetery at Middletown.

Thus lived and thus died Willbur Fisk, a man of sterling honor, of strict integrity, of fervent piety, and genuine humility. As a man of learning, he was more than respectable; as a preacher, he had few equals, and still fewer superiors; as a gentleman, his society was courted by the intelligent of every land; and as a literary teacher and president of a college, he probably had not a superior. His personal appearance was much in his favor. With a beautifully formed head, and a pleasing countenance; a spare, but erect and well-proportioned frame; an easy manner and a benign disposition, he was in all respects the perfect model of a MAN, whether physically, mentally, or morally considered. But he has gone, and left a Church in tears; yet not without the hope of meeting him again in that land of beauty and delight, "where the weary are at rest."

A plain monumental shaft marks the spot where Fisk was laid, bearing on one side the simple inscription,

"WILLBUR FISK, S.T.D.,

First President of the Wesleyan University."

And on the reverse side, the simple dates of his birth and death. Lately, however, a more suitable and imposing monument has been erected at Wilbraham, Mass., the scene of his early literary labors. A splendid building has been erected near the site of the old Wilbraham Academy, at an expense of some ten or twelve thousand dollars, bearing on its noble front the impressive inscription,

"FISK HALL."

This edifice is designed as a suitable appendage to the buildings of Wilbraham Academy, and was solemnly dedicated to the service of religion and education, on the 12th of November, 1851. The portrait of the deceased Fisk, adorned the walls of the audience-room, and what added greatly to the interest of the occasion, was the presence of his intelligent and pious widow, who had repaired from Middletown, in company of some of the professors of the University, to the scene of her early days, as the companion of her deeply lamented husband. Several appropriate addresses were delivered on the occasion, and the virtues and talents of the deceased Fisk were descanted upon in appropriate terms. Let "Fisk Hall" stand, therefore, as a monument not only in memory of him whose honored name it bears, but as a feeble testimony of the respect with which his name is still remembered in the Methodist Episcopal Church.

STEPHEN OLIN, D. D.

CHAPTER XVIII.

STEPHEN OLIN, D.D. L.L. D.

As the subject of this chapter has but recently deceased, and as no written life has as yet appeared, it will be impossible for the writer of these chapters to give more than a meagre account of this truly great, and in some respects, wonderful man. Yet a man who was so well known, and so deservedly esteemed as was President Olin, has no doubt left a memorial of his greatenss on the minds and hearts of all who were so fortunate as to cultivate his friendship, or to form even his acquaintance. It is the latter circumstance, which impels the author to attempt a sketch of his life and character, more especially as the subject of the chapter was in a most emphatic sense, an eminent Methodist minister, as well as one of nature's noblemen.

Stephen Olin was born in the town of Leicester, Addison County, State of Vermont, on the 2d day of March, 1797. His father, Judge Olin, was a man of great respectability, and filled for a length of time, the office of Lieutenant Governor of the State of Vermont. Stephen, at a very early age, manifested a love for study, and after having undergone the requisite training in the district school of his native town, he was in due time initiated into the higher grade of schools, so plentifully found in his native State; and after having completed his academic course of study, he entered Middlebury College, which is located but a few miles from the place of his birth. His room-mate, and confidential friend during his stay at College, was Mr., now Hon. Myron Lawrence, of Massachusetts. These young men were competitors for the highest graduating honors, and so equally balanced were each of their claims, that the faculty of the institution had the matter under deliberation for two weeks, after having disposed of the other appointments to the students; and in the final arrangement of parts, both were allowed to share in the laurels. The valedictory, however, was given to Olin, but being confined to his room by sickness, Mr. Lawrence had the honor of its delivery. The President of the College, however, was free to acknowledge, that Olin displayed the greatest amount of talent of any young man who had ever passed before him in examination.

After having graduated, Mr. Olin's health being frail, and his resources limited, he concluded that a residence at the South would be a benefit to both the one and the other. He accordingly bade farewell to his native hills, and went to South Carolina, and providentially found an opening for the use of his talents, as Principal of Tabernacle Academy, in the Abbeville District.

Up to this time, Mr. Olin was designed by his father for the bar, and as yet he had made no profession of religion. Indeed, so far as he had any definitely formed views of religion, he was inclined to skepticism and infidelity. As the academy*

* The following relation, Dr. Olin, while he was in Augusta, Ga., gave of his introduction to the Tabernacle Academy: "On leaving college, I came to this State (Georgia), with the view of teaching, and expected to be employed in Putnam County, but was disappointed in obtaining a situation there. I was stopping, without any employment, at a public house in this city; and on taking up a paper, my eye lit upon an advertisement for a teacher, in Tabernacle Academy, in Abbeville District, South Carolina, which lies up the river from this place. Guided by the light of that advertisement, I made my way up the river, and arrived at the place of the location of the Academy; a place

of which he had been chosen principal, was situated in the midst of a Methodist community, and was patronized by that denomination of Christians, he was required by the standing rules of the institution, to open and close the exercises of the school each day with prayer. He hesitated at this point, doubting in his own mind whether he could make an intelligible prayer. After having tried his skill, however (probably in secret at first), he consented to the requirement of the trustees ; but now his conscience began loudly to accuse him of mocking God, by going through a daily round of devotional exercises in the presence of his pupils, which in his case was the result of stipulation—of bargain with the managers of the school, without any religious convictions or feelings on his part.

As a sense of the impropriety of this course pressed more and more heavily upon him, he was led to examine in the most serious manner, the evidences of Christianity. This serious investigation, resulted in the full and clear conviction of the truth of revealed religion, and of the importance and

which I found to my astonishment, to be almost bare of houses, it being a mere country place. I inquired for some suitable one to whom I might make known my business, and was directed to the frame of a new building, partly covered, where I should find one of the trustees of the Academy. I there found a man at work on the building, with his coat off, and shirt sleeves rolled up, whom I found to be the trustee to whom I was directed—a Rev. Mr. Glenn, whom I afterwards found, whatever may have been my first impressions, to be an excellent man. On inquiring where the Academy was, I was pointed to a log-cabin, as being the building; but said Mr. Glenn: 'Our new Academy,' meaning the building then in process of erection, 'will be finished this fall. You will teach in that till the new one is finished.' I engaged for $700 per year. I began in the log-cabin. The door was hung on a couple of sticks, and the windows were miserable; I drew my table to the wall, where I was supplied with light that came in between two logs. In a few weeks, the school was removed to the new building. I had a large number of scholars, and continued in that Academy three years."

necessity of conforming to her requirements. Upon further examination, he discovered himself to be a poor lost sinner by nature, and that unless he found deliverance through the blood of the Redeemer of mankind, he must be lost eternally. He, accordingly, resolved in the strengh of God, to become a Christian, at the hazard of the loss of fame, honor, and wealth. One morning, he went out to a spot in the vicinity of the academy, and kneeling down before his Maker and Judge, he sought his favor, he sued for pardon, he invoked the blessing of a clean heart; and in answer to the prayer of faith that would take no denial, soon he found peace in believing, and Stephen Olin became a "new creature," "old things having passed away, and all things having become new." The surrender of his soul and body had been complete; his pride of intellect and of education had been subdued; his powers were forever consecrated to the service of Cod; and as a result, his sense of the divine favor was clear, and his conversion convincing to himself and others.

As soon as Mr. Olin became a Christian, he saw the importance of openly professing his faith in Christ, and as the only consistent way for him to do so, was to identify himself with the visible body of Christ, he soon united with the Methodist Episcopal Church as a probationer,—a step which all whether learned, or unlearned, rich or poor, must take before they can gain admission to membership in the Methodist Church. After a probation of six months, Mr. Olin was received into full communion, having given evidence in the meantime, of his conversion and upright walk. Shortly after his connection with the Church, he felt that he was called of God to preach the Gospel. Among his friends in Abbeville who took a deep interest in his spiritual welfare, was the late Rev. James E. Glenn, at that time the stationed minister in the place, and a man of some celebrity as a preacher, who perceiving in young Olin the elements of future greatness, at once encouraged him to make a proper use of his talents as a public speaker, and for the purpose of affording him an opportunity for so doing, frequently took him with him, to his preaching appointments on the Sabbath, where he would follow the preacher with an exhortation to the congregation, and then close the exercises by singing and prayer. Soon the exhortations of Mr. Olin, became the most interesting part of the services, so that the *preacher* was completely eclipsed by the glowing, burning eloquence of the *exhorter*.

As soon as his engagements with the trustees of the academy, would allow—he, having in the meantime, obtained license to preach—he offered himself, by the persuasions of his friends, to the South Carolina Annual Conference of 1824, as a Methodist travelling preacher, and was received, and stationed in the city of Charleston, S. C. His first sermon in that city was delivered while the Conference was still in session, and in the presence of most of the preachers. His subject was the conversion of St. Paul,—a most appropriate one for the occasion.—One who heard him at that time, says in reference to the sermon :—

"It was night, and at the old Trinity Church. He rose in the pulpit, tall and ungraceful; went through the introductory exercises, particularly the prayer, with a simplicity of manner, and an earnestness of tone and style of supplication, very different from the ordinary style of such a service; read out his text, closed the Bible and turned it round; laid his hands upon its corners, and began preaching. He had no divisions in his sermon, and yet it was the very soul of method, so clear that you saw through all its connections at a glance, as he went along.—He struck at once into an original track of thought—profound, searching, brilliant, chaining the attention. His sea-line took all the soundings of the human heart; his analysis was master of the deepest intricacies of human motive and passion; his imagination soared into the heaven of invention; his action at going off, awkward, and his long arms thrown about without the slightest reference to rhetorical canons, presently seemed the fittest in the world to accompany an intellectual handling of the subject, perfectly *sui generis*, the like of which had never before been known. Soon his mind was glowing at a white heat; the mass of thought ran like molten gold, poured from inexhaustible sources; and his intellect seemed to have a range wide as the compass of heaven and earth. He commenced preaching at seven o'clock, and the bells of the city were ringing for nine as he closed; and there we were utterly unconscious that even twenty minutes had elapsed, all tremulous with excitement; the tall, awkward man, with his singular gesticulations, unique manner, everything—literally everything—lost sight of, forgotten, in the grand, glorious, majestic truths of the gospel, which flashed like chain-lightning around that old, high, ungainly pulpit, for the nonce a throne of thunders."

The description thus given of Mr. Olin's first sermon, by the graphic pen of Rev. Dr. Wightman, of South Carolina, throws considerable light upon his early efforts in the pulpit, and it is no wonder that the same writer observes, that, "Never in the memory of the oldest Methodists, had so powerful a preacher burst with so sudden a splendor, and tremendous an effect upon the Church."

Mr. Olin remained in Charleston but six months, when he was compelled on the approach of hot weather, such was his state of health, to seek a few months' relaxation, in a more northern clime. He returned, however, to Charleston on the setting in of winter, and at the next session of the Conference, was re-appointed to the same field of labor, with the hope that if his health was not sufficient to endure the labors of the pulpit, he might be able to edit a religious paper—the Wesleyan Journal,—which had been projected, and the prospectus drawn up by Mr. Olin's hand had been issued,—but these hopes were not realized, as before the time of publication had arrived, he was again compelled to leave the city. But although disappointed in becoming the editor of the Journal, he furnished from time to time some very able papers for the same, which were greatly admired.

In 1826, Mr. Olin having passed through his two years, probationary course, preparatory to his admission to the Conference, was, notwithstanding his feeble health, received into full connection, and ordained deacon, but was left without an appointment. The next year he sustained a supernumerary relation to the Conference, and was stationed in Athens, Ga., during which time he endeavored to render himself as useful as his health and strength would allow; but at last despairing of ever being able to do effective labor as a travelling minister, he located in 1828, much against his own inclination, and that of the Conference. Shortly after his location, he became united in marriage to Miss Bostwick of Milledgeville, Ga., a young lady of ardent piety, of lovely appearance, and of some wealth. He re-entered the travelling connection in 1832, by joining the Georgia Conference.

In the year 1830, Mr. Olin was elected Professor of English Literature in the University of Georgia, although his health still continued very poor, and he was barely able to attend to the daily recitations of his students. His popularity as a teacher was so great, that during the year 1833, he was elected President of Randolph Macon College, Virginia, and in the following year, he entered upon the responsible duties of his presidency; and although his fame had preceded him in taking charge of the institution, yet he more than met the expectation of his warmest admirers. In the spring of 1837, his health again failed, and in company with his beloved wife he set sail from America, for an extensive tour in Europe and Asia.

Having arrived at Paris, by way of Havre, he remained

upward of a year in that city; and while there, the late celebrated Dr. Chalmers, of Scotland, visited the place, and Mr., now Dr. Olin, although in rather a precarious state of health, could not deny himself the privilege of hearing that great man preach, especially, as the two men were, in fact, very much alike in many particulars, as it relates to physical appearance and zeal in the pulpit. Although cautioned against making the attempt, he ventured, and such was the effect of the sermon upon his exceedingly nervous system, that he immediately took to his bed, and had a severe illness of six weeks' continuance, which all but carried him to the grave. Through the good providence of God, however, his health was so far restored, that he ventured to make a tour of England, Belgium, and Italy. While in the latter country, he had the misfortune to lose his beloved wife,* an affliction doubly severe, as he was thus left alone in a land of strangers. After spending three months in Rome, he turned his face to the East. He has left two volumes of "Travels in the East" of surpassing interest, and although it might be pleasant to the reader to quote largely from his work, our limits will only allow us to trace his course from one place to another, and refer to a few interesting incidents occurring during his travels.

Dr. Olin sailed from Athens for Alexandria, in Egypt, on the 19th day of December, 1839, on board the French war-steamer Lycurgus, and after a pleasant voyage of about a week, he found himself in the city of the Ptolemies. "We

* Mrs. Olin died in the south of Italy, being seized with a wasting disease, in the end of March, and which proved fatal on the eighth day of May, 1839. She was buried in a small Protestant cemetery, in the environs of Naples, about a mile from the city. In reference to this lady, the doctor says, "Rarely endowed with the talent of doing good, and communicating happiness, and a bright example of the conjugal virtues—patient, indefatigable, inventive; full of cheerfulness and hope, and courage and faith, she was the angel of my sick-room, who watched by my restless pillow night and day."

had no sooner reached the land," says the doctor, "than a score of donkeys, and their drivers rushed towards us from all quarters, and we were nearly trampled under their feet, as well as stunned with loud vociferations, before we were able, with the help of a young Irishman connected with one of the hotels, to engage as many of these indispensable animals as were necessary to carry us through the narrow, dirty streets, to the quarter of the city inhabited by the Franks. Walking is quite out of the question with all who have any objection to being covered with mud, and jostled and trodden upon by loaded camels. One of these huge animals kneeled down upon the beach, alongside our boat, and waited patiently till our baggage was piled upon his back, and bound with ropes.

"We then set off for our hotel, urging our way through dense crowds, whose strange looks and costumes, assured us that we were at length among a race of men unlike anything we had seen before. We passed through the bazar, which I perambulated twice more in the course of the day. The streets are very narrow, and appear much more so, from projecting casements on either side, which nearly meet. The gloom is increased by awnings of boards, and sometimes of palm leaves, extending across the street, and forming a kind of roof, which excludes the rays of the sun, without, however, being so well constructed as to shed rain. The goods are exhibited in stalls of very inconsiderable dimensions, open in front, and even with the street. The seller commonly sits cross-legged within upon a mat or carpet. The customer does not enter the stall, for which there is not sufficient room, but stands in the street while he examines the article which he wishes to purchase, and negotiates the price. When not engaged, the merchant commonly has a long pipe in his mouth, with the bowl resting on the ground. Clad in a long flowing robe, which is confined just above the hips with a broad, silken girdle, of the most showy colors, his head adorned with a huge white or scarlet turban, his legs uncovered almost to the knee, his feet also bare, or in red or yellow slippers, he sits listless and at ease. He makes no demonstrations of eagerness to sell his wares: he eyes you coldly—you are apt to think contemptuously, as you pass. He smokes deliberately and incessantly, and now and then strokes his long beard, which falls down upon his bosom.

"An endless train of camels, laden with immense leathern bags full of water, building materials, sacks of flour, barrels of sugar, and everything, which in other regions is transported in carts, fills the narrow street, threatening to overturn you and your diminutive steed. A host of donkeys and their drivers; women, their legs bare to the knee, but with their faces carefully veiled; a promiscuous crowd of men of all colors, and all costumes—gorgeous, fantastic, wretched, many of them nearly naked—with their loud confused din of outcries and vociferations, form a scene that is quite indescribable. One's head soon grows dizzy with the strange sights and strange sounds."

We must leave the doctor's description of the city, and accompany him on his visit to the Catacombs. "On our way, we encountered two funeral processions. The first was that of a small child. The body, in this instance, was deposited in a basket, and carried upon the shoulders by a man who preceded the rest of the company. A number of persons, perhaps a dozen, men and women, followed in rather a disorderly manner, looking about with the utmost unconcern, but chanting in mournful strains. The other funeral was much more numerously attended. The body, which was that of an adult person, was carried by four bearers upon a bier. There was no coffin, none being used in burying the dead in this country; instead of which, the corpse was dressed in grave-clothes, and covered with a large shawl. It was borne head foremost. A number of shabby-looking men went before the bier in a sort of straggling procession, chanting as they advanced. It was followed by a train of perhaps twenty or thirty women, who were veiled and clothed in white. Their dress and whole appearance were poor and mean, leaving one to conclude that the profession of mourner, to which they belonged, is not lucrative. They are said to get not more than one piaster—less than five cents per day. They sang a dirge in very melancholy and piercing tones, and their attitudes and gesticulations were those of vehement and overpowering grief. They tore their loose disordered hair, and smote their breasts with frantic violence, carefully avoiding, however, the infliction of serious injury, by staying their convulsive hands before they quite reached the head or bosom. The rending of the garments was done with similar violence, but with the same harmless results. A number of them carried in their hands blue handkerchiefs, or strips of cloth, which they alternately stretched across the shoulders or back of the neck, and then raised with both hands high above the head, jerking them with much apparent violence, though the worthless rags resisted their efforts, and received no damage.

" This was all ludicrous enough. Another exhibition, equally characteristic of the manners of the country, which we met with in the same excursion, was much more serious. We were stopped by a large crowd, which quite filled the street near one of the public warehouses. I heard heavy blows, followed by piercing cries, in the midst of the throng of rather shabby-looking people. Urging on my donkey to the spot, I saw an athletic man inflicting merciless blows upon a female, with a heavy stick. She cried out piteously, but without any effect. The crowd looked on with interest, and apparent satisfaction, and no one attempted to interfere. I inquired of the young Arab whom we had employed as a dragoman, what was the meaning of this outrage. He answered with an air of great indifference, in his bad English :

'It is an Arab man licking his woman.' I asked him if this was a common practice. He answered, 'Yes; the wife do bad, and the Arab lick 'em.' I afterward learned that this sort of domestic discipline, is universal in this country. No one supposes it is wrong, or that the conjugal relation can exist on better terms. A European lady, resident in Alexandria, who happened to be with us at the time, informed us that she had lately inquired of a favorite servant, after the health of his wife: 'Very well,' he said, 'better than common the last two days,' since he had given her a good flogging. She told him that Englishmen did not whip their wives. He replied that it was 'indispensable to whip Arab women, otherwise their husbands could not live with them.'"

After a visit to Mohammed Ali, Dr. Olin began to make preparations for a visit to Cairo; and after a rather unpleasant voyage on the Nile, he arrived at the point of debarcation on the 1st of January, 1840. In this city he remained three weeks, busily employed in visiting the various objects interesting to the traveller, in and around the city. On the 7th, he visited the celebrated Pyramids of Ghizeh. The largest of these, the doctor describes as being 732 feet square, 474 feet in height, and covering nearly thirteen acres of ground, and being composed of 202 tiers of square blocks of limestone, each tier varying in thickness from two to four feet, and forming one of a series of steps from the bottom to the top, by which persons may safely ascend to the area of about thirty feet square on the summit of the pyramid. This pyramid, called the Pyramid of Cheops, is supposed to have been built 2123 B.C.

Dr. Olin one day met with a wedding party, in the streets of Cairo, which he thus describes: It was "composed of many persons mounted on donkeys and camels, with one or two elephants in the cavalcade, some fantastically dressed in many colors, some singing or playing on rustic musical instruments, some seated with their faces towards the tails of their animals, all boisterous and reckless, and using all sorts of waggish and comic arts to amuse the rabble. They were followed through the principal streets by a vast multitude, that completely closed up the way, and put a stop to all passing and business. Nobody interfered with them, and they were allowed to keep up, as long as they pleased, a scene of uproar and confusion which in any other part of the world, would have been put down at once by the police. This forbearance on the part of the public authorities from interrupting the people in their humble enjoyments, is a pleasing evidence that sentiments of kindness may be felt by the most tyrannical rulers, and that long-established customs may secure some trifling immunities, where political institutions afford no protection."

Having visited all the curiosities in, and around Cairo, the doctor and his company prepared themselves for a voyage up the Nile, and after spending some ten or twelve days in ascending this noted stream, and observing everything worthy of attention, the doctor soon found himself in view of the monuments of ancient Thebes, at which place he spent a number of weeks, visiting in the meanwhile, the Cataracts of the Nile in Upper Egypt, with numerous other curiosities of nature and art. When he had completed his observations in Upper Egypt, he descended the Nile to Cairo again, and soon began to make preparations for a journey across the desert, to Jerusalem, which he commenced on the 2d day of March, in company with a Mr. and Mrs. Cooly, and an English gentleman by the name of Carrington, together with four other gentlemen, who afterward joined the company. The caravan consisted of about thirty camels, and nearly as many Bedouins to guide and take care of them, together with eight or ten servants—in all nearly fifty persons, and all armed to the teeth with guns, pistols, swords, knives, &c., with the exception of the doctor, who thought it full as safe to leave all "carnal weapons" behind. He had three camels for his own personal use, and the conveyance of his baggage and food in the desert. As an indispensable article, he was obliged to carry from twenty-five to thirty gallons of water, besides a tent and other articles of convenience.

On the 6th of March, our travellers reached Suez, a town of fifteen hundred, or two thousand inhabitants. This place was peculiarly interesting to the doctor, on account of its being in the neighborhood of the locality where God displayed his miraculous power in opening a way through the Red Sea, for the passage of the children of Israel, in their flight from the land of Egypt. After stopping a short time at this place, the caravan took up its line of march for Mount Sinai, in the neighborhood of which, the travellers arrived on the 13th. When they arrived in sight of the mountain, the doctor observes: "It was a time of profound, overwhelming emotion. I was on holy ground, and for the time seemed one of the living mass of millions who, three thousand years ago, stood upon this plain full of trembling and awe, with their faces turned towards the frowning, flaming battlements, where their captain had gone up to talk with the Lord. I could not withdraw my full eyes from the 'Mount of God'—the holy place where the Almighty had dwelt, and shown his glory; nor when I thought of the circumstances of terror and majesty with which he was pleased to invest his transient dwelling place, could I fix them steadily there."

After resting in the convent during the night, Dr Olin and a companion ascended the mountain, described by the resident monks as the true Mount Sinai of the Scriptures. The doctor felt convinced that the monks were in error in this particular, and on the 16th, he ascended the northern summit, which is no doubt the true "Mount of God;" and when on this summit of Sinai, he reverentially read the Decalogue, which was first promulgated by the Almighty on that spot, amidst the thunderings and lightnings of that solemn and awful occasion. After his ascent to Mount Sinai, the doctor visited the "Rock of Horeb," and which he fully believed to be the one smitten by Moses, as described in the book of Exodus.

On the 18th of March, Dr. Olin resumed his journey toward Palestine. On his route he passed "Mount Hor," and arriving at the ruins of Petra on the 30th, he remained for some time to examine the ancient remains of temples, tombs, &c. &c. While here, he was greatly annoyed by a set of savage Bedouins, whose sole business appeared to be to tease and annoy the traveller by attempting to extort money under the pretence of acting as guides, guards, &c. As a portion of the account is interesting and somewhat amusing, we will give it in the doctor's words.

"The morning after my arrival, I succeeded in reaching the north extreme of the valley, before my absence was discovered, but I soon perceived a most villainous robber-looking man approaching, armed with a long knife and matchlock. As I was quite out of sight of the camp, I reconnoitred the savage with some attention. He soon attempted to make his benevolent object known, though I did not at first understand him, nor feel very sure of his intentions and character, as he came from an opposite direction to that of our camp. In order to aid me in comprehending the import of his communication, which I afterwards learned was to inform me that I was in imminent danger without a guide, he drew his knife, and went through all the forms of cutting his own throat, and then raised his crazy old gun to his face, pointing it directly at me, to signify that I was as likely to be shot as butchered. I made him comprehend as well as I could, that I had no fears, and should break the head of any Arab, who might render such an act expedient. He continued to accompany me, a measure to which, as I could not possibly prevent it, I at last consented.—I took care for some time to keep him in advance, and always in my eye.

"I had hardly become reconciled to such company, before a second man made his appearance with similar objects and claims. I insisted on his leaving me with so much earnestness, that he at last stopped, but stood for some minutes as if doubtful whether to go away, or stay by me. I made him understand, that I would give him no bucksheesh though he followed me all day; and the other man fearing that his own pay might be diminished, aided me so effectually, that the warrior at length left us. A little before sunset of the same day, I had walked from the camp, to examine the theatre not far distant in the mouth of Wady Syke; and having paid my guide for the day and dismissed him, was alone. Soon I perceived the discarded applicant for my patronage in the morning, coming towards me accompanied by two other armed Arabs. He at first urged me to go farther into the gorge, which I of course declined. He then demanded bucksheesh for having guarded me through the northern part of the valley in the morning. I told him he had not served me, and I would give him nothing. He spoke to his companions, and then turned again to me, repeated his demand with much violence of language and gesture, all three at the same time advancing towards me with a threatening aspect. I had not so much as a stick for defence; but I answered sternly and loudly, at the same time walking quickly towards them, and raising my hand with an air, from which they might infer that my bosom was full of deadly weapons. These fellows take it for granted, that all Franks are well armed, and they reverence nothing so much as percussion locks, which, indeed, are dangerous antagonists to their crazy matchlocks. They retreated precipitately at this bravado, and left me to my occupation."

On the 2d of April, the doctor left Petra. Passing Mount Hor, where Aaron the brother of Moses died, he proceeded to the site of ancient Carmel, and on the 7th reached Hebron, where after making a short stay, he proceeded to Bethlehem, the birth-place of the Saviour of the world, and on the 9th entered the city of Jerusalem. A day or two previously, the doctor had received a severe injury in his back by a fall from his camel, and when he arrived at Jerusalem, he was scarcely able to support himself. He proceeded directly to the house of one of the American missionaries, where he was cordially received by the Rev. Mr. Lannean, who at once recognized the doctor, and called him by name. Here the doctor was confined to his bed for eight days, receiving in the meantime, all the care and attention possible, from the kind-hearted missionaries of the Presbyterian and Episcopal Churches, and on Good Friday, he had the unspeakable privilege of partaking of the Lord's Supper, on Mount Zion, there being a large number of strangers present from Great Britain, Germany, and the United States, together with the resident Protestants and missionaries. The services were conducted principally by clergymen of the English Church, Dr. Olin assisting in the same.

After gaining sufficient strength, Dr. Olin began his work of examining all that is interesting in, and around Jerusalem, and on the 20th made an excursion to Jericho, on the occasion of an annual festival which is held for the purpose of commemorating the baptism of Christ in the River Jordan. The number of persons encamped before Jericho on the occasion, was estimated by him at 2500, including a singular variety of languages and costumes. There were Copts, Greeks, Armenians, Catholics, and Protestants, from almost every Christian nation under heaven, the most of them pilgrims, who had assembled for the purpose of engaging in the ceremonies and bathing in the sacred stream. Having visited the Jordan, our traveller turned his course to the Dead Sea, where he tested, as nearly all travellers do, the buoyancy of its waters. Having satisfied his curiosity thus far, he returned again to Jerusalem.

On the 27th of April, Dr. Olin and company bade farewell to the Holy City, on their return to the Mediterranean; and after passing through different places of interest and note, worthy the attention of the Christian traveller, they arrived at Beyrout in Syria. After leaving the latter place, they sailed for Smyrna, where they arrived safely on the 25th of May, but where before landing, they were condemned to a fifteen days, quarantine, which expiring on the 9th of June, they immediately took passage for Constantinople. Here Dr. Olin was seized with a fever, which confined him for eight days, part of the time in a miserable filthy hotel, until he removed to the residence of the Rev. Mr. Hamlin, the American missionary, where he experienced all possible kindness and attention, and where he unexpectedly met as the wife of Mr. Hamlin, a young lady, with whom he had been formerly acquainted in Dorset, Vermont, a few miles from his own native town. After his recovery, he spent about a week in Constantinople, when he sailed for Vienna, in Austria, passing through the Black Sea, and up the river Danube. He arrived in the capital of the Austrian dominions on the 13th of August where he was again seized with a raging fever. Here, too, he experienced unremitting attention, from the missionaries of the American Board, and after a month's confinement he took his departure for Switzerland; from thence to Paris; and crossing the Channel, he found himself in London; and after spending a week in that city, he was again prostrated by sickness, but his strength again rallied, and on the 4th of October he sailed for Boston in the steamer Acadia, when after a rough, but otherwise pleasant and short passage, he once more set foot on the shores of his native land.

We have thus followed Dr. Olin on his Eastern tour, and after passing through many dangers, he is again restored to the bosom of the Church of his choice, and by that Church is received with open arms and affectionate sympathy, after an absence of over three years. We shall now lose sight of him as a tourist and traveller, and trace his subsequent career as a minister and teacher.

As his health was still poor, he thought it inadvisable to take up his residence in the South; consequently, in 1842, he accepted the Presidency of the Wesleyan University, in Middletown, Conn., which important relation he retained for nine years, until the close of life. He entered upon his duties with an enlightened zeal, and well supplied the place of the lamented Fisk, in that important institution. Feeling lonely in his widowhood, he was, in 1843, united in marriage to Miss Lynch, the daughter of the Hon. Judge Lynch, of New York city, with whom he spent the remainder of his life pleasantly and happily. While employed as President of the University, he did not content himself merely with going through the routine of duties peculiar to his station, although these were sufficiently onerous and burdensome, but he was in the habit of travelling extensively, especially in the Northern and Eastern States, in waking up the minds of both preachers and people, in behalf of the cause of education. The ministers of the various Annual Conferences, patronizing the Middletown University, will long remember with pleasure and gratitude, his pious efforts in this direction. One occasion the author especially remembers, when the doctor, addressing the Black River Conference, in reference to the importance of the Methodist Church providing the means of education for the young, exclaimed in substance, "Must our children suffer, because they are the children of Methodist parents? Shall our son, doomed to ignorance for want of proper facilities to acquire knowledge, rise up, at some future day, and exclaim, with sorrow, '*I too might have been educated, but,—my father was a* METHODIST !' "

It was not only in the cause of education that Dr. Olin, during his presidency, exerted himself, but the Bible cause, the missionary cause, and all other benevolent enterprises are greatly indebted to his tongue and pen, for an advocacy of their respective objects and claims. Since his return from the East also, he has been in the habit of using his pen. His "Travels in the East" have been greatly admired, and have met with extensive circulation. His written addresses to the students and graduates of the University, are unequalled in power of thought; and no doubt many a young man has been saved to the Church and the ministry, by a perusal of the same. It is understood also, that he has left a large number of manuscripts of various kinds, which will no doubt, before long, be given to the Christian public.

During Dr. Olin's connection with the University, he was subject to occasional attacks of disease, and while the exercises of the commencement in 1851 were being held, he was suddenly prostrated upon the bed of sickness. During his illness, a promising son was torn away from the embrace of his parents by death, and in a few days after, the noble form of the father became cold and lifeless, and was borne away to the silence of the tomb. He died at his residence in Middletown, Conn., of typhoid fever, on the 16th day of August, 1851, in the fifty-fourth year of his age, and twenty-seventh of his ministry. His remains were interred in the College cemetery, near those of the lamented Dr. Fisk

Dr. Olin's death produced a degree of sadness throughout the length and breadth of the land, not only in the bosom of the Methodist Church, where he was best known, and perhaps best loved, but all evangelical Christians seemed to feel that the universal Church had suffered a serious and irreparable loss in the death of this truly great man; and even the citizens of the nation, as may be inferred from the tone of the secular press, felt that one of nature's choicest specimens of manhood had been cut down in the midst of his usefulness.

We have called Dr. Olin a great man. This is emphatically true of him in *every* respect, whether we view him as a man, a citizen, a scholar, a Christian, or a Christian minister. He was a self-made man; for although born of honorable parents, he was obliged to depend upon his own resources, principally, for all the knowledge which he ever acquired; and when we take into consideration his continued ill-health, and his frequent attacks of disease, is it not wonderful that such a man should have accomplished so much in so short a space of time? Dr. Olin's "physical and mental proportions were alike gigantic. His intellect was of that imperial rank to which but few of the sons of men can lay claim. At once acute, penetrating, and profound, it lacked none of the elements of true mental greatness. We have known many men far superior to him in acquired learning; but for breadth and comprehensiveness of range, for vigor and richness of thought, for fertility and abundance of invention, we have never met his equal. The great things that he did in preaching, in talking, in writing for the last thirty years of his life, were accomplished rather by observation and thought, than by reading or study; of these his uncertain health made him incapable. Yet his acquisitions were of no mean order; a broad and deep foundation had been laid in the severe studies of his youth and earlier manhood; and he had a wonderful sort of intuition, if such it may be called, into all forms of human thought and knowledge. His judgment was so profound that on all subjects of an ethical, political, or religious character, his *à priori* judgments were of more value than most other men's conclusions on the largest collection of facts would be.

"But grand as was Dr. Olin's intellectual being, his moral life was still grander. So overshadowing, indeed, was its majesty, that we can hardly contemplate any portion of his nature apart from it. The whole truth, were we to set it down as our eyes see it, would perhaps be judged by those who did not *know* Dr. Olin, to be but another addition to the fond exaggerations of friendship. We see so much earthliness in men—even in men of deservedly high name and station, that it is hard to believe in a life free from this base alloy. If man *can* be free from it, he was. He walked on in the daily path of life, spending his great mind in the service of the humblest of his fellows, more cheerfully than if he had been serving kings—in the world, working for the world, but not of it. Presenting in himself an embodiment of the loftiest ideal of human purity and love, it was the effort of his life to raise others to breathe in his own celestial heights.

"Not that he *felt* himself to be thus elevated. The crowning beauty of his whole nature was its humility. Severe as was his virtue, he knew too well, that after all, it was not *his* evei to know or think himself more virtuous than others. And so, charity, the meek attendant of humility, was ever by his side. In all things else but intellectual and moral pride, he would have been a fit companion for those great spirits that taught of old in the Stoa, or discoursed of virtue and beauty in the groves of the Academy. He had their supreme love of truth—he had their profound contempt for all that is low, grovelling, and earthly,—but he had, too, what they had not: a clear apprehension of the relation between man and his Creator, and a deep sense of the corruption and debasement of humanity, as estranged from God. And the basis of his high morality was laid in pure religion—in an humble and total self-consecration to the service of God his Creator, and in a most ardent love of Christ his Redeemer. He had but one aim in life—to realize a high degree of Christian holiness, and so to promote Christ's kingdom upon earth. To this point all his studies tended,—for this, all his intellectual treasures were lavished,—for this, he freely spent his worldly goods,—to this, he devoted health, and strength, and life.

"The highest style of man, is that which combines a loving heart with high intellectual and moral power. A more genial and affectionate nature than Stephen Olin's, we never knew. His religious affections overflowed in the broadest Christian sympathy for the race; while upon his family and friends, he lavished a wealth of love which few men are endowed with. His social life was all affection and tenderness. His friendship! O how pure, and deep, and ardent it was! Could we unveil the inner sanctuary in which the sacred things of love and friendship are, and must be, guarded, we could show many a treasure—all the fruit of his overflowing heart. With his friends there was no restraint or reserve. His whole heart was poured forth in the gushing flow of sympathy. He delighted, too, in all the manifestations of affection—'in the *detail* of feeling—in the outward and visible signs of the sacrament within—to count, as it were, the very pulses of the life of love.'

"With such qualities of mind and heart, it is not wonderful that he was pre-eminent as a preacher. In over-mastering power in the pulpit, we doubt whether living, he had a rival, or dying, has left his like among men. Nor did his power consist in any single quality—in force of reasoning, or fire of imagination, or heat of declamation—but in all combined. His course of argument was always clear and strong, yet interfused throughout with a fervent and glowing passion—the two inseparably united in a torrent that overwhelmed all that listened to him. His was indeed, the

'Seraphic intellect and force,
To seize and throw the doubts of man;
Impassioned logic which outran
The hearer, in its fiery course.' "*

* Methodist Quarterly Review.

As a pulpit orator, Dr. Olin had indeed few, if any equals; the few sermons, addresses, speeches, &c., which the author has had the privilege of listening to, as falling from the doctor's hallowed lips, have left an irresistible impression upon his mind, that as the like he never heard before, so the like he will never hear again from the lips of mortal man. Nor is the author alone, in forming this estimation of Dr. Olin as a preacher—the Rev. Dr. Wightman, of South Carolina, in speaking of a number of sermons which he had heard Dr. Olin preach, remarks that they were the grandest exhibitions of intellectual power and gracious unction which were ever witnessed in this, or any other country. "The like," says the doctor, "we despair of ever hearing again on earth. Even then, the working of his mighty intellect reminded you of a steam-engine, of vast power, set up in a frail frame-work, which trembled with every stroke of the piston, and revolution of the wheels. The whole of this prodigious movement was pervaded with so remarkable a simplicity of spirit, and so utter an absence of the least appearance of self-glorification;—the preacher was so evidently, so thoroughly absorbed in his subject, so swept onward by a resistless desire to have the Gospel made the power of God to the salvation of his hearers, that no lingering suspicion ever darkened the mind that he was playing the orator. You would as soon have looked to see the waters of the Niagara pause to dally with the wild flowers on the margin, as have entertained the remotest suspicion that Dr. Olin was paying the least attention to the rhetorical fringes of his sentences, or putting himself, or the elaborate composition of the sermon forward as an object of admiration. Indeed, you had time for nothing but to tremble, while he unlocked the mysterious chambers of the heart, and let in daylight upon your dim moral perceptions; or to lay hold upon Christ, as he made the way of justification by faith plain, and led you on to Jesus the Mediator of the new Covenant, and to the blood of sprinkling, in a path all luminous with the light of life; or to exult with a believer's bounding joy, while he pointed out the massy structure of your Christianity—its base, durable as eternity—its capital, high as heaven, and lost in the splendors of God's throne. Astonishing was the effect occasionally produced by his preaching. We have known instances of clear and happy conversion, while he was delivering a sermon. A memorable instance of the power he wielded, occurred in one of the towns of Georgia. His text was, 'If when we were enemies, we were reconciled to God by the death of his Son, much more being reconciled we shall be saved by his life.' An indescribable awe seized the congregation while he unfolded the glorious peculiarities of the Christian scheme of salvation, and scores literally *rushed* to the altar, when he finished the discourse."

As the head of a College or University, President Olin was probably unsurpassed by any living teacher. He was a man of whom his students and fellow-professors felt justly proud, not so much because of his greatness, as the goodness of his heart, and the undying interest he felt in their welfare, both temporal and spiritual; and so greatly was he beloved, that very few cases occurred during his presidency, either South or North, requiring the exercise of severe discipline. He was, in fact, a *father* to his students, for he acted a father's part in counselling, advising, expostulating with a degree of pathos and fervency, which he only could exhibit, and which proved his deep anxiety for the well-being of his pupils. During his Presidency of the Wesleyan University, a glorious revival of religion occurred among the students, which spread into the town, and extended to different denominations and churches; and although confined a portion of the time to his bed of sickness, he was frequently present at the students' class-meetings, and other seasons of social worship. But we must leave the subject, praying that Stephen Olin's mantle may fall on the shoulders of some of his surviving brethren or sons in the Church and ministry.

THE END.

www.ingramcontent.com/pod-product-compliance
Lightning Source LLC
LaVergne TN
LVHW011158110826
845150LV00006B/1251

* 9 7 8 1 4 2 5 5 4 5 5 7 4 *